Money-Go-Rounds

Cross-Cultural Perspectives on Women

General Editors: Shirley Ardener and Jackie Waldren,
for the Centre for Cross-Cultural Research on Women, University of
Oxford

Money-Go-Rounds

The Importance of Rotating Savings and Credit Associations for Women

Edited by
*Shirley Ardener and
Sandra Burman*

Routledge
Taylor & Francis Group
LONDON AND NEW YORK

First published in 1995 by Berg Publishers

Published 2020 by Routledge
2 Park Square, Milton Park, Abingdon, Oxon OX14 4RN
605 Third Avenue, New York, NY 10017

Routledge is an imprint of the Taylor & Francis Group, an informa business

ISBN 13: 978-1-8597-3170-3 (pbk)

Contents

Preface

Sandra Burman and Shirley Ardener

Once upon a long time ago, Shirley Ardener wrote a paper on 'The Comparative Study of Rotating Credit Associations', then defined as: an association formed upon a core of participants who make regular contributions to a fund which is given, in whole or in part, to each contributor in rotation. It was an analytical survey of the literature, which followed a fieldwork-based study of the operation of 'contribution clubs' among a section of the Igbo of Nigeria. After publishing the survey, her attention largely turned to other topics, and ROSCAs went on the back burner for a while. Over recent years a new and growing interest in ROSCAs by theoretical and developmental economists has occurred, and more recently scholars from countries with developing economies in which ROSCAs flourish have been increasingly drawn to them, considering them to be indigenous institutions more adaptable to their countries' economic needs than models introduced from industrial societies elsewhere. Ardener's interest was rearoused in particular when ROSCAs were widely discussed at a conference in Leiden in 1988 on the political economy of Cameroon, a country in which she had spent many years. It then seemed logical to her to combine her interests in ROSCAs and gender by convening a workshop which would bring new material together. Fortuitously, by 1991 her colleague Sandra Burman had collected some interesting material on ROSCAs in the course of her wider studies on women's lives in the difficult urban conditions of South Africa. As a result of this conjunction of interests, contacts were made and in January 1992 an international workshop on women's use of ROSCAs was held in Oxford.

The emphasis here is on associations where money is collected and distributed by one or other method of rotation, because this principle makes a practical difference, and has particular advantages and disadvantages. A great variety of other institutions offer credit facilities and provide people with a wide choice. Obviously, within the scope of this book it is has not been possible to include detailed material on all of these, although mention of some is occasionally made.

This volume, based upon the workshop, brings together new studies from different disciplines and experiences. Most authors are social anthropologists or have had some anthropological training: Almedom, Ardener, Besson, Khatib-Chahidi, Miyanaga, Nelson, Niger-Thomas, Rowlands and Summerfield. Burman works in the field of socio-legal studies; Bortei-Doku, Lembete, Mayoux, Sethi and Srinivasan are in social studies; while Aryeetey, Deng, Hospes and Light are more familiar with economics than the rest of us. As the authors of the various papers set out their observations, a certain amount of repetition occurs which has been retained in this book to underline particular parallels and convergences.

There is one reprint in this collection. The editors have acceded to requests by the other contributors who felt that, because Ardener's earlier paper is in a journal which is inaccessible to many, it would be useful for a facsimile to be included here, retaining the original page numbers as this text is also referred to from time to time not only by the authors here but also in the general literature on ROSCAs. It gives a general overview of ROSCAs which may be read first by those unfamiliar with the theme. Further, despite or more properly because of, the study's antiquity, it can be used for making a comparison with the new material in the chapters below, thus highlighting the continuities and changes over the years.

The chapters have been arranged in three parts, the first two dealing with Africa and Asia, and the third with diaspora communities in Europe, America and the Caribbean. There is very little documentation of the use of ROSCAs in Europe and the Americas, apart from immigrant communities. We know that diddlum and knick-nack clubs existed among working girls in England in the nineteenth century (see Tebbutt 1883). The tontine of Europe was not exactly a ROSCA in the terms of our definition, being an investment club whose share-outs increased as deaths diminished the membership; nevertheless, the term tontine is widely used for ROSCAs in francophone areas. Many mutual aid societies which collect for special purposes (slate and Christmas clubs, for example) which usually require a banker can be found in England today, but these do not embody the principle of rotation. Perhaps more material will be forthcoming. We could not find an available contributor with new material from Latin America although ROSCAs have been reported (see Ardener appendix, below and Low 1995).

Most authors have occasionally used local non-English terms for

ROSCAs. These have been kept, as they will be familiar to members of the communities in which they are found and to regional specialists. Some of these terms remain unchanged in the plural use in the local language. In this book, however, they have sometimes been made plural by the addition of the English 's' suffix, to fit more comfortably into their English sentences. We hope this solution is acceptable. A list of terms for ROSCAs in a large number of languages can be found in Low (1994).

The workshop on which this book is based was held in the congenial surroundings of the Cherwell Centre in Oxford, and was convened by the editors for the Centre for Cross-Cultural Research on Women at Queen Elizabeth House, Oxford University's international development centre. The project received support from Oxfam and the Ministry of Overseas Development, and we are grateful to these bodies, and to others (including the British Council) who funded some of the participants. Four of the papers presented at the workshop (those by Joy Hendry, Sophia Koufopoulou, Sarah Massengo and Sue Szarbo) could not be included here because they were either not completed in time or did not focus sufficiently on associations that rotated and therefore fell outside our remit. We benefited from the contributions of these participants to the debates and where appropriate their material has been referred to. Two papers, by Summerfield and Miyanaga, were written especially for this volume.

The editors invited a colleague at our Centre, Alaine Low, who acted as rapporteur at the workshop, to prepare a bibliography of material on ROSCAs available from records in Oxford, and this is published as a separate working document (Low 1994). Low's study was not restricted to articles on women's participation, although these had special mention. It is intended as a companion text to our volume on women.

We are indebted to various helpers with the preparation of this manuscript. In particular Rosie Hill, but also David Hawke, Judy Mabro, Ian Fowler and Greeta Ilott, whose copy-editing skills (and in the case of the latter two their invaluable expertise on word processors) solved many problems and greatly helped the authors and the publisher. David Hawke also compiled the index.[1] We are also grateful to The Royal Anthropological Institute for permitting us to reprint Ardener's 1964 survey. The drawing on the cover is by Rhoda Michuki and was first included in a cyclostyled publication (see Wainaina 1990).

Notes

1. The index has covered most names and places mentioned, but the details of ROSCAs, and many themes raised throughout the book recur so frequently that it was not practical to index them all comprehensively.

Bibliography

Ardener, S.G. (1953), 'The Social and Economic Significance of the Contribution Clubs among a Section of the Southern Ibo', *Conference Proceedings.* N.I.S.E.R., Ibadan, Nigeria.

—— (1964), 'The Comparative Study of Rotating Credit Associations.' *Journal of the Anthropological Institute* 94 (II) pp. 201–28.

Low, A. (1995) *A Bibliographical Survey of Rotating Savings and Credit Associations,* Oxford: Oxfam and CCCRW.

Tebbutt, M. (1983), *Making Ends Meet; Pawnbroking and Working-Class Credit,* Leicester: Leicester University Press (Methuen).

Wainaina, N. (1990), (cyclostyled), *Indigenous Savings and Credit Schemes for Women in Kenya,* Nairobi: Swedish Development Authority.

Notes on Contributors

Astier M. Almedon, who read Human Sciences at Oxford and carried out fieldwork in Ethiopia for her doctorate, works at the London School of Hygiene and Tropical Medicine. She has published in the field of health care and nutrition.

Shri Anand, who works for The Karnataka Department of Sericulture, assisted Linda Mayoux with the fieldwork used in the study here.

Shirley Ardener is Director of the Centre for Cross-Cultural Research on Women at Oxford University's International Development Centre, Queen Elizabeth House. She carried out anthropological fieldwork for many years in Nigeria and Cameroon. She has published on these countries and has also edited and contributed to a number of books on, women in various aspects, in the Centre's series.

Ernest Aryeetey is an economist at ISSER at the University of Ghana. Since taking his doctorate at the University of Dortmund he has published a number of important studies. He is interested in regional policy, human settlement development planning and development finance.

Jean Besson studied social anthropology at the University of Edinburgh, and taught at the Universities of Edinburgh and Aberdeen before becoming Senior Lecturer in Anthropology at Goldsmiths' College, University of London. She has carried out fieldwork in Jamaica and the Eastern Caribbean, and has published widely on Caribbean peasantries, gender and development.

Ellen Bortei-Doku is a rural sociologist at the Institute of Statistical, Social and Economic Research (ISSER) in Ghana, working mainly in gender studies, rural development and social policy issues.

Sandra Burman is a Senior Member of the Centre for Cross-Cultural Research on Women at Oxford, and Director of the Socio-Legal Unit of the University of Cape Town. She has been published widely on the social consequences of law in South Africa, and has edited two books on children in South Africa for the CCCRW.

Zhong Deng received her doctorate in sociology from the University of California at Los Angeles. Using the Chinese census, her thesis completed a cohort analysis of status placement in the Peoples China from 1949 to 1982, documenting the interruptions caused by the Cultural Revolution. Dr Deng has also written several articles on Chinese economic thought.

Otto Hospes is Assistant Professor and Lecturer in Credit and Cooperatives in Developing Countries, Department of Agrarian Law and Rural Finance at Wageningen Agricultural University, Holland. He carried out fieldwork in Indonesia, and since then his work has been published extensively.

Jane Khatib-Chahidi is a social anthropologist who conducted fieldwork in Iran, and later in Turkish-speaking Cyprus where she has taught at the Eastern Mediterranean University in Famagusta and the International American University in Kyrenia. Two of her articles on Islamic themes have been published in books sponsored by the CCCRW.

Nozipho Lembete (Kubeka) holds degrees in social science from the Universities of the Witwatersrand and Cape Town. When a social worker with NICRO, a national organization in South Africa for social work among prisoners and their families, she worked for Sandra Burman as a part-time research assistant both in Cape Town and Johannesburg, while their research on ROSCAs was in progress.

Ivan Light is Professor of Sociology at the University of California at Los Angeles. He has a long-standing interest in ethnic and immigrant entrepreneurship, and has published a lot in this area. His most recent book is *Race, Ethnicity and Entrepreneurship in American Cities*, (Aldine de Gruyter).

Linda Mayoux, based in Cambridge, is a freelance consultant currently working with the Open University in England. She has undertaken several research projects on gender and small-scale enterprises which required fieldwork in Asia, and has a number of publications to her name.

Kuniko Miyanaga is an Associate Professor in social anthropology at the International Christian University in Tokyo. A one-time visiting scholar at the Institute of Social and Cultural Anthropology at Oxford, she has surveyed here the literature on Japanese ROSCAs and translated into English some of the key data in Japanese.

Nici Nelson is a Senior Lecturer in Social Anthropology at Goldsmiths' College, London. She has carried out fieldwork in Kenya over many years, and her work on urban Nairobi has appeared in numerous publications.

Margaret Niger-Thomas, based in Mamfe Town in Cameroon, formerly studied sociology and then anthropology at Yaounde University in Cameroon. She is President of the Manyu Women's Self-Reliance Cooperative. After several years teaching in Mamfe, she spent some time at the CCCRW, Oxford, as a Visiting Study Fellow. She is currently conducting research at the Afrikacentrum in Leiden, Holland.

Michael Rowlands is a Professor at the Department of Anthropology at University College, London. He has over a long period undertaken fieldwork in Cameroon on pre-colonial economic history and material culture, and has numerous publications to his name.

Raj Mohini Sethi is Professor in the Department of Sociology at Panjab University. She is interested in gender issues, rural development, and socio-legal studies, on which she has published.

Shaila Srinivasan was a Lecturer in Sociology at Delhi University before completing her doctorate at Nuffield College, Oxford, on patterns of Asian entrepreneurship in Oxford. She is currently an out-reach worker with the Ethnic Minority Business Service in Oxford.

Hazel Summerfield read the Human Sciences degree at Oxford, and later took legal qualifications which she applied to her work as an immigrant/ refugee advisor at a legal advice centre in London patronized by immigrants. She has a paper in the Centre's book *Migrant Women* which compares the experiences of two ethnic minorities living in the same neighbourhood of London.

1

Women Making Money Go Round: ROSCAs Revisited

Shirley Ardener

This book deals with a financial system, the rotating savings and credit association, which is remarkable for its wide distribution, its variety of forms and functions, and its relative durability in situations both of high financial insecurity and of prospering industrialization. Although the ROSCA can be placed within a broad set of institutions which provide credit and mutual aid, it can be more discretely isolated by the basic definition: *an association formed upon a core of participants who make regular contributions to a fund which is given in whole or in part to each contributor in turn.* While special attention has been given to disaggregation of the material by gender, many general principles are discussed below which throw light on household participation (see, for example, respectively Rowlands' contribution, and Light and Deng's chapter below). Indeed, when dealing with issues related specifically to the activities of either men or women, obviously the role of, and lessons for, the other always arise. We hope therefore that the volume will make a contribution to all who are generally interested in ROSCAs as well as those concerned with women's activities.

The definition given above for a ROSCA permits the inclusion of a wide diversity of groups, some with quite complex structures. It excludes a great variety of savings and credit institutions which do not embody the principle of rotation. Some of the elaborated features of ROSCAs are common to some of these other institutions which do not distribute cyclically. Savers often have a wide choice. An interesting question is why so many choose ROSCAs.

My 1964 paper, which is reprinted at the end of the book for reasons explained in the preface, disputed the assertion by Clifford Geertz (1962) that ROSCAs, though useful in an intermediate stage of development, would necessarily fade away as more developed financial institutions replaced them. My views were endorsed by a Sudanese banker then staying in Oxford who himself participated in a ROSCA composed of fellow bank employees. Events have confirmed my stance since: while in some places ROSCAs may have become less important in proportion to other credit institutions, elsewhere they have spread or burgeoned more vigorously than ever. They have done so in financial climates and cultural contexts where other credit systems have faltered, due to the inability or unwillingness of creditors to meet their obligations. The Cameroons (the field I know best) is one area where current economic activity, at all levels, depends heavily on participation in ROSCAs of a variety of forms and scale (see Niger-Thomas and Rowlands below and Nzemen, 1993). Indeed, they have been seen there as expanding in significance in reaction to the insecurity of the banking system, but also as then having actually disrupted the banking system itself.

It is tempting to say that it is in regularly harsh economic climates that the ROSCA comes into its own, that it is then that it is particularly needed. Where incomes are very low, where there is no formal social security network, where ill health stalks and a variety of calamities hover, a system of low-cost ROSCAs, as has operated in West Africa for many years, helps to meet the challenges for all but the very impoverished or destitute. ROSCAs are also sometimes initiated in rapid response to the sudden need for liquidity to take advantage of unpredictable flows of desired durables (such as bicycles), as occurred after the cultural revolution in China (personal communication, Zhang Yongjing; see also Bortei-Doku and Aryeetey for Ghana).

But if ROSCAs are popular among the poor and in fluctuating economic conditions, they also thrive among some relatively affluent economic strata (see below). Indeed they are often popular with the intellectual and political élites who have easy access to formal banking systems. In Taiwan, for example, as Besley and Levenson report, estimates of up to 80 per cent ROSCA participation have been made. They say: 'Our study confirms the importance of informal finance, even in an economy that is undergoing significant modernization . . . If ROSCAs do serve a function in consumer demand for durables, as our analyses suggest, then attempts to force movement of savings towards the formal sector should take account of the productive role that the informal system plays' (1993:28–9).

Formal/Informal Distinction Blurred

Not only do ROSCAs themselves flourish today, the discipline of regular contribution-paying in ROSCAs may have enabled new forms of financial management to emerge. For example, the Indian *chit* funds have been said to provide ideas for the establishment of credit unions and even the well-known Indian Grameen banking system. At the workshop, ROSCAs were said to provide a captive membership which can be harnessed for other purposes. For example, in South Africa financial institutions, anxious to get their hands on the large sums invested in ROSCAs, are introducing new arrangements for them, and even utilizing ROSCAs to provide security for housing loans (see Burman and Lembete). In Ghana a modern growth has been the itinerant (male) banker who tours the markets collecting dues from market women, who receive their savings at the end of the month, less the banker's commission. It is surely significant that this mobile banking system is known by the same term (*susu*) as that used for the traditional ROSCA (Bortei-Doku and Aryeetey). Moreover banks in Ghana are tentatively attempting direct involvement in this field. As noted long ago, familiarity with banking systems does not preclude the use of banks by members of ROSCAs; indeed contributions may be paid by cheque, and it is not uncommon, if the member receiving the lump sum has no immediate needs, for ROSCA cash to be deposited in a bank until required (as in Ethiopia, see Aredo 1991, and below p.15). The notion that the formal and informal economies operate as totally independent sectors is thus no longer tenable.

Although formal systems are available to more people than ever, many of the reasons for the attractiveness of the so-called informal ROSCAs remain those pointed out many years ago. A Ghanaian (see Bortei-Doku and Aryeetey) or a Cameroonian (Niger-Thomas), or an Indonesian (Hospes), will often belong to a number of ROSCAs, paying off for some funds received while contributing to sums which can be called on in an emergency. Here local rather than bureaucratic knowledge is critical: the traditional social obligations to help kinsmen, and sometimes neighbours and workmates, quickly come into effect as word gets around among members of the ROSCA, who will adjust the order of rotation to enable the unlucky one to receive a turn. The speed with which ROSCAs can usually react to their members' needs can rarely be matched by distant, impersonal, banking systems. Some members are prepared, even prefer not to take an early turn. Even when no direct financial dividend is given to late takers, and despite the lack of the use of the capital sums which early recipients enjoy, they may prefer the element of insurance which waiting provides.

We can note here, in considering the 'cross-over' between sectors, that the 'captive membership' can be harnessed for other than financial purposes. Associations designed to meet other aims will set up a ROSCA to take advantage of their discipline and moral imperatives. In Indonesia, for example, family planning organizations directed to providing contraceptives for women have set up ROSCAs to ensure that women present themselves regularly for medication (Hospes).

Default

The overriding priority given to meeting ROSCA obligations, and the consequent comparative rarity of default, is a notable feature of these associations. The disgrace and humiliation which can fall on a defaulter is much feared. It is reported from Kenya that the entire group of twenty-six members of the Kauwi Kiseveni Women's Group will visit a defaulter, accompanied by the sub-chief, and take away any item worth the debt, including a husband's property. It is not surprising to learn that 'the stigma that follows such an act is a deterrent to most would-be defaulters', and that the group has survived a long time – since the 1970s (Wainaina, 1990:29). Also of importance are the serious consequences for any defaulter if lost trustworthiness leads to exclusion from further participation in ROSCAs, particularly where they are securely embedded in the local social and economic system. To avoid the shame and the social and economic deprivation arising from default, resort may be had to money-lenders, sale or pawning of assets, or even to malpractice, in order to find ROSCA contributions (see, for example, Summerfield on Somali practices, or Ardener 1964).

However, an important element in the stability of many, if not all, ROSCAs is that it is in the interests of most or all of the members to ensure that there are no defaulters. A defaulter threatens the system, and a failed ROSCA can damage the reputation of an entire group, such as that described by Niger-Thomas for Cameroon. To avoid this becomes an issue for the group, and the organizer might lend money to a contributor unable to meet a due, or another member might help, or the defaulter might be permitted to pay late (perhaps by a post-dated cheque, though this is not popular), or to borrow from a hardship or loan fund to which members have contributed. In certain cases, such as in businessmen's clubs in Ethiopia (see Aredo, 1991), members must provide guarantors who will take on responsibility for any failure by a member to pay (see also Miyanaga on Japan).

The fact that members of a ROSCA can rely on a nil or low default rate is especially crucial for the poor; as Light remarked at the workshop, 'peasants are risk-averse: they can't afford it', and as Rowlands said: 'security, rather than credit' is critical for them. The result is that among Mamfe women, for example, as Niger-Thomas reports, the risk may not seem great: 'members don't see it. They find their own level of contributions.' In South Africa women were bemused when asked about default: 'it was clearly unthinkable' (Burman and Lembete, below).

Coping with Inflation and Disruption

Important elements in determining the success or failure of ROSCAs are the impact of inflation, of a sudden general financial crisis or recession, or of social disruption such as war. It is then that default may become overwhelming. After the war in Vietnam, in the 1970s ROSCA participation slumped (Linda Hitchcock, 1993: personal communication) – though, interestingly, it has been reported (see Aredo, 1991) that ROSCAs actually developed in Ethiopia in the devastation following the Italian war in response to the needs of reconstruction, as they did among Armenian women war refugees in desperate need in the Lebanon (Hamalian, 1974). In their recent paper, Besley and Levenson provide graphic representation of the slide in ROSCA participation from 1983 to its low in 1985, when all economic activity in Taiwan was in shock; they do not go into any detail of how confidence was restored but it quickly rose to near earlier levels. In fact the strength of the structure of the ROSCA is that it permits some flexibility, and frequently can meet the challenge of acute financial pressure, recession or inflation. For example, when payments of contributions are difficult to make, the rotation can be extended for everyone by increasing the periods between payment, thus allowing more time for the collection of dues; or payment may be postponed for a period, as happened in Ghana in the 1980s due to the impact of the implementation of structural adjustment programmes (see Bortei-Doku and Aryeetey); or seasonal adjustments can be made, perhaps over Christmas or the Hindu Diwali celebrations – times when expenses are high (see Niger-Thomas, and Bouman 1979) – or when school fees must be met.

A clever form of inflation- or deflation-proofing has been developed by tying the lump sum to the local price of a fixed amount of gold or silver, or zinc sheets (as described by Khatib-Chahidi and Hospes), the contribution each time being varied according to metal prices. Where a local currency is subject to wild variation, the lump sum may be tied to a hard currency such as sterling, the dollar or the deutschmark, though the contributions are paid in local currency, as in Cyprus. Indeed, it has even been suggested that the spread of ROSCAs in Turkey in the 1980s was actually due to inflation (ibid).

Loss of value of the lump sum, due to inflation, might also be considered to be mitigated, met, or exceeded, where the recipients towards the end of the cycle of rotation receive more in relation to the total sum of their contributions than do those who receive their take-outs earlier in the rotation. Examples are Japan (formerly), Taiwan and India, where members competitively offer bids to 'purchase' or 'win' the lump sum, the 'price' paid being distributed to members, or where members competitively offer to pay in bigger contributions than later takers. In South Africa the pay-out is sometimes clearly regarded as a non-refusable loan, the recipient being forced to meet the appropriate interest (see below). But the 'surplus' value a member receives over what she or he has paid in is not always seen as interest due for allowing earlier payments to be used as credit; this may have advantages, for example for Muslims whose doctrines prohibit usury.

It is probably very significant that the ROSCA capital sum is not always seen by a member as a loan; early recipients are getting money due to them; it is their own right which they are taking, albeit early in the cycle. They may be grateful to their fellow members, or to an organizer, for letting them take their money early, but it is their own entitlement, which they will get anyway – sooner or later. This does not necessarily lessen the critical awareness that it is an amalgam of contributions from all their fellow-members. Indeed, this may distinguish money acquired through a ROSCA from loans from other credit institutions, and introduces a sense of equality and mutuality between members, which might be a, or even the, critical social consideration (as explained below).

We may note the language used by Chipeta and Mkandawire (1991:10) in describing the meaning of *chiryelano*, the term used in Malawi: '*Chiryelano* is co-operation in consumption . . . it is not entirely correct to apply the term "savings" to this practice. It is even more objectionable to add the terms "credit" and "rotating" . . . for although receiving creates an obligation to give, strictly speaking it is not lending and borrowing that this practice entails.' The language sometimes used in the Mediterranean is also suggestive. As the item bought with the accumulated capital is passed to the recipient, it is referred to as a 'gift' (see Khatib-Chahidi for Cyprus, and Koufopoulou (1992) for Turkey) and as the participating members conduct their proceedings in members' homes they are called 'guests' (ibid). We are now in that complex moral field of gift exchange which has received so much attention from social anthropologists since Mauss (1921); the literature is extensive (for a recent contribution see, for example, Davis, 1992). Elsewhere we hear of members 'playing' or 'bidding' for – sometimes 'winning' – the fund, which itself might be known as the 'prize' (see, for example, Mayoux, Sethi and Besson); in his interesting analysis von Pischke (1991) uses the term 'unprized' for members awaiting their turn to receive. Thus the element of chance enters, with overtones of gambling, of participating in or playing a game – a leisure, rather than economic, activity. Pignede (1966:146–7) writes of 'money games' in the Parbat District of Nepal, 'where Gurung women and girls appear to be especially fond of them'. Here again we are far from the language of banks and government offices or aid agencies. Here, also, is excitement; here is successfulness. If to be beaten in the bidding might seem like failure, it is only temporary; for such members live to bid another day, and finally even those that wait will receive – and receive even higher 'prizes'!

Social Responsibility

Fundamental to the strength of many ROSCAs is being seen as having moral and social dimensions. In communities where social solidarity is stressed and mutual aid obligations have a very high priority, any activity based on private advantage and on individual competition becomes problematic. Personal economic success not shared may be incompatible with family and community acceptability. Carsten (1990) shows that women in Langkwi, Malaya, in organizing ROSCAs (here *kut*), 'actually create a community of households, a female community, by linking houses together in a chain of . . . consumption' – centered on the *dapaur* the household cooking pot or consumption unit. Carsten notes that:

> significantly, this consumption is shared between houses rather than involving one individual household. Houses or hearths are linked together in a chain of equal and shared consumption of the same articles. And in this way, there is an avoidance of an association between the house and the

accumulation of money, i.e. of values which somehow negate the house. In other words, just as in budgeting and individuating effects of money, this is also present in the way money is saved.

In such circumstances respondents in a ROSCA may stress its social aspects. Thus when we read that 'ROSCAs among women from the Horn of Africa are valued even more for their social support than for their financial benefits' (Almedom), we may ask whether this emphasis may not be used to mask the significance of their economic value and hide the fact that not all members gain equally, both features to which it would be inappropriate to draw attention.

That it is possible to claim (see Rowlands for Cameroon) that participation meets, or even demonstrates, a member's social responsiblity, may be a key element in their success. The names of some associations illustrate this stress on social solidarity and responsibility. For example, in Ghana we find an association named 'Our Well-Being Depends on Others' (Bortei-Doku and Aryeetey); in Mamfe, Cameroon, one association operates under the title 'Let's Try and See' and another fourteen or so 'Modest Sisters' have been meeting monthly since 1983, contributing to a monthly lump sum equivalent (in 1991) to £2,800 (see Niger-Thomas). In Indonesia the 'Dedicated Women' subscribe to their ROSCA when they meet for religious study in the local Islamic university (Hospes); and we can note that Indian women conduct their ROSCA in association with their religious recitations (Sethi; cf. Hospes for Indonesia). The imagery in the names of these associations is important; it is not of the kind usually encountered in the formal banking sector.

In our preface to Low's survey (1995), Burman and I suggested that for some the 'social' element 'sugars the pill' of crude economic materialism; moreover it has practical functions. The money, time and energy spent on socializing, far from being 'wasteful' or 'uneconomic', may be an essential requirement for justifying membership and thus the financial viability of the ROSCA. Even in ROSCAs where the membership does not gather together, the essential idea that participation is a joint activity for communal advancement may still be relevant (see Niger-Thomas). There are situations, of course, where ROSCA participation is seen as a purely individual concern (for example in the commercially organized *chit* funds in the Indian subcontinent, as described by Sethi). And ROSCAs based on individual advancement can exist side by side with those with social or communal activities. It might be argued, however, that because the latter exist they may be important in many situations for the general acceptability of the more individual type, and because of their customary low default rates set a standard that ensures the very survival of those with private objectives.

That the purely social element is highly valued by many who join ROSCAs is, of course, undeniable. This may, as some have suggested, be particularly important in urban situations where kin-networks are attenuated (see Burman and Lembete for South Africa, and Almedom for Ethiopians) and among immigrants (Summerfield on Somalis in London, Almedom on Ethiopians in Oxford, and Light on Koreans in Los Angeles), where they may act as substitutes for family ties. Burman and Lembete show how ROSCA members' assistance may take the place of marital support in one-parent families. Further, those who move to towns in their own countries, or emigrate abroad, live among strangers. They may be even less at ease and able to cope with bureaucratic structures (staffed with unfamiliar figures following complex rules) than they were at home. It is interesting to note, however, that in Turkey (see Khatib-Chahidi) ROSCAs, far from being necessary substitutes for family ties, were sometimes blamed for having actually weakened them, and that Summerfield believes that ROSCAs 'can facilitate' divorce initiated by Somali women in London. To sum up, in ROSCAs kin ties may be used, avoided (as in Ghana), replaced or break down.

The obligation on members of a ROSCA to meet to pay their contributions may provide justification, structure and discipline to their social gatherings. But because the social element is elaborated, and because its expense may even account for a significant part of the funds collected, we should not overlook the fact that socializing may have a cost-effective benefit. Members may receive considerable economic returns apart from ROSCA cash. From other members they may get valuable information on a wide range of topics, advice on many issues, or unpaid labour, and so forth. Rowlands describes how Bamileke businessmen in Cameroon, by establishing networks of trust built up by membership of ROSCAs, share news and arrange business deals on a large scale. Almedom describes how Ethiopian women in war-torn Addis Ababa exchange information at ROSCA gatherings. Light and Deng discuss the extraordinary success of Korean families in Los Angeles as a result of their ROSCA networking; while Burman and Lembete show how ROSCAs among the rising middle-class lighten the burdens of urban living in South Africa by enabling women to draw on each other's professional advice without pay. In all these situations friendship networks are a resource, because 'social collateral' is a prerequisite not only for successful entrepreneurs but often also for social and economic survival.

It is important to realize that this may be as true for the very affluent as for the poor and middle classes, since the rich may have much to fear in a social or political environment where power and patronage can change hands suddenly, where families can rapidly slide down the social ladder, losing their status, privileges and economic advantages (even their civil liberties) as political regimes take new turns. For élites belonging to prestigious circles, including ROSCAs with exclusive memberships, there may be more than simple direct economic advantage in this form of capital accumulation. The indirect economic and political benefits of membership, of networking, may be very large. It is not surprising, therefore, to find that in some territories, such as Indonesia and Korea, the wives of élites are among those women most active in ROSCAs.

As the African material by Burman and Lembete and by Niger-Thomas illustrates here, the social element in the ROSCA permits displays of ever more elaborate social forms and graces, in which free rein is given to sartorial and other elegances. In Cyprus, too, domestic skills can be called on (see Khatib-Chahidi). Sometimes, as in some ROSCAs in South Africa and Turkey, the meetings are accompanied by lavish entertainment in luxury hotels, a casino, or (in at least one documented case) a military officers' club (Burman and Lembete, Khatib-Chahidi, and Koufopoulou (1992)). Such socializing among members or former members (see Sethi for India) reinforces or provides social identities and potential support networks.

Reputation

Similarly an essential part of the social capital required by an entrepreneur or anyone depending on another's goodwill – and who doesn't? – is a reputation for reliability and trustworthiness. This is especially critical for anyone like the poor and women who may have few land rights or real estate – a situation often found in Africa and Asia. Regular participation in a ROSCA can enable those with few material assets to build a reputation. The importance of the latter to women in the Caribbean has been well documented by Besson, who uses her data to show below that women's participation not only enhances their own personal status but contributes to the common good by the building of a distinctive 'Caribbean counter-culture of reputation and indigenous development' linked to the colonial experience.

Disaggregation: Difficulties and Advantages

In focusing a workshop and book on the activities of one section of the population, namely women, we did so because the detail and special relevance of their activities is often indistinguishable from men's in the general descriptions, though they may not be in reality. Indeed, many authors (see for example, Bortei-Doku and Aryeetey below) have difficulty when trying to disaggregate the available published material in order to detect whether or not women's participation even exists, let alone is peculiar to them in any way. For example, in the recent study by Besley and Levenson (1993) on Taiwan, age and income of head of household are determinants in the data, head of household being defined as the person with the highest income regardless of relationship or age; gender is not treated as significant. Yet as Light and Deng show, treating households as units may mask women's entrepreneurial inputs. The nominal role of Japanese men is noted by Miyanaga. On the other hand, where men finance a wife's contributions to a ROSCA, as reported by Niger-Thomas, their importance too may be obscured. Burman and Lembete have noted that secrecy regarding joint subscriptions to a ROSCA may adversely affect women in the event of a divorce (see below). Apart from any intrinsic interest, such questions are of particular importance for those devising development programmes for women. That aggregation also provides a confusing picture of men's behaviour is, of course, no less true, an inference which is an important lesson from women's studies generally. Ideally we should separate for examination not only data on men and women: it has also been argued that the category 'woman' (just like the category 'man') can usefully be unpacked further (see, eg. Ardener 1978). And certainly many have argued that 'the household' as a unit of study can obscure more than it reveals. As Guyer and Peters (1987:210) summed it up: 'the household is of variable structure; is both channel and outcome of broader social processes; and is the site of separable, often competing, interests, rights and responsibilities. It is as much a "segmented" unit as are labour markets, segmented by gender, age, clan, ethnicity and so on.'

And as Clare Madge shows in her study of allocation of responsibilities for different elements in household expenditure among the Jolas of Gambia, this can vary between households, over time, and according to changes in agriculture and other factors. Madge describes how these Muslim Jolas women contribute to their *kafo* groups (ROSCAs), which act as financial centres for the whole village. Her work reinforces our contention that particular studies on ROSCAs need not only to disaggregate gender membership, but also to include clear contextual analysis – something all too rarely provided.

Other Points

An important contribution of our exercise lies in revealing the need, and making suggestions, for further research. While we await more disaggregation, producing richer texts and more profound analyses, we can perhaps highlight a few more points revealed by the studies presented at the workshop and in this book. We can note, for example, that women have proved themselves very reliable debtors; indeed, as Bortei-Doku and Aryeetey have reported for Ghana, they may have a better record on default than Ghanaian men. Certainly the strictness of the Kenyan women noted above suggests that this may be so, and I believe the experience of the Grameen Bank in India supports this; it is a proposition that could well be tested in other areas. Anthropologists have long recognized the importance of debt relations, not only because where harshly applied they can lead to impoverishment, but because in many communities they possibly reinforce existing kin ties of mutual support and dependency, or produce new beneficial socio-economic networks. Nelson shows how Kenyan women make use of debtors as a resource when ROSCA payments are due. Personal debtors act almost as bankers for the creditors; we should not forget here that for most of us here banks are our debtors. But in Africa, for example, laying out money converts it into social capital, a key element in social survival and economic prosperity. Thus in his interesting analysis below Rowlands discusses how the behaviour of some successful Cameroon businessmen is geared to the widening (rather than narrowing) of debtor/creditor circles, in which ROSCAs play an important part; he links this activity to indigenous philosophical understandings where money has many of the same connotations as transmittable 'vital life substances', and he attributes the exclusion of women from ROSCA circles to these beliefs, also arguing that women's different sense of mutual assistance retards the development of their participation in large-scale ROSCAs. Carsten (1990:135) also sees that women's economic co-operation is 'very different from its male counterpart',

> money is removed from the context in which it is earned by men, an individualistic and commercial one, and circulates through the activity of women in associations which have their basis in kinship and locality and

which involve the participants in economic exchange which is firmly based on the morality of kinship and community. Once again "individual male money" becomes "shared-female-kin-money".

Although several authors in our book note that all-women ROSCAs tend to be smaller and have lower contributions, it remains to be seen whether this will always be the case as more women gain the experience and confidence to carry out larger-scale projects as some are already doing, and whether they will then still support ROSCA associations to the same extent.

The balance between consumption, consumer goods, and entrepreneurial investment in the use of the accumulated capital of ROSCAs certainly requires more detailed work. That women, as might be expected, use their ROSCA accumulations for food for their families is attested by Almedom and Mayoux. That they use it to buy necessary household equipment (see e.g. Niger-Thomas on 'kitchen ROSCAs', et al.) or clothes (see, for example, Sethi) is also unsurprising. Indeed we should note that such household expenditure is seen by Kenyan women as very important, being a prerequisite to 'uplifting women's economic status' since 'women who do not have these basic items are shy, even to come out and meet with other women, or to allow visitors to their homes' (Wainaina, 1990:29); without them they cannot play a full part in public affairs or the economy. The importance of ROSCAs in meeting South African women's aspirations to upward social mobility is well brought out by Burman and Lembete. But the proportion of their ROSCA capital accumulations which women spend on housebuilding and entrepreneurial activity (as demonstrated by Wainaina and Nelson for Kenya, by Bortei-Doku for Ghana market women, by Niger-Thomas for Cameroon middle-class women, by Burman and Lembete for South African women, by Mayoux for poor silk-spinners in India, by Besson for Caribbean importers and by Hamalian for Armenian women money-lenders and wholesalers in the Lebanon), has received less prominence than their expenditure on perishable and durable consumer goods. We are fortunate to have in our book Nelson's detailed longitudinal study (all too much of a rarity) of a group of women beer-brewers in a depressed area of Nairobi, who by forming a successful ROSCA acquired the initial capital, organizational skills and confidence to deal with formal authorities, and thereby to acquire land, loans and ultimately substantial property assets. The broader study by Wainaina (1990) usefully complements Nelson's in-depth work here. Further uses of ROSCA money are reported by Summerfield, Besson and Srinivasan, who describe how women in immigrant communities meet the air fares of family members, visitors, immigrants, and refugees to the United Kingdom, while Summerfield briefly mentions that ROSCA accumulations handled by women were devoted to the costs of the Somali civil war.

Just as Rowlands has linked the particular success of Bamileke businessmen in Cameroon to their devotion to ROSCAs, so Light and Deng have argued that the notable success of Korean clothing manufacturers in California has been aided by their use of ROSCA membership. Hospes, too, describes the accumulation of capital in Indonesian ROSCAs by all sections of the population – from, for example, police officers to traders to relatively impoverished housewives – where membership of ROSCAs may be single-sex or mixed. Most Bamileke ROSCAs, however, are single-sex, perhaps reflecting the almost independent (at times almost parallel) lives led by many married couples in Cameroon. In contrast, among the Koreans in Los Angeles described by Light and Deng, women play a large part in family-based ROSCA activity. Traditionally, and today, Korean women manage the household accounts; in California this is often extended to business finances. The evidence collected by Light and Deng indicates that Koreans in California became more involved in manufacturing clothes than they had been in Korea, and made more use of ROSCAs than they did in Korea.

Empowering Women

Irene Tinker and others have noted that income, including credit, does not necessarily empower women if the power relationships within the household and in society do not permit this and stay unchanged, but despite this caveat Tinker (p.46) feels that in the long run 'credit programmes that encourage women's empowerment, and provide support against those who would object to this shift in power, are essential if women's conditions are to improve'. ROSCAs are one way that women seek to empower themselves by mutual support.

One of the merits of ROSCAs for some women is that they (collectively or individually) can be the decision-makers when spending the capital they thereby accumulate. Collective choice occurs where the initial compact between members requires that the capital sum be spent on particular items (this is widespread; for example, see Niger-Thomas on 'kitchen *njangis*') when the recipient might be accompanied to the market to effect the purchase, or the ROSCAs in Cyprus where one member purchases in advance the gold coin or bangle for the next recipient. Burman and Lembete give a number of examples for South Africa, in one of which members pressed recipients to bank most of their lump sums. In Kenya the recipient of the lump sum may have to report on her expenditure to other members and have it recorded (Wainaina, 1990). The interest shown by women members of some ROSCAs in the purposes to which each puts her savings exemplifies the notion that the association should be of mutual benefit; since each member has contributed to each lump sum, all have an interest in seeing that it is wisely and appropriately spent. Males are often kept out of women's ROSCAs; some do not find them a comfortable environment. Nelson gives details of Kenyan women's vigorous rejection of male attempts to enter the entrepreneurial circle which developed out of their ROSCA activities, fearing they would lose control and even be bankrupted by them.

Secrecy

Women's control over ROSCA accumulations may be preserved by elaborate ruses which prevent a husband from knowing when his wife receives her money, lest she be subject to unwelcome persuasion or pressure to meet his needs (Niger-Thomas, for Mamfe, Cameroon). And women may sometimes feel that it is more appropriate to save through a ROSCA for expenditure they do not wish to meet directly from housekeeping money given by their husbands – for example on helping their own mothers (Wainaina, 1990). As Hamalian records in rich detail, Armenian women in the Lebanon keep their affiliations to *shirkets* carefully selective and strictly secret. Indeed, *shirkets* can almost be seen as a network of secret societies of immense financial importance to the economy, with an organizer exercising power rather like that attributed to the secret gnomes of Zürich! In contrast to their public standing, among members of these secretive ROSCAs the leading women may be known, rather engagingly, by such terms as 'Happy Lady', referring to their duties as hostesses, joke-tellers even, when entertaining the members (Hamalian 1974) – once again, the public stress being laid on sociability rather than on their indubitable economic effectiveness.

A reluctance to talk about ROSCA membership can also arise where they are viewed by respondents as 'old fashioned', 'primitive', or unimportant (see Miyanaga for Japan) and people of West-Indian background in the UK have been known to speak rather disparagingly of them; indeed, the West-Indian born kitchen staff at Queen Elizabeth House (one of whom is a member of a 'partners'), were divided on the issue. At our workshop the Oxfam representative, Sarah Massengo, in her interesting presentation on mutual aid associations in Tanzania, initially omitted to mention that the five members of her own Oxfam office formed a regularly renewing ROSCA circle: this seemed to her unremarkable. The Koreans of California contacted by Light and Deng were at first reluctant to talk about ROSCAs (despite their crucial economic importance for them) because, as well as feeling they might be regarded as old-fashioned, they thought (erroneously) that they were illegal. Indeed, ROSCA money is sometimes referred to as 'black money' (see Light and Deng). Part of the Koreans' worry was that (as is probably the case generally) members may not report as profits the 'interest' or 'bonuses' (the excess of their capital take-outs over payment in) when declaring their income for tax purposes.

There may be a further worry, as is true in California, that the 'interest' charged in ROSCAs exceeds the legal limit. Where registration is technically required, there may have been no compliance, and secrecy is therefore preferred; it is notable that sometimes where ROSCAs are organized by government officials, or registration is enforced, the number of recognized women organizers has fallen (Mayoux for India, and Hospes for Indonesia). By and large, individual ROSCA activities are not considered to be a matter for the state to know about – unless there is default by a member or organizer (which may be covered by normal debt or bankruptcy legislation), or in cases of probate claims (as I was told occasionally happens in Oxford in the case of deaths of the older generation of those born in the West Indies). As Sethi notes, special legislation does exist in India; more detailed study of the legislation pertaining to ROSCAs is certainly desirable.

Embeddedness

I welcome the recent mathematical testing of the 'real' economic benefits of ROSCAs in accumulating capital, as against other methods of saving, and of the various methods of deciding priorities of distribution of the sums collected. There are, however, some social scientists who might consider that searching for statistically acceptable 'hard facts' by use of mathematical modelling often adds comparatively little to our understanding of the social significance of ROSCAs in relation to the complexity of some of the methodology employed. Indeed, I suspect that if they knew of it they might look quizzically at some of the recent work on ROSCAs by the economists from Princeton, Pennsylvania, Boston and Harvard (including Besley, Loury, Coates and Levenson) and Light's detailed analysis below of material collected by mail shots. Nevertheless, such work introduces intriguing new analyses.

A sceptical case *was* put by Chapman (1992a and b), a social anthropologist now in business studies at Bradford. At a business-studies conference he argued that in the last thirty years social anthropology has reacted against methodologies formerly held: 'not (only) for fashionable reasons, but because positivist, behaviourist, "scientific", ambitions started to seem logically incoherent and obstructive'; anthropologists have preferred semantic analyses. In discussing single-strand analyses, and the problem of separately analysing categories like 'politics', 'religion', 'kinship' – and by inference economics – Chapman points out that Evans-Pritchard, in his classic study of the Nuer, showed that:

> the structure was the political system – politics and kinship were indissociable; the economy was organized through this tribal and lineage structure, and production derived from, and served the ends of, this structure – economy, politics and kinship were indivisible; and the religion was so tightly bound into all of these features – into the integrity of lineage, the bonds of kinship, the rituals of diplomacy, the orchestration of consumption patterns – that the attempt to study 'Nuer religion' involved a rehearsal of the entire social and intellectual structure of Nuer life; and there was no 'law' that was not a refraction of the power and imagery of the systems already described ... [Thus] our own division of fields of study and areas of life – politics, economics, law and religion – was of only very limited use in the organisation and presentation of results; any attempt to force it on the analysis, could only have impoverished or distorted the picture of the Nuer that emerged. An immediate response to this might be to argue that ... a developed society, with its division of labour, naturally differentiated the domains – politics, economics, law, culture and religion – which in primitive societies were muddled up. This will not do, however. (Chapman 1992a:12)

These observations will seem (as Chapman agrees) commonplace to social anthropologists and many others, including economists. They are set out here as a reminder that when discussing ROSCAs any attempt to understand their vigour and survival (or weakness and demise) by splitting their aspects into discrete economic, social, ethnic, religious, or gender terms, and omitting the 'imagery of the systems', is doomed to let reality escape. The social and economic benefits commingle; finally they are inseparable. The economic underpins the social, while simultaneously the social supports the economic. The economic *is* the social and the social *is* economic. Further, as many of the papers in our book show, prescriptive kinship or communal obligations, attitudes to the person, and ideas about concepts such as 'progress', 'responsibility' and the like, lie at the very heart of ROSCA operations (see Miyanaga for Japan). Cosmological perceptions are likewise embedded in ROSCAs, as is demonstrated by Rowlands in his discussion of ROSCAs in Cameroon.

Chapman discusses the theme of 'honour and shame', and considers 'patronage', and how in the Mediterranean/North African zone these interact with priorities regarding 'probity' and 'corruption', all the subject of much in-depth research by anthropologists. He notes how notions about such matters in the Mediterranean zone differ widely from those found in, say, northern Europe (Chapman 1992b:9–10). Indeed, perceptions of these kinds vary from area to area, and have a crucial bearing on the success or failure of ROSCAs, in contrast to other formal loan schemes, where priority to repay money received is often determined by different moral judgements. Rowlands says of these: 'for most Cameroonians, there is no assumption that money borrowed must be repaid'; no bankruptcy proceedings are taken in Cameroon. Foreclosing a debt is to be avoided. Moreover, Rowlands speaks of Cameroonians 'converting debt into a social resource'. Thus we often find that the obligation to pay ROSCA dues is seen as understandably or justly eclipsing all other demands, as a moral, or traditional, or perhaps even religious duty not applicable to other debt payments. We have rightly been warned about being 'romantic' where ROSCAs are concerned. Nevertheless, it is clear that the rewards of ROSCA membership are simultaneously material and immaterial – perhaps that is their strength. Recent interest in ROSCAs by indigenous users who see them as non-western, authentically traditional, even 'ethnic', and providing a go-it-alone solution to the desperate problem of international economics and unremitting debt, may strengthen their future.

References

Ardener, S. (1964), 'The Comparative Study of Rotating Credit Associations', *Man* 94, 2, pp. 202–28.

—— (1978), *Defining Females*, London: Croom Helm. 1994 Reprint, Oxford:

Berg.

Aredo, D. (1991), *The Potentials of the IQQUB as an Indigenous Institution Financing Small- and Micro-Scale Enterprises in Ethiopia*, The Hague: Conference Paper.

Besley, T., Coate, S. and Loury, G. (1990), *The Economics of Rotating Savings and Credit Associations*, Harvard: John F. Kennedy School of Government.

—— and Levenson, A. (1993), *The Role of Informal Finance in Household Capital Accumulation: Evidence from Taiwan*, Princeton: Woodrow Wilson School of Public and International Affairs. Discussion Paper.

Bouman, F.J.A. (1979), 'The ROSCA. Financial Technology of an Informal Savings and Credit Institution in Developing Countries', *Savings and Development*, 3:253–76.

Carsten, J. (1990), '"Cooking Money", Money, Morality and Exchange', in M. Bloch and J. Parry, (eds) pp. 117–141.

Chapman, M. (1992a), *Social Anthropology and International Business – Some Suggestions*, Brussels: Academy of International Business Annual World Conference. Conference Paper.

—— (1992b), *Patronage and Corruption, Honour and Shame*, Reading: European International Business Association Annual Conference. Conference Paper.

Chipeta, C. and Mkandawire, M.L.C. (1991), 'The Informal Financial Sector and Macroeconomic Adjustment in Malawi', *African Economic Research Consortium*, Paper 4, Initiatives Publishers, Nairobi.

Davis, J. (1992), *Exchange*, Milton Keynes: Open University.

Geertz, C. (1962), 'The Rotating Credit Association: a "Middle-Rung" in Development', *Economic Development and Cultural Change*, I (3).

Guyer, J.I. and Peters, P.E. (1987), 'Conceptualizing the Household: Issues of Theory and Policy in Africa' *Development and Change*, vol. 18, no. 2, pp. 197–215.

Hamalian, A. (1974), 'The Shirkets: Visiting Patterns of Armenians in Lebanon', *Anthropological Quarterly*, vol. 47, pp. 71–92.

Koufopoulou, S. (1992), Unpublished paper presented at CCCRW workshop, Oxford.

Madge, C. (1991), *Intra-household Use of Income Revenue and Informal Credit Schemes in the Gambia* (mimeo).

Messerschmidt, D.A. (1973), 'Dikhurs: Rotating Credit Associations in Nepal', in *The Himalayan Interface*, J. Fisher (ed.), Amsterdam. pp. 141–65.

Nzemen, M. (1993), *Tontine et développement ou le défi financier de l'Afrique*, Cameroon: Presses Universitaires du Cameroun.

Pignede, B. (1966), *Les Gurungs: une population himalayenne du Népal*, Paris: Mouton.

Pischke, von J.D. (1991), *Finance at the Frontier*, Washington: The World Bank.

Wainaina, N. (1990), *Indigenous Savings and Credit Schemes for Women in Kenya* (cyclostyled), Nairobi: Swedish Development Authority.

PART I

Africa

2

Building New Realities: African Women and ROSCAs in Urban South Africa[1]

*Sandra Burman and
Nozipho Lembete*

Our interest in investigating specifically women's rotating savings and credit associations (ROSCAs) arose from work Sandra Burman conducted on the support networks of single mothers in urban areas, using Cape Town as her sampling area. As interviews progressed, it became evident that ROSCAs were not only widespread throughout the African townships but much used by single mothers. As a result, we conducted a set of interviews specifically on ROSCAs both in Cape Town and in the highly urbanized triangle formed by Pretoria, the Witwatersrand and Vereeniging (the 'PWV'), to help us evaluate their importance to such women, and this dictated the framework of our research. However, our interviews revealed women's use of ROSCA's to be so varied and vital that to describe them as support groups fails to convey more than a part – albeit a major one – of their multi-faceted functions. This paper is therefore a discussion of the roles ROSCAs play in the lives of women who use them, and their possible importance for women in a future South Africa.

Background

ROSCAs are known by various names in South Africa, many regional. The more common ones include *stokvel, gooi-gooi, umgalelo, mahodisana,* and *umshayelwano,* though most of the terms are also used to cover burial societies, non-rotating savings clubs, and various other types of mutual aid societies.[2] We are, however, confining our discussion below to associations 'formed upon a core of participants who agree to

23

make regular contributions to a fund which is given, in whole or in part, to each contributor in rotation' (Ardener, 1964:201).

Although ROSCAs have operated in South Africa since at least early this century, there is very little detailed anthropological work on them, and what there is was generally done several decades ago (notably Kuper and Kaplan, 1944; Hellman,1934,1948; Brandel-Syrier, 1962, 1971; Wilson and Mafeje, 1963; Mayer and Mayer, 1971). More recently work by Cross (1986; 1987) on rural ROSCAs, and by Kokoali (1987) on religious organizations in the little town of Paarl, includes some discussion of ROSCAs. While the investigation described in this paper was in progress, reports on four small studies of urban ROSCAs appeared (Thomas, 1989a and 1989b; Webb, 1989; Lukhele, 1990; Ross, 1990), but of these only the study by Ross, which was formulated in conjunction with our investigation and used the same questionnaire, concentrated on women. Data therefore tends to be regional and sparse. However, a market research survey of 1,300 African adults in the main metropolitan areas except Cape Town and the squatter areas, undertaken in October 1989 by Markinor, the largest independent South African-owned market research organization, provides an indication of the size of the phenomenon in urban areas – although it must be borne in mind that ROSCAs also exist in rural areas, where some 60 per cent of Africans in South Africa still live. Markinor concluded that a quarter of the African adult population in metropolitan areas were members of ROSCAs, burial societies, or communal buying groups, with ROSCA members constituting less than a sixth of this total (Scott-Wilson and Mailoane, 1990). By 1991 a subsequent Markinor survey, which included Cape Town and squatter areas, showed a membership of 28 per cent, a result of both expanded survey coverage and a general increase in the size of ROSCAs (*Business Day,* 1992). Some 60 per cent of ROSCA members are women (Lukhele, 1990), and according to the Markinor study are likely to be aged between 24 and 49, in the higher monthly income groups, and working. This prosperous profile is, however, somewhat misleading when applied to Cape Town's ROSCAs.[3]

Kokoali (1987) suggests that ROSCAs began as savings clubs among contract labourers, especially on the mines, and Lukhele (1990) writes that women have been intimately involved in ROSCAs since at least early this century, when their traditional role as the brewers of beer evolved into that of running shebeens – places where beer (and later other alcoholic drinks) was sold and 'parties' organized as vehicles for ROSCAs. In those days 'respectable' Africans did not usually belong, but as Lukhele (1990:8) explains, African women running shebeens 'began to use the stokvel as a means of protection from police harassment [for selling illicit liquor]. When a stokvel member was arrested, the others would help with the home and children until the member came out of jail. In this way stokvels became more than just organisations for circulation of money and evolved into comprehensive support systems for members in time of hardship.'

Nowadays some ROSCAs have members of both sexes; others of only one. They vary greatly in size and to a lesser extent in mode of operation. Thomas (1989b), on the basis of fieldwork in Cape Town, tentatively divides ROSCAs into three categories. First, those with small membership, dealing in relatively small amounts of cash, which usually do not lend out money and operate primarily as savings groups. Second, those which save with a specific goal in mind, such as the purchase of some expensive item. These have variable membership size and may have an additional fund to lend on interest. Many of this type of club do not have rotating payouts, but some do in the sense that, for example, a special deal is struck with a shop to buy the required items (such as, for example, a fridge), and as enough money is saved for one to be bought the person with the first turn will receive one, and then saving will resume for the second, and so on. Thomas's third category is 'high-budget rotating credit associations (HBRCAs), which may have over 100 members, deal in very large amounts of money, and whose main function is lending of funds, often at high interest rates, to members' (p.6). Our research indicated that this last category of ROSCAs is dominated by men, although women may be members.[4] In Cape Town, groups composed entirely of women largely fall into the first category – that of small groups operating primarily as general savings and credit clubs. In Johannesburg, however, women's groups are also found more frequently in the second category – that of clubs which save with a specific expensive purchase in view and which more frequently lend money on interest.

Recently the potential of ROSCAs as vehicles for the financial betterment of Africans in South Africa has become increasingly evident. As far back as 1984 a study by the Perm Building Society drew attention to this huge untapped savings market in the African community. A special account was designed to suit the needs of non-rotating savings groups and ROSCAs which operated a lending fund – a book-based account with no charges, elected office-bearers authorized to sign for withdrawals, a better-than-average rate of interest paid monthly and rising as the balance increased, and no minimum balance imposed to keep the account open. After piloting, this Club Account was formally launched in 1988, and proved so successful that it has been copied by other financial institutions, which are competing vigorously for group savings and have introduced such additions as training schemes in meeting and money-management skills for *stokvel* chairpersons.

Meanwhile, in 1987 the community development organization Get Ahead (financed by US Aid, fifteen foreign governments, and a wide range of South African corporations) set up a Stokvel Loans programme, on the basis that peer pressure and group involvement would ensure debt repayment. The aim of the programme was to put emerging African entrepreneurs on the first step up the economic ladder, and most of the programme finances informal ventures. Get Ahead lends an initial R500 a member to a group with a minimum of five members and a maximum of ten. All members must know one another, and not more than two family members are allowed in a *stokvel*. The group has to function as a conventional *stokvel* for a month before receiving the loan and throughout the loan repayment period. The leader of the group is expected to collect the *stokvel* savings and the loan repayments each month and hand the latter to Get Ahead. If the loan is paid back in full and on time, the *stokvel* group may apply for a second loan of about R800, and after that a third of R1,000 – the maximum given by Get Ahead at the time of writing (1992). Interest on the loan is set at 32 per cent, but 10 per cent of this is set aside for the customer and given back after a year, when the loan is repaid. The group is encouraged to use this 10 per cent as a deposit on its next loan. Thus the interest paid on the loan is effectively 22 per cent. Get Ahead has branches throughout the country except in Cape Town, where it was forced to suspend its branch because loans were not secure in the squatter camps (*Business Day*, 1992).

In 1988 the National Stokvel Association of South Africa (NASASA) was created by the man who became its president, Andrew Lukhele, to fight for the rights of *stokvel* members and promote recognition of *stokvels*, especially by formal financial institutions, as a source of informal credit. NASASA has been very active in Johannesburg, the financial centre of South Africa, where most of its membership is based, with the result that various imaginative schemes are currently being implemented to tap the considerable funds collected by *stokvels* (R84 million in metropolitan areas, according to Markinor's 1991 survey, and R1.6 billion nationally, according to preliminary research by the National Building Society) (*Business Day*, 1992).

The aim of several schemes which have NASASA's backing is to increase the stock of much-needed housing for the African community, both for ownership and renting. In a bid to overcome the difficulty that *stokvel* members do not qualify for loans, NASASA and specialist financial services group Syfrets have clinched an agreement enabling *stokvels* to invest money in Syfrets-administered unit trusts. The aim is to divert the millions in *stokvel* savings from banks and building societies to unit trusts, which can then serve as collateral for home loans. This has the added advantage of ploughing African savings back into the African community which generated them. The scheme also, very importantly, removes the eroding effect of inflation on *stokvel* savings, and can be used for raising loans for African businesses too. Again, other financial organizations are enthusiastically starting to market unit trusts to the African community; the Old Mutual insurance company, for example, uses a comic paper format, featuring an imaginary township savings group as characters, as a marketing tool.

Another brainchild of NASASA is the Stokvel City Housing Project, focusing on building informal homes in site-and-service areas or upgrading the ubiquitous backyard shacks that house many township dwellers in formal housing areas. The strategy is to provide access to cheap, convenient building materials through the creation of depots selling these on a cash-and-carry basis in the townships, where training in building skills is available. Loans, generated by the NASASA Unit Trust and the Independent Development Trust (IDT), are to be made to men and women who form housing *stokvels* to buy materials, with NASASA as a financial intermediary. At the time of writing the Development Bank of South Africa is also involved in discussions with NASASA on providing additional financing in the housing market.

With all this evidence of recognition by the formal sector of *stokvels* as an important unit in South Africa's financial system, the South African Reserve Bank has embarked on a campaign to define the role of the informal financial sector within present deposit-taking institution legislation. The bank has made it clear that it wants to act not as a regulator of *stokvels* but rather as a facilitator of their development, adding legitimacy to a market already functioning efficiently. The bank therefore proposes that while *stokvels* should remain largely self-regulatory and exempted from the Deposit Taking Institutions Act, they should be registered with NASASA and comply with all the self-regulatory guidelines, while NASASA should work in co-operation with the bank's supervisory department.

It is against this background of the growing strength of ROSCAs as the formal sector awakens to their importance in South Africa's financial future that the role of women in ROSCAs must be viewed.

Fieldwork

The primary research on which this paper is based is, first, detailed interviews with nineteen women, belonging to ten different ROSCAs in Cape Town and six in the PWV area (five in Johannesburg and one in Pretoria) – comprising two metropolitan areas with rather different economic and demographic profiles in their African populations. The PWV is the largest metropolitan area in South Africa, with Africans from all parts of the country congregating there. They constitute the greatest concentration, from all over South Africa, of well-to-do Africans, although the area also contains many who are very poor. Cape Town's African population, in contrast, is mainly Xhosa-speaking and is probably still the poorest African population of South Africa's major cities, as already explained.

Our sample of women members of ROSCAs reflected something of this wide range of demographic and economic backgrounds: *inter alia* they included not only Xhosa-speakers but also those whose home languages were Zulu, Tswana, and Northern Sotho. However, as single women they were probably not representative, in the sense that they were usually poorer than women of similar occupational and family background but different marital status. Our broader study dictated a focus on unwed mothers, who constitute a very high proportion of mothers in urban areas but who are in general a disadvantaged group compared with other single mothers, and even more so when compared with married women.[5] Moreover, obtaining a statistically random sample was impossible, given the financial constraints of our research funding, which forced us to choose interviewees on grounds of availability and access rather than representativeness. We have, however, been able to draw on a further four detailed interviews with women (not selected on grounds of marital status) in two ROSCAs, undertaken by Fiona Ross using our questionnaire, and her research findings are included in our figures.

Our and Ross's detailed interviews on ROSCAs produced data on groups which varied considerably in size, type of membership, length of time in existence, and mode of operation. Since our primary interest was in discovering the roles ROSCAs could play in the economic and social arrangements for single mothers, we needed such a varied sample. Our questions set out to investigate the importance of ROSCAs to women from different backgrounds and with different experiences of such associations, rather than to estimate women's importance within the range of ROSCAs operating in urban areas.

In addition to the interviews specifically on ROSCAs, the paper draws on detailed life histories of divorcees, wives married by customary law only, and unmarried mothers. All were interviewed in Cape Town over the past twelve years as part of various investigations by Sandra Burman into socio-legal aspects of divorce and illegitimacy. Seventeen interviewees provided some information on their membership of ROSCAs. They came from a wide range of economic backgrounds, but again economic constraints prevented any attempt at statistically random selection, so that it would be misleading to draw conclusions from the percentage of interviewees who were members of ROSCAs.

Finally, to place our interviewees' ROSCAs in the contexts of other alternatives offered by social and economic credit- and aid-giving bodies, interviews were conducted with three single mothers belonging to non-rotating savings clubs, as well as a number of organizers of, and researchers on, various institutions involved in forming mutual assistance groups and/or giving credit in the townships. These covered such organizations as the Cape Credit Union League, the National Stokvel Association of South Africa (NASASA), non-profit-making companies operating loan schemes for informal sector entrepreneurs, and *manyanos* (Christian women's church groups).

Profile of the ROSCA Interviewees and Composition of their Clubs

Interviewees

All fifteen of our interviewees were single mothers, three being divorced and the remainder never having married. In four cases their children lived with maternal relatives, not their mothers, but the mothers all contributed to their expenses. The additional four women interviewed by Ross were all mothers, three of them living on their own: one was married, two were separated and one had never married. The total sample thus consists of nineteen women, eighteen of whom were in effect single mothers and one married mother. It should be noted that the fact that a woman's offspring have reached adulthood does not usually mean that the woman is relieved of duties of child-care and support; on the contrary, her obligations frequently increase with the addition to her household of grandchildren, often without much or any financial support from their parents. Of the nineteen women in the sample, only one was no longer responsible for children: her offspring were adults caring for their own children, and no longer lived with her.

The Cape Town women ranged in age from 24 to 45, most being in their late twenties or early thirties. The majority had not completed the possible twelve years of schooling before leaving school, two remaining only till passing standard five (seven years of schooling) and others for varying extra numbers of years. Three of the women had full- or part-time domestic jobs, two were cleaners (at a station and in a restaurant), one was a bakery attendant, one a saleslady in a shop and one an 'unskilled' crèche worker; but most (eleven) had trained as nurses, teachers, or secretaries and were using their qualifications in such posts. This last group claimed in general not to earn money outside their jobs, but information from the less skilled workers indicated various additional sources of income – as is to be expected, given the very high rate of participation by women in the flourishing informal economy in African townships. Of the eleven who revealed their earnings in the formal economy, only one earned over R1,000 per month (R1,700 per month gross), and at least seven earned less than R400 per month, one single mother earning only R120 from a part-time charring job. However, in at least one case additional earnings from the informal economy usually more than doubled the interviewee's meagre earnings, raising her income to R1,000 in good months.

The six PWV women interviewed were aged between 26 and 39, half being in their twenties. At least three had completed school, and two had degrees in social work. The two latter were working as social workers, two others were clerks (one with a jewellery firm, the other with a clinic), one a teacher, and the sixth the branch manageress of a small up-market shop. Two reported additional sources of income outside their jobs: the senior social worker sold beauty products on a part-time basis, and one of the clerks received frequent financial assistance from her mother. Five of the six told us their monthly earnings: all earned R1,000 or over, the highest being R1,760.

The ROSCAs

Our and Ross's detailed interviews on ROSCAs produced data on sixteen clubs, which varied in size from five to forty-five members, three being of twenty or more. All six PWV ROSCAs had only women members, in most cases by deliberate choice of the members: and at least three specifically excluded men. As one group expressed it, they preferred it that way simply because they felt that 'men can find it difficult to work with ladies. They may feel they are being controlled'. Another group told us that they had only women members as they felt women understood one another better. In contrast, most of the ten Cape Town clubs did not in principle exclude members on grounds of gender, but three had only one male member and in one other case the only male in a club of forty-five had left after one rotation, as 'he just didn't seem to feel comfortable with the ladies only.' In practice, therefore, five clubs had only women members, and two – each a club of six close friends – said that they preferred to keep it that way, the explanation offered being in one case that a man might feel uncomfortable as the sole male. One well-established club of twenty-two women was specifically a women's club. At least two Johannesburg and one Cape Town club had only unattached members, the Cape Town club (of six) including both men and women.

Apart from gender, criteria for membership were many and varied, influenced primarily by the requirements of trustworthiness and an ability to pay – or at least an inability to vanish into thin air. Thus some clubs specified that people should be over (or under) certain ages. In one case it was stated that members must be employed, and in others that members must receive a constant income – an important qualification, given the present very high rates of unemployment in the African community and the uncertainties of such informal sector trading. Several clubs were composed largely or exclusively of people in the same occupations at the same places – nurses, clinic workers or cleaners. Others were from different occupations but the same workplace. One was composed exclusively of members of the same church, while membership of another one was limited to the same block of flats. Some clubs were formed by a small band of close friends, others specifically admitted members of the same family. In one case six of the eleven members were from the same nuclear family – a mother and her five daughters. One club of both men and women co-workers, all single, said that they preferred people who were not married as they felt marriage led to decreased reliability: married people were more likely to default on a contribution, pleading family problems, whereas single people had fewer responsibilities. (In contrast, however, two interviewees told us that married people were viewed as desirable members, as marriage made for responsible behaviour.) All the clubs required that new members be recommended by an existing member, a process in some cases reinforced by a semi-formal ceremony of introduction to the group and explanation of the constitution. No interviewee reported formal references being required, beyond that of the introducer.

The length of time those interviewed had been members of their clubs also varied. Two had been members for some three years, two for between two years and thirty months and three for between twelve and twenty-four months, but most had joined within the preceding year.

Operation of the Clubs

The Formalities and Social Arrangements at Meetings
We were interested in how often clubs met, how formal the meetings were, what effect this had on knitting the club together, and how much social life they provided for their members. It transpired that three of the clubs did not have any meetings, although two were hoping to introduce them. Of the remaining thirteen clubs, eleven met monthly and two fortnightly.

Clubs that did not have meetings had various features in common. All were small – one of seven members, the other two of five each. One of the latter did not have meetings because four of the members were nurses who worked different shifts and also lived in different parts of the Cape Town metropolitan area. The club therefore revolved round the organizer (there was no formal executive), who was the only member who had met all the others, three of whom were her friends. (The fifth member was the boyfriend of one of the others.) However, it was a requirement of membership that each member should have at least one close friend in the group, and the operation of the club depended on close friends taking responsibility for contacting each other when necessary. The constitution laid down that the member who was to be paid must receive the money by at least the fifth day of the calendar month, and members took the time limit very seriously. If there were any delays or other problems, they tended to telephone the organizer. How the money was actually transmitted was left to the discretion of individuals. Although no formal records of payment were kept, the organizer kept her own. Similarly, the other club of five had a fixed payment date of the first day of the calendar month and members either paid in person or gave their contributions to the unofficial organizer, who was one of the three co-founders and the person who had recommended the other two members. Members either worked together or lived near other members, so there was contact between them even without formal meetings. The organizer kept a list of the order of rotation, but no receipts were issued. In contrast, the third group had no person who acted as organizer, since all members worked at the same clinic and merely ticked the rotation list, which hung in the office of the founder of the club, who had recruited the others. Payment in kind (at the time of interview, in soap powder) had to occur within the first week of the month.

Not only did some of the clubs not have meetings, but only five had a name – there was no correlation between this and the size of the clubs. Only one club – a relatively long-standing one of twenty-two members

– had a formal uniform, but two others, both in Johannesburg, explicitly expected members to dress smartly for meetings. Although all clubs had some basic rules, the constitutions of some were much more formal than others. Almost half had no formal executive officers. Meetings generally took place at members' houses (often that of the recipient of the pay-out) except where the group revolved round a place of work or a church, in which case meetings at these venues were more appropriate. In the case of some big clubs, meetings had to be held in larger venues, such as schools. The most affluent clubs in Johannesburg sometimes held meetings in hotels.

Procedure at meetings varied in degree of formality, several beginning with a prayer and then regularly following the same agenda. Most clubs which had meetings appeared to operate on the basis of group decisions, but with two exceptions – one being a small club of six where the secretary made most of the decisions but where group pressure no doubt curtailed any autocratic tendencies. The other exception was one of the two clubs composed of both men and women (we were not told the exact composition but there were twenty-four members), where the chairman had an unusual degree of power. The five-person executive did not include a treasurer, the chairman doubling as both. He was responsible for all banking; with other executive members he decided the order of rotation, making the decision one week in advance of payment, with no safeguards against favouritism beyond the secretary's records to show that nobody was paid twice in a rotation. However, we were assured that all the executive members were elected by the ROSCA at the beginning of each rotation, with an eye to leadership qualities that included an ability to listen to other people's views and problems.

A feature of all ROSCA meetings in our sample was of course the receipt of contributions from members and the handing over of money to the person whose turn it was to receive it; this will be discussed in detail below, together with loan schemes. But in addition some clubs operated a system of fines for various offences, either using the money for refreshments or banking it and dividing it – and the interest it generated – between members at the end of the year. Two clubs levied a fine of R10 (that is, 10 per cent and 20 per cent of the contribution respectively) for non-attendance (even if the contribution were sent). It was felt that attendance at meetings was essential to reinforce group relationships of trust and unity. The former club also fined a member an additional 20 per cent of the contribution if payment was late, while the latter (a club of twenty-two members) imposed a sizeable fine for talking during meetings, and fined members wearing the club uniform improperly. An unusual feature in a society not noted for its punctuality was that several clubs placed considerable emphasis on members arriving on time, and fined latecomers. Of the nine Cape Town clubs which had meetings, two fined members R1 and R3 (enough to hurt) if they were late – though we were not told what counted as late – while of the four PWV clubs which had meetings, one stressed that punctual attendance was important – on the dot of 2 p.m. – and two others fined latecomers heavily: in one case, R5 if late by half an hour; in the other, 'R2 if late, even if by a minute'. While not all of these punctual clubs paid particularly high contributions, most had other features compatible with an upwardly-mobile membership.

Such features could also be seen in the type of socializing at the meetings of the more affluent clubs. The largest group in the sample (with forty-five members) served no refreshments at meetings, although it provided a useful forum for members to meet and make friends; but this lack of food was unusual. The normal pattern was for refreshments to play an important role at meetings. In some cases in our Cape Town sample the person who was about to be paid out served light refreshments and cool drinks; in others the club provided, either from small set refreshment contributions by members or from the fines-kitty. One Cape Town group of which we were told (outside our sample) had a membership of sixty-six men and women, organized in six groups of eleven, with one from each of the six groups receiving payment at each meeting.[6] Meetings were considerable occasions, with impressive party fare and photographs of the six recipients dressed in their most elegant clothes, while other members wore either smart suits and ties, if men, or the club uniform of black skirt, white shirt and black tie, if women.

The PWV clubs were even more lavish: two provided three-course meals, usually at the home of the person who was to be paid but sometimes at hotels; and a third planned to do so the following year. In at least two cases members made a sizeable set contribution towards this. In another club – the Ladies Elegance Society – members contributed even more towards a party with music and dancing, again sometimes at a hotel. Items discussed over the three-course meals included in one case 'marital problems, children and beauty tips', in another 'general matters, relationships, politics and dresses'. One of these clubs had, as an official on the four-member executive, a Public Relations Officer, whose function it was to organize social occasions, including trips to such places as Sun City (South Africa's most lavish casino at the time of writing) or to the adjoining state of Swaziland. Interestingly, this club of eleven had two 'half members', who belonged for purely social reasons, contributing towards meals and the compulsory gifts but not the basic contribution, and receiving no payout.

As can be seen, therefore, socializing of various types played an important role in all the clubs that had meetings. However, none of the ROSCAs in our sample – nor any other women's ROSCA of which we were told – had anything approaching the lavish two-day parties described by Lukhele (1990) of mixed-gender ROSCAs on the PWV, where the payouts and receipts from the parties were so large that one recipient used his to buy a farm, and another 'six buses and nine small businesses'. While it is not unknown for the parties of women's clubs to include outsiders (whose contributions and gifts on such occasion can be of sizeable economic importance), in Cape Town these are usually other women and the parties are generally smaller and more sober occasions than those of men's, or many mixed-gender, ROSCAs. However, in Johannesburg, where NASASA is based and is most active, it serves as a network for information on parties, to which all members are often invited. Women's clubs which belong to NASASA are therefore more likely to have men at their parties as guests, in which case the party takes on a different nature.

Contribution, Payouts and Loans

In the Cape Town ROSCAs in the sample, the average contribution per month (whether paid monthly or fortnightly) was conspicuously lower than in the PWV sample. Members paid less than R100 in half the clubs, the two lowest being R25 and R30 and the highest R200. In contrast, only one Johannesburg club paid less than R100 (and paid only in kind), while the highest contribution was R250. At least seven of the sixteen clubs definitely allowed some form of doubling (payment of more than the minimum contribution when the payer had money to spare, on the understanding that the recipient would repay the amount when the payer's turn came round for receiving the kitty).

Most allowed members to swop payout turns between themselves, though several stressed that this was discouraged except in emergency situations. It was apparently feared that allowing swops could cause squabbling.[7] We were told of at least two clubs which prohibited all swopping. Most clubs paid out the entire kitty each time, to only one person, and entirely in cash – though the most affluent club accepted payment by cheque. Four clubs also accepted payment in kind as part – or, in one case, all – of the contribution: one club was currently paying entirely in soap powder; one Johannesburg club paid R100 in cash and R50 in either groceries (from a list supplied by the recipient) or cash, if this was requested a week in advance; another paid R100 in cash and R20 in the form of a compulsory gift of some small household item; and one Cape Town club paid R50 in cash and R10 in the form of a gift of the payee's choice (the payee making up the difference in price if it exceeded R10).

The exceptions to the general rule that clubs paid out the full amount were all connected to loan schemes. In one case less than two-fifths of the R50 contribution (from each of the twenty-four members) was paid out to the person whose turn it was, the rest being banked by the treasurer and used as a loan fund for members at a spectacular interest rate of 20 per cent per fortnight. The banked funds were then divided between all members at the end of the annual rotation. In another case the member was paid out in full but then required to put R300 (half the payout) into the club's loan account. Recipients of loans (to members, or through them in the case of non-members) were charged interest of 10 per cent over a three-month period; in the event of non-payment a further 10 per cent per month was charged for each month the debt was outstanding, failing a satisfactory arrangement with the executive. None of the PWV clubs in the sample had loan schemes, but one (of eleven members) would contribute towards a member's expenses in a crisis: the example was cited of a member involved in a strike, who had not been paid one month. The member was expected, when her turn for the kitty money came round, to pay back the amount advanced to her, but there was no mention of interest. (The supportive ethos of that club is illustrated by the fact that members automatically contributed R5 each in the event of the death of a member's close kin; similarly in another PWV club members each contributed R50 in similar circumstances as 'a sign of sisterhood, since death is unplanned'. In neither case was the ROSCA seen as doubling as a burial society.)

One Cape Town club merits special mention, in that it was exceptional in several ways. It meets the Ardener definition cited above, but the payout, although made according to a rota, was viewed as a compulsory loan on which the member had to pay interest. The rota was compiled by all members placing their names on it in advance, and each was obliged in her turn to borrow a minimum amount. If the person at the head of the list did not want to borrow the entire kitty, loans would proceed down the list until the entire amount from contributions and loan repayments for the month had been paid out. The club had been in existence for many years, and past experience had led it to decide that a rota was necessary to avoid favouritism.[8] Interest was charged at 20 per cent per month, but was not compounded unless the borrower failed either to make repayment within three or four months or to report a difficulty to the group. As the entire fund was lent at every meeting, the club did not use banks and obtained a higher rate of interest than the bank would have given. The composition of the club had dictated its mode of operation: originally its membership comprised mainly uneducated women, but the difficulties of record-keeping and interest calculations led to the recruitment of better-educated members, and by the time of the interview it was composed of forty-five women from a wide variety of backgrounds including teachers, domestic workers, hawkers and nurses.

Logically, record-keeping would appear to be important for the running of ROSCAs, but we found that in fact some of the smaller ones kept no records at all except whatever notes members (or an organizing member) might have made for themselves. In others the executive kept a record of contributions and payouts, or else had a minute book – in which, presumably, this information was recorded. Most did not issue receipts. (This was in marked contrast to Thomas's report (1989a) on the immaculate record-keeping in the mainly larger ROSCAs he investigated.) Where a club had a building society or bank account as well, that would of course provide a partial record of club finances, but it could necessitate checks on the scrupulousness of the treasurer. We were told of the solution adopted by one club (not in the sample) which was given a plastic card for access to their account via a machine. The club decided to give two office-holders each half of the machine number needed for access to the account, while a third held the card. All three thus had to visit the machine together to withdraw money from it: one to insert the card and the other two each to punch in half the number, retreating some distance after doing so to ensure the secrecy of the number. Presumably the three could have colluded to cheat the club but this arrangement provided some safeguard against temptation overcoming one member – a modern version of the three-lock trunks used by some early English Friendly Societies.

Disputes within Clubs

Given these somewhat scanty arrangements, we investigated whether there was much dispute over payments, absconding of members, people leaving before the end of a rotation, or executive corruption. None of the sixteen clubs had ever had anyone abscond, and only one reported having to evict a member for defaulting on her payments. Several said that they had never had anyone leave even at the end of a rotation, and the rule seemed to be fairly general that nobody would be allowed to leave during a rotation. Some women were bemused when asked what would happen if someone did not pay her contribution: it was clearly unthinkable, given the basis of trust on which the clubs were formed and the strength of public opinion in the townships – in some cases reinforced by a high level of violence. (One woman from an Informal Housing Area, for example, when asked about potential enforcement of payments, spoke of the group beating the person into submission.) Of our seventeen interviewees outside the survey sample who told us about their ROSCA membership, only one reported having left a ROSCA, in that case because she no longer had an income with which to pay her contribution; and the mother of one of our ROSCA interviewees had also been forced by financial problems to withdraw from (another) ROSCA the preceding year.

Nor could any woman interviewed tell us of disputes with office holders; this probably results largely from the limited power of executive members in clubs where none of the kitty is banked or where members' turns are largely decided by consensus within the group. In the club with twenty-four members and a powerful executive, mentioned above, problems were potentially more likely; but mismanagement of funds was controlled by publicly counting at every meeting the money collected from contributions and loan repayments. Deductions to pay officials were not permissible. Our interviewee could not tell us whether there were disagreements over the chairman's decisions about the order of rotation and, if so, what happened.

How much of this apparently trouble-free organization was a result of the relatively small size and weak executives of women's ROSCAs, and how much a consequence of the way women, compared to men, operate in a club, is difficult to judge. Certainly large ROSCAs, which invariably have a high percentage of male members, are by all accounts much more troubled by disputes and corruption.[9] To place the scale of our fieldwork clubs in perspective, it may be helpful to contrast them with a large ROSCA of which an interviewee for a different study in Cape Town supplied details in 1985. That club, which was both a burial society and savings club, had 200 members, although we were not given the details according to gender. She paid R80 per month, which was equivalent to more than R200 in 1991 and higher than any contribution paid in our Cape Town sample for this study. The payout was between R20,000 and R40,000 (enough at the time to buy a house, a car and a business) depending how many branches one joined: our interviewee belonged to three. (A number of branches would all be present at a meeting.) The organizers took R1,000 of each payout to a member and placed it in a savings account (from which the member received the interest) until it was ascertained that all the member's debts within the ROSCA – from other members having 'doubled' during the rotation – had been paid. Given the size of the ROSCA and the correspondingly weaker social pressures, this was presumably a cheaper and less time-consuming option for the executive than possibly having to resort to lawyers to recover debts from the payee. However, despite a powerful executive, the club had an unusual feature which, if it indeed operated as promised, would serve to curb executive corruption to some extent. This was an arrangement whereby one could 'insure' one's investment by 'signing for one's children'; the list of their names was then sent to a lawyer, so that if one died before one's turn came round, the children benefited from the payout instead of the organizers. This particularly appealed to our interviewee, given her divorced status and the fact that a rotation took several years, but unfortunately we did not discover whether non-executive members, especially women, were in fact protected by this measure.

Members' Uses and Perceptions of Their Clubs

To assist us in assessing the financial importance of ROSCAs to their women members, we asked the women interviewed how they had used or intended to use their payouts. This revealed a variety of needs, pressures and aspirations, few of which appeared to be frivolous. Some were of a universal nature: for example, the safeguarding of children's futures by depositing the money in savings accounts or buying insurance policies, payment of crèche charges, payment towards building an extension to a home, payment of accounts, or the purchase of large items (such as a fridge or a room divider) or luxuries such as clothes or a bicycle for a child. Other goals had a very South African ring to them. One woman planned to save the money towards her aim of giving up her job as a crèche worker so that she could spend more time with her own child (who was not allowed to attend the affluent crèche); another had used her payout to buy a cow for a feast to introduce her child to the ancestors. A woman from Natal used her payout for a visit home – an expensive undertaking, as the visit was for a housewarming party to which she was required to contribute after the family had bought and extended a house. Another woman used her payout to build herself a shack in the back yard of her home, to obtain more privacy than was possible in her crowded four-roomed house. An enterprising entrepreneur used a payout to buy a dilapidated van, which at the time of interview she hoped a relative would repair so that it could be used to fetch produce from the Transkei for sale. She planned to save her next payout towards the conversion of the shack at the back of their home into a restaurant and bar, which would in turn generate more money. Another wanted to buy a house for her trips back to the Ciskei, her rural area of origin, but family demands were such that, when she arrived at her aunt's house there and found the family in dire need, she felt obliged to spend the money on supplying the household and having the leaking roof fixed. For her next payout she had lowered her sights to the building of an extra room on to her aunt's house, but a house of her own in the Ciskei remained a long-term goal.

From the earlier interviews outside the sample we gleaned examples such as the installation of electricity in a home, or in one case contributing to a father's business in the Transkei and helping him to expand it. One woman, who had already had two other payouts, had used the first to renovate her home, the second to put the finishing touches, and planned to use the third to buy a car. But sometimes the money had merely fended off disaster, as in the case of a woman who used it to pay her rent arrears.

A few clubs had clearly enunciated views on how the payouts should be spent, or even imposed actual restrictions. Thus a six-member ROSCA encouraged members to buy expensive household items they could not otherwise afford, or to extend their houses. We were told that members, when visiting the payee's house, liked to see how the money had been spent – 'it pleases them'. Another group of six, all single and working together, as a policy decision urged each other to bank at least 60 per cent of their payouts and show the others proof of this, although their work was not well paid. Yet another group of six, all women living in the same block of flats, decide at the beginning of each rotation how the money should be spent. For their first rotation members were restricted to purchases of underwear or nightwear; for their second (the current one at the time of interview), they had decided that everyone should buy curtains.

As it is very difficult to leave a ROSCA during a rotation, which in the case of larger clubs may continue for several years, we asked, at the end of each interview, whether in the light of her experience the interviewee still thought ROSCAs useful institutions, and if so why. All without exception still approved of them, some volunteering such enthusiastic comments as 'everyone should join one'; at least one interviewee hoped to join a second one as soon as her salary increased.

(Two others already belonged to a second but non-rotating savings group.) All were very decided that the clubs were of great importance for single mothers.

Reasons for this support proved to be quite varied. Naturally, financial considerations loomed large, though frequently linked with social ones. Some interviewees thought ROSCAs 'the best way to save money', because the social pressures imposed by a club made it virtually impossible to default on payments. Moreover one could not withdraw money on impulse, as could be done from a bank or building society account. Some mentioned that savings made the purchase of larger items possible without resort to hire purchase: one told us, for example, that her desire to join a club dated back to a visit to a friend who had invited her to see what the payout had bought: 'she had a new, beautiful bedroom suite'. Others, who had already used their payouts for such purposes, indicated that not only their lifestyles but their self-esteem had been augmented. As one woman – a cleaner at the railway station – told us, after she had bought linen from her pay-out she felt very proud of herself; as her ROSCA usually liked to hear what members used their payouts for, she had happily shared this with them. Some women saw payouts as a way of supplementing their regular salaries, for example for end-of-year payments for Christmas, and school uniforms for their children's new school year. One interviewee explained that she belonged to get more money than she put in, since her club had additional income from both fines and loan interest, which was split between members at the end of each rotation. Another woman, whose club had an additional system of compulsory gifts, spoke of the extra motivation to belong which it provided, enabling her to collect household items that she would probably never buy for herself. Above all, interviewees stressed that the savings themselves, the possibility of loans from the ROSCA or of swopping turns in emergencies, and the close friendships resulting from the club, all gave additional security in times of unexpected financial demands. (Most would probably have had difficulties in obtaining a bank loan.) Many stressed the usefulness of ROSCA money in freeing them from reliance on frequently unreliable or uncooperative men who had fathered their children, a major concern given the serious deficiencies of the South African maintenance system (Burman and Berger, 1988). Several spoke glowingly of how their payouts enabled them to save for their children's education, as well as to buy their children toys and clothes which they could not afford on their earnings.

Given the lack of interest payments in the majority of ROSCAs in the sample, an obvious question was whether the women were aware of the interest most were forfeiting by putting their money into their ROSCAs rather than a bank or building society. However, investigation of their additional savings methods showed that they were aware that banks, for example, paid interest. We obtained information on this point from eleven of the nineteen interviewees: only one (from an Informal Housing Area) did not have a bank account, and she was planning to open one in order to save at least R20 per month. She said she had realized that she could not do without a savings account book. Others also told us of separate savings accounts, and in two cases fixed deposit accounts; whether these were with banks or building societies was not always clear. Some had their salaries paid into the bank, and at least one mentioned the interest gained from the bank as a motive for this, although her ROSCA operated without interest payments.

Undoubtedly an important reason why women ROSCA members were prepared to forego interest from their savings, where applicable, was the social role of the clubs, which loomed large in a number of answers and often had financial implications too. Some interviewees emphasized that they valued their clubs as forums in which to collect advice from other members on how to save and use money constructively. At the upper end of the income scale, a member of one of the most prosperous clubs explained that the club had a number of professional members who acted as a resource for the others; she, as a social worker, found that she also had much to contribute to the group – which no doubt increased both her status and her self-esteem. In common with several others interviewed, she indicated that as a single mother she could be lonely at weekends and over holidays; her membership of the club gave a sense of belonging. It was also helpful to share information with other divorcees, and led to a productive use of leisure time. Her club actually organized excursions for its members and had ambitious travel plans for the future, including trips to Botswana, Mauritius and even further afield overseas. She found it a highly stimulating group. Similarly, another told us that she had joined to make friends from other backgrounds, occupations and townships outside her usual circle, but this obviously was less of a motive in the case of small clubs. Typically in such cases membership was viewed as a way to see friends regularly. One woman from the PWV told us that members of her ROSCA had mostly been at school together, but until the formation of the club no longer saw much of each other. She regarded the club as a way of having fun which was also productive. Another PWV club had been founded by four friends, who had been at university together but subsequently found that their busy careers prevented them from seeing each other, although working in the same city. Several of those interviewed had been founding members of their clubs: at least two were the main instigators of their respective ROSCAs, one choosing to form a new club rather than join an existing one so as to operate only with close friends. Interestingly, Ross's informants, who came from lower income groups, stressed to her that membership of a ROSCA carried with it prestige in the community. A number of other interviewees probably indicated much the same, though they expressed this in a more personal way, several of the poorer telling of their desire to join a ROSCA after seeing how friends, by saving together, could buy expensive things. Among the more affluent, entertainments such as lavish dinners and expensive travel no doubt had a similar effect – an interesting change from Brandel-Syrier's (1971:47) findings in Johannesburg in the early 1960s that the educated considered ROSCAs primitive.

Conclusions

In the light of the information supplied by the women in our survey, we found various erroneous ideas prevalent among some of the researchers we interviewed who did not actually work in the townships. It was thought that as banks became more accessible, both geographically and culturally, ROSCAs would fall away, and that this was indeed happening. However, this expectation was based on an assumption that ROSCAs were continuations of some earlier 'traditional', communal life style, less strange and hostile than banks (an expectation also found in the literature: see e.g. Geertz, 1962). Such ideas have been under fire recently (Boonzaier and Spiegel, 1988; Thomas, 1989a), and all our evidence supported these criticisms. Moreover, what became abundantly clear was that, far from being the resort of the poorest in the community, ROSCAs were available only to those who had a job or a regular source of income to meet contributions without fail, unless (as in one case from outside our sample) a relative – in this case a son – could be found to pay for the woman instead. The very poorest in need of credit would usually be obliged to resort to township loan sharks, who charge interest of 50 per cent or more; indeed, our earlier interviews provided an illustration of a divorced woman who was obliged to do just this because her income had been too uncertain for her to join a ROSCA.

It was, however, the flexibility and resulting variety of the institution that led us to regard it as a possible portent of the future. From our sample of ROSCAs it was evident that, rather than acting as support groups for those in need of a crutch, the clubs were vehicles for the upwardly mobile from *every* income group who could afford to belong to them. This is borne out by Lukhele (1990:32), who reports that ROSCAs 'are becoming increasingly popular among young upper-income Africans, whose clubs are fashion-orientated'. He reports that ROSCAs with members of one or both sexes adopt the name of some famous make of clothing and use payouts to patronize their favourite stores: among his examples is that of a women's group which named itself after an expensive Johannesburg shoe store. Moreover our data show that, as needs changed, so did the clubs, adopting new modes of socializing and enforcing new values such as punctuality. In addition, although the clubs often consciously retained long-standing systems of communal support in times of crisis, such as donations to express sympathy on a close relative's death, the motivation for these old institutions might be described in a new terminology of 'sisterhood', highlighting a new feminist consciousness. It was noteworthy that both PWV clubs which presented club donations to bereaved members 'as a sign of sisterhood' contained a high percentage of well-educated professional members. While we would not suggest that women in 'traditional' African society did not consciously rely on other women for support and assistance, the connotations of that interdependence are changing as women's place in urban society changes yet again and finds new expression.

Given the strong interdependence between members of ROSCAs, it is hardly surprising that they – and particularly women's ROSCAs – should serve as vehicles for women's support for each other. Nor is this a phenomenon peculiar to ROSCAs with only single women as members: in our sample a number of groups which included married women displayed it too, even if not expressing it in feminist terminology. The reasons given for excluding male members, such as feeling more comfortable with women and being able to work better with them, were examples of this. Seeing that the clubs also empower women by helping them to become to some extent economically independent of their husbands, families and boyfriends, and to create social standing for themselves within the community, it becomes obvious that they are a natural vehicle for liberating and strengthening women in a very patriarchal society. With the increasing economic power that current developments are making possible for ROSCAs, even the generally smaller women's ROSCAs are likely soon to be able to increase women's financial strength considerably too. Moreover, there seems every likelihood that as African affluence increases with the current political adjustments, women's ROSCAs will grow in number and influence.

While this may well provoke a backlash from those who feel threatened by women's increasing power, this is unlikely to be strong enough to prevent the ROSCAs from having notable consequences for the role of women in the new South Africa.

Notes

1. Our thanks go to our interviewees for their co-operation and help, and to Ms Ann Turner and Ms Amanda Tiltman for their research assistance. The research would not have been possible without the sponsorship of the Human Sciences Research Council, the UK Save the Children Fund, the Research Committee of the University of Cape Town, the UCT Foundation and the Wingate Foundation, to all of whom we are most grateful.
2. ROSCAs also exist among the Indian population in Natal, where the very sparse literature on them records the use of the names *chita* (Hindi) or *chitu* (Tamil) (Kuper, 1960).
3. The economic situation of Africans in Cape Town is still adversely affected by the consequences of the Coloured Labour Preference Area policy instituted in 1955 and abolished only in 1985. Under it, no job could be given to an African unless there was nobody classified as Coloured to take it. Training facilities for Africans, particularly women in Cape Town, were very limited. This, together with the legislation requiring suitable passes and aimed at excluding women and children from urban areas, generally left Africans, particularly women, in only the most poorly paid work (Burman, 1985). The effects of this are still visible in the economic profile of Cape Town's African population, compared with that of other major South African metropolitan areas.
4. In this kind of ROSCA a woman often contributes along with her husband, the contributions being in her husband's name. While doing research in the Southern Divorce Court, Sandra Burman encountered several cases of women bitterly (and inevitably unsuccessfully) opposing their husbands' divorce petitions, although no children, housing, or other property were involved. Investigations revealed that in these cases the woman had usually contributed to her husband's long-term ROSCA, which was due for payment soon and would in effect have provided both partners with a large lump sum, equivalent to a pension in the case of older spouses. While arrangements can be made in South African divorces for the future sharing of regular pensions, ROSCA payouts are not subject to them.
5. In 1989/90, the latest year for which statistics are available, 69.8 per cent

of African babies born in Cape Town were classified as illegitimate, and our research shows that these would have been born to women unmarried by civil *or* customary law, who would probably not have been living with the father, and who were unlikely to be receiving child support from him (see Burman and Berger, 1988; Burman, 1992).

6. Membership covered a wide range of occupations, from domestic workers to nurses and a (male) university professor.

7. Even where turn-swopping was not allowed, the expectation of a payout soon sometimes enabled women to cope with an emergency. Thus one was able to borrow the expected amount interest-free from her employer shortly before her turn, enabling her to reroof her mother's house in the Transkei immediately after the roof blew off in a storm.

8. Interestingly, this procedure had not been followed by a very similar club that we found had been formed a year before our interview and modelled on the long-established one. Regrettably, therefore, we were obliged to exclude the newer club from our sample as it did not rotate the order of loans. It preferred to invite members to apply at each meeting, though urging those who had not yet borrowed at least the minimum amount to do so within the 'rotation' or face exclusion without repayment of contributions.

9. One woman told us of her mixed-gender ROSCA, outside our sample, from which an office-holder had recently disappeared with a large sum of money. Members were scouring South Africa for him. However, his girlfriend (who did not know where he was) had not been obliged to withdraw from the club, and our informant was adamant that they had a lawyer (rather than more informal methods) ready to deal with him when he was found.

References

Ardener, S. (1964), 'The Comparative Study of Rotating Credit Associations', *Journal of the Royal Anthropological Institute*, XCIV, pp. 201–29.

Boonzaier, E. and Spiegel, A. (1988), 'Promoting Tradition: Images of the South African Past', *South African Keywords*, E. Boonzaier and J. Sharp (eds), pp. 40–57.

Brandel-Syrier, M. (1962), *Black Woman in Search of God*, London: Lutterworth Press.

—— (1971), *Reeftown Elite*, London: Routledge and Kegan Paul.

Burman, S. (1985), 'The Interaction of Legislation relating to Urban Africans and the Laws regulating Family Relationships', *Acta Juridica 1984*, pp. 89–104.

—— (1992), 'The Category of Illegitimate in South Africa: Its Size and Significance', *Questionable Issue: Illegitimacy in South Africa*, Cape Town: Oxford University Press.

—— and Berger, S. (1988), 'When Family Support Fails: The Problems of

Maintenance Payments in Apartheid South Africa', *South African Journal on Human Rights*, 4: pp. 194–203 and 334–54.

—— *Business Day*, 11 March 1992, Survey on Stokvels, pp. 12–15.

Cross, C. (1986), *Informal Credit – Or, How Does a Rural Community Capitalize Itself?*, paper presented at the Seventeenth Annual Congress of the Association for Sociology in Southern Africa, University of Natal, 30 June–4 July 1986.

—— (1987), 'Informal Lending: Do-it-Yourself Credit for Black Rural Areas' *Indicator SA* 4 (3): 87–92.

Geertz, C. (1962), 'The Rotating Credit Association: A "Middle Rung" in Development', *Economic Development and Cultural Change* 1(3): pp. 241–63.

Hellman, E. (1934), 'The Importance of Beer-Brewing in an Urban Native Yard', *Bantu Studies* VIII: pp. 34–60.

—— (1948 [1935]), *Rooiyard: A Social Study of an Urban Native Slum Yard*, Cape Town: Oxford University Press.

Kokoali, C. (1987), 'Umgalelo and the Failure of the Church? A Study in Voluntary Associations in Mbekweni Paarl', Unpublished M.A. Thesis, University of Cape Town.

Kuper, H. (1960), *Indian People in Natal*, Durban: University Press.

—— and Kaplan, S. (1944), 'Voluntary Associations in an Urban Township', *African Studies*, 3(4): pp. 178–86.

Lukhele, A. (1990), *Stokvels in South Africa: Informal Savings Schemes by Blacks for the Black Community*, Johannesburg: Amagi Books.

Mayer, P. and Mayer, I. (1971 [1961]), *Townsmen and Tribesmen: Conservatism and the Process of Urbanization in a South African City*, Cape Town: Oxford University Press.

Ross, F. (1990), *Strategies against Patriarchy: Women and Rotating Credit Associations*, Unpublished B.Sc. Hons. Thesis, University of Cape Town.

Scott-Wilson, P. and Mailoane, M. (1990), *Developments in the Informal Sector*, Unpublished seminar paper.

Thomas, E. (1989a), *Rotating Credit Associations in Cape Town: A View from Anthropology*, Preliminary Report to the Small Business Development Corporation.

—— (1989b), *Rotating Credit Associations in Cape Town*, paper presented at the Annual Conference of the Association for Anthropologists in Southern Africa, University of the Western Cape, 13–16 September 1989.

Webb, N. (1989), *Informal Credit Markets in Cape Town, Guguletu – A Case Study*, Unpublished B.A. Hons. Thesis, University of Cape Town.

Wilson, M. and Mafeje, A. (1963), *Langa: A Study of Social Groups in an African Township*, Cape Town: Oxford University Press.

3

The Kiambu Group: A Successful Women's ROSCA in Mathare Valley, Nairobi (1971 to 1990)

Nici Nelson

'Women in Groups can Solve their Problems Together'

Introduction

This is the tale of a successful Rotating Savings and Credit Association in a large squatter area of Nairobi known as Mathare Valley. The group, which will be referred to in this paper as the Kiambu Group (not its real name, for obvious reasons) has been successful for the following reasons. First, it has had a continuous existence (if not an exactly continuous membership) from 1971 to the present, a period of twenty-one years. Second, it is a ROSCA which evolved gradually over the years from an informal association to a formal, registered co-operative plus ROSCA and finally to a very successful land-buying co-operative. I question whether one can describe a ROSCA as successful when it has evolved into another form of economic association.

In this paper I give a brief background of Mathare Valley and the women who lived there and describe my twenty-year contact with the community of Mathare and the Kiambu Group. After a brief discussion of ROSCAs in general and the Gikuyu of Kenya in particular, I will give a history of the Kiambu group from 1971 to 1990 (the period of my last visit). I will then analyse why I think that consolidation and expansion of the Kiambu Group has been successful, discussing whether or not it can be called a successful ROSCA, and end with a discussion of Geertz's contention that ROSCAs were the product of a shift from a traditional agrarian social formation to a commercial one.

Mathare Valley, Then and Now

When I arrived there early in 1971, prepared to do fieldwork on the migratory and economic strategies of female heads of household residing there, the area had 60,000 people living in scattered 'villages' which had developed after the ending of the Mau Mau Emergency along the irregular valley of the Mathare River. In the ten years since the ending of the Emergency, poor rural–urban migrants (mainly Gikuyu) had spontaneously created housing on this piece of marginal urban land. Indigenous leaders, both men and women, had arisen from within the community, allying themselves with the then leading (and subsequently only) political party. They constituted themselves a KANU committee, cultivated patron–client links with the local MP, established their loyalty to the President (mainly through women's dancing groups which sang loyalty songs to the President at his country house) and eventually set up 'local' party elections to legitimate their leadership roles. By the late 1960s these KANU committees operated in each of the Mathare 'villages' much as the village elders used to in the rural Gikuyu context, dealing with local disputes and acting as a conduit of local opinion to the adminstrative Chief of the area. The major difference was that the Mathare committees included women as well as men, something that did not happen in the village (see Ross, 1973). This reflected the large number of female heads of household in Mathare, and women's relatively more independent economic position in the urban informal economy compared with the women farmers of rural Gikuyuland, who did not have access to land except through a father or a husband. These community leaders had weathered a serious confrontation with Nairobi City Council in the late 1960s, and the community had won the *de facto* right to continue to exist. For this reason community spirits in the early to mid-1970s were running high and the KANU political party leaders who had spearheaded the fight for existence were active and highly respected. Due to the ecological position of Mathare Valley, it was ideally sited for what Ross (1973) referred to as the 'entertainment industry'. Many women were attracted to the area by its economic opportunities for women, such as brewing local maize-millet beer (called *buzaa*) and/or 'sex work' (the exchange of sexual services for payment). It was on this category of women that I concentrated my research efforts.

Many changes have taken place in and around Mathare Valley and the areas to the north-east of the centre of Nairobi. In 1973 a small but significant area of 'rehousing' development was created further to the east, out along the Juja road extension. Several hundred low-cost housing units and site-and-service plots were available for rehousing Mathare residents in order that the units they already owned could be torn down. The number of the units in the scheme was derisory, and inevitably competition for the limited number of plots and houses was high. It was the political leaders and their closest clients who 'qualified'. One prominent local politician received a house, as did his wife, his girl friend, his grown-up daughter and his secretary.

This rehousing initiative triggered the departure from Mathare Valley of the most ambitious and energetic entrepreneurs *cum* local politicians, both male and female. At this time all the populist local leadership was thus 'bought out'; they abandoned Mathare Valley proper for more lucrative fields to the east of Mathare.

This process of economic differentiation was continued throughout the 1970s and early 1980s by a World Bank-sponsored, low-income housing project called Dandora. Several thousand low-cost housing units were allocated to the 'poor' of Eastlands. While laudable attempts were made to create tamper-proof schemes of allocation, it was inevitable that ways could be found round them. Many poorer clients were allocated plots on which to build, but sold out to richer people who could afford to keep to the building schedule required by the authorities.

The early 1980s were also marked by a presidential ban on 'traditional alcohol' and the granting of a concession to the Lonrho group for the commercial production of *buzaa* (maize-millet beer). The result was the collapse of the local brewing 'industry', throwing the poor female members of the Eastlands informal sector economy back on sex work, hawking and domestic work to earn a livelihood. At present the HIV/ AIDS crisis in Kenya makes the most lucrative of those three options a very questionable proposition.

By the mid-1980s, therefore, Mathare Valley consisted of very poor owner-occupiers or tenants of housing owned by absentee landlords, eking out a living hawking or seeking casual work (in the manual trades or domestic work). Mathare in 1990 was a much poorer place than it had been in 1972. It had also become a hopeless, apathetic, cynical place, where residents regarded their politicians as out to line their own pockets. Since all the local populist politicians and entrepreneurs had abandoned the place, it is currently without a truly local leadership or the vibrant, lucrative informal economic activity which characterized it in the 1970s.

As we shall see, the women who are members of the Kiambu Group were part of the local politico-economic élite which abandoned Mathare Valley.

The Research

In 1971 I began a research project in Village II which continued for three years. I followed the standard ethnographic methods of participant observation in all local activities and events, with extensive visiting, informal discussion, collection of life-histories, and focused interviews on a variety of topics. Finally I conducted a random-sample survey in Village II to collect basic demographic data on the women living in Mathare.

In 1974 I left Kenya for London to write up my PhD thesis at SOAS, University of London. Since that time I have been back to Kenya for short visits in 1978, 1983, 1985 and 1990.[1] In 1983 and 1990 I was there for three months each time, and did some small pieces of research, re-contacting my previous informants. Each time I visited Nairobi I spent a great deal of time with the president of the Kiambu Group, Mama Alice, and her daughter Alice, who was also the secretary of the group.

Rotating Savings and Credit Associations

It is not the purpose of this chapter to restate Ardener's conclusions to her 1964 survey. However, I should like to underline some of the economic and social functions ROSCAs perform which are particularly pertinent to this case study. They assist in small-scale capital formation (otherwise known as savings), provide a measure of security, and provide credit on a very small scale (something most economic institutions are unwilling to do). Such associations can enhance the social status of the organizer 'who gains status by demonstrating his powers of leadership and administrative ability'. As we shall see, this was definitely the case with the Kiambu Group's leader. Finally, they are associations often involved in shifts from one type of economic activity to another. Ardener disagrees with Geertz's contention that the ROSCA is a product of a 'shift from a traditionalistic agrarian society to an increasingly fluid commercial one' (quoted in Ardener, 1964:221), suggesting that they may be more a cause of the shift than a product of it. The Kiambu Group may have assisted its members' move from a fluid commercial economic activity of an informal variety to one of a more complicated institutionalized formal kind.

In pre-colonial Gikuyu society women's associations existed, usually based on kin and neighbourhood. These were commonly concerned with a rotating exchange of labour. Thus groups of related women would come together to prepare land, or to weed or harvest each other's fields. Muriuki (1974) makes no mention of this type of association, but his history is heavily political in emphasis, and as such concentrates on age-sets and councils of elders. Kenyatta (1938:59) mentions them only as male institutions but his account of Gikuyu life, written as it was in 1938, is predictably androcentric. Fisher (1954) claims that women's work groups of these types were an old Gikuyu institution. What I discovered in my own fieldwork was that in the second half of the twentieth century the Gikuyu developed ROSCAs. Neither my fieldwork nor the available literature makes clear the origins of the Gikuyu version of the ROSCA. The Gikuyu had an institution referred to as an *itega*, which was a contribution party, usually held when an individual had an important rite of passage (such as a funeral) or a crisis (like a serious illness) to finance. Guests would be invited and given beer and food, after which they would all make a 'contribution' to the giver of the party. Often these contributions were written down in a book; nowadays, in more sophisticated, 'modern' urban versions, they are announced over a public-address system by a compère, whose job it is to encourage and jolly the crowd into larger and larger contributions and shame the last-givers into outdoing the generosity of the first-givers. The term *itega* is now often applied to a ROSCA formed by a small group of friends, who make a rotating payment into a fund that is received by each in turn. The Kiambu Group was one such ROSCA in Mathare Valley.

The Kiambu Group ROSCA and Later Co-operative

In 1971 I very early become friendly with a pretty young teacher from Village II named Alice, and through her with her merry sister Rachel and her hard-working mother Mama Alice (after whom, as her favourite, she was named). One day Alice asked me if I would like to come to an *itega* with her. It was being held at her mother's house that day, and was called the Kiambu Group because all the women in it had been born in the district of Kiambu. I had already learned that the word *itega* in Gikuyu could denote a number of diverse events, but the common theme of them all was that those present made a contribution in money or kind. The only type of *itega* I had met at that point in my fieldwork was the one described above, meant to raise money to pay for an illness, towards the expenses of a funeral or wedding, or even to send a child to school overseas. However, I soon realized that this particular *itega* was a form of ROSCA. It had been started a few months before by Mama Alice, one of the richer women in Village II in Mathare Valley. When I began to attend their meetings in 1971 there were twenty members, all women from Kiambu who brewed *buzaa* beer and owned housing units in Mathare Valley. Many of them were KANU leaders or members of the Village Committee. The only exceptions were the three daughters of the two most powerful women in the group, the founder, Mama Alice, and the KANU leader of women, who enrolled their young daughters as members. These three young women were not themselves house-owners, merely *buzaa* brewers who lived in rooms belonging to their mothers.

The group was loosely organized at this time. Mama Alice, as the founder, was the president, and her daughter Alice acted as secretary, while Lucy (the daughter of the other KANU leader) was treasurer. Though at this time the group was very informal, it is interesting that the leadership structure mimicked that of more formally constituted groups. Alice and Lucy were officials because they were literate, while most of the older women were not.

At this time the group met once a week. The woman who would be receiving the fund that particular week would host the meeting and provide tea for the group. The contribution each week was K.sh 12/ plus a little extra to pay for the tea. That meant that each week someone in the group received at least K.sh. 240/. This was more than the then monthly minimum wage in Kenya (K.sh 150/), and was the amount a hard-working beer-brewer could earn in a month (see Nelson, 1978). The cycle of contributions took five months to complete.

As Ardener points out in her article (1964:208), the members of the Kiambu Group would certainly agree that ROSCAs help to build the 'habit' of saving, since the obligation to contribute regularly becomes a solemn duty and encourages people to save each week in a way which they would not otherwise do. Mama Alice said as much to me on several occasions, as did Alice and a number of the other members when I asked them why they chose to belong to the Kiambu Group. One quotation from Mama Alice will illustrate what I mean:

> It is good to have the group to answer to if you do not set that money aside each week. Otherwise, if you were on your own, when business is bad you might decide not to that week. The *itega* of the Kiambu Group teaches us the *faida* (profit) of learning how to save money regularly.

I followed the group throughout my fieldwork period until 1974. In 1972 their success had attracted more members, and the membership had grown to thirty. One or two of the new members were not from Kiambu, but were well known to existing members. Not all the new members were house-owners; at least half were highly respected but poorer 'clients' of the KANU leaders who were members. Membership of the Kiambu Group had become a resource which patrons could grant to selected clients. However, the new members had to be relatively successful *buzaa* beer-brewers in order to be able to meet the weekly contribution. Except for the aforementioned three daughters of two important members, the rest of the women were all over forty years of age. Perhaps a quarter of the members were childless, and some of them were considerably older.

The Kiambu Group decided at this time that it needed a clubhouse. The reason was that some of the new members no longer lived in Mathare, and it would be more 'convenient' (and I suspect more neutral) to have a single venue. They held a work party, and on the back of one of Mama Alice's houses (more a convenient than a neutral choice!) they built themselves a crude lean-to shelter with a cardboard roof. The room was furnished with benches and a table and chair at the front for the secretary to sit at while she collected and recorded the contributions. The table and chair were given by Mama Alice as befitted the generosity of a founder/patroness.

The women said that this group gave them access to a large sum of money, for which they could plan ahead. The commonest use for the money for those with children was to pay school fees. These women often described their membership as being 'for the good of the children'. Usually the childless women or older women with grown-up children used their money to capitalize a brewing business or obtain building materials to repair their housing units. It was obvious that in the context of the local economy the members of the Kiambu Group had above average incomes.[2]

The rota for turn-taking was set up by the secretary. The founder and the most important women in the group were usually at the head of the list; but the members' needs would be taken into account and there was a certain flexibility which allowed them to request a change of their position in the rota to meet an emergency. As Ardener points out, those members early in the rotation received an interest-free loan, so it was economically advantageous to be at the top of the list.

In 1972 the contribution-completion-rate was close to 100 per cent. Members rarely defaulted, and if they did it was usually for very good reasons (such as illness or a death in the immediate family). The correct procedure in this case was for the woman experiencing difficulties in paying her contribution to explain her problem and get the permission of the group to defer her payment. They always made good the default at a later date. Almost all the members I shall describe as 'Old Timers' were the earliest settlers of Mathare Village II, who had built housing units for residence and rental. As a result of this secure economic base, they were able to become large-scale brewers of *buzaa* beer and to carry out more wholesaling (a more profitable form of economic activity than just retailing). Each Old Timer wholesaler stood at the centre of a network of retailers to whom she regularly sold her beer. I have described elsewhere the delicate balance of credit which large-scale brewers had to maintain to maximize their profits (Nelson, 1979). The meeting was not always held on the same day of the week but I gradually came to recognize the signs which marked the day of the Kiambu Group *itega*. On that day I would inevitably find one or more of the members making the rounds of their brewing networks collecting a debt here or there to make up their contribution.

After two years of successful operation as a ROSCA, the shrewd, ambitious founder, Mama Alice, began to seek ways to expand the group's function and size. She approached another powerful woman in her group, a top KANU leader. They decided that the time had come to formalize the operation of the Kiambu Group. One of the first things they did was to buy a bound journal and instruct Alice, the secretary, to keep a complete record of the weekly meetings. She was already keeping a list of who had paid and not paid, but now she began to take something approximating to minutes. The KANU leader already knew about minutes as proper procedure for running meetings, and sent Alice along to the secretary of the Village II KANU Committee to find out how to keep minutes, conduct meetings and organize a group in the 'proper' (that is, modern) manner. From the beginning of 1973, more formal meetings replaced the former casual procedures.

In the early days, the *itega* took place on a mutually convenient afternoon, not always the same day. But there was no formal meeting in that each member would drop in at some point in the afternoon. They would spend five business-like minutes or two gossipy hours, as their circumstances permitted. Women would come, casually dressed and work-dirtied, straight from their brewing, selling of beer, or housework. After greeting those present, they would give Alice their money and then either sit and have a cup of tea or make their excuses and go back to work. After Mama Alice decided to modernize the group, the meetings were called for a certain hour on a given day, and women had to spend a certain period of time there. The formalization of the meeting was reflected in the increasingly formal dress and demeanour of the members. There was an air of seriousness about the meetings; there was less local gossip and more eager discussion of future strategies.

The next thing they did was to approach the Chairman of the KANU Committee for the whole of Mathare Valley. This man was also the 'founder' and Chairman of Village II (where most of the members of the Kiambu Group resided); he had been one of the first house-builders in the area, and had early on assumed responsibility for giving new arrivals 'permission' to build there. At this period he had been elected as Councillor for the whole of Mathare Valley; he was a man of many parts and many connections with the world of power and money outside the Valley. The women requested that he give them 'permission' to apply for co-operative status.[3] He at first refused them this 'permission'. Undeterred, members of the group who knew him best, who were also on the KANU committee, kept up an unremitting campaign for several months. They showed him the book of minutes they had been keeping, asked him to attend a meeting (an invitation he never accepted) and purportedly discussed their investment plans with him. It took several months of exhaustive persuasion and the mobilizing of all the women members of the KANU committee. At last he was persuaded that they were both serious and competent, and gave them the name of a lawyer to help them in their application. In the next six-month period the lawyer advised them how to draw up a charter and apply for status as a co-operative land-buying society. Overall, they paid him a fee of K.sh. 1,880/, a not inconsiderable sum which was raised by levy from the membership.

The leadership of the Kiambu Group also seem to have received advice on financial organization from the Chairman, who was himself a very canny businessman. Mama Alice explained to me that the Chairman had advised her that rather than continue to rotate their receipts, it would be better to reinvest all income into new investments. When Mama Alice relayed this advice to the Group, they saw the sense of it and agreed not to take anything out of the Group for the first few years. This point marked a significant change in the scope of activities of the Kiambu group. The existing membership tapped their networks, and women from all over Mathare and Eastleigh were included. Membership expanded during 1973 from the original 30 to 107. No longer was there any requirement that people be from Kiambu or own houses in Mathare. The major requirements for membership now seemed to be reliability and the resources to buy at least one 'share', worth K.sh 1,200. Although payment schedules for the shares were flexible (as will be seen below), two of the original members were forced to drop out because of the cost. They were older and not so 'well-up' (the local equivalent of 'well off'), being women who had joined initially as favoured clients of one of the KANU leaders but without the resources to buy a share. Needless to say, the other members with limited resources (the three daughters discussed above) had their 'shares' paid for by their wealthy mothers.

It was at this point that I realized the extent of gender antagonism in Mathare Village II. As it became apparent that the Kiambu Group was expanding and the prognosis for financial success was excellent, a local men's group asked to join them. The discussions about this proposed merger were very revealing. Even though the leaders of the men's group promised the membership that they (the men) would co-operate with the women and give them equality, the women refused. They refused with vigour and vitriol. 'Men will "eat all the money" and leave us bankrupt', shouted one angry woman in a meeting. Other typical comments were: 'men are corrupt', 'men do not have the true spirit of *harambee* (working together)' and 'they will take over and not let us speak in our own co-operative!'

At this time the Kiambu Group became a small ROSCA embedded in a larger umbrella organization which was a registered land-buying co-operative. The ROSCA continued to operate on a weekly basis in the same way as it had before, with much the same membership but with some differences. First, a new requirement was that everyone in the ROSCA had to be a member of the Kiambu Group Co-operative, so the two poor women who could not buy a share in the co-operative also left the ROSCA at the same time. Secondly, the pool of potential participants in the ROSCA and its weekly *itega* was larger, and the membership in any given cycle shifted slightly. After a single cycle of payments was completed, one or two women might opt out while a couple of others would join. There was tacit agreement that approximately thirty was the right size for a single cycle; Mama Alice told me that all agreed that a five-month cycle was the longest that most women could wait for a return on their investment. Mama Alice and her daughters, Alice and Rachel, were invariably part of every cycle. It was their way of keeping control over the Group.

Another change in the *itega* procedure at this time was the way the members used their 'fund', namely to pay off some of their arrears in 'share' buying. At one typical meeting in November of 1973, I recorded that twenty-eight of the thirty-two-member ROSCA were present. At this meeting, after the collection of the *itega* contribution, there was a place in the meeting's agenda for members to put money towards their shares. The woman who received the *itega* 'fund' promptly used most of it to pay K.sh. 150/ on her 'share'. Six of the most important older women were designated to carry the money collected for shares to the bank. At least two women had to go together when attending the bank.

The reins of leadership of the new Kiambu Group Co-operative stayed firmly in the hands of Mama Alice. She had been elected chairwoman of the Kiambu Group, a post she holds to this day. Her daughter Alice was elected secretary, a post she held until the early 1980s, when she became the treasurer. Mama Alice's other daughter, Rachel, was elected to the steering committee of ten. Thus effectively Mama Alice had a block of one-third of the membership of the steering committee of a co-operative with 100 members.

By the end of 1973 the group had collected K.sh. 20,000/. Mama Alice confided to me that her ambition was to buy a shop. It would be used for trade, and the 'poorer' members (that is, those who could afford to buy only one share) would be able to work in it. At this time it was obvious that the Kiambu Group was being stratified into an upper stratum of those who could buy multiple shares and those who were still struggling to buy their first share. The ROSCA continued to operate on a weekly basis.

In early 1974 there was great excitement in Mathare. The new housing units and site-and-service scheme plots in New Mathare were being allocated. The units were supposed to house the poorest of the poor. The reality was that all the KANU members and all their clients were at the top of the allocation lists. A significant proportion of the Kiambu Group ROSCA received an allocation either of a built unit or a plot under the site-and-service scheme – in a few cases, both. Despite this dislocation, the ROSCA continued to operate with the same pattern of using the contribution to pay off part of a share in the co-operative. Old Mathare Village II and New Mathare were within walking distance. The group had expanded (there were now 120 members) and had managed to accumulate K.sh.50,000/. They had just made a down-payment on a butcher's shop in Eastleigh, and were eagerly awaiting taking possession of the shop and starting to operate it. Just before I left Nairobi, Mama Alice elatedly told me that the books had been inspected successfully by the office of the Attorney-General.

At this point I lost close contact with the entire group. My information on its continued existence and operation ceases to be based on multiple interviews with a large sample of members, participant observation and casual conversations. My later data on the Kiambu Group consists of semi-formal interviews with Mama Alice, Alice and Rachel, and the important KANU Women's leader, in 1978, 1983 and 1990. All these women had been both close friends and chief informants. I had managed to keep contact with them. It is important to note, therefore, that the quality, and perhaps the reliability, of my data changes at this point as my resources narrowed. My informants consisted of members of one family who effectively were the leadership of the Kiambu Group.

In 1983 Mama Alice was still president, Alice was still secretary, but another woman (unknown to me) was now treasurer. Lucy, the previous treasurer, was no longer a member, having married and moved out of Nairobi. Mama Alice and her daughter reported that the Kiambu Group remained at 120 members but had made great economic advances. They had completed the purchase of the butcher's shop, started nine years previously. The rents they received for the shop were reinvested in more plots in the Eastlands area. Mama Alice, always as cagey and careful with her information as with her money, told me that there were 'many'. Alice later told me that they had eight plots. The financial situation of the Group was much more secure since a dividend had been instituted. The rents from these plots were used to pay off the mortgages; the remainder was partly used to pay a yearly dividend to each member, depending on their holding of shares. Poorer members in the group, that handful of members who owned only one share, were employed in various capacities, maintaining the properties, collecting rents, supervising and working in these properties.

The group had branched out into acquiring rural plots and had bought into four rural land-allocation schemes. In such schemes a large section of rural land would be divided amongst a group of share owners. These plots of land were often worked and/or supervised by the above member and employees. I have only the sketchiest idea whether these plots were individual plots, or shares of a coffee or tea estate worked centrally, with the membership charged for labour and input and given a share of the profits at the end of the year.

The remainder of the rents and profits from the plots were saved for reinvestment. In 1993 the group had deposits in three banks totalling K.sh48,000/, K.sh2,000/ and K.sh10,000/. The reasons why they had three bank accounts were, first, to spread the risk and, second, to widen their options for obtaining additional mortgages.

The ROSCA had ceased to operate two years previously. Alice maintained that it had outlived its usefulness. Those members who were successful (most of the membership) were now so well-off that they had bank accounts of their own, and were conversant with the ins and outs of interest payments and so forth. The poorer members, who were really employees in all but name, could not afford the contributions. In the last years the contribution had risen to k.sh 50/ and sometimes k.sh 100/. At this time the minimum wage was K.sh 550/ per month. Thus it can be seen that the weekly 'fund' for such an *itega* was nearly the monthly wage for an unskilled worker. This would obviously be out of reach of the poor employees in the group. Several of the older women, who had been committed to the idea of the *itega* more as a form of sociable solidarity than just a form of saving, had either retired from the group or died. The ROSCA had ceased to be after eleven years of existence. It had transformed itself into a co-operative, which eventually proved more useful to the members than the ROSCA.

In 1990 I was in Kenya pursuing entirely different research interests. However, I did visit Mama Alice and also her daughter Alice. Inadvertently I stumbled on another exciting development in the ongoing saga of the Kiambu Group. Mama Alice was now retired from any active work except managing her investments. She was still chairwoman and Alice was now the treasurer. I found Alice poring over an architect's drawing. This was a plan for a six-storey apartment block. It seemed that the latest project of the Kiambu Group was to tear down the one-storey butcher's shop (their original investment) in order to build an apartment block with shops on the ground floor. They were going to raise money from the membership to demolish the building and prepare the foundations. A levy of K.sh 2,000/ was being raised from each member.

This strategy very much reflected the current state of the land market in Nairobi. In the 1970s and early 1980s Nairobi expanded rapidly to the east, and it seemed at the time that there was unending land for exploitation by builders and developers. The availability of cheap land meant that most buildings were low, two-storey at the most. As Nairobi's population exploded in this period, development has gobbled up most available land and land prices have risen sharply. Therefore, people interested in investing in urban housing are now buying the older, low houses and replacing them with multi-storey blocks. The Kiambu Group, therefore, was moving with the times. On subsequent visits I learned that Alice was negotiating a loan from a finance company with a very short repayment schedule to get a lower interest rate. I was impressed by her financial competence and acumen, as she knowledgeably discussed repayment schedules, differential interest rates, collateral and equity with a sophistication which left me far behind. She confided that the Kiambu Group had profited greatly from the People's Bank, which had been organized in the mid-1980s by a populist politician who gave collateral-free, low-interest loans to the *maskini ya Nairobi* ('the poor of Nairobi'), to quote Alice.[4] The Kiambu Group had mobilized their networks to obtain some of this low-cost money, and it had been very helpful for their investment strategies before the People's Bank failed. As she spread her papers out on the table in front of her to illustrate the negotiations she had carried out with a wide variety of financial institutions in previous years, I remembered how once in 1972 a young nursery-school teacher from Mathare Valley had asked my help in setting up a system to record the receipt of members' payments towards their shares. In handling the affairs of the Kiambu Group, she had become an excellent administrator and financial expert.

By the time I left Nairobi, the butcher's shop building had been demolished and the site was being prepared for building. I have no doubt that the apartment block has been built by now. The last words Alice said to me on the visit could stand as a motto for this book. Standing proudly in front of her small house, she waved good-bye to me, and when I wished her and the Kiambu Group good luck with their new venture, she smiled and said,

'Women in groups can solve their problems together!'

The Kiambu Group: Did It Succeed, and If So, Why?

The Kiambu Group ROSCA was obviously successful in that it lasted with much the same membership for ten years, and there seemed to be a relatively low rate of default. In the three years in which I was in close contact with many members of the group and heard the weekly gossip of the *itega*, I did not record a single instant of wilful default. I recorded twenty-three instances of negotiated temporary default, and all were made good at a later date. Certainly in the early years one cycle was always followed immediately by another. In 1978 the cycles were still continuous. I am not sure whether or not there were gaps between the cycles after that period.

The Kiambu Group could also be said to be successful because of the way it ceased to exist. It did not come to an end because of scandal about the leadership or accusations of embezzlement and fraud. It ceased to operate because many women in the group had reached an economic level where they had personal bank accounts and received a higher rate of return on savings invested in other ways. Yet as I have demonstrated, the Kiambu Group ROSCA was directly responsible for the economic enhancement of its members and their ability to set up a successful land-buying co-operative.

Then why did the Group succeed? I think because of two factors: first, its organizational structure, and second, the objective conditions of Kenya during the years 1970–1990.

What were the important aspects of the Kiambu Group's organizational structure to which its success may be attributed? First, the members were relatively homogeneous socially. As I noted, all the members came from Kiambu district, and the resulting links of friendship and kinship were important in building trust and accountability, as was the fact that the first members had all been residents of Village II, Mathare Valley. Even when the membership was expanded, all the members lived in Eastlands, the area to the east of the city centre which included Mathare. The second important factor was the relative economic homogeneity of the group. There were a small number of women who might be called 'clients' of more affluent members, but in the beginning the economic differential was small. The gap in affluence between members widened after the allocation of houses and site-and-service plots in New Mathare, and the expansion of membership when the group formed a co-operative; this small group of relatively poorer women thus became virtual employees of the co-operative.

Another way in which social homogeneity was ensured was the Kiambu Group's refusal to include male members. The women preferred to maintain their solidarity as an all-female group.

All these factors meant that the members could call on multiple sanctions to prevent defaulting. The group could mobilize links of friendship or kinship, shared neighbourhood ties, lack of mobility (because they were all house-owners) and the importance for these women of maintaining a reputation for reliability and honesty in their roles as brewers or wholesalers of beer, landladies or politicians.[5]

It could also be said that the Kiambu Group was lucky in its leadership. Mama Alice, the founder, had allied herself with one of the most powerful women in Mathare Valley, and this lent the group great credibility. Mama Alice herself was an intelligent, hard-working and business-like woman. Her daughter Alice was very like her mother. The two women led the group with firm and presumably honest leadership. I infer that they were honest from their reputations. All the members of the group were canny, clever women who would have been perfectly well aware if their funds were being embezzled. If there was any peculation, it was done on a moderate and locally acceptable scale.

The leadership was also wise enough to take good advice when it was given, such as the Councillor's advice to postpone the granting of dividends to the members until the group was on a firmer footing. They avoided the temptation of yielding to take-over bids from already established men's groups which might well have stripped them of assets.

It is true that after the first few years the Kiambu Group did not seem to be run on particularly participatory or democratic lines. To call it a true co-operative would seem to be overly optimistic. A more accurate way of describing them might be an investment company run by Mama Alice and Alice, in which there were 100 investors. However, the centralized leadership was firm, intelligent and fair.

The Kiambu Group, after it had consolidated itself as a flourishing *itega*, successfully made the transition from a ROSCA to a ROSCA plus a co-operative. One of the reasons for this successful transition was that the leaders of the ROSCA had powerful patrons, who gave them some excellent advice and training in how to keep accurate records and run an organization properly. The literature on development is filled with complaints on how women's organizations are often badly run because women are less well educated and less exposed to modern institutions than men. It is difficult to mobilize women successfully into groups because their literacy and numeracy skills are poor and their experience with modern organizational procedures limited. These women had had enough exposure to modern organizational methods through their association with KANU to be clear what had to be done. They had access to male patrons who were ultimately willing to give them access to training, economic advice, and the necessary contacts. Having this back-up was important in the days when the co-operative was being set up, and undoubtedly facilitated its establishment and consolidation. But the early experience of running the ROSCA was invaluable in introducing the leadership to the procedures of a modern formal organization.

The Kiambu Group was successful also because all the members were already established, relatively prosperous businesswomen (though admittedly only within the informal sector of Nairobi). This meant that the members had both the resources to invest regularly and reliably, and the capacity to wait before they began to take out profits from their investment. Many nascent co-operatives founder because the members are anxious to have a return on their investment and do not leave enough in the re-investment fund. The fact that almost all the members of the ROSCA and the subsequent co-operative were also owners of housing units ensured their rootedness in the community and continued commitment to the group. The fact that they were older meant that they were not about to get married and leave the area (as did the young relative of the powerful KANU leader when she married). Urban co-operative ventures often fail because the membership is too fluid.

The Kiambu Group Co-operative was greatly assisted by the pre-existence of the Kiambu Group ROSCA. As I have shown, the 'fund' was one of the main ways in which some members saved the money to invest in shares of the co-operative. Admittedly, not all the members of the co-operative belonged to the ROSCA, but those who formed the important core of the co-operative did.

While these organizational and structural elements contributed to the success of the Kiambu Group, and however important they were, it must be recognized that an equally important factor was the combination of objective economic and political conditions in Kenya in the period 1970–1990. This particular historical moment in Nairobi and Kenya provided optimal conditions for the consolidation and expansion of an *itega* and the subsequent co-operative. The 1970s were a relatively buoyant time for the Kenyan economy, both formal and informal. For Mathare women the home-brewing of a local beer had a large market and no commercial rivals, and was only minimally illegal; the authorities did not regard it as a particularly important crime. The women had all arrived in Nairobi when there was a great expansion of self-built housing. Therefore they could consolidate their position in the urban area as landladies as well as brewers. A hard-working woman could, with reasonable luck as well as minimal investment and skills, make a better living than an unskilled labourer. Since the mid-1980s the informal sector has not been as lucrative an option for an unskilled, uneducated woman. A presidential decree against 'indigenous alcohol' in the mid-1980s effectively removed the option of beer brewing: the legal sanctions against brewers have since become draconian (Nelson, forthcoming).

Those women who set up the original ROSCA also benefited from the availability in the 1960s of much empty marginal land suitable for occupation and self-built housing. The members of the Kiambu Group had gained a significant foothold in the urban economy by building houses.

These Mathare women were fortunate in another respect. Just at the moment when the ROSCA was seeking to reform itself into an investment co-operative, many of the members received a new resource: the housing units and site-and-service plots in New Mathare. Political pressure had been applied to the Nairobi City Council 'to do something about squatters'. Many of the ROSCA members were part of the local political and entrepreneurial élite, which claimed a lion's share of the new plots. While these houses and site-and-service schemes were not free (the one entailed taking on a mortgage and the other a loan for building a house), they increased the owners' earnings from rentals. This further improved their ability to raise investment capital and reinvest the returns to expand the co-operative.

When the ROSCA was expanding and consolidating itself into an investment co-operative, there existed two excellent ways to make money which entailed very little effort on the part of the investors and which yielded a good return in a period of relatively low inflation. At this time there was a conjuncture of several historical trends. Urban land and building materials were cheap and available, while rental housing was lucrative. An owner could realize a housing investment within two years. During the late 1980s urban land became increasingly scarce, but the demand for rental housing in 1990 was still buoyant: hence the decision of the Kiambu Group to build an apartment block on their plot. It is possible that they may have entered that market after a recession depressed the demand for rental housing.

The second investment option which the Kiambu Group exploited to a lesser degree was investing in rural land. The late 1960s and 1970s saw a flourishing market in rural land. Buying into tea and coffee estates in the 1970s could produce quite spectacular returns. The Kiambu Group was wise to take advantage of this option when it was available.

Another condition which helped the Group was the fact that money was easily available to poor women of Eastlands, due to the existence of Ngumba's People's Bank.

Lastly, the Kiambu Group was founded during a period of relatively low inflation. It is known that in periods of high inflation, saving money through ROSCAs may become counter-productive for the savers. Money would lose its value during the period of the contribution cycle, with the later recipients subsidizing the early recipients of the fund if no steps were taken to adjust for this.

If the Kiambu Group were forming today it would have to deal with a very high inflation rate. The group would also have to raise much more initial capital as down-payment to enter the housing market. Interest rates are higher, repayment schedules shorter, and altogether money is very hard to come by. I am not sure how a co-operative eager to invest money would go about it in the early 1990s. Apart from the high inflation rate and cost of entry, opportunities are fewer, competition greater and the economy nearly stagnant. In periods of high inflation, the kinds of investments a group would consider must give a quick and high return, otherwise their savings will lose value rapidly. If, for example, such a group decided to invest in some productive enterprise, this would be an uncertain option, entailing as it does productive skills, sophisticated assessment of markets, and retailing outlets. It would also mean a slow rate of return, unacceptable in a high-inflation situation. In addition, deciding on one productive activity which a group of women is capable and willing to engage in is always the most difficult first step. Many a production co-operative initiative has foundered on the very question of what enterprise to begin. Investing ready capital in something like a housing market, which entails little risk and good certain returns, is much easier to agree upon. However, what does a group do if the cost of entry into such a market is beyond their reach?

Finally, I would like to consider whether the Kiambu Group ROSCA could be said to be successful if it transformed itself over the years into a larger co-operative. I think that overall the conclusion must be 'yes!'. Realistically speaking, it is unlikely that a ROSCA can have a permanent existence. The success of a ROSCA depends on a consensus on investment strategies. Life moves on; people's circumstances change and with them their view on how they should invest their surplus. In the second decade of the Kiambu Group ROSCA, the women who urged its continuation were those for whom this style of regular saving helped them either to keep abreast of their obligations to the co-operative, or to survive in an ever more uncertain economy. These members can be contrasted with those whose economic lives had become so varied and prosperous that they had expanded far beyond the confines of Old or New Mathare. For them the ROSCA had become no more than a pleasant way to spend an afternoon. There are other, easier ways to socialize. By then the fund was making only a minimal economic contribution to the lives of these wealthy women. The ROSCA had had a period of great importance at the time when these women were consolidating their businesses, and later creating, expanding and consolidating the co-operative. It was successful in both those aims, but it outlived its usefulness and was totally replaced by the co-operative, which had become a better strategy. However, it is true that without the Kiambu Group ROSCA, the registered co-operative would not have existed. Thus it can be seen to have been a success.

I would like to conclude with a slightly contentious observation. Ardener (1964:221) has claimed that ROSCAs were causative in a shift from a traditionalist agricultural society to a predominantly trading economy; which was her refinement of Geertz's claim that ROSCAs were a product of a shift from the one social form to another. My case study builds further on her observation. In this particular case – of a group of informal-sector beer-brewers and self-build house-owners seeking a secure place in the urban economy – the ROSCA assisted a shift from a more informal sector economy to the more complicated, formal sector area of co-operative investment and speculation in real estate.

To close, it would be fitting here to refine Alice's moral statement about the success of the Kiambu Group ROSCA, 'Women in groups can solve their problems together.' This would be a more accurate reflection of reality if the following clause were added – 'when the historic and economic conditions are favourable'.

Notes

1. My visit in 1990 was funded by a small grant from the ESRC. I was investigating the perception of the risk of contracting HIV/AIDS of young, sexually-active, unmarried women.
2. There was an observable correlation between economic success in Mathare Valley in the early 1970s (as either a beer-brewer or a house-builder and renter) and childlessness.
3. In the beginning of settlement in Mathare Valley in the early 1960s, certain older, ex-Mau-Mau, Gikuyu men established themselves as informal 'chiefs' of the area and claimed the unchallenged right to allocate building rights to those settlers who followed to build houses in the area. Sometimes a small payment was made to the leader and sometimes, when the petitioner was an attractive woman, he claimed his payment in sexual services.
4. In the late 1970s and early 1980s there was a proliferation of banks in Nairobi. One in particular had been formed by a politician eager to woo the residents of Eastlands: the Urban and Rural Bank (referred to locally as the 'People's Bank'), set up by Ngumba, an ambitious local politician. He had been Nairobi mayor in 1979 and had run unsuccessfully for the Mathare parliamentary seat in the early 1980s. He founded the Bank at that time in order to create local support. In its heyday it offered no-collateral, low-interest loans to the underprivileged, and the Kiambu Group managed to convince him that they qualified for such a loan. Alice was clear that this was a great help to them at a critical point in their economic development. The bank crashed in 1986 due to a combination of over-extension, unsecured loans and peculation. Ngumba fled the country, claiming to be a political refugee. He returned under an amnesty in 1991.
5. The reputation issue is very interesting. The fact that all women were involved with KANU, or were clients of those working for KANU, meant

that each member had a stake in maintaining a certain reputation for reliability and honesty. Many of the women were also wholesalers of *buzaa* beer; their reputations for reliability and honesty were essential for the maintenance of their extensive networks of retailers, who trusted that the beer would always be available when promised and would contain only the best ingredients. Certainly any gossip about a beer-brewer's default over *itega* payments or failure to keep up payments after having claimed the 'fund' would have swept Mathare Valley with the swiftness of a fire in dry timber. The gossip networks were very effective in keeping brewers and retailers abreast of the reliability of both fellow-brewers and customers (Nelson, 1978).

References

Ardener, S. (1966), 'The Comparative Study of Rotating Credit Associations', *Journal of the Royal Anthropological Institute*, XCIV (2):201.

Fisher, J. (1954), *The Anatomy of Kikuyu Domesticity and Husbandry*, Report for the Department of Technical Co-operation.

Kenyatta (1938), *Facing Mount Kenya*, London: Mercury Books.

Muriuki, G. (1974), *History of the Kikuyu: 1500–1900*, Oxford: Oxford University Press.

Nelson, N. (1978), 'Women Must Help Each Other', *Women Divided, Women United*, P. Caplan and J. Bujra (eds), London: Tavistock Publishers.

—— (1979), 'How Women and Men Get By: The Sexual Division of Labour in the Informal Sector of a Nairobi Squatter Settlement', *Casual Work and Poverty in Third World Cities*, R. Bromley and C. Gerry (eds) New York: J. Wiley and Sons.

—— (forthcoming), *Women Alone: Female Heads of Household on a Nairobi Squatter Settlement*.

Ross, M. (1973), *The Political Integration of Urban Squatters*, Evanston: Northwestern Press.

4

A Note on ROSCAs among Ethiopian Women in Addis Ababa and Eritrean Women in Oxford

Astier M. Almedom

Addis Ababa, capital of Ethiopia, is now home to over 1.5 million people.[1] Since the Revolution of 1974 which deposed Emperor Haile Sellasie, the rate of urbanization of the nation slowed down significantly, mainly due to the progressive economic decline resulting from the prolonged war in the North. The central government, both military and Marxist of a sort, was heavily engaged in armed conflicts with the peoples of the northern province of Tigray and Eritrea, a former Italian colony that was annexed by Haile Sellasie in 1961. The war with Eritrea spanned three decades, and that with Tigray nearly two decades, incurring enormous human and material costs. Ethiopia was set in a downward spiral of debts with several countries, including the former Soviet Union, which was the main supplier of arms. Millions of ordinary citizens suffered famine, and many of those unaffected by famine were demoralized, particularly women whose husbands, sons and often daughters as well were subjected to continuous harassment and forcible conscription. The prevailing repressive political climate discouraged the wage-earning section of the population from saving; instead a very short-term outlook was adopted by many. This was manifested by a widespread attitude of 'eat and drink and be merry, for tomorrow you die'.[2]

It was in these conditions during 1987–8 that I conducted a survey in Addis Ababa of mothers and their infants aged less than two years located in low-income households on the western edge of the city. The majority of interviews, which focused on infant feeding, health and growth, were conducted in Amharic by myself, with one female assistant. The women interviewed were hospitable and forthcoming, an important feature in this study where there were no gender barriers and a high degree of cultural compatibility between interviewer and respondents. During this survey I became aware that mothers were participating in ROSCAs.

Several authors have discussed the significance of *iqqubs,* or ROSCAs, in rural Ethiopia (Begashaw, 1978; Miracle et al., 1980; Padmanabhan, 1988; Aredo, 1991). The most systematic study of urban voluntary associations, including ROSCAs, in central Ethiopia was carried out by Gedamu in the late 1960s. According to him, 'voluntary associations are *ad hoc* structures which include both rural/monoethnic and urban/ multiethnic characteristics, as well as develop new and novel features in order to accommodate the specific needs and wishes of their members'. (Gedamu, 1972). Gedamu listed ten different purposes that were found in voluntary associations. Some of these are relevant to the data I present below. As the Addis Ababa data were collected, it became apparent that the ROSCA fulfilled three functions. First, it strengthened the urban networks of migrants to the city. Second, it also improved social support networks, in which women provided mutual emotional and moral support and exchange of information. And third, it indirectly benefited the women's weanling infants, by giving the mothers access to cash with which to purchase good-quality weaning foods such as *faffa.*

The sample has been described in detail elsewhere (see Almedom, 1991a; 1991b). A total of 113 mother–infant pairs were studied. Since people are reticent about discussing whether they belong to ROSCAs, questions were posed indirectly. The interviewee was first asked if ROSCAs were common in the area. If she answered 'yes' and was willing to add more information on the subject, then she was asked whether she belonged to one herself. It was found that 61 per cent of the women interviewed belonged to ROSCAs. Many of these ROSCAs were based on ethnic and religious affiliation, while others were based on friendship and neighbourhood only (see Table 4.1).

The frequency of ROSCA meetings ranged from two to six weeks, but once a month was the average. The form that these meetings took varied from coffee ceremonies – meetings where only coffee and roasted

Table 4.1. Distribution of ROSCAs among Sample Women.

ROSCA Membership	Number	Per cent
Yes	69	61.2
No	32	28.3
No information	12	10.5

cereal snacks and *dabbo* (a special leavened bread) were served – to meetings in which full meals were provided, followed by the coffee ceremony. Only women attended these meetings: they were often accompanied by their suckling infants. The children of the household and the neighbours would eat the left-overs of a large meal. The meetings were always held in the early- or mid-afternoon. In contrast with *idirs* (burial associations), when the men would be served first and the women second, ROSCA meetings gave the women a chance to eat the choicest foods themselves. *Tchat* (a mild narcotic leaf known in other parts of the world as *khat*) was never chewed during these meetings, though at other special sessions *tchat* was religiously chewed at length among Gurage women (Almedom, in McDonald, 1994).

The woman who hosted the previous meeting carried the small box used for collecting the money to the house of the new hostess. Towards the end of the meeting, the box was passed round and each participant put her contribution into it. The contributions ranged from 2 to 10 Ethiopian *birr*. Every member in the group contributed the same amount. Most of the money contributed was saved by the women from their daily housekeeping money and so was very little, but in some cases the husbands provided money for the ROSCA contribution. The money in the box would then be given to the hostess, who was free to use it; she kept the box until the next meeting.

The fund was spent by the women on a variety of things, including baptismal expenses and stocking their own food supplies. The women had been selected for interview on the basis of their motherhood; importantly, it was found that those who belonged to ROSCAs had better chances of providing good-quality weaning foods such as *faffa* (the locally-produced Ethiopian weaning food) than other mothers (see Almedom, 1991a). The funds formed a significant part of the available cash over which the women had direct control, with a consequent positive impact on the children. Other studies have shown that informal access to resources in cash or in kind play a very important role in the survival of the most needy sections of communities (see for instance, Rahmato, 1991 and Almedom, 1992).

ROSCAs among Eritreans in Oxford

The data from Oxford were collected after I discovered a small ROSCA which served as a support group among Eritrean refugees living there. A group of four Eritrean women living in Oxford held ROSCA meetings every week. This ROSCA was based on friendship, religious and kinship ties among the members. Each of the four members had at least four children. They divided their time between looking after their families and attending classes in their local community educational establishments. None of them was engaged in paid work or had an independent source of income.

Ideally, the hostess provided dinner and refreshments for all four members and their families. This relieved the others from the task of cooking for the rest of the family before going out to their ROSCA meetings. Therefore everybody attended the feast, but only the members (the mothers) contributed to the ROSCA. This ROSCA underwent several changes since its inception. Due to the pressures of language-learning and family commitments, the women changed the frequency of the meetings from weekly to fortnightly for a while, and my latest information is that, for the present, they do not hold formal meetings but just collect and rotate the fund. The women save some of the money from the State social security benefits and some from money given by their husbands each week. The amount contributed by each member is currently £40. The recipient therefore gets £120.00. The fund is spent on buying furniture for their homes or household appliances such as refrigerator/freezers, food-processors and washing-machines which ease their domestic work-load.

Discussion

The link between the purchase of good-quality weaning food and belonging to ROSCAs is an empirical one, and an attempt has been made to explain it in terms of the function of a ROSCA in providing disposable income to the mother.

However, ROSCAs had other uses besides the economic. The main difference between the conditions of Ethiopia when Gedamu did his study and those I experienced was increased repressiveness of the socio-political climate. As a result, the ROSCAs were a move away from organizations controlled by the state, such as the *idirs* (burial associations), which later became *kebeles* (neighbourhood associations). ROSCAs were free from political interference and taxation. At these meetings, women could air their common grievances about the absence of sons and husbands who had been forcibly conscripted to the ongoing war, discuss each others' problems, and benefit from the exchange of information. This aspect appeared to be more important than the financial function of the ROSCAs, though this retained significance.

Similarly in Oxford, unfamiliarity with the new social and cultural environment prompted the association of Eritrean women described above to form a support group in the form of a ROSCA. Through it their moral obligations and duties of reciprocity have been fulfilled, and at the same time solutions to immediate economic needs have been provided by the ROSCA. It is evident from these preliminary data that, whether at home or abroad, ROSCAs among women from the Horn of Africa are valued as much for their social support as for their financial benefits.

Notes

1. More detail on the history of Addis Ababa and the ecology of the study area may be found in Almedom, 1991a.
2. See Almedom 1991a.

References

Almedom, A.M. (1991a), 'Aspects of the Growth and Health of the Suckling and Weanling Infant in Ethiopia', Unpublished D.Phil. Thesis, University of Oxford.

—— (1991b), 'Infant Feeding in Urban Low-income Households in Ethiopia: I. The Weaning Process'. *Ecology of Food and Nutrition*, 25: 97–109.

—— (1992), *Evaluation of Relief and Rehabilitation Programmes in Eritrea, from a Gender Perspective*, Report to the Emergencies Unit, Oxfam House, Oxford.

—— (1994), 'Moral Virtue in *tchat*: The use of *tchat* among Urban Gurage Women in Ethiopia', *Gender, Drink and Drugs*, M. McDonald (ed.), Oxford and Providence, Berg Publishers.

Aredo, D. (1991), *The Potentials of iqqub as an Indigenous Financing Small and Micro-scale Enterprises in Ethiopia*. Paper to Conference on Small and Micro Scale Enterprise Promotion in a Changing Policy Environment, A Special Focus on Africa (Mimeo) The Hague, September 30–October 2, pp. 1–42.

Begashaw, G. (1978), 'The Economic Role of Traditional Savings and Credit Institutions in Ethiopia', *Savings and Development*, 4 (II), pp. 249–62.

Gedamu, F. (1972), 'Ethnic Associations in Ethiopia and the Maintenance of

Urban/Rural Relationships; with Special Reference to the Alemgana-Wallamo Road Construction Association', Unpublished Ph.D. Thesis, University of London.

Miracle, M.P., Miracle, D.S. and Cohen, L. (1980), 'Informal Savings Mobilization in Africa', *Economic Development and Cultural Change*, 28: 701–24.

Padmanabhan, K.P. (1988), *Rural Credit: Lessons for rural bankers and policy makers*, London: Intermediate Technology Publications.

Rahmato, D. (1991), 'Investing in Tradition: Peasant and Rural Institutions in Post-Revolutionary Ethiopia', *Sociologia Ruralis*, XXXI (2/3), pp. 169–83.

5

Mobilizing Cash for Business: Women in Rotating Susu Clubs in Ghana

*Ellen Bortei-Doku and
Ernest Aryeetey*[1]

Introduction

Over the past ten years in Ghana, local and international development agencies have become increasingly concerned about the financial needs of women. The principal reason for this interest is the recognition that finance and income-generation are key factors in the current attempts to improve the standard of living of women and their families. A lot of attention has been focused on problems of women's access to formal financial institutions. However, interest is growing in women's use of informal financial markets, based on a recognition that these markets are more accessible especially to low-income women.

This paper examines women's use of rotating savings and credit associations in Ghana. Our main interest is on their motivation for joining ROSCAs, and how the associations operate to meet the needs of the women. It also addresses the factors promoting the resilience of this form of savings. Some attention is also given to the modifications that have taken place in the activities and organization of ROSCAs, alongside the changes that have occurred in the Ghanaian economy. Finally, the potential for collaboration between ROSCAs and donor agencies interested in promoting women to maximize their income-earning activities is discussed. The paper is based on observations from the authors' fieldwork in the Greater Accra and Volta Regions, and also from Kumasi and Takoradi in Ghana. Altogether about 1,000 women in Southern Ghana have been interviewed on their participation in different savings institutions, as well as about fifteen ROSCAs.

In Ghana as a whole, informal savings mobilization and credit facilities continue to dominate the financial market, in spite of over thirty years of formal banking in the country. It is estimated that about 55 per cent of the total money supply in the country is held outside the banks (Aryeetey and Gockel, 1991).

The expression 'informal financial sector' is by definition the antithesis of the formal financial system. 'The formal financial sector is seen to include all financial transactions taking place within the framework of established financial institutions, covered by the banking law or other financial regulations of government, thus the informal financial sector absorbs all other financial transactions not covered by the above' (Aryeetey and Gockel, 1991, p.1). This catch-all definition for the informal sector would then include such schemes as the rotating savings and credit clubs, *susu* collector schemes, money-lending and to some extent credit unions.

The informal sector provides a crucial service for both men and women, enabling them to meet both consumption- and investment-related expenses. Regrettably, hard data on the gender composition of participants in the various types of informal savings and credit schemes is yet to be collected on a nationwide basis. But there are strong indications that women are as actively involved in informal savings and credit mobilization as men. The wide-scale involvement of women in trading, marketing and other informal-sector activities, where the informal financial markets are most active, supports this view.

Although the banks do not keep gender-segregated data, it is widely believed that women in Ghana are less involved in savings and loans schemes through the formal banking system than their male counterparts (Opoku, 1989). This admittedly impressionistic view originates from other firmly established facts about the operations of banks.

A strong bias towards big business in manufacturing, commerce, and agriculture has traditionally steered banks away from the micro-enterprises in which the majority of women are involved. Where there have been agricultural loans to small-scale farmers the facility has been more readily available for traditional export crops such as cocoa, in which only a few women may be involved.[2] Estimates of women's ownership of cocoa farms stand at about 20 per cent of cocoa farmers (Opoku, 1989; Bukh, 1979). In the Kwahu Praso Rural Bank, for example, 77 per cent of agricultural loan beneficiaries in 1988 were cocoa farmers. On the other hand loans to food-crop farmers comprised less than 1 per cent in 1988 (Opoku, 1989).

Factors contributing to the continued high profile of the informal financial market include the lack of proximity to banks in general, especially in the rural areas where for most communities the distance to the nearest bank can be more than 50 kilometres. However, this fails to explain the poor patronage of banking facilities among urban dwellers, who are often within one to five kilometres of a bank. In this case it is more the attitude and general operations of banks which have kept many potential customers away (Aryeetey and Gockel, 1991). Miracle et al (1980) identify a wide range of uncompetitive features of the banks in developing countries which encourage the continued patronage of the informal sector. These include among other things cumbersome savings and loans procedures and general discrimination by banks against low-income customers. For the estimated large number of men and women who do not utilize formal banking services, money-lenders, relatives and friends as well as trading partners are usually the main source of financial assistance.

For the purpose of savings most men and women keep their cash at home or save with ROSCAs and *susu* collectors. The ROSCA is known in Ghana as *susu*.[3] Rotating *susu* clubs have long existed here, although no date has been firmly associated with their introduction. The term *susu*, however, bears a close resemblance to the Yoruba term *esusu*, indicating that there might be a link between the arrival of Nigerian traders in the country and the proliferation of *susu*[4] (Aryeetey and Gockel, 1991). But the essential practice of rotating *susu*, namely the pooling of scarce resources by a group of people periodically for each member's benefit, is not new to Ghana. In most Ghanaian cultures there are age-old traditions for pooling labour, food, utensils and implements for mutual benefit.[5] It is likely that the pooling of cash resources gathered momentum with the increased monetization of the economy following the growth of the export economy in the latter part of the nineteenth century.

Gender and Membership of *Susu* Clubs

Susu clubs are generally open to men and women, but the venue at which a club is organized tends to influence the sex of its members. Three broad types of venue are common in Accra and Kadjebi, namely public institutions and neighbourhood clubs in urban centres and markets in both urban and rural areas.

The predominance of women at markets in Ghana is reflected in their high involvement in *susu* clubs in markets. Many market clubs have an all-female membership. Where there are male members they normally constitute less than 10 per cent of the total. It is common to find clubs that bear the name of the founder, and this serves as a good indication of the sex of the membership. In the Dodo Amanfrom market in the Kadjebi District, for example, the clubs are known either by the names of their leaders, who are often women, or by the foodstuffs they sell.[6] Except in a few instances, food retailing at the market in southern Ghana is done by women. *Susu* clubs in the urban markets of Accra are similarly largely composed of women.

Women are also widely represented in neighbourhood *susu* clubs in urban areas. In Nungua near Accra many of the *susu* clubs have been established by women bringing together friends and relatives rather than work-mates as is common in the market. However, even in these clubs the members tend to be engaged in similar occupational activities. In the urban-based public departments of the civil service men rather than women are the dominant force. Many of the clubs in various public offices in Accra have been formed by men, but the few women members tend to be quite active. The situation in public institutions is a reflection of the greater presence of men in formal institutions in the country. On the whole, the evidence we have so far indicates that women generally outnumber men in *susu* clubs. However, lack of evidence from other parts of the country makes it difficult to generalize this statement.[7]

At all the different venues where women and men organize rotating *susu* clubs there is a clear preference for single-sex groups. Where groups are mixed, memberships are either overwhelmingly female or predominently male.[8] Table 5.1 below presents a breakdown of the sex composition of the membership of rotating *susu* clubs observed in Accra and Kadjebi.

Table 5.1 also offers some support for claims that rotating *susu* clubs may indeed be more popular among women than men. About 70 per cent of the total membership (343) of the fifteen clubs observed are women. The majority of the members are economically active, working mostly as traders at the market-place. The clubs attract both the educated and uneducated. Many of the members in rural areas have never had formal education, as has been observed at Kadjebi. As can be expected, educational levels of members are higher in Accra, where several of the members have completed elementary school. Those in the public departments tend to have the highest education, many having completed secondary and vocational schools. Founders of clubs usually tend to be older than many of the members, whose ages range from mid-twenties to mid-forties.

Table 5.1. Sex Composition of Rotating *Susu* Clubs in Accra and Kadjebi Districts, 1991.

Susu Club	M	F
Accra District		
Public Departments		
1	44	1
2	7	3
3	3	7
4	24	1
Nungua Ladies' Club	0	35
Nungua Savings Club	15	15
Nungua Victory Bar Fan Club	10	70
Makola Market (Enam Obi So Na Obi Ye Yie)	0	10
Kadjebi District		
Dodo Amanfrom Market		
– Vegetable Sellers' Club	0	10
– Kofinyor Club	0	10
– Fish Sellers' Club	4	16
– Agbesino's Club	0	16
– Aboboitor's Club	0	10
– Akpletor's Club	1	9
Kadjebi Market	1	21

Source: Fieldwork, 1991.

Resilience of Rotating *Susu* Clubs: Organizational Features

A close examination of the organization and operations of rotating *susu* clubs helps to explain why the clubs have survived into the modern era in Ghana. Essentially the clubs are simple organizations directly tailored to the skills and resources of the members. As they set themselves the short-term goal of completing one rotation at a time, members are free to join or leave the clubs whenever they are no longer able to join in the next rotation.

Founding members of rotating *susu* clubs explain that they are motivated by a need to overcome frequent shortages of cash in their business activities, and in crisis situations. They team up with others whom they have observed to have similar problems. The founder of a club in Dodo Amanfrom Market has organized women who have borrowed from her regularly to form a *susu* club.

Survival of the *susu* clubs is enhanced by their flexible and cost-effective strategies. When necessary, the clubs have been able to suspend their operations for long periods, and then re-group after improvements in the economic circumstances of members. A club that has been operating for twenty-one years in the Dodo Amanfrom Market suspended its rotation from 1985 to 1990, due to economic hardships faced by the members. The fact that rotations are complete cycles on their own promotes such flexibility in the organization. Management and book-keeping in the rotating *susu* club is typically very limited. Clubs hardly incur any costs in this regard. In the clubs at the Dodo Amanfrom Market where the illiteracy rate is high the only records that are kept are on the periodic payments by members. Some of the clubs here do not even record this information, as the leader keeps an oral account of club payments. Record-keeping is relatively higher in the public departments than anywhere else, needless to say, because of the higher levels of literacy and organizational skills here.

The founder usually becomes the leader of the club. The market clubs of Kadjebi all have a very small executive, usually consisting only of the founder. In contrast, the public departments in Accra and the neighbourhood clubs at Nungua have more sophisticated executive arrangements, with up to ten officers in the large clubs. It is worth noting that even in mixed clubs women do dominate the executive where the founder is a woman.

Recruitment to the clubs is usually drawn from close and trusted associates of the founder. Women leaders in the Kadjebi District explain that they prefer to invite people to join their club, rather than wait to be approached by interested persons. Sometimes members are allowed to bring others along so long as they can vouch for them. A certain degree of homogeneity is regarded as important for maintaining harmony among the members. But there is little indication that membership in a *susu* club runs in the family. Many of the members we observed did not have any family members in the same *susu* clubs or others.

There are usually no formal application procedures or standard criteria for selection of members, save for their trustworthiness. In addition, members are normally expected to have a regular income. This does not always mean paid employment however; a member of the Victory Bar Fan Club at Nungua, for example, is unemployed, but she pays her contributions out of her housekeeping money.

Wide variations have been found in the size of rotating *susu* clubs, both in Accra and Kadjebi. Membership ranges from about ten in the small clubs to about eighty in the larger ones.[9] Many club members do prefer small clubs to big ones as that brings forward their turn in the rotation. But the prospect of receiving very small lump sums in such clubs, especially where members agree on very low contributions, often tempers the desire to keep clubs very small. Clubs also tend to differ by the types of functions they undertake. Two distinct types of functions in rotating clubs have been identified, including single-purpose *susu* savings clubs, and mutual aid *susu* saving clubs with multiple functions.

About two-thirds of the clubs that have been contacted describe themselves as purely savings clubs. This type is usually very basic in its organization. There is often no executive except the founder-leader, and perhaps an assistant. Either one of these people can be responsible for making the periodic rounds to collect contributions from members, and to hand over the lump sum to the next recipient. The members come together for the singular purpose of raising cash for each other.

In the periodic Dodo Amanfrom Market all the women describe their clubs as savings only clubs. In their case they never hold meetings although members are in frequent contact with each other as they all trade in the same market. For many of them, meetings would disrupt their retailing, which takes place only once a week. Some of the savings-only clubs in the public departments and at Nungua however hold regular meetings, at which they collect and disburse the fund. These gatherings are usually quite short, lasting only about thirty minutes.

Compared to the single purpose *susu* savings club, the mutual aid *susu* savings club is a much more elaborate organization.[10] About one-third of the clubs are of this nature. There are basically three main functions in this type of *susu*. The primary focus is on savings, but in addition the club provides limited social security for its members. Socializing and entertainment within the club is also seen as one of its attractions. In the mutual aid *susu* clubs, the women place a premium on being able to count on each other. This is usually reflected in the names they adopt. For example a *susu* club in the Accra Makola Market is known as 'Enam Obi So Na Obi Ye Yie' which can be translated as 'Our Well-Being Depends on Others'. The typical types of mutual aid provided by the clubs include donations for funerals, child-outdooring,[11] marriage celebrations, and health care. The clubs make additional contributions towards the provisions of refreshments for their get-togethers. Through all these situations members also count on each others' moral support, apart from the donations.

Mutual aid *susu* clubs are generally associated with the better-off clubs, as in addition to the regular savings contributions the members have to make additional payments for donations and refreshments. A *susu* club in the Dodo Amanfrom market has been forced to abandon mutual aid functions because as the leader explained 'the women cannot afford it'.

Motivation for Savings and the Process of Mobilization

Over 80 per cent of the women and men in *susu* clubs that we contacted are in it primarily for economic reasons. Their main objective is to obtain bulk money to support their business activities. This particular type of savings is chosen by many because of the savings discipline that social pressure from the group imposes on them. As indicated in the previous section, there are also strong social advantages for those who can afford to participate in mutual aid *susu* clubs which are not offered by formal savings, or other informal financial schemes.[12] But for many people the social benefits are regarded as secondary to the economic advantages.

The significance of rotating *susu* savings for women's economic activities where it is practised in Ghana can best be understood with some insight into the financial dealings of the women. Several women engaged in trading, food processing or farming, obtain their goods or inputs on suppliers' credit terms. Where the sums involved in this transaction are large, the women often need credit to pay off their debts. The *susu* lump sum becomes an important cash fund for this purpose. Fish sellers in the Dodo Amanfro Market regularly trek to Dambai on the lake to buy smoked fish, which they obtain on credit from the women fish dealers. The visiting traders use their membership of rotating clubs to pledge the prompt payment of their debts as soon as they receive their funds. This strategy works because they can rely on other women from the Dodo Amanfro Market who are at the time trading at Dambai, to confirm their claims of *susu* membership. This is important as it shows the extent to which *susu* club membership boosts the credit-worthiness of the women.

The method of savings mobilization in the *susu* clubs in Accra and Kadjebi are quite similar to the procedures that have been noted elsewhere in West Africa (Ardener, 1964). Basically the founder and the members negotiate a uniform amount that is to be paid at regular intervals by each member. The amounts and intervals vary according to the needs of the members. They usually rely on the estimated sizes of their 'large' expenditures together with their regular earnings, to guide them in identifying an appropriate amount.

There are no remarkable differences in the amount of payments in Accra, Nungua and Kadjebi. In all the places individual contributions range from about ¢1,000.00 to ¢40,000.00 a month (approximately 1.50 pounds Sterling to 60.00 pounds Sterling per month at current exchange rates), showing that there is a fairly wide margin between the poor and better-off clubs. The higher rates of contributions are, however, more common in Accra than in Kadjebi.

Multiple contributions are practised in some of the clubs, where the better-off members are allowed to 'throw more than one hand into the fund'. Only one 'hand' can receive the fund at a time, however. Therefore a member who contributes more than one 'hand' receives the lump sum for each 'hand' at a different time. As multiple payments help to boost the size of the fund, it is regarded as an advantage to have some relatively wealthy members in the club. Criteria for homogeneity among members, as noted, earlier therefore, does not preclude wealth.

Many clubs favour weekly intervals in the payment of *susu* contributions, since this shortens the waiting period for all members. The weekly interval is very popular among the market women. At Dodo Amanfrom this coincides with the periodic market held every seven days. In the public departments in Accra the contributions are paid monthly, to coincide with the payment of salaries and wages.

The order of the rotation is a very important factor in the *susu* club. Most women have an idea of exactly when they would like to receive their fund. In order to avoid conflict, the leaders may introduce balloting or negotiate the rotation with each member. Balloting is common in the public departments in the urban areas, while negotiations are favoured at the markets. As can be expected in negotiated rosters, the leader and other core members tend to have the earliest turns. *Susu* club leaders are, however, quite flexible about making changes in the rotation to accommodate the emergencies of members. People are therefore allowed to take the fund out of turn, so long as they can find a member with whom to exchange turns.

Although many clubs appear to be functioning all right, there are signs that the relatively harsh economic environment has placed a strain on the payment of contributions among some members. The liberalization of the economy (World Bank, 1987) under the Structural Adjustment Programme (SAP) over the past two years has apparently had negative consequences on the purchasing power of people. The process has been accompanied by the removal of subsidies on health, education and transport, and the deregulation of prices of basic consumption goods. Traders complain that sales of their goods have been dropping during this period. *Susu* members fear that they may soon be unable to fulfil their obligations towards their clubs. Some have already been affected in major ways as is shown in the following illustrations. A club leader at Makola Market recently failed to hand over the lump sum to the next recipient, because she had diverted this money to pay off her own debt. In another instance at the Dodo Amanfrom market, a club member pleaded to be released from further participation in her club because of financial constraints. About 43 per cent of *susu* club members we contacted in Accra had failed at least once to pay their contributions on time in their current rotation.

Nevertheless, the rotating *susu* clubs pride themselves in maintaining strict discipline over payments among their members. The social pressure to sustain payments is such that at Nungua some members borrow money to pay their contributions rather than suffer the humiliation of non-payment. Mutual trust, obligatory feelings and perhaps personal pride are among the driving forces that sustain regular payments. Among women whose alternatives for obtaining bulk money are truly limited, such as the market women of Dodo Amanfrom, the default rate is quite low. It appears that more men than women have failed to pay one or more of their contributions over the past one year in the clubs we surveyed in Accra and Nungua.

Club members who persistently do not pay their contributions may be dismissed before the end of a rotation; they will be required to repay the club if they have already collected the lump sum. Most of the hardships associated with *susu* payments have been experienced by people in self-employment, rather than those in wage employment. Apart from dismissal there appear to be no other measures taken directly such as fines or police action, to punish delinquency on the part of members.[13]

Utilization of *Susu* Funds

As mentioned earlier, the majority of the women in *susu* clubs use their fund as working capital: 'It is cash we mobilize for business' (working capital is *dwetire* in Twi, *shika tso* in Ga and *Gati* in Ewe). Stocks of trading goods and farming inputs are replenished or expanded from this source. Typically women and men decide on their own how to spend the *susu* fund. Only about 10 per cent of the women rely on others (usually their husbands or friends and relatives) to help them to decide the use of their fund.

The fungibility of money, however, makes it quite likely that the funds are not used exclusively for business or any other single purpose. *Susu* members in both Accra and Kadjebi do admit that their funds are put to multiple uses, but they maintain that the dominant use is for income-earning activities. Table 5.2 below describes common uses of the *susu* funds in Accra. In general, Miracle and others (1980) found a broader scope of uses of *susu* funds in Nigeria and Cameroon than is evident in the Ghanaian situation so far.

Other expenses paid for by the fund include a wide range of consumption items, which serve the dual purpose of non-financial savings as well as personal items, depending on the needs of the club member. Personal items such as cloth, jewellery, and building materials are often sold to generate cash in emergency situations.

The highly sex-segregated division of labour in both the Accra and the Kadjebi districts presupposes that women and men have quite different uses for their *susu* funds. On the contrary, Table 5.2 suggests that this difference may not always be significant. Even in areas of activity commonly associated with men, such as the payment of school fees and house construction, some women expend their resources on these areas.

Nevertheless, with respect to economic activity, men and women tend to be involved in sex-stereotypical activities. Most women in *susu* clubs in Accra and Kadjebi are involved in female dominated activities such as petty trading in foods and manufactured goods, or food crop farming. In the public departments the women are usually secretaries and typists.

Table 5.2. Utilization of *Susu* Funds among Members in Accra.

Type of Expenditure	Men (7)*	Women (16)*
Working Capital	4	16
School Fees	2	1
Household Goods	1	1
House Repair	–	1
Building Materials	1	1
Personal Items	1	3
Save Cash Elsewhere	–	1
Lend to Spouse	1	–
Lend to Relative	–	1

Source: Fieldwork, 1991.   * Multiple answers.

On the other hand, men in *susu* clubs are likely to be artisans, or in the public departments, clerks, technicians, and administrators.

Changes in Rotating *Susu* Operations

Enormous changes have taken place in the Ghanaian economy, as indicated earlier, which have altered people's financial needs and their views and attitudes to financial transactions. While differing in terms of policy thrust, these changes basically helped to cultivate a need for liquid assets among people. Between 1975 and 1985 the national economy was characterized by high levels of inflation and severe shortages of some basic consumer items. Under those conditions there was an increased need for liquidity, in order for consumers to take advantage of chance supplies of goods on the market. The need to hold money increased significantly (World Bank, 1987), which damped interest in savings clubs. Following the adoption of a structural adjustment programme (SAP) after 1983, which included stringent fiscal and monetary policies and a liberalization of prices, households had considerable difficulty making ends meet with reduced real incomes. Thus there was little room for savings, whether formal or informal. With the greater need for cash, people were less willing to tie up their capital in credit arrangements such as suppliers' credit facilities, even though these continue to play a significant role in trading and farming transactions in the country.

The growing demand for ready cash has forced women entrepreneurs in particular to turn to a variation in *susu* savings which guarantees them more frequent access to their savings. This modification of the rotating club is known as the *susu* collector system, which has been discussed in detail by Aryeetey and Gockel (1991). The system has been described as mobile banking elsewhere (Miracle et al, 1980). In Ghana the majority of collectors are men from primary and middle school teaching fields, who undertake collection on a part-time basis. Only twelve women have been found in a collector's association of 500 members in the Accra District. It is believed that the dangers involved in carrying large sums of money around in the past discouraged women from taking up *susu* collection. High levels of illiteracy among market women may also have been a major constraint, because of the rigorous record-keeping involved. Other factors inhibiting women may be the sheer physical energy required to undertake the long walks around markets and shops. The situation is expected to improve as more women become educated and aware of security provision. The collector invites customers to save with him on a daily basis.[14] At the end of the month women receive their savings minus a day's contribution, which is the collector's fee for the service he provides. Not only do women not earn interest on their savings, but they receive less than they have saved![15]

Women point to some important advantages of the *susu* collector system over the rotating club. In the collector's club all the women receive their savings fund at the same time. Members therefore do not have to endure long waiting periods, as happens in the case of later beneficiaries in the rotating club. Each woman decides the amount of savings she will deposit daily with the collector, thus eliminating the constraint of having to make uniform contributions as is required in the rotating club. This enables women to save as little or as much as they can afford. Also, the collector often provides loan facilities for his long-term customers in addition to their savings. This individual savings plan also makes it possible for the saver to terminate her participation in the scheme without the shame and financial stress associated with leaving the rotating club before the end of a cycle.

But to some extent, the types of social scrutiny and social affiliation that underlie the recruitment of members to a rotating club, have also been found in the *susu* collector's club. Women usually make extensive enquiries about a collector before approaching him; a good recommendation by his other customers is therefore quite crucial. Similarly, goodwill and trust are necessary to sustain the relationship between a collector and his customers.

The risk element in *susu* savings is nevertheless much higher in *susu* collector operations, and cases of embezzlement by collectors are not unusual (Aryeetey and Gockel, 1991). Notably, *susu* collectors are hardly to be seen in the small periodic rural markets like Dodo Amanfrom, where it is more difficult to keep track of the collector if he does not live in the same village. Some of the rotating club members in this market once saved with a collector who did not live in Dodo Amanfrom; he embezzled their money and absconded. At the large daily markets in Accra, Kumasi and Takoradi collectors are very popular; over 77 per cent of the women traders in these markets save with a collector. By all indications very few men save with a *susu* collector. The reasons are not yet clear. Where men in rotating clubs have other savings accounts, these are normally with the banks or credit unions. Apart from the markets, *susu* collectors also operate in public departments and high-density residential areas.

Another variation of the rotating *susu* club to be found in a few places is the savings and loans or fixed-funds club (Miracle et al, 1980). In this case the club starts off as a ROSCA, but members delay taking their funds until a time when they need the money. Sometimes members decide to lend out the money amongst themselves and to non-club members at an interest, such as occurs in some of the public departments in Accra. In other instances the club uses the bulk fund as working capital, to set up a trading business. For example, a club in Accra used to buy soap with the fund, which was retailed to other colleagues. This was quite successful when there were acute shortages of basic domestic items on the market, but not at present, and the practice has been stopped. At the end of the savings period all the club members share in the profits, and receive back the amount of money they have saved. In Accra a popular time for paying back savings to members is at Christmas, or at the beginning of the new academic year in September, when parents have to pay school fees and replace school apparel and books.

In spite of the changes that have occurred in the system of *susu* savings, the rotating clubs continue to operate alongside the widespread *susu* collector system. As mentioned above, in the rural areas one is more likely to encounter the rotating club rather than the variations that have been described. It is not uncommon to find women who simultaneously participate in the rotating and collector modes. Aryeetey and Gockel (1991) indicate that about 3 per cent of women saving with *susu* collectors also belong to rotating clubs. The figures may be higher in some cases. About 60 per cent of the women we contacted in Accra who are currently involved in rotating *susu* clubs also save with a collector.

Conclusions and Policy Implications

The rotating *susu* club continues to play a dynamic role in helping to meet the cash needs of women traders and farmers. It is founded on principles of mutual trust, obligatory relations and homogeneity. In rural areas, reliance on rotating *susu* by women appears to be the result of fewer opportunities for securing financial savings than are available to their urban colleagues. The extensive flexibility in the operations of the club enables it to survive even under adverse economic conditions. This is shown by the ability of the club to rejuvenate after long periods of inactivity.

For both women and men involved in *susu* the main attraction of the club is economic, though they acknowledge the importance of their social relations with the other club members. In those clubs where members desire greater social involvement and support from each other the club operates as both a savings and a mutual aid association.

It appears that innovative credit schemes sponsored by donor agencies that utilize the operating principles of informal groups tend to be more successful than those that do not (Jackelen and Rhyne, 1991). But while donor agencies may be interested in using the principles of informal groups, they are often less enthusiastic about using the existing informal institutions themselves to enhance the retailing of credit (Aryeetey, 1992). Fortunately, some donor agencies are beginning to show interest in the immense potential for collaborating with informal savings and credit institutions such as the rotating *susu* club. Exactly how this can be done is what remains to be clarified. Attempts to find out the views of participants on this specific issue have been fruitless so far. The women at Dodo Amanfrom Market, for example, see help from outside in terms of 'loans for the *susu* members'. How or under what conditions this could be done in the context of the *susu* club is not explained. Others in Accra suggest that they should be given loans to expand their businesses, which will enable them to mobilize larger contributions to pay to the club.

An option would be to extend loans to members in order to boost their contributions. However, there is no guarantee that these loans will be used for *susu* contributions. Secondly, since the *susu* fund is interest-free and the borrowers will have to repay at least the amount of money they have borrowed, there is no benefit to be gained by the participants in such an arrangement.

There is also the possibility of matching funds that have been raised by women in *susu* clubs with loans from external agencies. The potential difficulty with this approach is how to devise adequate arrangements for ensuring the repayment of the loans. Judging from past experience with numerous credit schemes for small-scale entrepreneurs in Ghana, there is the apparent lack of commitment to loan repayment among borrowers when the loan is from external sources.[16] From our own observations it is difficult to conceptualize how external funds can be injected into a system such as rotating *susu*, whose sustainability seems to depend so much on the existing dynamics of economic activity and flow of income among the members. It has indeed been pointed out that members' commitment to the club stems from mutually shared values regarding indebtedness to one's neighbour. Aryeetey (1992) observed that recipients of the *susu* fund are bound to honour their payments to the club, by the fact that they have taken money from their friends; failure to do so is seen as depriving these people, with whom one shares goodwill, of their means of livelihood. Peer pressure of this nature has been instrumental in forcing most *susu* members to complete the cycle faithfully. On the other hand, they do not identify with the external 'benefactor', and have not yet developed sensitivity to the interests of the nebulous unknown donor agency that advances them loans. Default in the repayment of external loans therefore does not carry the same social stigma as it does towards one's neighbour.

Perhaps one needs to turn to some of the innovations that have taken place in *susu* savings mobilization, to find informal institutions that hold a potential for collaboration with external financiers. The one that readily comes to mind is the *susu* collector, especially now that more women are taking an interest in working as collectors. The collector can serve as an intermediary between lending agencies and the *susu* members, as many collectors are already in the practice of advancing loans to their clients. The Women's World Banking office and the State Insurance Corporation in Ghana are already experimenting with such a programme, but no official results have been published.

Among the poor, wealthy women traders and farmers, and for men and women in the public departments, rotating *susu* clubs remain a safe, simple and inexpensive system of savings mobilization. Its strengths lie among other things in the mutual dependence that each member experiences in relation to the other members in order to raise the *susu* fund.

Notes

1. Dr Ellen Bortei-Doku and Dr Ernest Aryeetey are Research Fellows at the Institute of Statistical, Social and Economic Research, University of Ghana, Legon Ghana.
2. Amarnor in his study based in the Asesewa District notes, for example, that Rural Banks 'are instructed to restrict loans to cocoa farmers, salaried employees and traders with collateral' (1992:14).
3. Maison (1988) describes rotating *susu* clubs as popular and widespread, but does not provide any quantitative measure of their presence.
4. ROSCAs are also known here as *eso dzodzo* (Ewe) and *adesa* (Kotokoli).
5. Labour pooling, for example, is known as *nnoboa* in many parts of southern Ghana.
6. Little (1957) observed that rotating *susu* clubs in Keta consist only of

women.

7. Gabianu (n.d.) has described *susu* clubs as a popular means of saving mobilization among women. See also Little (1957).

8. Slover (1991) indicates that about 50 per cent or more of ROSCAs in Zaire consist of single-sex groups.

9. Slover (1991) found in Zaire that about 75 per cent of ROSCAs have a membership of ten or less.

10. Some clubs appear to be dominated by mutual aid rather than savings interests; for purposes of analysis it may be useful to distinguish between the two wherever it is practical to do so (Ardener, 1964). The evidence here is that the two activities quite often overlap.

11. Child-outdooring ceremonies are held all over Ghana, at which eight-day old babies are literally brought out into the open yard to be introduced to the outside world (Sarpong, 1974). It is an occasion for naming the child according to the customs of his or her lineage, and for thanksgiving and merrymaking.

12. IPC (1988) lists mutual trust among members, orientation towards community development, clear leadership and elaborate control mechanisms as some of the attractions of rotating *susu* savings.

13. Ardener (1964) describes various penalties that are imposed on delinquents in other parts of West Africa.

14. A frequency of two and three times a week has been observed at Nungua.

15. This has raised questions about the significance of interest rates in promoting savings mobilization in formal banking institutions (Aryeetey et al, 1990).

16. There are several that can be cited; they include the Commerbank Farmers Association loan scheme put forward by the Ghana Commercial Bank, and the People's Participation Project loan scheme sponsored by the Food and Agricultural Organization through the Ghana Commercial Bank.

References

Amarnor, S.K. (1992), *Ecological Knowledge and the Regional Economy: Environmental Management in the Asesewa District of Ghana*, presented at the Conference on the Social Dimensions of Environment and Sustainable Development, Valletta, Malta, 22–5 April 1992.

Ardener, S. (1964), 'The Comparative Study of Rotating Credit Associations', *The Journal of the Royal Anthropological Institute*, vol. XCIV, Part 2, pp. 201–29.

Aryeetey, E. (1992), *The Complementary Role of Informal Financial Institutions in the Retailing of Credit: An Evaluation of Innovative Approaches*, presented at the UN Regional Symposium on Savings and Credit for Development in Africa, Abidjan, Cote d'Ivoire, 27–30 April, 1992.

—— and Gockel, F. (1991), *Mobilizing Domestic Resources For Capital*

Formation in Ghana: The Role of Informal Financial Markets, AERC Research Paper 3, AERC, Nairobi.

——, A. Kyei and Asante, E. (1990), *Mobilizing Domestic Savings for African Development and Diversification: A Ghanaian Case-Study*, Research Report, Workshop of the International Development Centre, Queen Elizabeth House, Oxford University, July 1990.

Bukh, J. (1979), *The Village Women in Ghana*, Uppsala: Scandinavian Institute of African Studies.

Gabianu, S. (n.d.), *The Susu Credit System: An Indigenous Way of Financing Business Outside of the Formal Banking System*, prepared in connection with Long-Term Perspective Study, Special Economics Office, Technical Department, Africa Region, World Bank, Washington D.C.

Interdisziplinaire Projekt Consult (IPC) (1988), *Rural Finance in Ghana: A Research Study on Behalf of the Bank of Ghana*, Accra.

Jackelen, H.R. and Rhyne, E. (1991), 'Towards a More Market-Oriented Approach to Credit and Savings for the Poor', *Small Enterprise Development*, vol. 2, no. 4, pp. 4–20.

Little, K. (1957), 'The Role of Voluntary Associations in West African Urbanization', *American Anthropology*, 59, pp. 579–96.

Maison, G. (1988), *Credit Delivery System For Small-Scale Operators: Problems and Prospects*, Report of FAO/Ghana Workshop on Informal Financial Systems, Accra.

Miracle, P., Miracle, D.S. and Cohen, L. (1980), 'Informal Savings Mobilization in Africa', in *Economic Development and Cultural Change*, vol. 28, pp. 701–23.

Opoku, I. (1989), *Gender Differences and Access to Credit: An Example of the Kwahu Praso Area*. Unpublished Long Essay, Department of Geography, University of Ghana, Legon.

Sarpong, P. (1974), *Ghana in Retrospect: Some Aspects of Ghanaian Culture*, Accra: Ghana Publishing Corporation.

Slover, C.H. (1991), *The Effect of Membership Homogeneity on Group Size, Funds Mobilization, and the Engenderment of Reciprocal Obligations among Informal Financial Groups in Rural Zaire* paper presented at the Seminar on Finance and Rural Development in West Africa, OSU/CIRAD, October 21–25.

World Bank (1987), *Ghana: Policies and Issues of Structural Adjustment*, Report No. 6635-GH.

6

Women's Access to and Control of Credit in Cameroon: The Mamfe Case

Margaret Niger-Thomas

A small but increasing number of Cameroonian women who earn regular salaries qualify for bank loans. The majority of these women are, however, excluded from modern banking and credit facilities. Most of them, whether living in large modern cities, semi-urban[1] areas or villages, depend on farming and petty trading for their main source of income. The growing desire of women in Cameroon to obtain credit and engagement in what they like to call 'big ventures' has led to women's active participation in the different types of 'informal' credit institutions which are widespread in the country. In order to be creditworthy, women have to save. Their ability to save has been shown by V. Delancey (1978a) in her study of women at the Cameroon Development Corporation (CDC). In another study she remarked that 'It has often continued to be assumed that Africans have a very low propensity to save. This has been based upon the false beliefs that Africans need and desire only a certain small quantity of money in combination with a high preference for leisure' (1978a:1). In Western Cameroon, at least, the pursuit of leisure is not the motive for saving. There are other priorities, such as educating children, building better homes, investing in health and income-generating activities. Women as well as men are actively engaged in these pursuits. The willingness of women to take risks, and their ability to assume the responsibilities inherent in accepting credit and to use it for investment in productive activities, is quite remarkable. Nevertheless, women's access to credit in Cameroon is typically limited to the informal sector.

My study is based on my personal experience of the Sub-divisional town of Mamfe, in the Manyu Division of the South West Province of Cameroon. According to the 1987 census, Mamfe had a population of 47,218, of which 13,844 was urban and 33,374 rural. The original inhabitants of this town are the Banyang people who occupy the Banyang homeland lying in the central area of the basin of the Upper Cross River. The economy is based on farming and petty trading. The urban centre is the location of government services including hospitals, administration, schools and colleges.

In the course of my fieldwork I interviewed 120 women who belonged to twenty out of a total of thirty-five women's groups in Mamfe. Those interviewed included salaried civil servants, weekly wage-earners, farmers, market women and housewives. Two questionnaires were drawn up. One was designed for interviews with workers in the bank and credit sectors on women's participation in these institutions and to collect statistics within a range of such institutions. The other was meant to determine how women raise money and use it through the use of indigenous credit systems, notably the 'meeting' and *njangi*.

Women's Access to Modern Systems of Credit

Two main types of modern credit institutions are found in Mamfe: banks and credit unions. The first bank was opened in 1945, while the credit union[2] became operational in 1969. These modern systems flourish in this 'semi-urban' area, although their economic effectiveness has fluctuated over the years. This has been partly because the members of some local credit unions know the value of borrowing but fail to do the necessary prior saving; an example is the Ogomoko local credit union (cited by Delancey, V., 1978a:9). The banks also started well but some went bankrupt including the Cameroon Bank, which folded in 1989; its failure was said to be due to over-lending to incompetent parastatals, the issue of 'political loans' or over-interference by the government. It was only in 1991 that its customers received their deposited savings. In 1991 the sole bank still working in Mamfe, the BICIC Bank, almost collapsed and many people withdrew their money. People are now afraid to place their savings in the bank. The credit union, which was considered a substitute for the bank, is seen as no better placed because the money saved in the credit union is itself banked. Some civil servants who gave the bank monthly transfers from their salaries into the credit union's account have stopped their orders. The bank is only used by some customers to receive their monthly salary cheques. This is very common among the women who hold current accounts in the banks. With this loss of confidence in banking, more people than ever before join indigenous savings associations.

Women's activities are highly gendered. Most women either market foodstuffs, some of which are seasonal, or cultivate and process them. In Mamfe very few women are salaried workers with monthly wages passing through a bank. Out of the 120 women I interviewed only about 20 per cent are customers of the bank or credit union.

Table 6.1 below shows women's use of banks and credit unions in Mamfe between 1985 and 1990.

Table 6.1.

Customers Using Modern Credit Institutions	Bank Customers	Per Cent of Women with Bank Accounts	Credit Union Members	Per Cent of Women Members in Credit Union
Total No. of customers	10,719	–	2,304	–
Total No. of women operating an account	3,219	30	618	26
Total No. of customers receiving loans	1,245	–	648	–
Total No. of women receiving loans	150	12.5	192	29.5

Due to the nature of women's economic activities their access to formal credit systems is greatly limited. Of women who save through and borrow from formal credit institutions, the percentage who actually used the bank within the period of five years studied was 30 per cent; almost the same percentage (26 per cent) used the credit unions. Of the total number of women operating accounts in the banks, only 12.5 per cent had been given loans. This might be due to the constraints on, and 'real cost' of, the small capital sums needed by women. The interest charged was usually very high and the collateral required is hard to produce since women are not customarily owners of land or buildings. This limits their demands for loans from the banks. On the other hand, more women have been given loans from the credit unions (29.5 per cent). The reason is that the credit union permits customers to borrow up to three times the amount of their savings. This suits women, given their low income and the difficulty they have in accumulating large sums. These loans were taken out to pay hospital bills, educate their children, and in order to develop their businesses. But considering the high yearly interest rates on the loans, women cannot afford to borrow all they need from these modern institutions and have to look for alternative credit facilities.

Women's Access to Indigenous Credit Systems

Before the advent of modern credit institutions, indigenous forms of credit had been in existence. Given the limitations of the formal credit systems, women have relied on what they had been accustomed to. In Cameroon most studies reveal two very common local credit associations: the 'meeting' and *njangi* (ROSCAs). In Mamfe, among the Banyang, the terms *bechoko* ('meeting' or 'sitting') and *nchuop* (*njangi* or 'contribution') are often used.

The 'Meeting'

A 'meeting' is simply a forum where a group of people meet at agreed times for a common purpose. The 'meeting' seems to have developed from traditional gatherings in villages in which the settlement of disputes and the celebration of births and deaths brought people together; palm wine and food were served. Two categories of meetings are now found in Mamfe which I will discuss here: ethnic and gender-based meetings. In the former, as implied, membership is drawn from men and women of the same ethnic group. Besides strengthening cultural bonds it offers mutual assistance to members. Such groups will create a 'sinking' or 'trouble' fund into which members pay a compulsory fee varying between 100–500frs (500=£1 in 1991). An ethnically oriented meeting often operates a 'thrift and loan' scheme which permits members to save money in various amounts. M. Delancey (1978:3) describes this type of savings club as a 'proto-credit union'. It is indeed a kind of savings bank in which funds are held throughout the year. All such savings are shared out in November in preparation for Christmas. While several studies of African savings systems have dealt with this type of meeting, which has something in common with English working-class 'Christmas Clubs', little or no attention has been paid to the second type, which is limited to women.

In Mamfe, 'meetings' for women only are numerous. As in the ethnic group meetings a 'sinking fund' and a thrift and loan scheme exist. In most women's 'meetings' saving is compulsory, as is a contribution to a 'sinking fund'. In the ethnic group 'meeting' saving is optional. The compulsory saving for women is an inducement to qualify for loans. These loans are made to women at low interest rates of about 10–25frs per 1,000frs (2–5p per £2) per month. Apart from the loans raised, a special savings fund is created to enable women to purchase identical material with which to make clothes; thus there is a common 'uniform' dress. In Mamfe the 'meeting' uniform is unique to the Banyang women, whose husbands do not provide them with any clothes except at Christmas, some not even then. These elegant uniforms are compulsory, and women value them. To save for them some housewives extract bits of cash from the weekly housekeeping money given by their husbands. A woman may belong to many different 'meetings', for each of which she is expected to buy the uniform appropriate to that particular 'meeting'.

The Njangi

The second informal sector credit institution found in Mamfe and much used by women is the ROSCA commonly known as *njangi*, or by the Banyang as *nchuop*. This credit system is familiar to most Africanists as *esusu* (or *susu*: see Bortei-Doku in this volume), and is called *tontine* in French. Several writers have described this association as it exists in various parts of Cameroon. They include M. Delancey (1978:13–14), Meyer (1940:113–19) and Illy (1973:300–6). Ruel (1969), in his discussion of voluntary associations among the Banyang, offers no evidence for these institutions.

There has been speculation about the origins of *njangi*. M. Delancey (1977:319) describes *njangi* as 'the monetized form of a traditional method of organizing cooperative labour, namely what might be called a rotating land-clearing association'. These activities, known to the Banyang as *ntem*, were often done on a rotatory or reciprocal basis according to the needs of members. Compensation for work done was made in food and palm wine. This was a simple economy. As the economy evolved and became monetized, cash replaced food and wine, being seen as a more satisfactory compensation which met a greater range of demands. As the economy evolved further, it produced an élite group resident in the towns who acquired property, such as farms, in the villages. They hired the services of the *ntem* groups and paid them in cash, plus food and wine as a complement. In this new economic order there were specific rates of cash payments for work done which were lower for members of the *ntem* groups than for non-members. As farmers sold their farm produce for cash, the money realized facilitated the introduction of a system of periodic financial contributions within the rotating labour group. Within the *ntem* group a new term developed, *nchuop* ('contribution', or *njangi)*, a concept operating on a money basis but rooted in the pooling of and reciprocal use of labour resources. As noted, the above evolutionary scenario is hypothetical. The spread of the ROSCA model from nearby Nigeria or from the coast cannot be ruled out.

Types of Njangi

I have distinguished two types of *njangi* in Mamfe: the personal and impersonal.

In the personal *njangi* members come together at a given time and place. Regularity is the watchword in terms of the day, place and time of contribution. Fines are imposed on defaulters.

Some of the most important differences between ROSCAs are in the ways in which advantages are distributed or balanced between members (Ardener 1964:201). This is clearly seen in the impersonal *njangi*, where the organizer is the only office-holder and often the first member to receive the fund. Quite often the recipient gives her a token amount for her time and effort. While almost all types of *njangi* have some form of social activity apart from raising funds, the impersonal *njangi* in which members don't meet is an innovation in Mamfe and in Cameroon as a whole. With the continuous shift away from the bank and even the credit union, civil servants aiming at raising loans to meet large family needs prefer to join an *njangi* without being obliged to cater for and entertain members. This kind of *njangi* is not only economical in that no extra money is contributed or spent on entertainment and fines; it also saves time. However, such an *njangi* can also present risks in cases of default. In the two cases I studied, members seemed to make conscious efforts to pay their shares to the coordinator in the last week of the month, or the first week of the month at the latest, when the amount contributed is handed over to the receiver.

Operations can be in the form of cash, kind or even both. Another variety which mainly involves cash contributions is the 'disproportionate *njangi*'. Here members contribute according to their ability to pay. In paying back, the receiver of the fund also contributes what she received from each member. This type of *njangi* is mainly found among women wage-earners. It acts as a forum for keeping women together. Other varieties of the personal type include the 'equipment' and the 'kitchen' *njangi*. The equipment *njangi* is meant to provide some expensive durable equipment which is usually not common or easily purchased. It permits members to contribute money over a period and assists them to equip their households. The items saved for include building materials, refrigerators, gas cookers, fans, a set of upholstered chairs, TV and video sets, and sewing machines. In Mamfe and elsewhere in Cameroon the equipment *njangi* is common among well-to-do women, whether married, unmarried or widows. The contributions are collected by the treasurer in advance and handed over to the receiver. The receiver must purchase the item of equipment she lacks and display it to the members on the day of the *njangi*.

Another type of special-purchase *njangi* is the 'kitchen *njangi*'. It mainly helps women to buy relatively low-priced kitchen utensils. Unlike the equipment *njangi,* which is meant for a richer class of women, the kitchen type is open to all classes of women: of the women interviewed, 75 per cent belonged to a kitchen *njangi*. In these the contributions are made in advance and given to one member, who buys any kitchen utensils she desires. In some cases two or three members of the group, excluding the recipient, are assigned to purchase the article which the recipient might have indicated and to present it on the day of the *njangi*. What is important is that the use of the money is determined by the group. The kitchen *njangi* operates on the basis of both cash and kind. In the case of cash, members contribute money and purchase the kitchen utensil according to the expressed wish of the receiver. The *njangi* in kind involves the collection of an agreed item; it could be soap, vegetable oil or the like. These items are collected and given to the receiver. This may be the same person whose turn it is to receive the kitchen *njangi* in cases where contributions of cash and kind are both required.

The following is a general description of the functioning of a personal *njangi*. Membership varies from five to fifty. Beside ethnicity, two main criteria stand out: status and occupation. Each group has its officials, notably president, secretary, treasurer, discipline and social officer. These form the executive, which determines the tone and direction of the *njangi*. Usually the president is the person who has initiated the idea and has organized the *njangi* into a cohesive group. Leadership positions are renewed yearly in some groups. The role of the secretary is to record the order of rotation and contribution. The treasurer collects the contributions at each sitting and hands the fund to the recipient. At times the president appoints one member to hand over the amount collected. The treasurer also collects fines from defaulters. There are always some kind of refreshments at the end of each *njangi* sitting, offered by the person whose turn it is to receive the fund. In one *njangi* the recipient may provide a crate (20 bottles) of beer from the contribution she receives. In some groups members contribute for refreshments sums between 300–1,000frs cfa (worth 60p–£2 in 1991); the currency (cfa francs) used in Cameroon is backed by the French government. This depends on the level of contributions of the group. The total amount collected is handed over to the next recipient for the purchase of food and drink. In some groups the current recipient is given the entertainment money collected to subsidize her expenditure. The role of the social officer is to supervise and organize the refreshments at each sitting. The discipline officer maintains order during the sitting.

In the impersonal *njangi* members know each other but do not meet on set dates or at set places; the coordinator collects the agreed amount from members and hands it to the receiver. She selects trustworthy members, usually wage-earners or civil servants whose income flow is regular. Contributions are made at the end of the month when salaries are paid out. The recipient is determined by the organizer according to the needs expressed by the group's members. All contributions may not necessarily reach the coordinator on the same day. Sometimes, when members do not send in their shares, the coordinator has to collect the money. Nevertheless, there is a constant payment of the accepted share for the period of time agreed upon. The success of this type of *njangi* lies in the confidence members have in the organizer as well as in each other.

In the impersonal type, the organizer has a triple function; acting as president, treasurer and secretary. Since members do not congregate, there is no form of entertainment. Uniforms are not as common in *njangi* groups as in the 'meeting', where they are obligatory.

In women's *njangi* groups contributions in cash vary between 100–100,000 frs cfa (20p–£200 in 1991). The 100frs contribution is common in the 'market women *njangi*' which operates on a daily basis. Fifty-five women are involved; all are petty traders dealing in foodstuffs and other daily needs. The collector is usually one of the members who is literate. She keeps a register of all the members and the order of rotation. She moves around at a given time of day by which each member must have sold at least one item to raise 100frs cfa. A total of 5,500frs (£11) is usually handed over to the recipient of the day, in the order of rotation in which their names appear in the register. It therefore follows that in about two months the round ends, each member having received 5,500frs. However, the *njangi* continues immediately, the positions in the rotation being reversed in the new round: that is, the last person on the register becomes first to receive. This goes on throughout the year. By the end of the year the *njangi* would have had six rounds and every member would have contributed and received 33,000frs (£66).

The money received from this form of *njangi* is used to buy wholesale items for retail. Apart from such 'market women *njangi*', and others organized by traders which operate daily, all other women's *njangi* groups meet weekly, fortnightly or monthly, usually on Fridays, Saturdays or Sundays. Many *njangi* start at the beginning of the year and end within the last three months of the year. Some start at the beginning of the school year – that is, in the month of September – and end in July. They are, however, renewable: even if some members drop out, new ones are recruited to ensure continuity.

The women of Mamfe value *njangi* as the only way to guarantee savings. Once a woman becomes a member of a group, she is obliged to save. This motivates her to work even harder, which the 'meetings', where saving is not obligatory, fail to do. Sometimes when a round of *njangi* ends the group may decide to take a break of a month or two before starting again. It is common with those *njangi* which end in October or November to begin again in January. The break provides rest from the worry of obligatory savings; it also enables members to plan projects individually for the next phase. In certain groups where the membership is large and the target period for completing the rotation must be met, the total sum is doubled: two members receive funds at every sitting. This kind of doubling, which allows a member to make more than one contribution and receive more than one allocation of funds, is common among women in Mamfe. This has also been cited by other authors (Embree, 1964: 142, Ardener, 1953: 130).

Quite often contributions are paid at the home of the member receiving the fund. Some groups have permanent meeting-places, such as the organizer's home or office or the members' place of work. Various factors determine the order of rotation. In some groups it is determined by lot. After drawing lots, members may exchange positions through negotiation or even buy desired positions. Once lots have been drawn for the first round, the order may simply be reversed at the end of the *njangi*, or members may draw lots for positions at each round. In others, the organizers determine the order, taking into consideration a member's needs. In such cases the organizers are sometimes bribed, the bribes varying from a crate of beer to a cash amount of 5,000frs (£10). Apart from this, *njangi* officials are never paid, but are usually compensated by refreshments. Uses of contributed funds for purposes other than *njangi* turns is rare, except in a few associations for the provision of entertainment, and the amount is then fixed. *Njangi* recipients are not required to pay interest as such. This is one of the reasons why women are so inclined to *njangi*; it is believed that any amount of money can be raised through this credit association without paying charges or interest as levied by the bank and thrift and loan societies. Nevertheless, defaulters pay variable fines in kind and cash; for example, in an association where the amount of the contribution is 50,000frs cfa (£100) each month, maybe 3,000frs (£6) is levied if the defaulter has already received her share of the *njangi* and 1,000frs (£2) if she has not. In others it may be a crate (twenty bottles) of beer and ten bottles of beer respectively. It is very dishonourable to be in debt to a *njangi* and unable to pay it. To avoid commitments they cannot fulfils women in Mamfe choose from among different kinds of *njangi*, taking into account their class, occupation and status. It is rare to find defaulters deliberately failing to pay their shares, or punitive sanctions go beyond the fines of the association. Another way in which some groups curb defaulters is to place members whose reliability is doubted towards the end of the rotation. Guarantors are not needed in the *njangi* as found in the 'meeting', where guarantors have to co-sign a contract for a loan to be made from the 'savings bank'.

If a salaried member is transferred to another area before the end of an *njangi* session, she continues to send her money regularly. If she has not received her share before leaving the district, she comes back to receive it, using a friend's house when it is her turn to entertain the group. If a member dies before she has had her turn, the members for whom she contributed will also contribute on her behalf at the time she was supposed to benefit. A member of her family would be invited to receive her share, or the president would take the money to a member of her immediate family. A problem arises if a member dies after having received her turn. It is usually difficult to find a member of her family willing to continue the contribution or pay off those from whom the deceased had received. Such cases, however, are very rare.

Case Studies

While women were interviewed individually about their access to and use of credit, a number of *njangi* groups were also studied to find out what was particular about each group. All-female groups in Mamfe are identified by name. These are chosen by members to reflect their activities, the ideals of the group, ethnic or cultural attachments, or on purely social grounds. Hence such names as 'Mo-ngho' (Smoke) for an *njangi* of women who prepare and sell food, 'Harmony Sisters', 'Semo-Sengho' (Let's try and see), 'Bechoko Bo Meh' (Sitting for those who own the land), 'Ideal Sisters', 'Jolly Sisters', and 'Modest Sisters'.

I was a member and treasurer of the group called 'Modest Sisters' from 1983 to 1990, before I decided to join an impersonal *njangi* group (see below) due to the pressure of the numerous activities I was engaged in. 'Modest Sisters' is an *njangi* group or ROSCA that has been running for over eight years. Its members are well-to-do women, either civil servants or big business women. It started in January 1983 with a monthly contribution of 25,000frs cfa (£50). After two years the amount was increased to 50,000 frs (£100), and two years later it went up to 100,000frs (£200). This group has always had between twelve and fourteen members – fourteen in situations in which some members pair up and contribute 50,000frs each to make up a share. This *njangi* meets at 7.00 pm on every last Saturday of the month, and runs throughout the year from January to December. It meets in rotation in members' houses and positions are arranged by drawing lots every year. The total amount raised at each sitting is 1.2 million frs cfa (£2,400), which members put to various uses. *Njangi* money is used for personal or family building projects, to send a child overseas for further education, or to pay school fees. Some women invest their money in big businesses, such as travelling overseas to buy and sell foreign goods; others buy a car, while others give part of the money received from the *njangi* to their husbands. This happens in cases where the husband has been giving his wife some money to make up her share each month. Apart from the shares contributed monthly, 2,000frs (£4) is also contributed at each sitting, of which half goes to the receiver for refreshment and half is kept by the treasurer for what the women call the 'Husbands' Day Party'. Since the group is limited to married women, members invite husbands to a sumptuous entertainment once a year: each member of the group also brings along another couple. The party is usually organized in mid-November or on the first Saturday of December in a member's house with adequate sitting and dancing space. On this occasion one of the husbands is made 'master of ceremonies', and other husbands are given the opportunity to make speeches.

This was one of the most successful female *njangi* groups I studied in Mamfe. Many factors contributed to its success. First, rules and regulations binding the group are strictly adhered to. Fines are levied on defaulters, 500frs (£1) for lateness without justification, 2,500frs (£5) for failure to contribute one's share on the *njangi* day if one has not 'received', and 5,000frs (£10) if one has 'received'. In the seven years during which I was a member of the 'Modest Sisters', only six irregular situations were recorded, excluding lateness. In four cases fines were paid for failure to contribute a share on *njangi* day, and there were two dismissals from the group. In 1989 the secretary of the group was dismissed by members for refusing to pay her fines. Also, in 1986, one of the members who always sent her share and failed to attend regular *njangi* sittings was warned and finally dismissed at the end of the year. Members are, however, so ashamed of default that if a member has not got her salary before the day of the *njangi*, by prior negotiation with the recipient she can offer a post-dated cheque, although this is not encouraged.

Another reason for the success of this group is that there are always women keen to replace members transferred to other areas. Some men ask their wives to join the group. Sometimes they contribute half their wives' share. In 1990 the group carried out an unusual activity. Generally women in Cameroon control the use of their money, especially when it is their own earnings. Having concentrated on themselves and their families for many years, the 'Modest Sisters' decided to extend their largesse to a philanthropic cause. Each member donated two bedsheets and two pillow-cases to the children's ward of the general hospital in Mamfe.

The 'Jolly Sisters' is one of the groups in Mamfe which carries out a series of activities at one sitting. It consists of twenty-four members, all married women, teachers, nurses, traders, housewives and office-workers, who meet fortnightly at 4.00pm on Saturdays in a member's home. The activities of the group during the first half-hour of a sitting include discussions on health and nutrition, or sometimes a member gives a practical lecture on how to prepare a particular food item. After the discussion the members contribute 2,000frs (£4) to both a 'sinking fund' and a 'kitchen *njangi*', and cakes of laundry soap costing 200frs (40p) to an *njangi* in kind given to the recipient, in whose house the group meets. In this group there is also a non-compulsory thrift and loan saving scheme in which any amount desired can be saved, and at every other sitting of the month a voluntary cash *njangi* of 25,000frs (£50) involving eight members, and one of 5,000frs (£10) involving twelve members, are held as well. Again, while members are not obliged to join the monthly cash *njangi*, everyone participates in the fortnightly 'kitchen' and 'soap' *njangi*. These activities are accompanied by food and drink offered by the hostess. *Njangi* groups in Mamfe not only enable members to raise loans without interest, but also act as a means of disseminating knowledge through the discussions that go on in them. Though an item like soap can be bought easily, it gives satisfaction when a large quantity is stocked in a woman's house for daily laundry and washing in the kitchen. 'Soap' is like the 'broom' given by a Bakweri mother in Cameroon to her young daughter on her wedding day: it is a symbol of cleanliness.

Another striking feature of all female *njangi* groups in Mamfe is that some women would not allow their husbands to know when they received their *njangi* funds. This was noticeable among the 'OPSANS' (a group of past students from the same girls' secondary school). In one of the member's houses where the 'meeting' and the *njangi* were taking place, the hostess who was the recipient that day asked another friend to receive the amount in her place. She also asked the person handing over the money to do so in such a way that she called upon the hostess's friend to receive it in the hearing of the hostess's husband and friends present on that occasion. At the end of the sitting, the friend secretly handed the money over to the intended recipient. In this case the members of the group understood what was going on, but the visitors present did not. This attitude is becoming more and more common among women in Cameroon and other parts of Africa, and can be seen in different walks of life, even among housewives who would not want their husbands to know when they have money. Even grown-up children working in towns and cities send money secretly to their mothers without their fathers knowing. Women have developed this attitude because of what they see as the selfish attitude of some men. A woman who knows that her husband spends the bulk of his income on drink and concubines at the expense of family needs would not let him know when she received her *njangi* fund. Some men do not believe that women need money of their own, even though they have to bear the bulk of family responsibilities. Hence women tend to develop financial strategies to preserve the money for their personal needs and family necessities.

The need to have credit and carry out what Cameroonian women call 'big ventures' is not limited to women living in Cameroon. Manyu women who lived abroad, especially those in Nigeria many years ago, were noted for two main achievements: building a house back home, and returning home finally with trunks of 'wrappers' (dress lengths) and other property. It is with this aim in mind that the Manyu women in London have organized an *njangi* within the Manyu Women's Meeting which takes place on every second Sunday of the month at a member's house, from 5-7.00pm. This not only allows for socialization and knowing who has just returned from Cameroon and who will be going back, but enables some women to raise large amounts of money, which is now very difficult to raise from the banks. The *njangi* consists of ten members, married and unmarried, contributing £400 at each sitting. Each

round continues throughout the year, with a month's break at the end of
a series; this period is meant to allow members to make up their minds
whether to continue or withdraw, and also to give time to others who
might wish to join the group to make the necessary arrangements. Like
most of the *njangi* groups back home, positions are determined by
drawing lots, but desired positions could be swapped by negotiation.
Defaulters pay fines of 50p for lateness and £25 for failure to pay a share
on the day of the *njangi*. All the members I talked to said that the £4,000
they had received from *njangi* funds was invested back home in a
building project in progress, to acquire a piece of land for a future
project, or to renovate their family houses in the village and give them
a modern appearance by converting them from mud-walled and
thatched-roofed huts to concrete, brick and zinc-roofed houses. Most
of these women go home for a period of two weeks to one month when
they receive their *njangi* contribution, or send money home to their
parents or relatives to supervise their building projects.

Unlike *njangi* groups in Mamfe, each member needs a 'shortee'
(surety) in order to be able to join a group. Moreover each member looks
for her own 'shortee', who must be a member of the women's 'meeting'
group. Sometimes a prospective *njangi* member may approach a person
who refuses to be a 'shortee', especially if the two women do not have
close, friendly ties. This may also happen if a woman doubts the
reliability of a member. The lack of a 'shortee' can stop a woman from
joining the *njangi* group in London. Three forms are signed by both the
member and the 'shortee', one of which is kept in the 'meeting' file, one
given to the 'shortee', and one is kept by the contributor. Whereas it is
only in the thrift and loan saving schemes that 'shortees' are needed for
loans raised, *njangi* groups in Mamfe and elsewhere never need
'shortees'. While at home there is a closer link between members of the
same society, and it is easier for people to know and trust each other, the
same does not necessarily apply to people from the same area living in
another country. If a member fails to contribute her share of the *njangi*,
the group always turns to her 'shortee'. This has helped to strengthen the
Manyu Women's Meeting and *njangi* in London.

Significance of Indigenous Credit Associations

'Women have been shown to save if savings have been a requirement to
credit' (Buvinic, 1979:iii). Women's ability to save gives them access to
credit, and the uses to which credit is put reveal that women can control

it wisely. When the formal and informal credit institutions are opened to women, the researcher's task has been to discover preferences and reasons for preferences. Several authors have shown that most women in the third world rely on indigenous credit associations, despite the presence of modern ones. It is in this light that this paper looks at the significance of indigenous credit associations in the Mamfe semi-urban area. These institutions have come into prominence because of the constraints of the formal institutions, which demand collateral security for loans. In the *njangi* groups, for example, every contributor is deemed creditworthy. This attracts the women, who have difficulty finding collateral security for loans. The kinds of economic investment engaged in by women include petty trading in foodstuffs, catering, urban transport, services, and departmental stores. Other areas of investment include the predictable demands of children's education and building, and unexpected demands such as hospital bills or expenditures on death ceremonies. *Njangi* also help to reduce the temptation to extravagance.

Apart from the economic aspect, members enjoy humane and social benefits when they come together in their *njangi* and 'meetings'. On such occasions innate qualities, such as leadership and a talent for oratory, are manifested and help in the selection of officers. People also make friends through these groups and learn from one another. The groups also help to improve the status of women in society by increasing their self-confidence. There is still illiteracy among women, who receive much less education, and this also limits their access to formal credit institutions. By turning for credit to the informal credit associations, women, no matter what their class or social status, can find a convenient, simple and accessible means of satisfying their wants.

Conclusion

Modern and traditional forms of credit association exist side by side. Before the advent of modern credit institutions it was customary to pool resources, either for mutual or individual benefit. Despite the presence of various types of modern institution, women in Mamfe evidently still hold fast to older values. But indigenous credit associations are fast becoming authentic finance houses, where loans can be raised and circulated for the benefit of members. While formal institutions for savings and credit can meet greater financial needs – and women do need them – the informal institutions are far from becoming self-destroy, and they are unlikely to be replaced by banks, credit unions and other seemingly more 'rational' types of credit institution in the foreseeable future.

Notes

1. 'Semi-urban' is a term used in Cameroon government publications to denote smaller dispersed centres of population with some urban services (such as piped water, electricity, schools, hospitals) which, together with interspersed or surrounding rural areas, form an administrative centre.
2. The credit union movement in Cameroon was introduced into the grasslands area by Roman Catholic Fathers. The first one was organized in 1963 by the Rev. Fr A. Jansen with ten men at St Bede's College, Njinikom.

References

Ardener, S. (1964), 'The Comparative Study of Rotating Credit Associations', *Journal of the Royal Anthropological Institute*, XCIV, pp. 201–9.

Buvinic, M, et al (1979), *Credit for Rural Women. Some Facts and Lessons*. Washington: International Centre for Research on Women.

—— (1953), 'The Social and Economic Significance of the Contributions Clubs among a Section of the Southern Ibo' *Conference Proceedings*, N.I.S.E.R., Ibadan, Nigeria.

Delancey, M.W. (1977), 'Credit for the Common Man in Cameroon', *Journal of Modern African Studies*, 15, 2, pp. 316–22.

—— (1978), 'Savings and Credit Institutions in Rural West Africa', *Rural Africana*, 2, pp. 1–8.

Delancey, V. (1978a), 'Women at the Cameroon Development Corporation. How their Money Works', *Rural Africana*, 17a, 2, pp. 9–34.

—— (1978b), 'Credit Union Activities in Cameroon. An Example of an Untapped Source of Investment Fund', paper presented at the *Annual Conference of the SEA*, Washington D.C.

Devereux, S., & Panes, H., with Best, J. (1987), *A Manual of Credit and Savings for the Poor of Developing Countries*, Oxford, Oxfam.

Embree, J. (1964), *A Japanese Village: Suye Mura*, London: Kegan Paul.

Illy, H.F. (1973), 'Savings and Credit of the Bamileke in Cameroun – A Study of the Internal Financing of Development', *Development Policy in Africa*, J. Voss (ed.), Bonn: Vealga Neue Gesellschaft.

Meyer, E. (1940), 'Kreditringe in Kamerun', *Koloniale Rundschau*, 31, pp. 113–21.

Ruel, M. (1969), 'The Modern Adaptation of Associations of the Banyang of the West Cameroon', *Southwestern Journal of Anthropology*, 20, 1–41.

7

Looking at Financial Landscapes: A Contextual Analysis of ROSCAs in Cameroon

Michael Rowlands

Introduction

With the collapse of communism, it has become clearer than ever that its opposing shibboleth, capitalism, is neither as homogeneous nor as global an order as we had been led to believe. The probability is that a number of different 'capitalisms' have emerged, historically based on precedent as well as on dissemination and local appropriation of basic ideas about commodities and markets from one source, 'The West'. If this is so, then there is an urgent need to provide ethnographies of the actual working of key aspects of capitalism as a local process, and surely one of these is the process of capital formation and investment and its reproduction. Ardener's precocious recognition of rotating credit associations is such an instance of how people conserved scarce cash within social domains that defined morally suitable goals and objectives. The key issue here is money and the social categories that may act to define its value.

One of the more persistent 'western' ideas about the circulation of money is that it has abstract and egalitarian consequences that dissolve 'traditional' social relations. In classic economic theory, money and markets function together to promote a liberalizing ethos of progressive individualism through the development of an entrepreneurial spirit. It is natural, therefore, that financial policy-making in development strategies has aimed to make cheap money available by distributing easy credit and building links between formal financial institutions such as banking and credit union organizations and informal savings groups. Starting from a particular contextual analysis of saving and credit in Bamenda, part of the Grassfields area of Cameroon, I will argue that people's perception of their local financial landscape springs from an opposing desire to maintain a strong social, and in particular a gendered, discipline on the circulation and consumption of money. Rather than the problem being one of too little money in circulation, it is believed to be more a question of the quality of money, or the scarcity of 'good money', defined by evaluating the purposes to which it is put.

Gendered Saving

The idea that money can be gendered in value does not affect the general perception that exchange rate and price ratio act as the principal determinants of circulation. Rather it turns our attention to what is done with money, in particular to the relative emphasis placed on saving for deferred consumption and immediate consumption.

ROSCAs are widespread in West Africa, and although they originated as precolonial trading organizations, have evolved in complex and diverse forms, particularly in urban settings where their relations with more formal means of saving such as banking and credit unions have never been adequately studied. The absence of attention is due to the tendency to follow the formal/informal dichotomy as a dualism between the dominance of formal economic versus informal social rationalities. This tendency to separate the social from the economic has resulted in very different perceptions of the relative difference in savings and lending behaviour in changing contexts.

In West Cameroon, ROSCAs (known locally as *njangis* or *tontines*) have for long been associated with the economic dynamism of the francophone Bamileke and the anglophone Bamenda. Nationally in Cameroon, the cultural stereotype of the 'Grafi' entrepreneurs from the Grasslands is often represented by the size and frequency of their contributions to *njangis* (or *tontines* in the francophone Cameroon). Big men in particular are widely recognized as capable of concentrating millions of local francs (cfa; the French-backed franc) through their *njangis* to pursue their business careers. Warnier (1993), in a short biographical history of Bamileke entrepreneurs, has distinguished several types based on their attitude to saving and investment. First there are the older men, now in their fifties or sixties, self-made men who originally started saving through local *njangis* and investing their returns in market activities or trading and built up substantial, if diversified, businesses which as often as not collapsed with the death of the owner. The business empire of the self-made man correlates nationally with a network of a dozen or so 'big men' who, whilst often illiterate, supported each other through extensive national and international transfers of money which totally avoided the formal banking system. Then there is a second generation of businessmen, usually with educational qualifications, distinguished by using government salaries and other forms of disposable income to get loans from banks or invest regularly in high-contribution *njangis* for business purposes. For these men, what others have called 'straddling' means that salaries from the public domain are the essential basis for entering into private business. Finally, the younger generation of men, often in their twenties or early thirties, consists of technocrats who look to foreign partners and foreign banks for capital to start new enterprises. Broadly speaking, these are least likely to rely heavily on ROSCAs to finance their enterprises. All three types co-exist at present in Cameroon, and reproduce their own business networks and aims. Whilst the older men are more concerned with converting wealth into titles in the village hierarchy, polygyny and the expansion of their households, the second group are more often involved in the ostentatious consumption of foreign goods, what Bayart has called 'la politique du ventre', the third group show signs of a more technocratic attitude, are critical of the older men, and see themselves at the forefront of a politics of renewal in contemporary Cameroon.

What tends to characterize all three generations of businessmen is their concern with the use of money to support male-dominated business networks. Wives, children and the needs of the household in Bamileke and Bamenda worlds are seen as definitely secondary to the use of available scarce cash for business. Stories are legion of businessmen who would refuse to spend money on clothes, medicines or education for their families and would build luxury houses for the government to rent, but live with their families in conditions of relative squalor. Such men would be described by their wives as 'slaves to money'. The younger men are less puritanical but to them too spending is strategic, which means the expansion of business networks and the maintenance of public confidence in the success of the business enterprise.

Hence it is not surprising that the attitude of women to men and money is deeply ambivalent and cynical. The problems of getting household money, or money for expenses, from husbands obsessed with economic success are the topic of everyday discussion in Bamenda. Rivalry between wives for the favours of polygynous husbands is the standard topic of moral stories, and the most frequent basis of witchcraft accusations by women against other women. Women's concern for money to pay for education, medical bills, clothes and so forth, is aroused principally by the needs of their children and the maintaining of their households. Men's ambitions are basically located out of the household, and require investment in usually male-dominated friendship networks and business partnerships. Men often express cynical views of women as profligate consumers who make relentless demands on them for money which they pass on to their brothers or mothers. The perception of many women that marriages are fragile, and that they therefore have a limited time to acquire resources, is based on the constant danger that they may well be left without resources and with young children to maintain, or be supplanted by a junior wife.

Gendered antagonism does shape attitudes towards the value of money. As noted by Niger-Thomas (this volume), it has been unusual, at least until recently, for women to invest in large-scale business enterprises, because they prefer *njangis* with fixed contributions and returns at specified dates, or smaller-scale trading and selling which provide regular small amounts of money to meet immediate needs. Accumulating scarce cash for immediate need and the security of a regular income, such as from rent, making clothes, and market activities, does in turn require the security of women's networks for mutual assistance. Women are the most frequent investors in credit unions in Bamenda, usually investing small sums each month and withdrawing savings at regular times, such as in September (when school fees are due) and at Christmas for household expenses. As in Manyu Division (cf. Niger-Thomas, this volume) women tend to form their own *njangis*, usually with special purposes in mind such as buying kitchen equipment, paying school fees, or simply to emphasize the ideal of mutual assistance and self-help. The value of money in this context is not only an expression of short-term satisfaction of particular needs, but is basically defined by what form of social relations it is converted into. Women who clearly are concerned with using money for gain to concentrate capital for investment in business are therefore more likely to be constrained by the demands that disperse available cash between family members, needs of children that may be attached to her through a variety of ties, and women's social groupings. The breakthrough into large-scale business enterprises is more difficult for Grassfields women, and requires their gradual separation from women's *njangis* in order to enter the more male-dominated business *njangis*. I would argue that businesswomen on any large scale are rare, precisely because they are more prone than men to disperse their savings and contributions through these social networks of mutual assistance.

Mutualism and the Extension of Debt

Debt in Bamenda is a valued practice, tied to reliance on mutual assistance and trust, to encourage diversification in the means of making money. The strategy of belonging to several ROSCAs, for example, serves to extend a personal debt portfolio as widely as possible. Strategizing on the timing of contributions, and the pay-outs from the different ROSCAs one belongs to, is certainly an essential element of business and political success. But the critical underlying assumption is that all members are committed to helping each other through lending their savings. The importance of valorizing debt in the maintenance of business networks is most clearly seen in the astonishing fact that, whilst bankruptcy proceeding legally exists in Cameroon, it is rarely taken advantage of by creditors. Why is this?

The scale of personal debt in Cameroon is unknown but considered generally to be enormous. Since the 1970s until the late 80s, the state-controlled funding agencies (FONADER, CCCE, and so on), and all the banks, gave easy loans on doubtful securities, most of which went into business enterprises and ostentatious consumption. In the present period of economic crisis the state, as the largest and most insolvent debtor, has caused the collapse of innumerable businesses through withdrawal of contracts. This has resulted in turn in the implementation of structural adjustment programmes requiring tighter fiscal regulation, and the loss of civil servant salaries as the security for loans.

Very few of these failed business enterprises end up in bankruptcy court due to disgruntled creditors attempting to retrieve something from the wreckage. The reason most frequently given to account for this strange state of affairs is that, for most Cameroonians, there is no assumption that money borrowed must be repaid. People look immediately to the possibilities of rescheduling debts through collective bargaining with creditors and converting the debt into a social resource. To settle a debt in such circumstances would be unthinkable since it destroys the social network on which it is founded. Much better to force the banks into bankruptcy than finally settle a loan. The implication, of course, is that the social networks of mutual assistance on which debt is founded involve kinds of indebtedness additional to money. Credit typically implies a means of obtaining resources which are likely to be used for many other purposes than the enterprise for which the loan was ostensibly intended. Not only does a typical businessman or businesswoman have a wide range of activities in their portfolio, but as often as not their accounting procedures for knowing where money is at any particular time are remarkably crude. Not surprisingly, this seems to be linked to the fact that it is not immediately accountable money that is valued, nor the redemption of debts that is rigorously pursued, but rather the spreading of the obligations to help (that is, lend money) to as wide a network as possible.

There is a saying in Bamenda that it is through family that one loses money. Giving to agnates is in many ways regarded as an absolute loss, since there is neither any compulsion on them to redeem the debt, nor does it form a useful investment in personal networks. Yet there is an immense pressure to redistribute wealth to close kin to meet their needs, which is supported by the frequency of witchcraft accusations made by younger, wealthier, men against their older paternal relatives in the village. Unlike most of the other peoples of Southern Cameroon, the Bamileke and Bamenda have a reputation not only for being mean with money and for not spending it on luxuries, but also for preventing wastage of resources in unproductive spending.

Debt, Kinship, Succession and Inheritance

This Weberian ethos is linked closely to the kinship system which systematically prevents partitive inheritance through naming a single successor who inherits the wives, land and movable wealth of a father. The successor is named by the father before his death to a number of close friends who promise to have him elected to the title. The chosen heir must possess certain personal qualities, intelligence, generosity, and strength of mind, as well as demonstrating his fecundity through having produced a first child. Succession to title is seen as the opposite to a successful career in business, politics, and so on. All such ambitions have to be given up, and the successor is supposed to resign himself to a life of restraint and relative seclusion. The chosen heir will often resist the choice and attempt to escape. In the course of the funeral, his peers will seize the successor and prevent him fleeing, strip him of his clothes, rub him with palm oil and camwood and install him, often quite forcibly, on his predecessor's seat, then dress him in his clothes and make him wear his regalia of title-holder. The emphasis is on restraint and containment in using force, to compel a successor to honour the debt of the father.

As Pradelles (1991) has shown, the system of partial succession in the Grassfields is linked to a perception of debt in the exchange of women. By including father, son, and father of the mother in a triadic model of paternity, in fact two very different forms of debt are created. Whilst the relation of father to son is strict and authoritarian, that to the mother's father is overtly less power-laden but none the less more threatening. The Bamileke call the mother's father the 'père de dérrière', as the man who provided the woman by which the man was able to have sons and daughters. The wife-giver is therefore the man who has allowed the husband to fulfil his debts to the dead by providing them with living successors in sons and daughters. It is he who has given them to the successor and who can take them back again. If the husband were later to forget the gifts due to the mother's father at the birth of children, or to share the bridewealth received at the marriage of a daughter, the children will suffer illness and possibly death as a consequence of not maintaining the debt. The debt to the dead by the living father or to the mother's father by the daughters' children and husbands is therefore unbridgeable and unrepayable except in the form of continuous giving, in order to prevent vindictive behaviour by the dead towards the living.

A belief in the impossibility of discharging a debt because reimbursement would destroy social networks is therefore deeply rooted in the basic ontology of Grassfields societies. Personal fortunes are made on the principle of acquiring non-reimbursable debts. The living have obligations to the dead that can never be discharged, as do juniors to elders, wife-takers to wife-givers, but whilst the obligation of sons to fathers is total, fathers have no obligations to sons. Not only is the father/son relation fraught and ambivalent, so is the relation between children of the same father and different mothers. Although they are under the obligations of 'those who speak with a single mouth', the rivalry between them over access to paternal resources renders agnatic relations tense and repressed. By comparison with the extensive debts of affinal links, agnatic ties are hostile and based on a desire to close the debt between living and dead. In the ambiguous and sorcery-prone ties of agnatic relations, we see the counterweight to the relations of mutuality found in the 'societies of friends' or ROSCAs.

The idea that debt is an obligation that can never be redeemed but only recompensed for, sanctioned by the disastrous social consequences of the anger generated by default, is therefore a key Cameroon Grassfields (if not African!) value. Since debts have primordial values, not only can they not be discharged, they must constantly be extended with the transmission of substances of all kinds in exchange (blood, semen, witchcraft substance, money). This centrifugal movement of obligation is at the same time counterbalanced by another value which is the ritualized incentive towards retention and containment of substances. The latter value is largely a matter of the transmission of ritual powers that have shifted historically from the matriline to a patrilineal principle in many Grassfields societies (cf. Fardon, 1988). Marriage, succession, the installation to lineage or clan titles, and funerals are strongly marked by the signs that prevent improper transmission and wastage of ancestrally derived vital substances. For instance, celibate men who never marry and lack children will be called *mu*, or 'children', as a sign of the absence of transmission, and therefore are unable to meet the debt to dead fathers. Moreover, as an encompassing notion, since women are principally the object and subject of transmission, the protection and transmission of such substances is seen as a largely male preserve, articulated on various occasions when the gap in the debt between living and dead has to be ritually closed. Funerals, including 'cry-dies', are such occasions, as are the births of first children to married sons or the setting-up of a separate compound, when the debts of the living to the dead have to be recompensed and contained. The associations of such occasions with anger and violence from disappointed or aggrieved dead are particularly strong, from which women and their fertility should normally be excluded.

Money has therefore many of the same connotations as other vital life substances in the Grassfields. It is a scarce resource, in particular social domains, that needs to be contained and not wasted. It shares procreative qualities with other life substances, witnessed in ideas of magical money or money-doubling. Certain men claim to have the ritual powers to transform the life substance of money so that it will reproduce itself, again a very widespread West African idea. Money is blessed.

Interfacing ROSCAs

If ROSCAs are embedded in a wider context of assistance through mutual debt, it is equally clear that they represent a particular manifestation of a principle of spreading risk that, whilst almost certainly precolonial in origin, has been transformed with the expansion of a money economy.

Although considerable variation exists, a consistent distinction is discernible in the organization of ROSCAs between those which emphasize mutual assistance for specific, often domestic, needs and those that are of larger scale and oriented towards profit-making activities. In francophone Cameroon, the distinction is made between *tontines de solidarité* and *tontines d'affaires*. The first is a ubiquitous form of association which is held at work or in people's houses, and unites people from the same origin or occupation. The contributions are paid monthly, over a fixed cycle, with the order of the rotation defined randomly beforehand. The amount of each contribution is usually small and the aims are limited and known to members; for example the aim might be for school fees, household needs, medical bills, Christmas expenses. Often people will stress that it is the advice and help they get from fellow members that encourages them to join, as much as the help it gives them to save. The emphasis therefore is on the achievement of mutually-defined goals through saving scarce money, rather than aiming to accumulate as such.

ROSCA or *tontine*, as a proper term, should probably be used to describe associations that are directed towards investment for profit. Not only is it a question of the amounts involved, often millions of francs CFA in Bamenda, but also the aims of members wishing to join such an association. In certain ROSCAs, a member's place in the rotation is determined by an auction which is run by the president of the association. The winner receives the money minus his bid, which is then put in a side fund to be shared out to all members in the final meetings. There are some members who never receive the fund but will sell their turn to other members who need the money. Lump sums are smaller and consequently money is more expensive at the beginning of the rotation than by the end, and the cost of obtaining early money has to be evaluated against the profitability of its use. More than likely such members will belong to several ROSCAs of differing size and will be able to use their dividends from lower-ranking clubs to pay their contributions to those of a higher rank.

What both types of ROSCA share is the key value of the social and personal commitment to debt as a means of providing mutual assistance. Members constantly stressed that ROSCAs are not the equivalent of banks or credit unions, since the aim of each ROSCA meeting is that by the end of the meeting all the resources shall be distributed and in members' hands. The rigid hierarchical organization of ROSCAs combined with the duties imposed on the president and treasurer is the means by which this happy solution is achieved. The claim that ROSCAs are very different types of organization from the other financial institutions available to its members does seem to be borne out by the practice. Unlike other means of acquiring capital, such as bank loans, salary payments or embezzlement which are accumulative in principle, the aim of contributing to ROSCAs is additive. The aim is not to accumulate wealth but to add on the number of debt partners that can be turned to in times of need. Money that has been socialized in this way is distributed so that the organization is not seen to make any profit; only the individual members do.

Western-inspired institutions that lend or pay salaries, in contrast to the ROSCA principle, are seen to make money from its members. Money paid in taxes, lodged in bank accounts, used as payment, all have non-ROSCA qualities of 'thing-ness', or of commodification, rather than those associated with the expansion of networks of indebtedness. This might suggest a gift-versus-commodity duality, on Melanesian lines, but in both settings it would ignore the evidence for commercial interest and gain. Instead, it suggests the existence of two capitalist logics – one perhaps more mercantilist in its orientation than the other. The incompatibility between the two, the accumulative western concern with rational calculation in contrast to the West African additive principle of converting and diversifying wealth into social networks, suggests that ROSCAs developed at the interface between these two logics. ROSCAs form the means by which 'free money' can be converted from the logic of wages, bank loans, and development aid into socialized capital for the funding of indigenous businesses.

In current debates on rural funding in development policies there has developed considerable caution over the effects of easy-money strategies. Rationing of low-priced loans to the rich, and misallocation of funds in the period when the provision of cheap money or credit was thought to be the best way to encourage rural development, undermined confidence and trust in public financial institutions. The tendency has been to question the value of permanent financial institutions due to the risks of increased formalization and bureaucratization by comparison with ROSCAs and other informal systems, where impermanence is a built-in characteristic. The problem with dualistic arguments that simply oppose the logics of formal and informal credit facilities is precisely that they distract our attention from the interactions between them and how they mutually constitute each other's activities. The banking system in Cameroon, for example, is not distinct from informal systems such as ROSCAs since transfers of credit and cash flows exist between them. In a highly centralized one-party state such as Cameroon, the financing of ROSCA loans comes mainly from government salaries which are paid into personal bank accounts, and the treasurers of ROSCAs will invariably invest their side funds in bank deposit accounts to earn interest. It seems very likely therefore that the expansion of ROSCAs in the '70s and '80s in Cameroon is functionally linked to the increased circulation of cheap money during this period through the creation of various public institutions for distributing rural credit. The interface between formal institutions and informal self-help associations served to channel uncontrolled money into specific social domains which restricted its movements to aims established by the membership of the latter.

The existence of such an interface is long-standing, as are crises generated by the breakdown in the relationship. The excessive rationalism that structural adjustment programmes impose on debt networks is a case in point since the rise in unemployment, particularly among civil servants, undermines members' capacity to make contributions to ROSCAs. An historical parallel exists with the end of the slave trade in the first half of the nineteenth century and the shift of European interest from slaves to trading in commodities through the hulk system. The remains of disarmed merchant ships left in the ports were used as entrepôts, trading European goods against palm oil and other commodities. As competition between Europeans for primary products led to the withdrawal of credit in indigenous trade, the extensive debt networks that linked coastal trading partners to the hinterland collapsed and the instability which ensued required European intervention and, finally, colonial rule.

We may be dealing therefore with an historically well-tried mechanism of adapting global financial circulation to local social demand in which scarcity of money was the significant issue, as well as limiting by informal mechanisms the wastage caused by undisciplined circulation. If so, then the distinction between business *njangis* and those stressing solidarity also takes on significance as part of a wider hierarchy of informal means of restricting movement of cash from one social domain into another, on a par with the anthropologically famous accounts of spheres of exchange. Douglas's (1973) description of them as 'primitive rationing' systems bears close similarities and is ultimately the inspiration for this analysis, which shows ROSCAs playing a similar role in a widened cash economy.

Gendering the Interface?

The tendency for the value of money to be gendered by the different needs of women who maintain children and households, in contrast to men's preoccupation with economic success, should roughly correlate with the distinction between neighbourly 'meetings', which operate ROSCAs, and business *njangis*. Niger-Thomas separates *njangis* for kitchen equipment, school fees, or clothes which are run by and for women, from the business *njangis* which, whilst not excluding women, include only those that have gone into business in a sufficiently big way to stand on a par with men. But whilst this is undoubtedly the case, such a sharp distinction could run the danger of overdetermining the dualism that can all too easily be derived from the formal/informal; *njangi/*'meeting'; male/female; father/

son dichotomies that we have discovered.

In a significant sense it is the articulation between the categories that appears to constitute social life in Bamenda, and more widely in West Cameroon. A significant difference exists in the degree of articulation involved at different levels of mutual aid. Village 'meetings', for instance, are not directly linked to formal institutions; in fact they may well be supported by prominent men and women in national life precisely because they personify the authentic values of traditional village life, in contrast to the perceived materialism and greed of the cities. Even though the amounts involved are small, it is deemed essential that members should travel to the village or send representatives to attend the meetings. Meetings of the large *njangis*, involving contributions of millions of francs, can meet without prominent members, whose contributions may have been paid to the treasurer in advance. The notion that whatever the success achieved, it all started in the village through the self-help of a mother's sacrifice is a favourite theme in personal biographies and popular songs. The 'meeting', or *tontine de solidarité*, symbolizes the theme of mutual aid as a totalizing, unifying event, even though women may use it the more effectively to satisfy their needs. On the other hand, the expansion of *njangis* for business, or *tontines d'affaires*, is more directly articulated with the achievement of education and qualifications required to gain government salaries upon which a business career is founded. 'Straddling' has traditionally been dominated by men, due to their access to funds from male relatives which were used to send them abroad for training, often over long periods of time. That such investments should be made in men by men obeys a patrilineal logic made more complicated by the fact that gender difference is not necessarily a classificatory distinction but a more complex representation of the transmission of bodily substances. The transmission of wealth and body substances through agnatic ties is bound to more complex notions of the containment of ancestrally derived life essence (Warnier, 1993). The idea that men are containers of transmittable vital substances provides an idiom and an ethos for contemporary and past accumulation on which inequality and hierarchy in the Cameroon Grassfields is fundamentally based. Women married into the husband's agnatic group bring with them substances from the mother's father that allows him ferocious powers of life and death over her offspring. The purity of transmissible ancestral life essence is constantly endangered by the substance of affines that, activated by strong speech and blood, can destroy it (Pradelles 1991). The link between transmissible ancestral essence, wealth, accumulation, and procreation is such that it should remain separate from women capable of bearing children.

Rather than gender coinciding with the 'meeting'/*njangi* distinction, the bases of gender categories in attitudes towards the body suggest a more complex difference based on a combination of gender and age, agnatic and affinal kinship. The notions of success associated with hierarchy, titles and wealth in the Grassfields is associated with men because of an ideology of ancestrally transmittable substance from which women are excluded – except, that is, women who are past child-bearing and therefore no longer constitute a threat to a group of agnates. The possibility that the frequently-mentioned absence of child-bearing women from the ranks of successful businessmen and businesswomen suggests that kinship symbolism may be a more powerful influence in determining women's relative access to capital.

Conclusion

Economic studies of informal financial self-help groups have inevitably tended to examine them as simplified or alternative versions of formal banking or credit institutions. Assuming the merit of the latter in promoting sufficient savings for investment, the stress has been on establishing the grounds for convergence of formal institutions and informal groups in the development of finance. The provision of credit institutions or the forming of linkages between banks and mutual self-help groups have been the sort of strategies most actively pursued.

The tendency to see the informal as a 'local' version of the formal and global, whose logic can be combined in pursuit of similar goals, underestimates the historically distinct cultural and ideological imperatives of ROSCAs. In Bamenda, ROSCAs are part of an active appropriation of economic capital but in a context where money is scarce and evaluated along gender, age and ethnic lines. Scarce financial means effectively requires that distinctions be made between those that give priority to maintaining subsistence and providing security as against those committed to economic success. In both instances, mutualism and a willingness to extend relations of indebtedness are key values in maintaining security and capitalizing business enterprises. How these 'norms' are articulated and who defines them are a product of complex social processes that a purely economic approach will tend to avoid, or treat as variables merely affecting rational economic calculation. In this paper, gender, kinship, perceptions of the body and modes of cultural transmission have had to be (briefly) mentioned in order to highlight the complexity of an ethnographic approach to these questions. In the end, however, it is perhaps less a question of how indigenous African saving and credit arrangements can be integrated into a wider financial landscape than recognizing that the former are historically well adapted to appropriating the resources of the latter and can be relied upon to continue doing so.

References

Bayart, J-F. (1989), *L'Etat en Afrique*, Paris: Fayard.
Douglas, M. (1967), 'Primitive Rationing: A Study in Controlled Exchange', in R. Firth (ed.), *Themes in Economic Anthropology* London: Tavistock.
Fardon, R. (1988), *Raiders and Refugees*, Washington: Smithsonian.
Pradelles, C-H. (1991), *Ethnopsychanalyse en pays Bamileke*, Paris: E.P.E.L.
Warnier, J-P, (1993), *L'esprit d'entreprise au Cameroun*, Karthala.

PART II

Asia

8

Women's Differential Use of ROSCAs in Indonesia[1]

Otto Hospes

The new benevolent attention to rotating savings and credit associations is also directed to those in Indonesia that have only recently been praised for their impressive and promising qualities. For example, according to Kern (1986:118), former credit adviser with the USAID/Government of Indonesia Provincial Development Programme in East Java, 'one of the most interesting forms of rural financial institutions in Indonesia, as well as many other countries, is the Rotating Savings and Credit Association (ROSCA), or in Indonesian, *arisan*'. And Bouman and Moll (1992:215), who are rural finance analysts, state that 'The most ancient and widespread form of group finance in Indonesia is likely to be the rotating savings and credit association (ROSCA) called *arisan*.' However, any praise of ROSCAs has to be interpreted with great caution. First, I am concerned that it is not the self-regulative capacities of poor people that is acclaimed but rather the ROSCA as a model. (The use of the abbreviation 'ROSCA' is very telling in this respect. Despite my reservations, however, I have allowed the acronym in this paper, in conformity to the rest of this volume.) My second concern is that it is not the savings and organizational capacities and preferences of poor people that are praised but rather the ROSCA as a mechanism to mobilize rural savings.[2] And third, many acclamations are nothing more than lip-service or hypotheses. I have elaborated these points elsewhere in a longer version of this paper (Hospes 1992b).

Those who promote ROSCAs as a model or mechanism easily forget that, strictly speaking, ROSCAs do not behave; rather it is people who construct and reconstruct their own form of the association. No use is made of an actor perspective (cf. Long, 1989) in their methodologies and analyses. One of the consequences of this bias is the production of quite general and simplistic ideas on the significance of rotating savings and credit associations for particular groups or categories of people. Probably the most dramatic example in this connection concerns about half the world's population: women. Few studies attempt to differentiate women according to their socio-economic background and their use of ROSCAs. Below I describe how different groups or categories of women participate in different kinds of savings and credit associations. For this purpose I outline the diverse backgrounds of different ROSCAs in a small Indonesian town. In my view, such an outline is a precondition for a more nuanced look at women's differential use of these associations.

Comparative Studies

Although Geertz (1962) and Ardener (1964) published nearly three decades ago, their studies on rotating savings and credit associations are still unique works in the literature, and are much quoted. The contribution by Geertz contains one of the few and probably the earliest descriptions of ROSCAs in Eastern Java.[3] I am not aware of any documented case of ROSCAs outside Java except for Ambon (Hospes 1992a). As a young anthropologist, Geertz was much concerned with the 'shift from a traditionalistic agrarian society to an increasingly fluid commercial one' (1962; 260) in the so-called 'underdeveloped nations'. According to him, this process involves a problematic shifting of 'the whole framework of peasants from one emphasizing particularistic, diffuse, affective, and ascriptive ties between individuals, to one emphasizing – within economic contexts – universalistic, affectively neutral, and achieved ties between them' (p.260). Geertz conceives rotating savings and credit associations as a product and conductor of this transformation: 'the rotating credit association has been found associated with a lesser or greater penetration of an elaborated, and ultimately international exchange economy into a primarily agrarian society' (p.261). He describes *arisan* on Java as 'a link between the largely unmonetized economy of the past and the largely monetized economy of the future' (p.245).

Geertz is one of the few who have tried to analyse the rise and evolution of ROSCAs (which he termed RCAs) from a general perspective of processes of social transformation. It should be emphasized in this connection that he is interested both in this type of association and in the family of institutions that 'not only spring up in the economic, but in the political, religious, stratificatory, familial and other aspects of the social system as well' (p.263). He conceives these institutions as 'middle rungs between traditional society and more modern forms of social organization' (p.263). Geertz seems to underestimate the very complex societal dynamics that evolve when an international exchange economy 'penetrates' a primarily agrarian society. It is hard to accept that an increasing interweaving of international, national and local economies provides the momentum for a modernization process that reduces these economies into phases of one and the same development plan. Yet Geertz treats whole countries and provinces as homogeneous economic units, including ROSCAs despite varying degrees of complexity. Second, Geertz's evolutionist model does not take into account the possibility of very different types of ROSCAs co-existing in one place or region. Third, Geertz (p.263) suggests that ROSCAs are 'irrational' when he predicts their transformation into banks, co-operatives and 'other rational credit institutions'. An ever-increasing number of sources doubt whether this is likely to occur. For instance Kurtz (1973), who describes ROSCAs (*cundina*) in urban Mexico and the USA, reports explicitly negative attitudes by the poor to financial institutions such as banks and savings and loan companies. Many people felt that banks were unfriendly or demanding, or placed restrictions on loans which the *cundina* did not (pp.55–6). On the other hand there is little evidence of ROSCAs which have transformed themselves into non-rotating savings and credit associations (Williams and Johnston, 1983; Prabowo, 1989).

In spite of the shortcomings of Geertz's analysis, I believe his approach is not to be set aside. My suggestion is to redefine his analysis in terms of his wider interests and drop the evolutionist bias. The idea remains of ROSCAs as flexible forms of co-operation that restructure social relations in changing contexts. Furthermore, a more differentiated look at people and development in particular regions is needed. Most case studies do not relate the diversity and development of these associations to local economic, social and political developments.

The article by Ardener (1964), is another classical survey of ROSCAs. Whereas Geertz uses a deductive approach and takes ROSCAs as a case study of the process of modernization, Ardener tries an inductive approach that results, not in a grand theory, but in some empirical generalizations and research questions. Ardener is not convinced by the evolutionist model of Geertz, and points to exceptions and contradictory developments (pp.221–2). The strength of Ardener's study is her systematic, detailed descriptive analysis of various types of ROSCAs. Her data collection enabled her easily to refute the 'theory' of Geertz. The shortcoming is the other side of the coin of an institutional analysis of ROSCAs, which ignores two important questions: first, the self-regulative and adaptive behaviour of members of ROSCAs, and second, the relative significance of ROSCAs compared to other savings and credit arrangements, methods, strategies and organizations.

Members of ROSCAs make rules and join associations that fit their employment conditions, income flows, savings and money needs. For example, because of fluctuating incomes, the actual rotation of a fund may not be regular (Hospes, 1992a). It is also possible – if unlikely – that ROSCAs evolve into non-rotating savings and credit associations (Williams and Johnston, 1983; Prabowo, 1989).

Self-regulation of ROSCAs implies endless possibilities to meet members' diverse financial needs and objectives: for example, indexed contributions, mutual exchange of turns, competitive bidding, borrowing from the organizer, and shared or multiple membership. Therefore it is very tempting not to study the use of alternative savings and credit arrangements, methods, strategies and organizations. However, it is exactly this kind of study that gives an opportunity to better understand the relative significance of ROSCAs. We must remember that it is people that count: people make rules, adapt rules and compare rules and the resources of different saving and credit arrangements.

Studies of ROSCAs in Indonesia

According to Geertz (1962), the most elementary form of ROSCA in Eastern Java is found in Modjokuto, a town-village complex where: 'interest is not calculated, rotation is determined by lot or by agreement, memberships tend to be small, and a separate staff does not exist' (p.243). Geertz emphasizes that the *arisan* is 'commonly viewed by its members less as an economic institution than as a broadly social one whose main purpose is the strengthening of community solidarity' (ibid.). More commercial forms of *arisan* in rural areas evolve as a result of processes of commercialization and urbanization. The minds of people change: there is 'an increased sensitivity to and understanding of the economic aspects of the rotating credit association, as against its symbolic, ritualistic aspects'. It is in urban contexts that the most clearly and specifically economic *arisan* can be found: the market *arisan*, which is characterized by daily contributions, no meetings, fixed order of turns and a large number of members.

The Asian Development Bank conducted a comparative study of informal finance across a common set of issues in five Asian countries, including Indonesia. Although in his overview Ghate (1992:93) states that 'ROSCAs are widespread in Indonesia', this has yet to be fully documented; I have referred to some of the literature in Hospes (1992b). I have had to resort to personal communication with fellow researchers[4] – a method that was also employed by Ardener (1964) – to provide some of the case material below from Sumatra, Sumba and Sulawesi.

Slaats-Portier (personal communication 1991) reports that on North Sumatra *arisan* became the dominant term for ROSCAs in the 1980s, replacing that of *jula-jula*, which was much heard in the 1970s. *Arisan* are organized by officials of the Family Welfare Programme (PKK) and the organization of female civil servants (Dharma Wanita). Some women consider *arisan* appropriate instruments to satisfy their consumption needs quickly. Traders respond to this need, and use *arisan* to safeguard their sale of luxury goods.[5] Wijngaard and Hoeve (pers. comm. 1991) report that ROSCAs in Tukka, a village on North Sumatra, are specially organized to finance one of the following expenditures: weddings, house construction or university education. The finance of weddings is the most popular aim of the associations. One of them is called *julo-julo adat nako*. Like most of the ROSCAs that are organized to finance weddings, the contributions of this association are in meat (cf. Geertz, 1962:246: *paketan daging*). Each of the ninety-two members contributes one kilogram of meat to the wedding fund a few days before the marriage. The ultimate sanction for default is public confiscation of household goods.

Van de Ven (pers. comm. 1991) mentions several *arisan* of female teachers who work at the same school in Hiang village, Jambi Province of Sumatra. He also reports on *kelompok gotong royong*, a common denominator of a variety of local co-operative undertakings. One such is a praying and singing society (*penghajian*) that maintains a weekly *arisan*. The members also work in small labour groups to finance the purchase of meat for the fasting month (*Lebaran*). The labourers do not want to get paid immediately, but collect their income just before the fasting month.

According to Vel (pers. comm. 1991), *arisan* on Sumba are found only among salaried people. Her observation that money is a scarce good on this island is a plausible explanation of the limited occurrence of ROSCAs with contributions and distribution in cash. With respect to two older types of associations on Sumba, it is better to speak of a rotating 'pool' (instead of a rotating 'fund'), as in the case of a group of male labourers who together cut *imperata* grass. Their daily yield is divided among members on a rotating basis to be used for roof repairs. The second type is a group of men and women from well-to-do households who annually contribute a large amount of rice to a pool that is cashed by the winner to buy zinc sheets for roofing. A new version of associations with contributions in kind has recently been introduced by the local project society, assisted by Vel (pers. comm.): women have been organized in a group that makes mats of *pandanus* leaves, to be sold every two weeks for the benefit of one of the members. Usually the recipient uses the fund to buy household utensils.[6]

Tang (pers. comm. 1991) distinguishes two types of ROSCA on South Sulawesi: *mengandelek*[7] and *arisan*. *Mengandelek* is the popular term among *becak* drivers, fishermen and fishermen's wives. Daily contributions are made to funds which are distributed every ten days. Whereas the rise of *mengandelek* dates back to the 1950s, *arisan* (or the use of the term *arisan*), evolved in the 1970s. Officials of the Family Welfare Programme (PKK) organize *arisan* of neighbours (*dasa wisma*), who contribute on a monthly basis. *Arisan* with a monthly contribution are also common among teachers.

Papanek and Schwede (1988) in their 1972–1974 survey found that 106 women among 146 lower-middle and middle-class Jakarta women belonged to one or more *arisan*. Drawing lots was the typical mode of rotation. The respondents belonged predominantly to *arisan* formed among friends or work colleagues (57 per cent of 262 memberships); there were also seventy-five neighbourhood *arisan* (29 per cent) and thirty-eight kin-group *arisan* (14 per cent). The authors conclude that '*arisan* are ad hoc social institutions that depend for their effectiveness on pre-existing bonds that form the basis of mutual trust' (p.92). Most savings were intended for the acquisition of capital assets: land, house, car, motorcycle, household equipment, jewellery. According to Papanek and Schwede, some urban women commented that '*arisan* were helpful in protecting small sums against casual requests by men and children because all family members could understand how shameful it would be not to make one's promised contribution at the next meeting' (1988:95). Others commented that 'husbands who might object to what they considered women's excessive socializing were mollified by the economic gains that *arisan* membership brought with it (ibid).

The specific urban setting and selection of middle-class women studied by Papanek and Schwede make generalizations impossible about Indonesian women's use of ROSCAs. The authors 'are not aware of any recent systematic studies of the role of *arisan* among women in Indonesia'[8] (p.92). A long time ago Geertz (1962) mentioned that the *arisan* became an 'extraordinarily popular institution' among 'people who represent a semi-urban, semi-rural proletariat, the members of which, though they have been forced to adopt many of the social, political, and economic patterns of the town, still cling to many of the values and beliefs of the village' (p.246). He added that *arisan* were most particularly popular among the women of this proletariat, 'who hold the purse strings in any case' (ibid).

Contributions

On Central Java, one of the eight prevailing forms of agricultural credit is the *arisan* (Lindauer, 1971). Lindauer observes that 'during the inflation in the Sukarno era, the contributions were linked to the price of rice or gold' (p.267, my translation). In the study on 'Informal Credit Markets in Indonesia' sponsored by the Asian Development Bank, three adaptations of *arisan* to inflation are casually reported: first, the agreement to make contributions in kind; second and third, to index the cash contribution to the price of a gram of gold or a sheet of zinc (Prabowo et al, 1989). Ghate (1992) mentions that 'apart from cash *arisan*, many of the *arisan* entailed contributions in kind (such as building materials, labor and foodgrains). Moreover some of the cash *arisan* were dedicated to the purchase of specific objects such as household utensils and furniture (popular among women) or livestock and roofing, piping and fencing material (which were popular among the men)'[9] (Ghate, 1992:94).

Non-rotation

In this connection the paper by Williams and Johnston (1983) provides an interesting final thought: they suggest that *arisan* on Java may in future evolve as non-rotating savings and credit associations: 'In order to avoid the *arisan*'s element of unpredictability, some groups are dissolving their *arisan* and forming *kelompok simpan-pinjam* (savings and loan groups)' (p.72). Prabowo (1989:9) remarks that 'Some *arisan* have developed lending and credit arrangements beyond those of traditional ROSCAs': the group fund is used for giving credit and does not rotate. Prabowo (p.10) adds that, 'In our survey such associations are identified as *simpan-pinjam, usaha bersama*, meaning to work together (my translation) or credit union' (p.10). Geertz (1962) does not include non-rotating savings and credit associations in his analysis.

Bidding for the Fund

To my knowledge the only published article dealing solely with *arisan* is that by Williams and Johnston (1983), who discovered *arisan* that are widespread on Central Java. According to them, two new types of *arisan* have emerged since Geertz published his survey in 1962. The first is the '*arisan* call' (cf. Prabowo et al, 1989), in which the rotation of the fund is determined by commercial bidding. They believe that it 'has gained great popularity among the urban élite since the mid-1960s . . . It is quite common for wives of high-ranking public servants and military officers to be members of 10 or more *arisan* call groups at the same time' (op. cit.:72). Further, 'this form of *arisan* is based on the Chinese *hui* ('association'), which has long been practised by the ethnic Chinese business community in Indonesia'. These findings imply a reassessment of Geertz's conclusion (1962: 247) that 'almost all urban *arisans* decide on the order with which the individual draws the fund not by agreement but by lot'.

Official *Arisan*

The second new type of *arisan* distinguished by Williams and Johnston (1983) is the 'official *arisan*', organized under the auspices of government bodies or official welfare programmes such as the Family Welfare Programme (PKK). This is primarily directed at women 'who, after all, are the members of the community who are most concerned with health, progress and prosperity of the family' (Rustam, 1986: 77). Rustam who, as the wife of the Minister of Home Affairs, is the chairman of the PKK at national level, says that the PKK has spread rapidly and evolved into a nation-wide movement after its official recognition in 1972. The organization of *arisan* is part of the PKK programmes on health and housing: the PKK 'sets up rotating lottery (*arisan*) groups to finance[10] the repair or building of houses, family lavatories and bath plus laundry units' (p.81). Martin-Schiller (1989) reports that 'the popular *arisan*, under the auspices of PKK (Program Kesejahteraan Keluarga – the government Family Welfare Programme) or other women's organizations, are purely women's activities' (p.36). Prabowo and others (1989: par. 4,2) speak of 'programmed' or 'dependent' *arisan* versus 'independent' *arisan*. The authors indirectly define 'programmed' and 'dependent' *arisan*: they deplore, with regard to five independent *arisan*, that 'it is difficult to compute the exact number because their activities are not registered in the district administration book'.

According to Williams and Johnston (1983), the *arisan* of PKK and other government or government-supported bodies function as a 'drawcard' used by government officials who 'have gradually intensified efforts to capitalize on the economic and social potential of the *arisan* in order to popularize women's activities and other development programmes' (p.67). However, in many cases, PKK meetings might have become little more than a brief *arisan*, as happened with a group of women radio listeners organized as part of a government programme for the dissemination of information (Martin-Schiller, 1989:36; see also Hesselink van Stelle, 1983:41). Williams and Johnston (1983:71) warn that 'in fact, high attendance at PKK meetings can easily be deceptive because participation in the *arisan* may become an end in itself, while the aims of the programme are overlooked'. In addition, they critically remark that 'a study of six villages in West Java found that *arisan* formed on official initiative tended to be less popular than those formed spontaneously by local people'.

Geertz (1962) mentions that 'the *arisan* is also quite popular among the élite of the town, those who, for the most part, live in the stone houses along the streets. In this group it is almost always based on one or another of the dozens of sodalities, political parties, youth groups, labour unions, charitable associations, school societies, women's clubs, athletic associations, which have proliferated on the urban scene since the Revolution of 1945' (p.247). An interesting but difficult question is what happened with these 'voluntary associations' and their *arisan* activities after the New Order ('Orde Baru') was established in 1965. Perhaps the central government recognition in 1972 of the Family Welfare Programme (PKK) can be interpreted as a new impulse towards what government officials describe as 'a voluntary movement operating at grass roots in country villages and wards' (cf. Rustam, 1986:77) and towards what government officials call '*arisan*'.

The Background to Women's Differential use of ROSCA: The Case of Tulehu

Perhaps the region in Indonesia that has longest been articulated with the world-wide economy is the spice islands of the Moluccas. The arrival of Portuguese traders in the sixteenth century marked the beginning of a dramatic expansion of trade networks that included this region. Other European traders followed and struggled for the privilege to buy cloves from local rulers. The Dutch East Indies Company (VOC) that took over control from the Portuguese in 1605 (Knaap, 1981a) forced the producers to sell all their cloves at a price of 56 rixdollars per *bahar* (550 pounds): five for the local rulers, one for transport and fifty for the producer. The

VOC was the first in the spice trade to pay its suppliers in cash. In 1863 Dutch governors had to end their policy of enforced cultivation because the new cultivation of cloves in African Zanzibar had pushed the world market price below the cost price of the Dutch (Knaap, 1981b). At independence in 1945 the new Indonesian leaders inherited a free market system. It was not until late in the post-colonial period that clove producers faced a monopoly on clove marketing and fixed prices again: Presidential Decree No. 8 (1980) orders that only government village co-operatives are entitled to buy cloves from the farmers for a fixed price. However, in spite of three hundred and fifty years of exposure to Dutch traders, missionaries and administrators, ROSCAs seem to be of late post-colonial origin in the Moluccan region.[11]

One reason why ROSCAs did not develop is the importance of sago and fishery in the local economy (Knaap, 1981a). Sago palms provide the traditional staple food as well as materials for house construction, and the sea provides fish, an integral part of the daily diet (Hospes, 1992a). The plentiful sago palms can be harvested all year round. Even more important, sago and fish were not exchanged for money until recently: they have been more or less subsistence crops. The paradise-like availability of sago and fish has for centuries been a brake on the gradual monetization of the local economy which followed the first contacts with foreign traders and rulers. There is little need for thrift and regular saving among sago and fish collectors. Traditional sago cultivation and fishing neither imply cash investments nor enable or give much sense to cash contributions to a common fund.

Another reason why ROSCAs did not develop is that clove trees yield abundantly only once in three or four years, and this does not make for regular saving. Furthermore, group saving by clove producers is difficult because clove production is very location-specific. Still, non-daily cash income can necessitate more or less regular saving, as in the many rice-producing areas of Indonesia where women used to save a spoonful of rice every day to bridge the difficult pre-harvest period. However, the abundance of sago and fish in the Moluccan region provided no reason to start regular saving in cash or kind. Periods of food scarcity rarely occurred. Money needs were extremely modest because sago and fish guaranteed most inhabitants a minimum living standard in terms of food supply and housing.

Within the last two decades the economy of Tulehu has dramatically altered since the village became a new regional trade and transport centre. Located at the north-eastern coast of Ambon island, it is a link between Ambon City and other ports of Indonesia on the one hand and the hinterland of the Central Moluccas on the other. The small town, which officially numbers 12,000 people (census 1989), attracts many migrants looking for work and education. About a third of its population consists of Butonese incomers who are much involved in the clove trade. Sumatran, Chinese and Javanese migrants from smaller but economically powerful groups, dominate as shopkeepers and restaurant owners. Many government services have offices in Tulehu, which is the administrative capital of a sub-district. In Tulehu ROSCAs are new phenomena since the 1970s. I distinguish three different situations which encourage the formation of ROSCAs: migration, government extension and organization, and increased money needs.

Migrants: Parallel Social and Economic Associations as Forms of Collective Self-help

To speak of a late 'origin' of ROSCAs in the Moluccan region is somewhat misleading. The first associations in this region were probably started by migrants (cf. Ardener, 1964:209). In Tulehu, Sumatran migrants started ROSCAs some fifteen years ago. Each week they came together to eat, drink and play *arisan*, to strengthen ethnic ties. They had earlier been exposed to ROSCAs in Sumatra, where they were called *bajulo-julo* (Hospes, 1992a).

The first Sumatran migrants of Tulehu started selling home-baked cookies as street vendors (*kaki lima*), then opened restaurants, and after a few years managed to establish medium-sized shops. With the help of these pioneers, new Sumatran migrants easily found opportunities to make a little income and ways to finance their larger business plans. They started to use *arisan* as efficient vehicles to save for investments. The socio-cultural *arisan* gradually became commercialized and discontinued weekly meetings. A pre-arranged sequence of receivers, instead of the lottery system, now determines the order of rotation; all participants bring their contributions each day to the group leader, and after ten days one participant comes to the leader to receive the deposits. The group leader is the first person to take the fund (Hospes, 1992a). Both Sumatran men and women participate in these commercial *arisan*. I found two *arisan* of Sumatran shopkeepers and restaurant owners of Tulehu: the first consists of ten men and three women, who each contribute Rp. 5,000 per day, except for two members paying Rp. 10,000 for two turns.[12] Every ten days the fund is distributed so that the full cycle takes nearly five months and the rotating fund amounts to Rp. 750,000. The full rotation is determined by lottery at the start of the cycle. The first turn forms the exception, the organizer receiving the first fund. The second *arisan* consists of fourteen Sumatran women with a daily contribution of Rp. 1,000. Four of them each have two turns and one member even has three turns, so that one cycle takes more than six months. Many Sumatran couples own two shops or try to open a second one. The wife manages the first shop and pays for daily household expenses. Possibly this explains the smaller standard contribution of the female *arisan*.

Parallel to the commercial *arisan*, other, non-rotating social savings and credit associations have evolved. In Tulehu an association of forty Sumatran households called *Ikatan Keluarga Saiyo Sakato* (IKSS) coordinates at least three activities. First, all forty households contribute Rp. 2,500 per month to a social fund, which the secretary deposits in a savings account at the Banky Rakyat Indonesia (BRI). The non-rotating fund is used for funeral ceremonies (Rp. 25,000 per case) and trips to Sumatra (one ticket per family). Second, most of the members of the IKSS contribute weekly to a fund for the annual *hari raya quarban*, an Islamic festival. A Sumatran shopkeeper, who is a *haji*, keeps this non-rotating fund. In 1989–90 thirty-four families together contributed about Rp. 40,000 per week. When a household is unable to save the required amount (the price of a goat or a seventh part of that of an ox) the savings are retained for the next season or returned just prior to the festival. Third, twenty-six women gather every month for religious classes at the local Islamic university. Their club, *Bando Kanduang* or 'dedicated women', keeps *arisan* every meeting. Each member contributes Rp. 5,000, while two members receive half a fund. The women also each contribute Rp. 500 monthly to a social fund for emergencies and birthday presents. Every three months the women come with their husbands to the Islamic university to discuss the progress of the *uang quarban* and have a big celebration.

Butonese migrants participate on a limited scale in labour associations with a rotating fund. In small groups they cut sago trees and distribute the proceeds of the sale of sago pith on a weekly rotating basis. Butonese migrants are much more involved in pre-harvest arrangements with Ambonese: they buy the rights to harvest clove trees for one or more (good) seasons.[13] The small Chinese and Javanese minorities of Tulehu are not involved in ROSCAs. But an old Chinese shopkeeper remembered *hui* as the Chinese name of ROSCAs that used to be popular among Chinese entrepreneurs in large urban centres of Indonesia.

Government Organization of Women

About ten years ago the first 'official' *arisan* was started in Tulehu by wives of police officers and the military. These run smoothly due to the regular income of their husbands. They are organized as part of semi-official women's clubs. Monthly contributions vary from Rp. 5,000 to Rp. 15,000. *Arisan* that result from government educational programmes perform rather poorly in Tulehu, like the one of the local Family Welfare Programme (PKK) which collapsed, failing to attract women to extension meetings. The *arisan* of the Office of Coordinated Services (Posyandu) has still to attract many women to the extension meetings. The monthly or fortnightly contribution is quite low, not exceeding Rp. 1,000.

It is difficult to describe the *arisan* of the government extension services in terms of the dualistic and evolutionary notions of social clubs that gradually transform into economic ones. There are no ethnic or neighbourhood ties that serve as a pre-existing social basis of *arisan*, and there are no future financial economic targets. Besides, these associations have no end dates. To a lesser extent this also applies to the *arisan* of wives of police and military officers. They live in compounds with their husbands, mostly migrants who happen to be stationed in Tulehu. In all these cases, however, the role of the *arisan* as an organizational tool or device to tie women to government programmes should not be underestimated (but see above for reservations).

Increased Money Needs and New Social Units

The most recent *arisan* of Tulehu are those of the native Ambonese. Three types have evolved in the last five to seven years: the *arisan* of economic peers who earn a regular income, the neighbourhood *arisan*, and the *arisan* of members of a religious society. The evolution of all three types is closely related to the increased importance of money in the local economy.

Until recently, Ambonese relatives and neighbours helped each other to build traditional sago houses on a more or less rotating basis (*masohi*). The forests provided all necessary construction materials. However, with the enormous incomes from the sale of cloves in the 1970s Ambonese villagers got a taste for building new houses with concrete walls and zinc roofs. As a result, the need to organize *masohi* faded. ROSCAs to finance the purchase of zinc roofs, as on Java, did not develop because for the

Ambonese the clove harvest provided the best single opportunity to invest in housing.

Arisan in Tulehu are not likely to be adaptations of *masohi*. The *arisan* of Ambonese people, who earn income from non-farm activities, satisfy needs rather different from the *masohi* of subsistence farmers. These non-farm activities are an example of the new economic opportunities in Tulehu, and also an expression of people's increased money requirements. When prices of cloves dropped in the 1980s, the farmers still had their increased money needs. Besides the zinc roof as the new standard of housing, rice had become the new standard of consumption, replacing the tasteless sago porridge. The growing opportunities to earn extra non-farm income were gratefully exploited, and *arisan* served as a tool for efficient cash-flow management. In contrast to the *arisan* started by Sumatran entrepreneurs of Tulehu to strengthen ethnic ties, *arisan* of Ambonese people who earn a regular income have no social or ethnic precursor. These *arisan* not only protect members against sudden expenditure; they also deter claims from family members.

Both men and women are involved in these *arisan*, which appear as new social units in increasingly commercial Tulehu. Those of the harbour labourers consist of men only; one small *arisan* for petrol vendors includes one woman; fish traders' *arisan* are a female affair, as are the *arisan* of market women. All contributions are made daily; memberships vary from three to twenty-five. Harbour labourers determine the full order of rotation by lottery at the very beginning of the cycle. The fisherwomen use both a lottery and a pre-determined order. Market women deliberate each time on who is to receive the fund next.

Neighbourhood *arisan* function less to strengthen neighbourhood ties than to collect money. Neighbours who are civil servants and pensioners, typically women, make daily or monthly contributions. But default has made this type of *arisan* less popular and less common in the many wards of Tulehu. People involved in neighbourhood *arisan* were typically women.

Every week members of a religious society come together to pray and sing Islamic verses. There are male societies as well as female ones. It is very striking that only female societies organize *arisan* at the end of the evening to stimulate members to participate in the meetings. I feel that this is not because women are less dedicated to Islam than men. The large involvement of women in street-vending activities and vegetable and fish markets, and their dominant role in managing the household purse, have made many women aware of the functions and possibilities of money. It is not only the lottery as the common method of determining the rotation of the fund that attract women who participate in *arisan*, but also the mere use of money. Most of the religious gatherings are held at the place of the winner of the fund, who pays for the tea and snacks at the next meeting. In one case the house of the leader, who is married to one of the most well-to-do men in town, is the place of weekly congregation. Besides the common contribution of Rp. 1,000 to the *arisan*, all 20–40 members also contribute Rp. 100 each to a non-rotating emergency fund.

Women's Differential Use of ROSCAs: Some Case Studies

I have just noted that there are *arisan* composed of female Sumatran shopkeepers, female Ambonese government employees, market women, female fish traders, female neighbours, and women who come together to sing and pray. My field survey in 1989 showed that sixteen out of twenty-four *arisan* consisted of women only, and four *arisan* had a mixed gender composition (Hospes, 1992a). Therefore one might safely conclude that ROSCAs are predominantly female affairs in Tulehu. The diverse socio-economic backgrounds of these Tulehu women, however, make it impossible to speak of women's use of ROSCAs without referring to the different groups or categories of women involved. To further illustrate my argument, I briefly describe four cases of women and their use of ROSCAs. Each includes some tentative conclusions on the significance of ROSCAs for the group or category of women as a whole.

The first case is that of Ibu Efi, one of thirteen members (ten men and three women) of an *arisan* of Sumatran shopkeepers and restaurant managers. Once every five months she receives the fund of Rp. 750,000. Her husband and brother-in-law are members as well. They all manage their own shops, and daily contribute Rp. 5,000 each to the *arisan*. Every ten days the fund is distributed. Two members of the *arisan* draw two times in one cycle, as they pay for two turns – that is, Rp. 10,000 per day. Ibu Efi runs the first shop her husband started before she had migrated to Ambon island. The young Sumatran woman explains that proceeds of the shop she manages are used to pay for food and medicines. She is also involved in another *arisan*, which includes Sumatran shopkeepers of Ambon City. There are sixteen turns and Ibu Efi pays for four of Rp. 1,000 per day. Every ten days the fund is distributed. She used her last four draws of Rp. 160,000 as follows: she sent Rp. 550,000 to her mother on Sumatra to purchase gold (Rp. 250,000) and to pay for her ticket to Ambon (Rp. 300,000). The remaining Rp. 90,000 Ibu Efi used for small consumption needs. The main reason for Sumatran women joining ROSCAs is not to protect small sums of money against requests by relatives or husbands in particular (cf. Papanek and Schwede, 1988). Close relatives live far away in Sumatra, and the local Sumatran migrant community has few kinship ties. On the contrary, ROSCAs are often used to tighten family relations. Many funds of the Sumatran associations have been used by female and male members to finance a journey to Sumatra. The wife's responsibility for one of the two shops of a Sumatran couple – which is common among the Sumatran community of Tulehu – suggests a rather independent position of the entrepreneurial wife *vis-à-vis* her likewise entrepreneurial husband. However, the domestic responsibilities of Sumatran women seem to limit their capacity to participate in ROSCAs with large contributions. Finally, the golden earrings and necklaces many Sumatran women possess suggest that they commonly use ROSCAs as a stepping-stone towards savings in gold.

The second case is that of *Posyandu*, short for *Pos Pelayanan Terpadu*, a small semi-official health centre. Right behind the building of the sub-district administration in Tulehu, the coordinator of the *Posyandu* organizes a meeting every fortnight. Every meeting consists of three parts: a health issue, an *arisan*, and gymnastics – in that order. According to the co-ordinator and her assistants, the meetings are meant to strengthen feelings of unity and mutual help among the forty female participants; and *arisan* should be seen as an integral part of this. The contribution is Rp. 1,000 each fortnight. At every meeting two folded pieces of paper, each with a name on it, are drawn from a glass full of papers: two women have to share the fund of Rp. 40,000. Although the *arisan* is clearly meant to attract women to meetings, it has not been important enough to guarantee a high degree of participation, for two reasons: first, the health centre is some distance uphill from the village centre, making this unsuitable for regular meetings. Second, the initiative to organize the meetings comes from above not only in a spatial sense but also in an abstract sense. Most of the Tulehu women do not appreciate these initiatives from semi-governmental bodies. An early collapse of the *arisan* is the result, as happened with the PKK unit in Tulehu, which had started an *arisan* that stopped rotating after a few meetings.

My third case is that of Ibu Aci, a member of two praying societies of elderly Ambonese women. Both societies meet weekly, and organize *arisan* when the late praying and singing has come to an end. As she puts it herself, Ibu Aci lives in a very small and ugly house, with her husband who runs a small shop in the front room. These externals conceal the fact that Ibu Aci is quite a wealthy woman, with an impressive savings account at a bank in Ambon City. In fact she makes millions of rupiahs from the inter-island trade in clothes sold on credit. She could afford to participate in an *arisan* with large contributions, like the *arisan* of Ibu Efi that collects Rp. 50,000 per member every ten days. However, the *arisan* connected to the praying societies only require a contribution of Rp. 1,000 per week. Obviously the *arisan* serves to stimulate women to attend the meetings regularly and is not a pure savings device. What makes the *arisan* of religious societies of elderly Ambonese women quite effective, unlike those of the Posyandu and PKK-unit, is that they reinforce existing ties of friendship, kinship and religion.

My fourth case is that of two Ambonese market women: Ibu Cum and Ibu Ida, who are the treasurers of two different *arisan* of vegetable-sellers and restaurant-keepers. Every day the members of these *arisan* bring their contributions of Rp. 2,500 to the nearby market stall of their treasurer. The daily contributions are not distributed immediately but are saved till the fifth day, when the women decide who will get the accumulated fund. Not surprisingly, Ibu Cum and Ibu Ida are known as very honest women. The substantial amount of daily savings underlines their responsibility as treasurers: Rp. 2,500 is about 30–40 per cent of the daily net income of a market woman of Tulehu. Ibu Ida's predecessor was the Sumatran restaurant keeper Pak Hab, who was married to an Ambonese woman. Pak Hab was one of the few Sumatran people strongly in favour of the integration of the Sumatran and Ambonese communities. In spite of his good intentions, he had to hand over the leadership of the *arisan* of Ambonese women because they felt a little ashamed (*malu*) of bringing their contributions to a Sumatran man – albeit a very friendly one. Ibu Cum has a much longer reputation as a solid treasurer than her friend Ibu Ida. Possibly her husband plays an indirect role in this connection: he is a high official in the Departmental Office for Education and Culture, earning a regular and considerable income. Somehow he managed to let his office donate Rp. 300,000 to his wife as the best market woman of Tulehu, as a board above her market stall shows. Ibu Cum can expect only few requests for money from her husband. This certainly does not apply to all market women, who are well aware that they cannot save individually at home without demands upon them. Therefore they use the ROSCA as a savings device to protect their small daily earnings against the many requests of relatives.

Women's differential use of ROSCAs in Tulehu cannot be understood without reference to the changing local society and rural economy. Put even more strongly, my case suggests that the study of women's use of these associations is an exciting but demanding attempt to understand change and continuity within different sets of relationships – migrants and their hosts, government employees and their clients, and small-scale entrepreneurs and their relatives. To look through the eyes of Tulehu women is to look through the eyes of migrants, target groups of government programmes, wives and mothers. Hence it is important not to use the label 'ROSCA' or the label 'women' in an undifferentiated way. Different classes or categories of women have their own particular and changing reasons to join, adapt or frustrate rotating savings and credit associations. Therefore the study of women's differential use of ROSCAs may provide much-needed pictures of people – and it is people that count.

Notes

1. The author is grateful for the constructive comments of Franz von Benda-Beckmann and Frits Bouman on an earlier draft of this article, now published as Hospes 1992a. This publication overlaps with the present paper, but does not cover identical ground. The Netherlands Foundation for Scientific Research in Tropical Countries (WOTRO) generously enabled me to conduct field research.
2. It is striking that among present-day policy analysts and development planners the term 'Rotating Savings and Credit Associations' (RoSCA or ROSCA) is standard, whereas in the older and more anthropological literature (Geertz, 1962; Ardener, 1964) the term 'rotating credit associations' is used.
3. I consider 'rotating credit associations' and 'rotating savings and credit associations' as synonyms (see also note 2) but prefer the latter because it suggests members' savings capacities and preferences.
4. All fellow researchers happen to be staff members, fellows, PhD students or graduate students of the Department of Agrarian Law at Wageningen Agricultural University.
5. This much resembles the practice of Ibu Isoh on West Java, as described by Veltenaar (1988:85–8): Ibu Isoh is a tailor, and organizes *arisan* to sell her products. In several villages she gathers about ten women willing to buy her clothes or embroidery. They regularly contribute to a rotating fund which is used to buy, for instance, a bedspread from Ibu Isoh. In some cases the bedspread *arisan* changes into one that serves to buy her table-covers. In other cases the members decide to start an *arisan* for purchase of zinc sheets (pan), *arisan* for plates, money *arisan* or gold *arisan* coordinated by Ibu Isoh who receives a small commission for her services. In 1988 she coordinated twenty *arisan* including four to buy bedspreads. At that time Ibu Isoh herself

participated in an *arisan* with a contribution of Rp. 100,000 per month (for a Bolivian version of this type of *arisan* see Adams and Canavesi (1992)).

6. In their survey of women's informal associations in developing countries March and Taqqu (1986) distinguish between 'rotating credit associations' and 'rotating labour associations'. However, the last example of Vel (pers. comm.) is obviously a mixture of both.

7. *Mengandelek* shows resemblance to the Dutch word *aandeel* ('share'). Scheepens (1974), who compared 'traditional savings and credit organizations and modern credit organizations of village Bojong' in West Java, found a similar term. He casually remarks (p.30) that 'some people told me that in early days there were also *arisan* (named *andilan*).' *Andilan* looks like the Indonesian pronunciation (*andil*) and noun (*an*) of the Dutch word *aandeel*. This suggests that Dutch colonial administrators or welfare workers might have stimulated Indonesians to organize themselves in *arisan*.

8. Hospes (1992a) contains general information on women's involvement in *arisan* on Ambon, the Moluccas. He also describes the case of a women's praying society which initiates *arisan* and business activities.

9. Scheepens (1974), Hesselink van Stelle (1983) and Veltenaar (1988) distinguish between *arisan uang* (which means 'money') and *arisan barang* ('goods'). In the case of *arisan barang* the fund is targeted to the purchase of glasses, plates, spoons, forks or pans. Patmo-Mingoen (1980), Jansen (1987) and Van der Brugh (1989) also distinguish *arisan uang* and *arisan beras* (*beras* means 'rice').

10. Rustam (1986), who wonders how to organize fund-raising activities to finance PKK activities, finds to her relief that 'fortunately, there are old customs for this kind of activity: women may be told to put a single spoonful of rice into another pot every time they cook; once a week all those spoonfuls are added to what other villagers have collected; when there is enough, the rice can be sold, and the "little money" needed is obtained' (p.80). Sinaga and others (1976) distinguish two types of local savings and credit groups of the West Javanese village Sukagalih: *arisan* and groups called *beras parelek* ('a spoonful of rice'). According to the authors, most of the women are members of *beras parelek* groups. All members save a spoonful of rice each day towards a collective stock that serves as a security fund for families who have run out of rice in the pre-harvest period (*paceklik*).

11. The historical studies of Rumphius (1910) and Knaap (1987) do not contain descriptions of ROSCAs on the Moluccas or Ambon island in particular: nor do the field notes of Kennedy (1950) and the comprehensive village study of van Fraassen (1972). Even van Paassen (1986), who conducted a socio-economic study of Tulehu, makes no reference to rotating savings and credit associations.

12. US$1.00 = Rp. 1,760 (July 1989).

13. Cf. Ardener (1964): 'Hill suggests that, in Ghana, they are unlikely to spread into areas where farmers can raise capital by pledging their farms, although

pledging of land among the Mba-Ise Ibo of Nigeria did not inhibit the development of rotating credit associations there' (p.206).

References

Adams, D.W. (1992), 'Taking a Fresh Look at Informal Finance', in D.W. Adams and D.A. Fitchett (eds), pp. 5–23.

—— and Canavesi, M.L. (1992), 'Rotating Savings and Credit Associations in Bolivia', in Adams and Fitchett (eds), pp. 313–23.

—— and Fitchett, D.A. (eds), (1992) *Informal Finance in Low-Income Countries*, Boulder: Westview Press.

Ardener, S. (1964), 'The Comparative Study of Rotating Credit Associations', *Journal of the Royal Anthropological Institute of Great Britain and Ireland*, vol. XCIV, no. 2, pp. 201–29.

Bouman, F.J.A. and Moll, H.A.J. (1992), 'Informal Finance in Indonesia', in D.W. Adams and D.A. Fitchett (eds), pp. 209–23.

van der Brugh, H.C. (1989), *Kredietmogelijkheden voor Vrouwen: een Case Study van een Dorp op Oost Java, Indonesie*, Unpublished M.A. Thesis, The Hague.

van Fraassen, Ch. F. (1972), Ambon rapport, Leiden, WSO.

Geertz, C. (1962), 'The Rotating Credit Association: a "Middle Rung" in Development', *Economic Development and Cultural Change*, vol. 10, no. 3, pp. 241–63.

Ghate, P.B. (1992), *Informal Finance: Some Findings From Asia*, Hong Kong: Oxford University Press.

Hesselink van Stelle, M.J. (1983), *Gotong Royong: samenwerking en hulpverlening in een Javaanse desa*, Unpublished M.A. Thesis, doctoraal leeronderzoek in de desa Oro-oro-ombo, Rijks Universiteit Leiden, Instituut voor Culturele Antropologie en Sociologie der Niet-Westerse Volken.

Hospes, O. (1992a), 'Evolving Forms of Informal Finance in an Indonesian Town', in D.W. Adams and D.A. Fitchett (eds), pp. 225–38.

—— (1992b), 'People that Count: the Forgotten Faces of Rotating Savings and Credit Associations in Indonesia', *Savings and Development*, 16 (4) pp. 371–96.

Jansen, A. (1987), *Allemaal Uitzonderingen? Verslag van een Leeronderzoek naar Inkomstenverwervende Activiteiten van Vrouwen in een Dorp in West-Java*, Unpublished M.A. Thesis, Rijks Universiteit Leiden, Instituut voor Culturele Antropologie en Sociologie der Niet-Westerse Volken.

Kennedy, R. (1950), *Fieldnotes of an Indonesian Journey: Ambon and Ceram 1949–1950*.

Kern, J.R. (1986), 'The Growth of Decentralized Rural Credit Institutions in Indonesia', in C. MacAndrews (ed.), *Central Government and Local Development in Indonesia*, Oxford University Press, pp. 101–31.

Knaap, G.J. (1981a), 'De Komst van de Kruidnagel', *Intermediair*, vol. 17, no.

5, pp. 23–7, 45.

—— (1981b), 'Monopolie en Monocultuur', *Intermediair*, vol. 17, no. 6, pp. 45–51.

Knaap, G.J. (1987), *Kruidnagelen en Kristenen: de Verenigde Oost-Indische Compagnie en de Bevolking van Ambon 1656–1696*, Unpublished Ph.D. Thesis, Floris, Dordrecht.

Kurtz, D.V. (1973), 'The Rotating Credit Association: an Adaptation to Poverty', *Human Organization:Journal of the Society for Applied Anthropology*, vol. 32, no. 1, pp. 49–58.

Lindauer, G. (1971), 'Formen des Landwirtschaftlichen Kredits in Central Java', *Zeitschrift fur Ausländische Landwirtschaft*, vol. 10, no. 3, pp. 266–72.

Long, N. (ed.) (1989), *Encounters at the Interface: A Perspective on Social Discontinuity in Rural Development*, Wageningen Agricultural University, Wageningen Studies in Sociology 27.

March, K.S. and Taqqu, R.L. (1986), *Women's Informal Associations in Developing Countries: Catalysts for Change?*, Boulder: Westview Press.

Martin-Schiller, B. (1989), 'Social Networks in an Upland Javanese Village: Family and Community', *Prisma: The Indonesian Indicator*, vol. 46, pp. 32–44.

van Paassen, A. (1986), *Sociale Zekerheid: Recht op Bestaan. Case: het Indonesisch Dorp Tulehu*, Unpublished M.Sc. Thesis, Wageningen Agricultural University.

Papanek, H. and Schwede, L. (1988), 'Women Are Good With Money: Earning and Managing in an Indonesian City', in *A Home Divided: Women and Income in the Third World*, D. Dwyer and J. Bruce (eds), Stanford University Press, pp. 71–98.

Patmo-Mingoen, H.K. (1980), *Ekonomische samenwerkingsvormen onder boeren in een West Javaans dorp...* M.A. thesis, Rijks Museum, Leiden.

Prabowo, D. (1985), 'Some Issues on Informal Credit Markets in Indonesia', Country paper commissioned by the Asian Development Bank, Manila, in conjunction with the preparation of the Regional Study on Informal Credit Markets in Asia.

—— (1989), *The Role of Informal Financial Intermediation in the Mobilization of Household Savings and Allocations in Indonesia*, paper presented at the Seminar on Informal Financial Markets in Development, Washington.

——, Sumodiningrat, G., Mangkusuwondo, G. and Prasetiantono, T. (1989), *Study on Informal Credit Markets*, Economic Research Centre, Universitas Gajah Mada, Indonesia, submitted to the Asian Development Bank.

Rumphius, G.E. (1910), 'De Amboinsche Historie', *Bijdragen tot de Taal, Land-en Volkenkunde van Nederlandsch-Indie*, vol. 64.

Rustam, K.S. (1986), 'Grass-root Development with the P.K.K.', *Prisma: The Indonesian Indicator*, vol. 40, pp. 77–84.

Scheepens, Th. J. (1974), *Socio-economic Research about Traditional Savings and Credit Organizations in Comparison with Modern Organizations in Desa*

Bojong, Jawa Barat, Indonesia, Unpublished field report, Wageningen Agricultural University, The Netherlands.

Sinaga, R.S. et al. (1976), 'Rural Institutions Serving Small Farmers and Labourers: A Case Study of the Village Sukagalih', *Agro Economic Survey*, Bogor.

Veltenaar, M. (1988), *Vrouwen en Inkomen in een West Javaans dorp*, Unpublished M.A. Thesis, Onderzoeksverslag doktoraalscriptie, Rijks Universiteit Leiden, Faculteit Sociale Wetenschappen.

Von Pischke, J.D. (1992), 'ROSCAs: State-of-the-art Financial Intermediation', paper presented at the *Seminar on Informal Financial Markets in Developing Countries, Washington, 1989*; final version published in D.W. Adams and D.A. Fitchett (eds), pp. 325–35.

Williams, G. and Johnston, M. (1983), 'The *arisan*: a Tool for Economic and Social Development?', *Prisma*, vol. 29, pp. 66–73.

9

Economic Kou (ROSCAs) in Japan: A Review[1]

Kuniko Miyanaga

In Japan the ROSCA is not a discrete institution but one form of a wider social system called *kou*. Sometimes spelt *kō*, the Japanese term functions both in the singular and plural. *Kou* is a traditional co-operative system which promotes group intimacy. Emphasizing prominent features of its practice, and following the distinctions established by Tokutaro Sakurai, it is commonly categorized in three groups, first *religious*, second *economic* and third *social*. It is the 'economic *kou*' that functions as a ROSCA.

Before I go on to review the basic characteristics of women's participation in ROSCAs in Japan, material available on *kou* in general is summarized in order to place this study in its proper perspective. It has seemed useful to offer my translations of some general Japanese texts, as these are not widely known outside Japan.

In 1962 Sakurai published *Kou-shuudan Seiritsu-katei no Kenkyuu* [The Study of the Formation Process of Kou Associations], a vast book of about six hundred pages in Japanese which became the first of his ten-volume anthology covering indigenous religious and social organizations in Japan. Sakurai's book presented an almost complete picture of what was known of *kou* at that time. There has not been much development of the subject since, apart from some follow-up studies (for example, see below).

Sakurai's description was, in a sense, historical. According to him, the association named *kou* first appeared in the ninth century. Its origin was religious, a *kou* being a group of people who gathered for religious pursuits under the guidance of Buddhist priests and temple officials. Avoiding a long historical description, it should suffice to mention here that, as it was later popularized and widely spread, the *kou* became more secular in its function in spite of its religious appearance. In other words, the ROSCA is a later, secularized form of *kou*. More recently, as the economy of Japan developed in the 1970s and 1980s, the economic element in the *kou* again became less and less significant and the social side more emphasized.

However, this historical change was not a unilineal development from the religious, through the economic, to the social type. These three features have overlapped, although the main emphasis has shifted from time to time. The social element which has been consistently observed throughout the history of the *kou* still continues today.

The common denominator of *kou*, as Sakurai argues, is drinking and feasting. Concluding a long-standing controversy about *kou*, in its great variety of forms, he says (1976:98):

> The formation of *kou* groups is characterized by shared drinking and eating as its absolute condition, regardless of their other purposes, which may be either religious or economic. The *kou* has always been popular for encouraging friendship through the social pleasure offered throughout its history, beyond controversy over -isms, and beyond classes and social differentiations.[2]

Practice and Function

The literature in English on Japanese ROSCAs was introduced by John Embree in his 1946 study *Suye Mura*, the first extensive ethnography of a Japanese village by a Western anthropologist. Embree (1946:111–12) describes *kou* (under the spelling *kō*) as part of the village co-operative system, and he illustrates the basic operation of the ROSCA in this way:

> If a man needs, say, 160 yen, then a group of, say, twenty friends can each contribute 8 yen towards the loan. This is repaid by him at the rate of 10 yen at stated intervals, in all twenty times. Thus, he pays 40 yen as interest on the loan. The *kō*, consisting of twenty lenders and the original borrower, meets as a rule twice a year thereafter in the eleventh and twelfth months by lunar calendar. At the meetings they each make a secret bid on a slip of paper. The man who bids lowest receives 10 yen from the original borrower and any other member who had already won, plus the amount he bid, say 4 yen, from each of the other members. People who have won cannot bid at future meetings and must pay 10 yen each time.
>
> Usually people bid high at first, desiring not to win, and bid low towards the end. For example, in a *kō* of twenty-one members the bids might run as follows:
>
> At the first meeting: everyone (twenty people) pays 8 yen to man in need – 160 yen. Second meeting: man who was in need pays 10 yen and others pay

lowest sum bid, say 6 yen (19 x 6 + 10 = 124 yen to the winner). . .

Sixth meeting: five men pay 10 yen each and others lowest sum bid, say 5 yen (15 x 5 + 50 = 125 yen to winner). . .

Nineteenth meeting: eighteen men pay 10 yen and others lowest sum bid, say 1 yen (1 x 2 + 180 = 182 yen to winner). Twentieth meeting: nineteen men pay 10 yen and others lowest sum bid, say 0 (1 x 0 + 190 = 190 yen to winner). . .

Last meeting: twenty men pay 10 yen, and the other automatically wins 200 yen.

Whereas the basic patterns in practice are outlined by Embree, its functions are better described by Sakurai (1962:382–83):

[The ROSCA in Japan, under the name of] such a *kou* as *tanomoshi* (or *mujin*), may be categorized into two groups according to their purposes. (From here on, *mujin* will be included in *tanomoshi*.) The original aim of this form of *kou* was to save a particular person or household from poverty, or to promote a particular business. Because such a person or household, or the business promoter, was commonly named as *oya* [parent], the *kou* was called *oya tanomoshi* (*oya mujin*). . . In contrast to this kind of *kou*, the second was called *oya-nashi* [no parent, or parentless] *tanomoshi* (or *oya-nashi mujin*); it aimed at the equal financing of all the participants and was not for the benefit of any particular person or business promotion. In the *oya tanomoshi*, even in cases where the recipient of the money is determined by lottery or competitive bidding, an exception is made, the first loan tendered automatically going to the *oya* [parent]. In contrast, the *oya-nashi* [parentless] *tanomoshi* gives no priority to any particular person, establishing the recipient each time by competitive bidding. The money then goes to the highest offer [of a discount].

Oya tanomoshi again breaks into two sub-categories: in one, the *oya* himself calls for and establishes the *kou*; in the other, the *oya*'s relative(s) or his sponsor founds the *kou* [in order to benefit the nominal *oya*]. For a *kou* to rebuild or renovate a temple or a shrine, as a rule the sponsor [who is a believer] will be the founder, [who leads the *kou* in order to raise a group donation among believers for the nominal *oya*, the temple or the shrine] indicating that it belongs to the second category. [Also in the second category,] if the [nominal] *oya* who is to be saved is the one who founds a *kou*, potential participants may feel too insecure to join, since the *oya* himself is too poor to be able to sustain the *kou* over time. In such a case, a friend or relative takes on the role of *oya-uke-nin* or guarantor.

The participants in general are called *kou-in*.[3] In *oya tanomoshi*, in relation to the *oya* participant, the other participants may be called *ko* [child][4] or *ko-kata* [one in a child-role][5] . . . The number of participants varies according to the geographic area where the *kou* is practised but, in general, in urban areas the number of participants tends to be greater and in rural areas smaller. In such rural areas, it is most common to have ten to fifteen participants, which is variable because the number of shares is determined by dividing the total amount of money to be raised by each reimbursement, and because a single participant may hold more than one share. For example, if two hundred thousand yen is the total amount that must be raised, and if one share is to be ten thousand yen, then twenty shares are offered. If each participant takes one share, there will be twenty participants. But if five participants each take two shares, there will be fifteen participants. The *kou*'s founder takes all responsibility for running it. He will offer the gathering site, and commonly he pays for the drink, the food, and the fee for the gathering site.

So far, no mention has been made of women's participation in *kou*. Ajio Fukuda, the leading authority on this matter in Japan, has told me that until recently *kou* membership was limited to men who represented their households. Women were allowed to assist in miscellaneous tasks but were neither official members nor important. However, there was one particular kind of *kou* which was organized for, and basically by, women. Embree describes an example in Suye as follows:

> Women's equivalent to men's *donen kō* [*kō* composed of the same age group] called women's *kō*, are also primarily sociability clubs for singing, dancing, and drinking. Being of the same age is not important because there are not enough native women of the same age to form a *kō*. Girls of the same age group marry out into different regions, and women who come in as brides do not necessarily form their friendships within the age group. Occasionally, a small group of women married within the *mura* [village] will meet for a *donen* drinking party, but no special *kō* is run. The women's *kō* are of the lottery type; dues vary from fifty sen [0.5 yen] to three yen depending on the group. For those who have won there is a [subscription of] ten- or twenty-sen interest. Fifteen or twenty sen are contributed for food; *shochu* [a hard liquor] is partly contributed by the hostess, partly brought by the members. It is worth noting that a man, usually the husband of the hostess of the day, is at the meeting. He keeps the books and is seated in the place of honour; meetings are four or five times a year.
>
> Sometimes a women's *kō* is called a bedding (*futon*) *kō*. In this case the winner is expected to use the money to buy new bedding materials.
>
> A variety of the women's *kō* (ostensibly a religious society) is the *Kwannon* [a Buddhisatra] *kō*, a social gathering of women at the Zen temple in Suye which also houses an image of *Kwannon*. Each member brings a measure of rice and twenty sen in return for which the temple furnishes *shochu* and food. The priest gives a talk and collects money offered to *Kwannon*. It meets on New Year's Day and once during the summer.

Then Embree returns to the description of the general characteristics of *kou* including women's *kou*:

> Some *buraku* [hamlets] meet twice a year, in the first and ninth months by lunar calendar, to hold an *Ise kō*, another semi-religious group. This has been described under *kumi* (see p.88).[6] It is the only *kō* where *kumi* are involved and is strictly a *buraku* affair.
>
> In the small, purely social, *kō* for one or two yen there are no regular heads, and no permanent books are kept. There is simply a check of names at each meeting to see that everyone gives his one or two yen as the case may be.
>
> *Kō* meetings occur with seasonal frequency. The economic *kō* are all bunched in the two or three months after the rice harvest. *Donen kō* usually meet three to five times a year – in periods when farm work is not so urgent: (1) around New Year's time; (2) spring *Higan* (equinoctial) holidays; (3) July, after transplanting and weeding are finished; (4) autumn *Higan*; and (5) just after harvest. Favourite times for meetings of women's *kō*, as one woman described it, are: the third month – flowers are in bloom, a good time to drink *shochu* and look at flowers from inside the house; the sixth month – rice-transplanting is just finished, so people take a rest; the twelfth month – to celebrate the end of the year. Such a meeting is termed *shiwase* [end-of-year party] *kō*.

We should note that the purpose of the women's *kou* is to solidify the group identity of members through regular meetings combined with drinking parties, and other aspects such as credit-raising and religious elements are considered by ethnographers, including Embree, to be pretexts for such meetings. Although these are treated as women's associations, it is notable that the husband of the hostess for the meeting functions as the accountant and is paid respect as the formal (which may mean simply nominal) director of the occasion.

Because the basic forms of ROSCAs among women follow those among men, detailed description of the women's practice is rare. Thus, the description offered by Smith and Wiswell (1982:40) is important:

> One common inspiration for their formation was the need to raise cash with which to pay medical bills or meet some other unusual or large expense. A women would then approach a circle of friends, neighbours, and kinswomen, and invite them to participate in a *ko-*. Assuming that she needed forty-five yen, the procedure might be as follows:
>
> 1. Needing forty-five yen, she asks fifteen women to contribute three yen each.
> 2. At the first meeting, the money is collected and it is agreed that there will be fifteen subsequent meetings, so that each member will win the draw.

3. At every meeting, the founder pays in 3.20 yen.
4. Every winner pays in 3.20 yen at subsequent meetings.
5. Lots are drawn at every meeting by those who have not yet won the draw.
6. The winner receives 3 yen from every non-winner, and 3.20 yen from the founder and all previous winners.
7. The last winner, at the sixteenth meeting, receives 48 yen (45 plus 3 yen 'interest').

As the schematic outline below shows, the later one draws the winning lot, the greater the amount of money one receives:

Meeting 1. Fifteen members pay 3 yen each to the founder: 45 yen.
Meeting 2. Lots are drawn, and the founder pays 3.20 yen to the winner and the fourteen others pay 3 yen to the winner:

$$1 \times 3.20 = 3.20$$
$$14 \times 3.00 = 42.00$$
Total 45.20

Meeting 6. Founder and four previous winners pay 3.20 yen each to the winner and 10 others pay 3 yen each to the winner:

$$1 \times 3.20 = 3.20$$
$$4 \times 3.20 = 12.80$$
$$10 \times 3.00 = 30.00$$
Total 46.00

Meeting 14. Founder and twelve previous winners pay 3.20 yen each to the winner and 2 others pay 3.00 yen each to the winner:

$$1 \times 3.20 = 3.20$$
$$12 \times 3.20 = 38.40$$
$$2 \times 3.00 = 6.00$$
Total 47.60

Meeting 16. At this last meeting, the founder and the fourteen previous winners each pay 3.20 yen to the only woman who has not yet won, making a total of 48.00 yen.

There are sixteen meetings of this fifteen-member *kō* because no lots are drawn at the first pay-in meeting, which is also the occasion for drawing up the rules under which the association will operate.

Although the credit-raising women's *kou* and men's *kou* are structured almost identically, there are some characteristic differences between them. Smith and Wiswell (1982:40) point out one difference as follows, again quoting from Embree's journal:

The scale of all of the women's *kō* was equally small. One that was having its last meeting after many years of existence was for one yen each, and ten sen for food. Previous winners paid 1.10 yen. 'Yesterday Mrs Tanimoto went to a *kō* in Fukada. It costs two yen, ten sen for *shochu*, and twenty sen extra for winners. It is a *futon kō* [bedding *kō*], and in theory one makes comforters and padded kimono with the proceeds, but they can be used for other things as well. Mrs Fujita won, and deposited the money in her savings account in the village office'.

Sanctions

Although most academics and the media have agreed that *kou*, including the ROSCA or economic *kou*, was a traditional or even 'backward' system, in the modern tradition (from the Meiji Restoration of 1868 until today) *kou* are viewed as an indispensable component of village social organization, because they promote solidarity and cohesion. The type of sanction associated with *kou* participation explains this circumstance.

In his 1982 book *Nihon Sonraku no Minzokuteki Kouzo* ('The Folk Structure of the Japanese Village'), Ajio Fukuda, concluding a long-term discussion among Japanese academics, argues first that the *ie* (the household) is the basic composite unit of the Japanese village, and second, that the household must fulfil two kinds of obligations, *gimu* (formal) and *giri* (informal). *Gimu* is a formal obligation to participate in the activities established at village meetings for the maintenance of the village. Failure to fulfil these obligations results in punishment, which may be as serious as exclusion from village activities. In contrast, *giri* is an informal obligation to promote harmonious relationships between households. The degree of intensity of efforts to fulfil *giri* creates differences in closeness among households, both connecting and isolating one from another in the village. Fukuda (1982:153) summarizes six major categories of *giri* obligatory actions. In order to be liked in the village, a villager must:

(1) greet and say hello to other villagers when he sees them on the road or in the field and keep the daily relationship peaceful; (2) pay a visit of greeting on such annual occasions as the New Year and *Bon*; (3) offer the co-operative labour expected of neighbours, *douzoku* [relatives in brotherhood], at the time of rice planting and harvesting, meaning participation in reciprocal production relationships; (4) fulfil responsibility by providing labour traditionally established for participants in village life relating to maintaining reciprocal organization at the times of weddings, funerals, and roof-thatching; (5) pay visits of greeting and give gifts of value established as appropriate for weddings, funerals, grieving periods, illness, and such; and (6) sufficiently

entertain participants in *kou* or gatherings when he has offered the sites for such gatherings. If he neglects to participate properly in these activities, an individual or his household members will be subject to harsh criticism and verbal abuse. It should be noted that in villages with advanced class differentiations, or with a ranking value system among the households, the degree of individuals' participation is not equal but may differ according to the position of the households on the village scale. Excessive participation will be criticized as much as insufficient participation.

It is important to note that in discussing *giri* obligations Fukuda refers to *kou* in his sixth point, and that in addition the fourth and fifth categories he identifies are directly related to *kou*, since *kou* are regularly formed to provide financial support and co-operation to those anticipating the responsibility of holding weddings, funerals, and roof-thatchings. There is no formal punishment for failure to fulfil *giri*. The sanctions are the constant criticism that results from such failure, in contrast to the admiration received for fulfilment. The nature of these motives and sanctions are psychological, and the *giri* obligation permeates every sphere of village life. Over generations, each household builds up a reputation in the village community.

Concerning *giri* as motivating the ROSCA (or economic *kou*), Kunio Yanagita, founder of the study of folk culture in Japan, writes critically about a shift from traditional *giri* expectations and the social sanctions which enforce them towards the legal regulation of the early period of modernity (1963:382–3):

> A much stronger sanction than legal documents used to constitute the foundation of the co-operative system. However, today such aspects as the feeling of *giri* which is obtainable in any modern credit association, no matter how friendly it is, and the commitment to the other participants, have been gradually reduced, since economic *kou* associations began to be formed among strangers, through the mediation of the founder.

In this context, Sakurai (1962:402–3) also emphasizes mutual support and solidarity as the basic characteristic of the ROSCA. He points out that the economic *kou* without *oya*, or 'parent', is a new phenomenon, endorsing Yanagita's position:

> However, the majority of *tanomoshi* [economic *kou* or ROSCAs] formed among ordinary people, were not *oyanashi tanomoshi* [parentless ROSCAs], which may be seen as merely providing reciprocal financial aid for the participants, or as a system of saving and investment. Needless to say, the

structural element of the Japanese village is its family-like orientation. Here the kin groups called *maki, ikke,* or *ittou* are united in an extremely strong feeling of coexistence. This is reminiscent of the relationship between parent and child or between brothers. Thus, there is a strong co-operative feeling at work among them. When these co-operative feelings among the kin groups are expressed through *tanomoshi,* the form of *oya tanomoshi* [ROSCA with parent] appears. When someone within a kin group has suffered from a fire, or has lost his field to a natural disaster such as high tide, flood, or landslide, or when a working member dies of an accident, without fail his kinsmen get together to help. But when the disaster is beyond their capacity, they ask for help from other villagers. The individual's relatives and kinsmen become the founder and guarantors of a [ROSCA] *kou* and ask other villagers to participate in it. In the *kou* formed to save an unlucky child who has just lost his parents, it often happens that the participants hold only one meeting, at which all the money raised is given to the child. Even in cases where a promise is made that the child will reimburse the same amount (though with no interest added) when he is grown up, none of the participants wish to collect such reimbursement, and thus it is an act of pure charity toward the less fortunate one. This example should be sufficient to concude that by its very nature the *tanomoshi* [ROSCA] is traditionally meant to be a social aid.

Sakurai (ibid) continues the description of the *kou* as focused on mutual help and co-operation by observing:

It was extremely common in villages built on agriculture, fishing, or forestry to establish *tanomoshi kou* or *mujin kou* (both ROSCAs) for obtaining pots and pans or the furniture necessary in daily life or purchasing tools necessary for production. The former covers tables, chests of drawers, oblong chests, *tatami* mats, family altars, tombstones, blankets, and clothes. There are some large-scale *kou* such as *ie* [household] *tanomoshi* for building a house, roof *tanomoshi* and reed *mujin* for thatching a new roof. As for the need for materials and tools in productive activities such as agriculture, fishing, and forestry, *kou* covers a variety of purposes, from cow *tanomoshi* (for ploughing), horse *mujin,* boat *tanomoshi,* net *tanomoshi,* charcoal kiln *tanomoshi* (for making charcoal), gun *mujin* (for hunting), even to *dendouki* [electric machine] *tanomoshi* for the purchase of modern electrical machines, power cultivator *tanomoshi,* thrasher *tanomoshi* (for thrashing rice grains), machinery *tanomoshi* and truck *tanomoshi.*

In modern times, as part of the national policy of the central government, the ROSCA became regulated by law:

In its origin, the *tanomoshi kou* [ROSCA] began with a traditional and simple co-operative system. It changed greatly in its form and content as it developed later, especially under the influence of the modern capitalist system. Yet there also remains much of the original sentiment which attached to *kou* at the very beginning. The feeling of shared responsibility is especially distinctive, because the creditors are also debtors in [the ROSCA] *kou*, unlike the situation with a bank. As a result, once joined, a moral obligation to share responsibility to the end permeates the association throughout any difficulties. The *kou* regulations are most concerned about this aspect. The following are some examples. The regulation of Kyoushin *kai* [name of a particular *kou*] in Tokyo registered at the Tokyo Police Headquarters for June 1927–February 1929 says, 'Head and Director share the responsibility for this association,' emphasizing their responsibility. Also, the regulation for the Shinyuu *kou* [the name of another *kou*] in Hakodate for September 1913–August 1915 says, 'The loss caused by the debtor's inability to continue reimbursement should be borne by all the participants and should be reimbursed from the surplus of the association,' asserting that all the debts should ultimately be cleared through co-operation among all the participants. For this reason, obtaining the *kou* loan came under rather strict conditions. That is, 'The debtor must have four guarantors who are the representatives of wealthy households in the same area.' When it is still thought to be insecure, part or all of the guarantors must be participants in the same *kou* as the debtor himself, in an attempt to maintain maximal security . . .

The above examples are of *tanomoshi kou* which provide financial aid among city residents. Therefore, practice is modernized and systematized by legal regulation. Establishing assets for security or fines for delayed payment are components of the modern banking system. Nevertheless, the deep sentiment from the pre-modern co-operative system remains as an undercurrent, the shared responsibility of participants being emphasized (Sakurai, 1962:395–6).

In the same social context, Nobuhiro Yagihashi (1991:110–12) also reports that in 1915 the National Government established a law, *mujin-gyo hou* (the law concerning ROSCAs), pointing out that its popular practice necessitated such regulation:

Mujin-gyo hou, promulgated in 1915 by the Government, was intended to place *kou* under more strict regulation by providing licenses. This situation in turn tells how much the economic *kou* was needed in the community. In November of 1934, the Ministry of Agriculture and Forestry published the results of research on *tanomoshi kou* conducted in January of the same year. This report documented for the first time the total number of *tanomoshi kou*, which was 298,696, with the total amount of debts as much as 471,000 yen . . . All over Japan, such economic aid associations functioned actively. But at the same time they were committed to the risk of holding a great amount of debts.

Sakurai (1991:390–91), explains why people dared to take such economic risks:

> The roles of such modern monetary organizations as banks, credit associations, and national loan associations in economy and business should not be underestimated. However, the recipients of the privilege of benefiting from association with the modern monetary organizations are limited to manufacturers with large capital, trading firms, and security companies. Some intermediate and small-sized businesses may benefit, but the privilege is a remote one for ordinary people. They may have to resort to pawnbrokers or loan brokers, even knowing that the interest they charge is high. In this situation, the *tanomoshi* [ROSCA] is formed in many urban areas. It has been reported often enough in newspapers and weekly journals that the *kou* causes a big problem when its operating money fails to rotate, as it is based on the collection of small sums from mine workers or small and powerless businessmen. In taking a risk by joining private banking organizations that cannot be secure, the difficulty of the lives of ordinary people oppressed by capitalism is illustrated.
>
> Even in the city, the situation is as bad as that described above. For small farmers and small fishermen in the villages, the situation is even more serious . . . It is as miserable in isolated islands and villages which are self-contained and operate in handicapped productive conditions. In such areas, the modern banking system is as useless as feeding cats with gold coins. It is understandable that the villagers have to rotate their limited goods and money among themselves.

Disappearance and Transformation

Sakurai's description applies to Japanese society as it was until the 1960s. However, since then society has changed drastically. Yagihashi's report entitled *Kou-Shuudan no Henyou* ('The Changes in Kou Association') is most interesting in this context, showing the major social changes concerning *kou* between 1936 and 1986. His report compares two studies, one made in 1934–36 under the supervision of Kunio Yanagita, and the other in 1984–86, which is a follow-up of the first, done by the Institute for the Study of Folk Culture at Seijo University. Yanagita's research includes over sixty mountain villages, and the follow-up covers twenty-one of them, tracing the changes during the fifty years between the two studies.

Yagihashi points out (1991:112) that the most distinctive change is the disappearance of *kou* in general, and that the disappearance of *tanomoshi* as the representative economic *kou* is especially conspicuous:

> In any case, how could it happen that *kou*, which used to constitute communal living, have all disappeared? The major reason, it is clear, is that small-scale co-operative financial aids are no longer necessary, as banks and agricultural associations which play a part in each household have usurped such functions over time. Furthermore, the standard of living in Japan in general has improved through the period of high economic growth and it has become possible to live without depending on a system like *kou*.

In the same essay (pp.118–19), Yagihashi also remarks:

> The disappearance of most of the highly economically-oriented *kou* indicates the end of the age during which *kou* were essential for living. As unity becomes loosened in the community, the relationship between households becomes distant, resulting in an economy that has become self-sufficient in each household as an isolated social unit. Moreover, various lending banks have become participants in household or individual budgets, accelerating the disappearance of *kou*. Furthermore, financial aids for those in a socially weak position have shifted from the community level to the individual level, based on various insurances and security systems.

Yet some *kou* still continue today. While the ROSCA, or economic *kou* has disappeared, the social *kou* organized for the purpose of a funeral still flourishes with little changed. According to Yagihashi (1991:120):

> Norikazu Tanaka in his report says, 'The funeral has not changed except that the body is now cremated.' Also, Kazuhiko Hirayama analyses the data gained in our follow-up research as follows: 'The folk culture concerning the funeral has changed little, and the mutual co-operation among villagers as related to the *funeral* has not changed. In their consciousness, the resistance to changing such a matter must be great. And also, the funeral, unlike a wedding or the birth of a child, is still most often performed in the household of the deceased ... It would suffice to say here that, for maintaining daily living, among *kou* that used to be essential for mutual help or co-operation, those with a high economic function have disappeared and those that are highly ceremonial continue.

Another kind of *kou* also continues today, but it has been transformed into a club or salon, and functions under many different names, with more emphasis on aspects of pleasure. However, such institutions are no longer formally recognized as *kou* (Sakurai 1976:97):

Recently, under high economic growth, the sight-seeing trip, including going abroad, has become popular and more expensive. Today, tourist bureaux, public communication associations, agricultural associations, and fishing associations encourage farmers and fishermen with more income to spend their surplus on recreational activities. However, the basic pattern follows the pre-modern pilgrimage *kou* for going to temples and shrines. For example, in business corporations rational management has been adopted and social organization modernized, the labour union is more respected, and the recreational and welfare system has been highly equipped. Yet it is common for each work unit to organize a pleasure trip once or twice a year. In urban areas, each month neighbourhood friendship associations accumulate certain amounts of money in the bank to organize recreational trips. This custom is still popular. These are not called *kou*, but they are the application of the pre-modern *tanomoshi kou* [or ROSCA] to our contemporary life.

Yagihashi also points out that with the transformation of today's *kou*, it has become more open to women. As it loses its traditional identity as *kou*, and changes into a loose club of sorts, it also loses the rigid gender division set by men. It may also be that women are more economically active. However, at the same time, such modern associations are socially peripheral and are no longer seen as an essential and indispensable component of the highly-developed economic system of today's Japan.

Notes

1. This brief report on ROSCAs in Japan has been made possible by kind advice from Professor Ajio Fukuda, a prominent scholar in the study of folk culture in Japan. I must also thank Professor Itoko Kitahara, Mr Daiichi Nakagawa, and Dr Noriko Kawahashi for helping me find materials. In the process of obtaining materials from Japan, I also depended on Professor Minoru Kasai, our Divisional Chairman at the International Christian University, Tokyo, Ms Takako Igarashi, his administrative assistant, and Mr Tsutomu Miyamoto, graduate student, who volunteered to collect data and send it to me in Oxford. Ms Jane Uscilka helped me refine my English. The text has been revised and edited by Shirley Ardener and Sandra Burman with my agreement to properly fit the overall perspective of the book. My stay at Oxford University was sponsored by the Japan Foundation.
2. Translations from the Japanese throughout are by the present author.
3. *In* means member in either plural or singular.

4. *Kou* may be spelled in English as *kō* or *ko*, the latter being a homonym with *ko*, meaning child. However, they are two different words for which two different Chinese characters are used in Japanese writing and two different pronunciations.

5. As *oya* [parent] and *ko* [child] are used as a set, *kata* emphasizes the role of one in relation to the other.

6. *Kumi* is the primary grouping unit of *buraku* [hamlet] which is described in detail on p.88 of Embree's book.

References

Embree, John F. (1946), *A Japanese Village, Suye Mura*, London: Kegan Paul, Trench, Trubner & Co. Ltd.

Fukuda, Ajio (1982), *Nihon Sonraku no Minzokuteki Kouzou* ['The Folk Structure of the Japanese Village'], Tokyo: Koubundou.

Hirayama, Kazuhiko (1988), 'Hanseiki-go no Minzoku to sono Kinshitsu-ka – Sanson no Baai' ['Folk Culture a Half Century Later and its Homogenization – The Case of Mountainous Villages'] in *Chiiki Bunka no Kinshitsu-ka ni kannsuru Sougou-Kenkyuu: Jinrui Kagaku 40 Kinen-go* ['Integrating Research Concerning the Homogenization of Regional Cultures'], Tokyo: Seijo University.

Sakurai, Tokutaro (1962), *Kou-shuudan no Seiritsu Katei no Kenkyuu* ['The Study of the Formation Process of Kou Association'], Tokyo: Yoshikawa Koubunnkan.

—— (1976), *Shinkou Denshou* ['Tradition of Belief'], Nihon Minzokugaku Kouza Series Vol. 3, Tokyo: Asakura Shoten.

Smith, Robert, and Wiswell, Ella Lucy (1982), *The Women of Suye Mura*, University of Chicago Press.

Tanaka, Senichi (1987), 'Shuushou' ['The Final Chapter'] in *Sanson Seikatsu 50 Nen: sono Bunka Henka no Kenkyuu – Shouwa 60 Nendo Chousa Houkoku* ['50 Years Living in the Mountainous Village: The Study of its Cultural Change – Research Report in Shouwa 60'], Seijou Daigaku Minzokugaku Kenkyuu-jo [Institute for the Study of Folk Culture, Seijo University], Tokyo.

Yanagita, Kunio (1963), *Teihon Yanagita Kunio Shuu dai24kan* ['The Standard Collections of Kunio Yanagita's Writings vol. 24'], Tokyo: Chikuma Shobou.

Yagihashi, Nobuhiro (1991), 'Kou-shuudan no Henyou' ['The Changes in *Kou* Association'] in *Shouwa-ki Sanson no Minzoku Henka* ['The Change of Folk Cultures in the Shouwa Period'], Seijou Daigaku Minzokugaku Kenkyuu-jo The Institute for the Study of Folk Culture, Seijo University], Tokyo.

10

Women's ROSCAs in Contemporary Indian Society

Raj Mohini Sethi

In recent years Indian society has witnessed the proliferation of non-banking financial institutions. The rapid growth and spread of these institutions in most parts of the country calls for an evaluation of their overall position in our society today. Their importance lies in the fact that they help to channel non-active, liquid, household savings that are an extension of traditional forms of money-lending; they provide friendly, easy and informal access to credit in contrast to the indifference of the official machinery of the formal banking system. Two types of *non-bank formal financial institutions* have been broadly distinguished: the first consists of mutual savings institutions, savings and loan associations, the post office savings system, and credit associations; the second consists of insurance schemes, pension and provident funds and similar financial schemes. Apart from these, a large number of *informal institutions* have increasingly been providing savings alternatives to the Indian populace. This category includes indigenous money-lenders and bankers, and also a variety of rotating savings and credit associations (ROSCAs) which maintain an element of secrecy and are outside the purview of the central bank control. Although there is an awareness of the activities of these informal financial institutions, there is a dearth of literature and reliable information on them. The present paper attempts to help to fill this gap, and gives a sociological explanation of the importance of one of these non-bank financial institutions for contemporary Indian society in both rural and urban settings, and among the wealthy as well as the poor. It looks at the genesis, structure and role of a particular form of ROSCA in India, in which the members contribute towards a common fund which is given to one member after another by rotation.

The data for this paper has been collected from both secondary and primary sources. The primary data was initially collected by one of my students, Ms. Mandeep Kaur,[1] for her M.Phil. programme, and later was supplemented by me through in-depth interviews concerning various ROSCAs in Chandigarh, Punjab and Haryana.

Origin and Spread

The indigenous institution frequently called *kuri*, *chitty* or *chit* fund was a means of obtaining credit from one's friends and neighbours in the village to meet certain exigent expenses such as those of a daughter's marriage or of one's father's *shradha* (ancestor worship). A woman in need of money or grain would coax her neighbours to contribute a fixed measure of grain every month. For example, if she could persuade nine of her neighbours to contribute five kilograms of rice every month, in the first month she would collect fifty kilos of rice, including her own contribution. The next month again fifty kilograms of rice were collected and handed over to another contributor, until all had received this amount. A system of drawing lots in advance was developed to avoid conflict over who received the total contribution. The terms *kuri*, *chitty* (*chit*), or *narukku* derive from Indian words meaning 'writing', 'a piece of paper' or 'paper cutting'. On each paper (*chit*) the name of one contributor was written, and the *chit* was then folded and put into a vessel containing some rice. After putting all the *chits* into the vessel, one person was asked to draw the lot signifying the 'prize-winner', who always gave a feast (Logan, 1887:1:173; Sim Cox, 1894:568; Aiyer, 1925 cited in Nayar, 1973:2; Government of Travancore 1930:1:Para 229; Government of India, 1930:1:Para 76, and Nayar, 1973:2).

The emergence of ROSCAs in Indian society is attributed to the character of the self-sufficient village communities, where, for lack of space in their households, small farmers and tenants would ask landlords to take care of their surplus grain. Sometimes they were cheated of the grain by the landlords; and to avoid this, households developed a tendency to use up all the produce immediately after the harvest season in various ceremonies and festivities, with the result that later, when they fell short of their day-to-day requirements, they resorted to borrowing from landlords and others. Under these circumstances, to reduce their dependence on loans, the women (to whom rice, the commodity of contribution, was easily available in the household) developed a habit of saving a handful of grain from every meal and investing that in a ROSCA. Women often became members of ROSCAs without the knowledge of the male members of the household. When the ROSCA fund accrued to these women they could encash the grain and buy household utensils, or if the fund was big enough, gold ornaments.

In the initial stages, membership of ROSCAs were confined to a few families living in a village neighbourhood unit, and individual contributions were very small and relatively easily available. Confining membership to the neighbourhood helped to verify the integrity of the contributors and the prospects for the continuance of the rotation. Their popularity assisted many women to become specialists in organizing and promoting them. With the passage of time, these rice *chitties* also gained popularity with other sections of village communities, such as landlords, tenants, farmers, indeed almost all classes in agricultural communities, who invested their savings in associations composed of persons of their own rank. It is said that the substitution of money for rice accompanied the decline of the barter economy. This changed the membership of ROSCAs as traders, merchants and salaried persons started subscribing to them (Government of India, 1930:1:481; Nayar, 1973:4–5). Some state authorities became concerned enough to introduce controlling legislation as early as 1918 (see below).

The relative informality and flexibility of ROSCAs not only helped to enlarge their membership but also facilitated their spread to other parts of the sub-continent. The *All India Rural Credit Survey* for the district of Quilon[2] (Reserve Bank of India, 1958:113) mentions that in 1930–31 there were 10,289 ROSCAs with a total capital investment of Rs. 25,800,000, while the *Madras Provincial Banking Enquiry Committee Report* (Government of India, 1930:1, Para 494) notes the existence of 4,159 ROSCAs in five districts of Madras Presidency alone during this period. The *All India Rural Credit Survey* (Reserve Bank of India, 1958:118) further mentions that in the 1930s and 1940s there was a considerable decline in the number of registered ROSCAs because of the emergence of the market economy and the decreasing isolation of the village community. This entailed a greater risk to ROSCA savings because of the possibility of embezzlement and evasion, and the emergence and encroachment of other financial institutions such as the co-operative bank and the savings bank. However, ROSCAs seem to have survived all the obstacles to their growth, and by the close of the 1940s there was an almost two fold increase in their number. Until 1970 their numbers doubled every year in the states of Kerala and Tamil Nadu. Initially the spread of ROSCAs was confined to the Travancore, Cochin, and Malabar areas and the southern parts of the Madras Presidency. Later they spread northwards into the states of Maharashtra, Delhi, Uttar Pradesh, Punjab, Haryana, Chandigarh, Bihar, and West Bengal. Nayar (1973:157–62) mentions that in the 1940s ROSCAs were unknown in most of these states. It was only when they matured as financial institutions that they crossed the boundaries of the southern states. It cannot be ascertained exactly when the institution appeared in the north, but today it seems to be quite common in the rural and urban areas of most of these states. However, in the rural areas of Punjab and Haryana ROSCAs were relatively unknown until the 1950s, probably because people were obliged to help their kin in all crisis situations (author's interviews).

Since the 1950s ROSCAs have become popular with almost all sections of the female population, at least in the urban areas of this region. Unfortunately the reports about registered ROSCAs do not break down membership by gender, but there is little doubt that women were active in these associations throughout. The Chit Fund Act 1982 which required the regulation of *chit* funds has not been implemented in the states of Punjab and Haryana, but has been in the Union Territory of Chandigarh.

Mandeep Kaur's study (1989:22,69,71) gives some information about the number of unregistered ROSCAs. It shows that 286 out of 827 adult women living on the Panjab University Campus were members of one or more ROSCAs and the total number of ROSCAs to which they subscribed was 273. Her data further shows that 81 per cent of the women learnt of the existence of ROSCAs during the last fifteen years, 8 per cent during the last eight years, and the rest during the last three years. However, the remarks made by one of my respondents succinctly describes the spread of these associations in the north. A woman aged 83, who had migrated from West Pakistan after partition, remarked:

> In the mid-1920s, when my husband was posted at Lyallpur, I came across some Muslim women living in my neighbourhood participating in *kametis*. They used to contribute four annas every month. I never participated in them. I never heard of them since then. Recently, during the last seven years I heard women talk about *kitties* in which they were participating in the Central Club Chandigarh.

Our data further indicates that the oldest form of ROSCAs subscribed to by the women of this region were called *kametis*.

Structural Forms

The *Report of the Central Banking Enquiry Committee* (Government of India, 1931:Para. 261) pointed out the existence of two types of savings schemes in South India: *nidhis* and *chitties*. The former has been described as a 'terminating society' of members who make a term-based monthly contribution of a fixed amount, which is available to members for loans. However, the *nidhis* have now lost even this characteristic, have become either recurring deposit schemes or fixed deposit schemes under the banking system, and are registered under the Indian Companies Act. Since *nidhis* do not distribute funds on a rotational basis they have not been considered as ROSCAs in this paper. The *chitties* described in 1931 were ROSCAs with a loose organization of a small number of people, and were originally confined to the village, where the periodical contributions were made both in cash and kind.

Today ROSCAs are known by different names according to region, social class, form and scale. In south India they are called *kuris*, *chitties* or *chit* funds. In the north, among the lower socio-economic groups they are known as *kametis*, the emphasis being on a savings function: they are similar to the *sahaya* or *thathu* (Mutual Aid) *chit* funds of the south. ROSCAs patronized by the middle and upper classes in the north are called *kitties*, and again the emphasis is on socialization and entertainment (author's interviews; Mandeep Kaur, 1989:51–9; Reserve Bank of India, 1954:2:64–7). The survey data collected by Mandeep Kaur revealed that 79.17 per cent of women members of *kitties* had family incomes above Rs. 5000 per month. Among those who subscribed to *kametis*, 70.49 per cent had family incomes below Rs. 3000 per month. Of the *chit* fund subscribers, 53.57 per cent had family incomes of less than Rs. 3000, and another 39.29 per cent less than Rs. 5000 (Table 10.1).

Table 10.1. Family Income and ROSCA Membership.

Type of Association	Monthly Family Income in Rupees at 1988 prices (percentages in brackets)			
	<3000	3000–5000	5000+	Total
kitty	–	10 (20.83)	38 (79.17)	48 (100.00)
kameti	86 (70.49)	29 (23.77)	7 (5.74)	122 (100.00)
chit fund	15 (53.57)	11 (39.29)	2 (7.14)	28 (100.00)
auction	2 (100.00)	–	– (100.00)	2
Total	103	50	47	200

ROSCAs may differ in order of rotation, or commodity subscribed to, or religious or other values. The order of rotation may be determined by consensus, the drawing of lots, or auction. Consensus-based ROSCAs are mutual aid associations known as *sahaya chit* or *kameties*; while *thathu chit* funds or prize (lottery) *chit* funds are lottery-based ROSCAs in which the 'prize winner' is determined by the drawing of lots. Auction-based ROSCAs are usually referred to as *auction chit* funds. Their subscribers have a very wide social base, being drawn from the landowners, tenants and other social classes in the rural areas, and also from various social groups in the urban areas (Krishnan, article published in *All India Rural Credit Survey* 1954:II:66–7). Their method of operation is also different, and in this system under-bidding is resorted to for determining the recipient or 'winner'. The person with the lowest bid takes it, while the difference between the bid and the fund collected is equally divided among the remaining subscribers. The common factor in commodity-based ROSCAs is the type of goods purchased with the lump sum, such as sarees, kitchen utensils or other consumables, which are the special attraction for contributing regularly towards the common pool. ROSCAs based on religious or other values, such as *sukhmani recitation kitties*, attract members around a common value, and the periodical contributions make it incumbent on the members to attend the meetings regularly. The following comments by subscribers and organizers of ROSCAs in my interviews illustrate the point:

> I am a member of a *kitty* group where we can buy only sarees or household utensils against the *kitty* lump sum. This way I have acquired many sarees or household utensils which would be otherwise difficult to acquire because of the tight family budget.

Another woman, who organized *kitties*, observed:

> I gave up my teaching job and started organizing my own *kitties*. I organize three to five *kitties* at a time. Each *kitty* lasts for ten months and each woman has to pay an instalment of Rs. 50 per month. Once a woman joins the *kitty* she is allowed to choose any household item from my 'shop' [a garage or room in her own house] worth Rs. 500, and continues paying the instalments thereafter. This way I earn an overall profit of 20 per cent on each item that I offer against the *kitty*. It is an insurance against women dropping out of the deal. The organization of *kitties* provides me an assured clientèle.

Another *kitty* member made the following observations:

I am a member of two *kitty* groups. In one the major attraction for the members to come together is for socializing, while the other is a sort of religious meeting and is called the *sukhmani kitty*. In this meeting the women come together to recite *sukhmani* [the Psalm of Sikhs], which lasts for an hour and a half. Thereafter the women feast together. In both the groups we draw lots at each meeting to determine who gets the *kitty* lump sum and the turn for organizing the next *kitty*, and in the case of the *sukhmani kitty*, who also gets the turn for organizing the next *sukhmani* recitation function. The *kitty* subscription compels the women to meet around a common value and express solidarity with one another.

Membership and Organization

The number of members in a ROSCA varies from five to several hundred, depending upon its nature and type. ROSCAs patronized by women are, however, usually small groups of around twenty to seventy persons. Membership of ROSCAs in which the order of rotation is based on consensus or drawing of lots is usually limited to twenty or thirty women, while membership in groups where auctions take place is seldom less than fifty, but normally not more than seventy. However, auction-based ROSCAs, or lotteries which carry a 'prize fund' that are organized by individuals or by state governments, usually have several hundred or thousand members. Membership of a particular ROSCA may be based on sex, age, religion, ethnicity, locale, social standing or personal character of the individual, or on the purpose for which it was formed.

A study of ROSCAs among students on the Panjab University campus in Chandigarh (Mandeep Kaur, 1989:60–1) revealed that membership was restricted largely on the basis of gender and age; locale, occupational status and educational status were of lesser importance to the members. Further, membership of some ROSCAs is confined to the educated élite, while in others it is limited to the illiterate or semi-educated. The data shows that all the *kitty* members in the sample were either college graduates or post-graduates (with at least a Bachelor's or Master's degree in Arts or Sciences), while 72.13 per cent of *kameti* members, 89.28 per cent of *chit* fund members and all the members of auction-based ROSCAs were at most high-school graduates or illiterates. In both situations, the age of the members usually ranged between 21 and 50 (94.50 per cent). Although most women's ROSCAs are largely composed of housewives (50.5 per cent), they are also gaining popularity among working women, professionals and couples. In the Union Territory of Chandigarh members generally belong to the twice-born castes of Brahmins, Khatris, Aroras, Jats or Baniyas (97.0 per cent). The representation of lower castes in these ROSCAs is very small, although very often they have their own ROSCAs.

Most ROSCAs have one organizer, the rest of the members having equal status. Some ROSCAs, such as *kitty* groups, have no particular organizer; the person who gets the lump sum is also responsible for organizing the next meeting. In other associations, the organizer is generally the person who originated the group and is considered to be the 'hub of the chitty wheel' who keeps the wheel moving. The money accruing to the members, fixing of the rate of interest on loans, bringing together and motivating members to save – all depend upon the initiative, ability and far-sightedness of the organizer. The organizer is also responsible for the many functions of the association, such as enrolling members, maintaining attendance and other records, and preparing the *chits* for the draw. In case of default, the organizer decides the penalty in consultation with the other members (Nayar, 1973:116; Kaur, 1989:74; Author's Interviews).

Some ROSCA organizers invest part of the savings in banks or the stock market, and are required to prepare the annual balance sheet for the auditors. As compensation, the organizer gets a fixed amount from each instalment, and may sometimes ask for an out-of-turn payment of the 'prize' or lump sum, to which members usually willingly agree. The organizer's dividend is larger than that of the ordinary subscribers. In south India, however, *chit* fund groups have functioned more like 'joint stock companies' with a board of directors rather than a single organizer (Nayar, 1973:117). In all such complex forms of ROSCAs, the organizers as well as the subscribers are usually men. Of the thirteen ROSCAs registered between 1978 and 1992 in the Union Territory of Chandigarh, only four had names that could be associated with women (information supplied by the Department of Finance, Union Territory of Chandigarh).

The task of organizing ROSCAs is not simple. Organizers face several problems, of which the most serious is default by contributors. This becomes acute if the membership runs into hundreds or more and is scattered over vast areas, in which case ascertaining the integrity of the subscribers and the organizer becomes impossible. Interpersonal relations are the key to instilling confidence. Failing them, untrustworthy subscribers and unscrupulous organizers often dupe gullible contributors. Many pay their contributions for the first few instalments, but after receiving their turn to take their money declare bankruptcy and stop paying dues. Because of these risks, the organizer keeps the lion's share for herself.

A further major problem is that of unscrupulousness on the part of the organizer: she/he may advertise the scheme, collect subscriptions, pay out the money collected to a few subscribers, and then disappear. The capital may also be manipulated by the organizer for her or his own benefit. These problems generally arise in *chit* fund type ROSCAs which have a large membership and where the organizer is more or less anonymous, not known personally to most of the subscribers. This type of ROSCA is not usually organized by women. In Mandeep Kaur's data (1989:52) only 1 per cent of women subscribed to *chit* fund groups in Chandigarh. However, some of the problems mentioned above, such as default, are common to all ROSCAs.

Legislation

As noted above, since among the masses ROSCAs have come to stay, some state governments have enacted legislation, including registration, to check malpractices. The first such legislation was introduced in the erstwhile state of Travancore as far back as 1918. It is known as the Travancore Chitties Act of 1918 (Government of Travancore, 1930:1:Para. 235). This committee made a detailed study of the effects of Chitties Regulation III 1094 M.E. (Chitties Act of 1918) and made suggestions for its amendment, and in 1945 it was replaced by the Chitties Act 1120 M.E. Later, in 1964, the law was again amended to a form that is still operative (Reserve Bank of India, 1958:116; Nayar, 1973:129). Similarly, the State of Kerala passed the Cochin Kuries Act in 1931–2 and the State of Madras enacted the Madras Chit Fund Act of 1961, later amended (in 1969) and now referred to as the Tamil Nadu Chit Funds Act. The Madras Chit Fund Act of 1961, amended in 1969, has also been extended to the union territory of Delhi and the states of Punjab and Haryana. The main purpose of introducing these legislative provisions has been to keep a check on the activities of the ROSCA organizer by fixing two items: first, the organizer's 'prize' amount payable in advance at particular points in the rotation; and second, the organizer's remuneration or commission, which may not exceed 5 per cent of the agreed contributions. When such legislative provisions are non-existent or not enforced, the organizers have often listed the names of bogus subscribers to enhance their profits (Nayar, 1973:129–31). Recent enquiries with the Finance Departments of the Governments of Punjab and Haryana revealed that the Madras Chit Fund Act of 1961 had not been implemented in these two states but that it had been in the Union

Territory of Chandigarh. However, because of the increasing frequency of default and embezzlement all over India, the Government of India enacted The Chit Funds Act 1982 (Act No. 40 of 1982), which extends to the whole of India except the state of Jammu and Kashmir (*All India Reporter*, journal section, 1983:26–44). The act has not been promulgated in the official gazettes of the Punjab and Haryana governments, but has been notified in the Union Territory of Chandigarh. Enquiries from the Finance Department Chandigarh in February 1993 (personal communication) revealed that eight *chit* fund ROSCAs had been registered before the passage of the act and only five after it. Four of the eight *chit* funds were registered under women's names, but after the passage of the act, during the last ten years, only one ROSCA had been registered with a woman's name as the organizer. Women's ROSCAs operate largely at the informal level; both organizers and subscribers feel shy of operating at a formal level and turning their institutions into officially recognized financial institutions.

Order of Rotation and Subscription Amount

The order of rotation, which is a basic feature of all ROSCAs, can be weekly, monthly or even half-yearly, depending upon the financial position, locale, or even gender of the subscribers. For most women's ROSCAs it is monthly or bi-monthly, and it takes between six months and three years to complete one rotation. Mandeep Kaur's study (1989:70) shows that nearly half (43.96 per cent) of women's ROSCAs in Chandigarh lasted three years, 30.4 per cent lasted two years, and 25.64 per cent lasted between six months and one year. Her data further indicate that ROSCAs are usually renewed as soon as the existing order of rotation is completed. The *Report of Travancore-Cochin Banking Enquiry Committee* (Government of India, 1956:124) and also Nayar (1973:59) record that in this state 297 out of 480 ROSCAs were conducted on a monthly basis, five were bi-monthly, fifty-nine quarterly, fifty-four operated twice a year, thirty-eight at the time of harvesting, and twenty-seven on a yearly basis. The *All India Rural Credit Survey* (Reserve Bank of India, 1958:118–20) also reported that the duration of ROSCAs in Quilon district varied between twenty-eight and eighty-four months, while the average duration for all the centres in the survey was thirty-five months. However, it is not possible to ascertain how many of these ROSCAs belonged to women, as separate figures for men and women organizers were not available.

A particular feature of ROSCAs patronized by women is that the total sums handled by them are relatively small, the interval between instalments short, and the discounts bid at each instalment, where these occur, small. Contributions to ROSCAs are made in cash and range from 50 to 5,000 rupees. Mandeep Kaur's data (1989:68) shows that 54.0 per cent of women subscribers to ROSCAs on the Panjab University Campus contributed Rs. 50 or less for each instalment, 36.0 per cent contributed between Rs. 100–200 and only 10 per cent between Rs. 200–400. However, the following response of a business woman interviewed by me completes the picture:

> In the early seventies I became aware of *kitties* and soon thereafter I became a member of one such group . . . At that time the monthly contribution used to be 25 rupees only. Later, it was increased to 100 rupees and still later to 200 rupees. Today, I am a member of two *kitty* groups where the contributions are Rs. 2000 each. Instalments for one group are paid monthly, and for the other twice a month.

The amount of each contribution is pre-determined and fixed by general agreement among members or by the organizer before the start of the rotation. Even where every member contributes the same amount and gets an equal lump sum, the gains of all the members are not the same, since, unless there is bidding for discounts, such ROSCAs involve the giving of interest-free loans to all but the last contributor in a particular rotation (Ardener, 1964:211). ROSCA funds are often non-transferable. The prize money given to the winner of certain games (such as those known as *tembola*) played at the time of a ROSCA meeting is collected through additional subscriptions of 10 or 20 rupees.

The method of contribution is not always simple. It differs from one ROSCA to another and from one subscriber to another. Tables 10.2 and 10.3 illustrate two different methods of contributions: one of a simple consensus or lot ROSCA, in which all members pay and receive identical amounts, and the other of an auction-based ROSCA where the share of the discounts, or 'profits', is equally distributed among the members but the contributions and the lump sum amount received by them at each instalment is not equal. Apart from these, there are some auction-based ROSCAs where, in addition to the share of profit on the bid, the subscriber is also paid some interest if the organizer deposits or invests part of the lump sum in a bank or in a joint-stock company. However, we did not find any instance of such ROSCAs organized by women in Punjab, Haryana or the Union Territory of Chandigarh.

Table 10.2. Financial Arrangements of a Simple ROSCA (In Rupees).

Instalment	Amount subscribed	No. of subscribers	Prize amount
1	50	20	1,000
2	50	20	1,000
3	50	20	1,000
4	50	20	1,000
5	50	20	1,000
etc.			

Table 10.3. Model of Financial Arrangements of an Auction-Based ROSCA (in Rupees).

Instalment	Lump sum	AR	OC	TP	PS	AS
1	3,000	0	0	0	0	300.00
2	2,500	500	50	450	56.25	243.75
3	2,600	400	50	350	43.75	256.25
4	2,650	350	50	300	37.50	262.50
5	2,700	300	50	250	31.25	268.75
6	2,750	250	50	200	25.00	275.00
7	2,800	200	50	150	18.75	281.25
8	2,850	150	50	100	12.50	287.50
9	2,900	100	50	50	6.25	293.75
10	2,950	50	50	0	0.00	300.00

AR = Amount Reduced
OC = Organizer's Commission
TP = Total Profit Available for Distribution
PS = Pay-Out of Profit Per Subscriber
AS = Amount of Individual Subscriptions at each Instalment

Role of ROSCAs

The basic motive underlying the emergence of ROSCAs is economic – the accumulation of savings. Although ROSCA savings are small in scale they help to pool the savings both of those social groups that have little or no capacity to save and also of those that have it. Many a housewife is known to skimp and scrounge to keep aside a rupee or two from her daily household expenses and invest it in a ROSCA. The lump sum, or 'prize money', helps some more affluent women to buy gold as well as household goods. The uniqueness of ROSCAs lies in the fact that the residual savings of the family are put into circulation rather than lying dormant at home or in, say, a bank. ROSCAs, which encourage compulsory savings, have become substantial economic instruments, as shown by the findings of the *Report of the Agricultural Credit Review Committee* (Reserve Bank of India, 1991:562):[3] this states that the data for its Field Study 1 showed that 43.0 per cent of institutional borrowers were also obtaining money from these private informal sources. Data on borrowings of rural households indicate that 36 per cent of household credits were used for consumption purposes, 13 per cent for social and religious ceremonies, and the remaining 51 per cent for productive purposes. These figures further explain the popularity of ROSCAs as against co-operative credit societies, which cannot respond as quickly to borrowers' emergent needs.

The availability of credit through ROSCAs helped many women to become skilled entrepreneurs and achieve economic self-reliance. Many a housewife who felt the need to generate income has been using ROSCA savings as seed money for investments in small-scale business ventures, such as selling garments or household goods or setting up garden nurseries or beauty parlours. The following case illustrates the point:

> I used to play cards quite often and became addicted to the game. Once I lost a very huge amount and came under a heavy debt. It was a very depressing situation for me, and to get out of it I thought of doing something. My sister, who had a saree business, sent me a consignment of sarees. From their sale I earned a profit of Rs. 10,000. One of my *kitty* draws also came around this time, and I got a lump sum fund of Rs. 20,000. With this money in hand, I opened a boutique in 1986 and started organizing *kitties* to have a permanent clientele. Today, there is no looking back for me (author's interview with a successful boutique owner).

Apart from their economic value, ROSCAs are often also socially relevant. One fall-out of urbanization and industrialization is that familial bonds are not as strong as they used to be. The role of kin has become increasingly ambivalent, and urbanites have developed new support structures based more on neighbourhood and friendship than on kinship. This explains how ROSCAs are rooted in locale and friendship in the urban areas of the north. Housewives and professionals, in particular, have developed networks of social relationships cemented at ROSCA gatherings where regular entertainment is provided. Contact with ROSCA members also penetrates the private familial domain of the participants, members often being invited to social, cultural or religious functions organized at their homes. Solidarity is manifested in the moral, monetary or other support mutually given by members. Mandeep Kaur's study (1989:92,94) shows that around 75 per cent of ROSCA subscribers in her sample were able to establish new networks of social relationships, and 65 per cent of them continued with their ROSCA contacts on other social and cultural occasions as well. Around 60 per cent of all ROSCA subscribers in the study said that the members supported them both materially and morally whenever they faced a crisis. Once a bond is formed, it tends to persist even though the members cease to subscribe to a particular association.

Although ROSCAs help to integrate members into the mainstream of society, they may also become the sheet-anchor for small pressure-group politics, since they have a tendency to become exclusive. Entry to these groups helps members to achieve status, which explains why ROSCAs are patronized by professionals, businesswomen and executives, who use their membership network to work their way into prestigious social and economic positions.

Conclusions

Geertz (1962:260) linked the emergence of ROSCAs with development theory, and referred to them as middle-rung institutions that help in educating the peasant to meet the challenges of a changing economy – a shift from an agricultural to market economy. The Indian experience of ROSCAs points to contrary evidence, showing how these institutions are embedded in Indian village life. It also highlights their mass appeal, which is reflected in their continuity and spread to urban areas. Their popularity rests on their informality and flexibility as non-bank financial institutions in an otherwise formal and alien environment.

Notes

1. Mandeep Kaur (1989) submitted a M.Phil. dissertation entitled: 'A Sociological Study of Rotating Credit Associations Among Women'. Her study assessed the nature and extent of ROSCA participation by women residing on the Panjab University campus in Chandigarh. The study was done

on a sample of 200 out of a total of 827 subscribers or organizers.
2. The erstwhile District Quilon was composed of parts of the states of Travancore and Cochin.
3. The data was collected by the consultants of the *All India Rural Credit Survey Committee* between 1975 and 1986 and supplemented by the National Bank of Agriculture and Rural Development's 1986 evaluation study.

References

All India Reporter (1983), Journal Section, AIR, Nagpur.

Aiyer, S.S. (1925), *Economic Life in a Malabar Village*, Bangalore: The Bangalore Printing and Publishing Co. Ltd.

Ardener, S. (1964), 'The Comparative Study of Rotating Credit Associations', *Journal of the Royal Anthropological Institute*, vol. XCIV, Part 2.

Devereux, S. and Pares, P. (1987), *A Manual of Credit and Savings for the Poor of Developing Countries*, Oxford: Oxfam.

Geertz, C. (1962), 'The Rotating Credit Association: A Middle Rung in Development', *Economic Development and Cultural Change*, vol. 1, no. 3.

Government of India (1930), *The Madras Provincial Banking Enquiry Committee Report*, Delhi.

—— (1931), *The Indian Central Banking Enquiry Committee, Part 1, Majority Report*, Calcutta.

—— (1956) *The Travancore-Cochin Banking Enquiry Committee Report*, Travancore.

Government of Kerala (1972), *The Kerala Chitties Bill*, Trivardrum.

Government of Travancore (1930), *The Travancore Banking Enquiry Committee*, Travancore.

Kaur, Mandeep (1989), *A Sociological Study of Rotating Credit Associations among Women*, Unpublished Thesis submitted for Master of Philosophy, Panjab University, Chandigarh.

Krishnan, V. (1954), 'The Trambraparni Ryot', abstract from Ph.D. thesis published in *All-India Rural Credit Survey Report*, II, pp. 64–7, Bombay: Reserve Bank of India.

—— (1959), *Indigenous Banking in South India*, Bombay: The Bombay State Co-operative Union.

Logan, William (1887), *The Malabar Manual*, Madras: Government of Madras.

Nayar, C.P. Somanathan (1973), *Chit Finance: An Exploratory Study of Chit Funds*, Bombay: Vora & Co., Publishers Pvt. Ltd.

Reserve Bank of India (1954), *All India Rural Credit Survey Part II*, Bombay.

—— (1958), *All India Rural Credit Survey, District Monograph Quilon*, Bombay.

—— (1991), *Report of the Agricultural Credit Review Committee. A Review of the Agricultural Credit System in India*, Bombay.

Sim Cox, E.J., (1894), *Primitive Civilizations, or Outlines of the History of Archaic Communities*, London: Swan Sonnenschein & Co.

11

Gender Inequality, ROSCAs and Sectoral Employment Strategies: Questions from the South Indian Silk Industry

Linda Mayoux and Shri Anand

In recent years there has been a shift in approach to women's employment strategies from individual 'income-generation projects' to 'sectoral strategies' attempting to address the needs of larger numbers of women within particular industries or sectors of the economy. This has been partly a result of disillusionment with isolated attempts to set up women's enterprises and co-operatives because of high levels of failure, and partly a recognition that such individual projects can have only a negligible impact on women's employment as a whole. The content of such 'sectoral strategies' has as yet been only very vaguely defined but credit has frequently been singled out as 'the missing factor' inhibiting poor women from increasing their incomes. The examples of the Self-Employed Women's Association (SEWA) and Working Women's Forum (WWF) in India have often been cited as examples of successful interventions, although increases in income have generally been small and women have not always controlled the income they earn.[1]

This article discusses the potential role of another form of savings and credit organization in the context of overall sectoral strategies for women: ROSCAs, or *chit* funds as they are termed in the area studied. The discussion is based on research on the silk-reeling industry in one major reeling centre, here called 'Silkapura', in Kollegal Taluk in the Mysore District of Karnataka.[2] In Silkapura ROSCAs have for some time been organized for men and have been an important feature facilitating the advance of male reeling labourers into entrepreneurship.

Recently women, including some reeling labourers, have begun to join these ROSCAs. As a form of credit for women, these organizations have a number of special features. First, the amounts of money in cash which can be accumulated are large relative to those normally available to women from other formal and informal credit sources. Second, unlike most bank credit available to women, there are no predetermined strings attached to the use of the money; furthermore the funds can be obtained without the consent of other family members, provided payment is satisfactory. Third, the purpose of these ROSCAs is solely economic; no socializing is required, and no attempt is made either by the members as a whole or by the women themselves to organize women around wider gender issues. We found that at least in some cases such organizations have played an important role in increasing women's control over resources which they can use to increase assets in the family. This has been important even in cases where men were spending much of their income on alcohol and gambling and where women would otherwise have limited prospects of saving or getting access to credit.

If any development of these ROSCAs by outside agencies as part of wider sectoral strategies were to take place, a number of questions and potential problems would arise. First, would attempts to change the membership composition to cover either women in general, or particular categories of women, such as reeling labourers, necessitate changes in their regulations, and would this alter their ability to respond to women's economic needs? Second, could social and/or consciousness-raising and/ or educational activities be added to such groups without reducing their economic value? It is argued here that such issues need to be discussed with the women involved, covering all the possible options. However, provided this is done and women's ability to join the existing organizations is not impaired, such development could be a valuable part of wider policy for assisting women in the silk industry, and also in others where women have a reasonably stable and independent source of income.

Gender Inequality, Poverty and Credit in the Reeling Industry: A Multidimensional Problem

Silk reeling is the process of transforming silk cocoons into raw silk, which is then passed on for further processing before being woven into cloth. In Mysore District, discussed here, reeling is mainly a rural occupation with a significant impact on the economy of those villages where it is concentrated. Silkapura and the surrounding villages form one of the highest rural concentrations of reeling enterprises and have experienced relatively successful entrepreneurship development over the past decade or so. By 1989 in Silkapura there were ninety-two registered silk-reelers on official lists. As described in more detail below, the industry requires substantial amounts of capital and involves considerable risk. Nevertheless, much of the expansion in recent years has been in small-scale units, many owned by former labourers, men from the Adi Karnataka Scheduled Caste. Some of these had become relatively affluent and were producing some of the highest-priced silk in the Bangalore Silk Exchange. By 1991 there were signs that this process of expansion was accelerating rather than slowing down (Mayoux, 1993a; Mayoux et al, 1992).

However, although male labourers have been able to become entrepreneurs, the benefits to women have been less clear. In Silkapura an unusually high number of women's names appeared on the list of registered reelers, but on closer investigation units were invariably found to be controlled by men. The units had been registered in women's names in order to get bank loans, either because these were thought likely to be more readily available for women, or because the relevant male family member already had an outstanding loan. Major problems for women were lack of access to adequate resources and restrictions on their movements outside the home, which made the crucial entrepreneurial tasks of moving in the 'male space' of the cocoon and raw silk markets socially unacceptable. Nevertheless, women were in some cases involved in the enterprise as supervisors, whether or not the unit was in their name. However, there were no women supervisors in the larger more successful family establishments, and it seems from interviews that those women who did supervise saw this mainly as a stop-gap measure until the business was prosperous enough for them to retire back into the household. In no case had there been any attempt to train daughters to improve their supervisory and managerial skills, as was frequently done for sons.

On the other hand, as elsewhere in the industry, women form a major part of the labour force: 59 per cent in the units interviewed in the area as a whole, of whom 12 per cent were girls. Most were Scheduled Caste, but some were landless women from middle-status castes. These women were concentrated in the middle- and lower-paid tasks earning Rs5–14 a day, and were prevented by discrimination from moving up to higher-paid 'male' tasks where earnings were Rs20–30 a day.[3] Wages were nevertheless higher than the Rs6 per day women would receive in agriculture. Regularity of work varied between reeling enterprises, being greater in the larger and more successful establishments which ran more or less all year, with double shifts in months of peak cocoon supply. In other units, however, employment could be sporadic and earnings irregular. There were also periodic crises in the industry because of trader boycotts or, as in 1991–92, cocoon disease. During these periods labourers who had worked for particular employers for a long time could take subsistence advances, subsequently deducted from their pay when work resumed, the amounts available depending on the success, as well as the discretion and goodwill, of the employer. Many women, however, had to find alternative employment in agriculture when employment was unavailable.

Nevertheless, despite the problems, for women employed in the larger units at least, earnings were reasonably secure and higher than in agricultural labour. On their own they only just covered subsistence, reckoned in 1991 to be about Rs15 per day for basic food and fuel for a family of husband, wife, and two children. If the family owned its own home and some contribution was made by male wages, women's earnings permitted households or individual women to make some savings. As in the case of Shri Basavaiah discussed below, with prudence, determination and co-operation by family members, labour households could save quite substantial amounts.

For women, however, poverty is a matter not only of income but of the extent to which they can control it. In this area, as in many societies, women's incomes were ideally put into a 'family pool' over which men, as heads of the households, had jurisdiction, women's power being generally limited to saying how much was spent on food, children's clothing and similar items. Major expenditure in areas where women were judged to have some knowledge, such as livestock, or which required diversion of funds from spending on children, would also ideally be discussed jointly. However, business affairs would be conducted by men, and women's opposition could be enforced only by various types of manipulation and 'informal' power.

In labourers' households this same ideal of male control prevailed, yet with a certain amount of consultation; the degree to which women retained control over all or part of their income depended greatly on the relationship between the individual man and woman. In a number of interviews it was found that a significant proportion of such 'family' income was spent by the men on their own luxury expenditure of drinking and gambling. These activities were widely recognized to be a serious drain on the resources of many families in all the caste groups from which female reeling labour was recruited. For example, one labourer interviewed had lost two children through malnutrition, but her husband was still spending a large proportion of the family income on such pursuits. Attempts by the women to dissuade their husband were often met with violence or threats of violence. These problems were seen by the community as a whole as 'private', and little support was given to the women. In other cases women's incomes were taken to further the education of male family members, men's political careers, or other chosen activities. As described below, in some cases where the maintenance of 'ideal' family arrangements was impossible, the women ROSCA members had managed to gain control of their income.

In Silkapura low wages, women's lack of control over their income, and their burden of unpaid work gave them little incentive to enter or stay in the labour market except under extreme necessity and/or when forced to do so by male family members. Those able not to work generally considered themselves fortunate. When family income improved as a result of male family members setting up reeling or other businesses, women generally withdrew from paid labour. This was leading to a shortage of labour with potentially serious consequences for continued expansion of the industry (Mayoux, 1992a).

Women and *Chit* Funds: A Way Out of Poverty and Dependence?

The silk industry as a whole is one of the few where a definite policy to improve life for women has actually been introduced, partly but not only prompted by stipulations attached to loans from the World Bank. Under these loan conditions the Department of Sericulture is required to appoint female staff at all levels, to introduce gender-sensitization, and to prepare an Action Plan for Women's Development. As regards reeling, this has meant that many training schemes previously directed to men are now exclusively for women. Other support for new reeling enterprises is similarly increasingly focusing on women in both the Sericulture Department and other government schemes like the Development of Women and Children in Rural Areas (DWCRA) credit scheme, under which a number of loans have been given for setting up women's reeling co-operatives. However, these schemes have so far yielded few successes, at best resulting in a handful of female entrepreneurs out of thousands of men in Karnataka as a whole. Many of the attempts to set up women's co-operatives failed (Mayoux, 1993b).

Significantly, there is no special legal protection for female labourers, despite the poverty outlined above. Legislation such as minimum wages, maternity provision and pension and insurance rights theoretically applied in the larger establishments, but its enforcement was not encouraged by the Sericulture Department and was consistently opposed at state level by the employers' association. Interviews with male labourers also indicated that the possibility of upward mobility for men has exerted downward pressure on female wages (Mayoux, 1992b). Attempts to unionize women labourers are likely to face considerable resistance, not only from the Sericulture Department and employers but also from male labourers and women's families, in the context of male upward mobility.

In Silkapura the discovery in 1991 of women labourers gaining access to substantial amounts of money through ROSCAs suggested the development of the latter as an alternative way of assisting women to increase their control over their income, and even possibly also their upward mobility to entrepreneurship – seen as the ultimate aim of most development programmes for women in the industry and also by a number of the women labourers interviewed.

Chit Funds and Male Upward Mobility

Chit funds have been extremely important for male entrepreneurs in the expansion of the industry in Silkapura. Reeling entrepreneurship requires substantial amounts of capital, and involves a considerable degree of risk – precisely those factors which make entrepreneurship for the poor difficult if not impossible. Capital is needed to buy machinery, and ideally also to build a shed, purchase cocoons, and meet labour costs and advances. Capital then continues to be required for the purchase of cocoons and to meet the costs of labour (including subsistence advances) and storage of silk when market prices are unfavourable. Moreover, because of the wide fluctuations in profit, capital is required to continue operation whilst sustaining what are on occasion substantial losses. For the smallest viable unit of four basin machines for fine silk production, and working capital (not including sheds), Rs50,000 was needed to operate at a reasonable level of profit with about two weeks' cocoon supply to play the market. With considerably less than this, a few entrepreneurs had managed gradually to work their way up from small-scale intermittent production of coarse-quality silk to larger-scale production of more profitable fine-quality silk. Nevertheless, the availability of credit was seen by most reelers as the key to success, and one of the main reasons why some reelers were successful and others not.

The availability of bank credit in Silkapura had been one of the decisive factors for smaller and poorer reelers setting up business, and one of the main reasons why more male labourers became relatively successful entrepreneurs than in other reeling centres in Karnataka. Obtaining general bank loans was on the whole problematic for poor would-be entrepreneurs, requiring security and involving relatively high rates of interest. Many, however, had received loans under special schemes targeted at disadvantaged and priority groups, in particular the Differential Rate of Interest Scheme (DRI) and the Self-Employment for Educated Youth Programme (SEEUYP). Here references rather than security were required, and interest rates in bank schemes were subsidized.[4] Until 1991, when political interference severely affected loan repayment, the record of repayment was generally good (Mayoux, 1993a; Mayoux et al, 1992). Nevertheless, obtaining such loans was also difficult. For those without contacts applications took a long time, and there were reports of demands for bribes from those required to give reports to the banks. Moreover, the terms of the loans under special schemes were not sufficiently flexible and in a number of cases had been tied to purchase of machinery and/or cocoons. Timing of loans was also often inflexible, depending on when loans were sanctioned. Some reelers had had to take their loans and show receipts at times when it was unprofitable to reel, many getting involved in falsification of documents and bribery in the process.

Informal sources of credit also existed. Many salaried or wealthy people in Silkapura saw money-lending on interest as an easy way to increase their assets, provided the business in which they invested was reliable. They charged high rates of interest and were generally reckoned to be an undesirable source of credit. Although caste was no barrier, and indeed some of those who lent money were Scheduled Caste government servants, some form of surety was necessary for larger amounts such as those required for reeling.[5]

In this context ROSCAs provided a valuable additional source of capital. *Chit* funds have existed in South India since about the beginning of this century (Ardener, 1964:203): they probably came to this area from Madras, of which Kollegal was a part during colonial rule. In other parts of India such *chit* funds have been registered, requiring the keeping of accounts and registers of contributors, the issuing of receipts, and so on (Ardener, ibid.:203; and see Sethi, this volume). The *chit* funds used by reelers in Silkapura are, however, illegal because unregistered, and organizers are unlicensed. The organizations are surrounded by secrecy; they are often used as a way of circulating untaxed income and 'black money'. Many members do not wish others to know that they have joined, and many conduct all operations through the organizer rather than attending meetings. As a consequence, members do not necessarily even know who the other members of the same *chit* fund are. This made it difficult to get detailed information, even after one of the authors of this paper actually joined one of the funds, although two of the organizers were friends of the authors. Some of the details below may therefore differ from those for other *chit* funds which operated in the past or may operate subsequent to the research. In particular the length of time and number of members varied, depending on the wishes of the organizer and of members.

Reelers and organizers interviewed in 1992 estimated that about 70–90 per cent of reelers in 1991 had at some time made use of ROSCAs, and their use appeared to be increasing all the time. In June–July 1992 there were five such associations operating for take-outs of Rs50,000, Rs20,000, Rs10,000, Rs5,000 and Rs3,000, all with twenty members and operating over a period of twenty months. The funds were set up by the organizers, who approached a number of people whom they considered suitable. The organizers at this time were all male teachers, and all were landless except the organizer of the largest fund, who had five acres of land. Organizers of the three largest funds were upper caste, and those of the two smaller ones were Christian.

Members of each fund came from a variety of castes and a range of occupations, so that they had differing credit needs. Reelers wishing to use the funds for productive investment in reeling itself need to join *chit* funds, as do others with differing credit needs. Reeling profits are highest at particular times of the year because of market fluctuations, and thus funds composed only of reelers would have all the credit demand concentrated in certain months. However, reelers could and did use the fund for other purposes also. Common combinations were government servants on relatively high but fixed incomes, reelers with varying profit levels who obtained high returns in favourable conditions, shopkeepers and the like. Labourers were involved in other funds for lesser amounts.

Rotation was decided by discount bidding. For example, the functioning of the Rs10,000 *chit* fund was explained as follows: in the first month all members would contribute Rs500. A member in great need of money would offer to accept a discount of, say, Rs3,000, and if no one else offered to accept a bigger discount, would thus receive Rs7,000. From the remaining Rs3,000 the agent would take 3 per cent commission, and the remaining Rs2,700 would be divided among the members, giving each Rs135 which would subsidize their contribution the following month. The fund would thus continue, usually with later recipients getting larger amounts as the competition decreased. It was said that those with lucrative sources of investment generally drew first, and those using the fund as a source of savings for such items as house improvement or dowry tended to draw last. The responsibility to ensure that all members paid lay with the organizer, who had to pay any defaults, and this was seen as justifying the commission. As the whole business was secret, community pressure was difficult to apply, but defaulters were unlikely to be asked to join any other *chit* fund. The organizers were generally well known to members, and although in the past one or two cases had occurred of organizers absconding with funds, default was very rare. In any case, risk was not confined to this particular type of savings organization (see below).

Many of the large- and medium-scale reelers obtained sums of Rs10,000 or more from paying monthly amounts of Rs500 upwards. Smaller reelers were involved in smaller funds. Male labourers moving up the ladder to entrepreneurship generally obtained credit from several different sources, credit from one source being an indication of reputation and reliability when applying for credit from another. One example was former labourer Shri Basavaiah, now one of the most successful Scheduled Caste entrepreneurs in Silkapura. Both he and his wife had worked as labourers since childhood, and Shri Basavaiah had been able to move up the promotional ladder to supervisor in a large reeling unit. Between them they had been able from their work to save Rs4,000, with which in 1983 they set up 2 *charkhas* (small coarse-reeling machines). Then in 1985 they succeeded in obtaining a bank loan of Rs15,000, and set up 6 *basins* (fine-quality reeling-machines); this loan they supplemented with Rs10,000 from a *chit* fund for working capital. In 1988 they borrowed a further Rs10,000 from a moneylender, and combined this with profits to build a proper shed. By 1991 Shri Basavaiah was producing some of the highest-priced silk in the Bángalore Silk Exchange, and was again a member of a *chit* fund to raise money towards building a second reeling unit in his sister's name.

Women and *Chit* Funds: Some Case Studies

For poor women obtaining credit is even harder than for poor men, because of lack of resources, prejudice in the lending agencies, and power relations in the family. In times of hardship women could and did borrow money from moneylenders if they had jewellery to leave as security. Most poor women, however, had very little property of this type, and as noted above interest rates were very high. Even though the bank was close by, women were very unlikely to get general loans because of the security required. Women were eligible for loans under all the special schemes, some like IRDP even having a target quota of 30 per cent for women, and others like DWCRA being exclusively for women. Nevertheless, as noted above, although a number of bank loans for reeling were in women's names, they had invariably been obtained and used by men. All the DWCRA reeling co-operatives in the area studied had failed, or were run by men using their wives as labourers (Mayoux, 1992c). Such loans were available only for entrepreneurship development, and as in the case of men were insufficient for this purpose and had to be combined with credit from other sources.

A number of savings and insurance schemes operated for women in Silkapura at various times. These all either involved relatively small amounts of money or had proved risky. About thirty women reeling labourers from the Scheduled Castes belonged to a Savings Society called 'Women's Association *Chit* Fund' (*Sanghada Chit*). This was a standard type of savings club exclusively for women, supervised by a voluntary organization in the nearby town and using the Silkapura Bank for deposits. However, the savings amounts were small and the maturation period long.[6] One well-meaning reeling entrepreneur who had wished to encourage savings and security for his female employees set himself up as an agent for the Life Insurance Corporation (LIC). A number of his workers joined this scheme[7] and gave regular sums from their earnings. However, when his business got into trouble during a period of cocoon disease he was not able to give his labourers work, and all the policies lapsed, much to the bitterness of the women. In general, savings schemes were treated with extreme suspicion because of the danger of the organizer absconding with funds, as had happened in a number of other cases, and outside organizations were suspect because of rumours of corruption. More formal types of savings schemes over a long period were seen as being too inflexible and risky because of possible problems of repayment, as in the case of the LIC scheme.

In this context, despite their risks, *chit* funds were seen as offering a flexible system of savings and credit run by people known to the participants over whom some degree of control could therefore be exercised. Exactly when women began to join the *chit* funds is unclear, and as with everything surrounding the funds precise investigation was difficult because of the secrecy and illegality of their operation. It is, however, definitely a very recent phenomenon, and may have begun with a few professional women teachers in the village who had male relatives already involved in *chit* funds. Even more recently, since 1989, some female reeling labourers began to join various of the funds. In June–July 1992 there were at least eight women *chit* fund members. One was a Christian nurse (salary Rs2,000 per month) separated from her husband who joined the *chit* fund for Rs10,000. It was run by an upper-caste man, an ex-student of her mother's. The other seven women were members of a Rs3,000 *chit* fund run by a man from the same community. Of these, one was the president of the women's tailoring co-operative in Silkapura who had joined with her husband, and another was a housewife who secretly saved from the housekeeping money her husband gave her.

The remaining five were landless reeling labourers, all Christians, one of them from a Scheduled Caste, all of whom worked for the employer mentioned above who had introduced the LIC scheme. As can be seen from Appendix 1, these five labourers came from a variety of family backgrounds. One was an older unmarried woman; another was a widow. Both these women were the main income-earners of their families and were in control of their incomes. One of the three married women and her husband had joined the fund together. For all these women *chit* funds were important as a source of savings and credit for relatively large expenses such as education fees, house maintenance and repair, the purchase of jewellery for a daughter's marriage, and so on. The other two married women had both joined without the knowledge or consent of their husbands, both of whom drank heavily and were a considerable drain on family resources. For both these women the fund was an important secret way of saving and keeping money; their ultimate aim was to start some sort of business to get a more reliable income.

The vital role of *chit* funds in giving some very poor women access to lump sums to improve their situation is illustrated by the case of Shanthamma. She joined several such funds, and appears to have been the first labourer in Silkapura to do so. In 1991 she was working as a reeling labourer earning Rs15 daily. Her husband was working for the same employer, but in the better paid task of rewinding, earning Rs25 a day. They had two children, both of whom went to school. Her husband's drinking was a major problem. For some time he had worked in Tamil Nadu for much higher wages but had been forced to come back after hurting his leg when drunk. Family income arrangements were a matter of frequent dispute and constant negotiation. When interviewed in 1991 the husband was paid weekly, and from his weekly income of Rs150–175 he spent Rs25–27 for the family's supply of the staple diet *ragi* (millet). The rest he spent on smoking, drinking, and occasional purchases of clothes for himself and his family. He commonly spent Rs15 a day on drink – the equivalent of all Shanthamma's earnings. He had received advances from the employer, putting the family in debt, but Shanthamma did not know to what extent because he refused to tell her. When interviewed again later in 1992 he was not working because the reeling unit was closed and he had not sought alternative employment because of ill-health caused by drinking. Shanthamma felt she could do nothing to prevent him drinking: if she said anything to him, there were serious arguments and he beat her. She said that she could not expect any help from the community leaders because most of the other men behaved in the same way.

In spite of threats of violence, however, Shanthamma had stopped giving her income to her husband but was saving what she could to use for the family's other food needs and her children's education. In 1991 work was quite regular, and with her savings, an interest-free loan of Rs3,000 from her employer, and one of Rs600 from her father-in-law, a sympathetic and religious man, she had managed over a period of two or three years to build a house on her father-in-law's land. Her husband had given her Rs300 towards the house, and when there was no reeling work had done some of the work on it, for which she paid him Rs5 a day. She had also taken a Life Insurance Corporation policy from the employer mentioned above, as she had been anxious to have some savings for her old age; but as noted above this lapsed when work stopped in 1992.

She was secretly a member of *chit* funds for a number of years. She drew Rs850 from one, and Rs1,200 from a second, using the money towards building the house and paying for amenities such as lighting. In late 1991 she joined another *chit* fund for Rs3,000. Even after reeling work stopped in 1992 and she became dependent on lower-paid agricultural labour, she was able, without any formalities, to join forces with another woman with whom she had worked, so that she could continue to pay into the fund. She was intending to use the money for clothes for the children for Christmas, and for house-building and repair. Much of the money would, however, go in general household expenses because of closure of the reeling unit. In future she had plans, on the basis of her reputation for ability to save and improve her situation, to get a bank loan and instal four reeling basins, so that both she and her sister could be assured of work.

Thus for Shanthamma *chit* funds were an important part of a savings strategy which gave her access to quite substantial sums of money for about Rs2-3 a day. Importantly, it was a form of savings and credit which she was able to obtain without her husband's knowledge or consent in a situation of poverty and family violence over which she had very little control. The money helped her to build and maintain her own house, and educate and clothe her children. This, however, is only part of a strategy, and is dependent on a reasonably regular source of income.

All the women interviewed (see Appendix 1), despite their problems and the fact that they could not always predict when money could be drawn, saw *chit* funds as a reliable and flexible form of savings and credit compared to the other options available. They felt that their money was reasonably accessible if they needed it, although they might receive a little less than they paid in. They trusted the organizers, who were well known to them. The savings period was also relatively short, and for a much larger amount than the Women's Association Chit Fund mentioned above.

Possibilities for Development? Some Problems and Questions

Chit funds thus have a number of advantages over other sources of credit and savings, giving women access to relatively large amounts of cash to use as they wish, with no questions asked provided they are able to continue to pay their instalments. These advantages and the fact that women labourers are already repeatedly using them indicates that they fulfil some of their needs. The question then arises, in the context of attempts to assist women within the industry, whether and how such benefits could be increased and/or extended to more women. In the context of the wider aims and sensitivities of development agencies in the industry, the development of such funds are more likely to be a viable and relatively uncontroversial measure than other possible solutions for women, such as unionization and the establishment of more explicitly feminist organizations. However, as many attempts to develop women's informal savings and credit organizations elsewhere have often been at best unsuccessful and at worst completely disruptive of their solidarity and support networks, such an intervention must obviously be considered with the utmost care.

A number of questions and potential problems surround their development by outside agencies as part of wider sectoral strategies. First, the local funds are currently illegal and agent-led, and any attempt at development would involve regulation and registration of some sort. Although this might extend the numbers of women involved beyond the narrow circle of acquaintances of organizers, and be less subject to prejudice, such measures would also make the funds more public, and jeopardize the secrecy so important for the two poorest women above. Second, the funds give women access to larger amounts of money than are usually accessible under formal women's schemes, and as in the case of Shanthamma involve informal arrangements between members for repayment. Funds introduced by outside agencies might need greater regulation to ensure repayment and to offer lower amounts, thus being less flexible and responsive to women's needs. Third, given the wider aims of development and the complex nature of women's poverty and disadvantage, it would obviously be desirable to add social, consciousness-raising, and/or educational activities to the economic activities. Again, it is not clear how this could be done without jeopardizing their secrecy. Such issues would need to be discussed with the women involved, covering all the possible options, but provided this is done and women's ability to join the existing organizations is not impaired, such development could be a valuable part of wider policy to assist women labourers in the industry, and also in others where women have a reasonably stable source of income.

Although such *chit* funds can be an important part of wider sectoral employment strategies, they are not in themselves sufficient if the aim is ultimately to develop women's entrepreneurship potential. In reeling and many other industries *chit* funds would need to be combined with other sources of credit if women (and men) were to have access to significant amounts of capital. However, there are ways in which this could be done in the Indian context, particularly with banks and insurance schemes. *Chit* funds would also need to be combined with other measures to yield improvements in women's position within industries – in the case of silk reeling, increased training opportunities and changes in the marketing system to enable women to take over higher-paid male labouring jobs and organize their own marketing. Significant change in women's position to increase their access to resources for investment in *chit* funds also ultimately requires more fundamental 'feminist' intervention aimed at wider structural gender inequalities. Whether or not such organizational developments could arise of their own accord from the organization of women's credit and savings groups remains to be seen.

Wages have not risen above subsistence levels even for skilled and experienced female workers, despite considerable expansion of the industry, and the disparity between male and female wages has increased in recent years. Whereas wages for predominantly female tasks are fixed at village levels, those for better-paid male tasks are negotiated on an individual level by labourers. Village-level wage rates are negotiated by men, and male labourers with aspirations to upward mobility do not see high female wages as in their future interest (Mayoux, 1992b). Moreover any suggestion of independent female organization was considered as contravening norms of male authority which was as rigorously supported by male labourers as by other men. Thus attempts at unionization of women labourers, though desirable, were likely to face considerable opposition at all levels.

Family Background and *Chit* Funds: Details of the Five Reeling Labourers Interviewed

DODDAMMA: Scheduled Caste; illiterate
Family situation: Age 45. Widow with no children. Living with, and helping maintain, her aged mother and lame, unmarried sister, with some help from married brothers living separately.
Control of income: Madamma controls the family income.
Other savings: None at bank. LIC scheme.
Previous *chit* fund: -
Current *chit* fund: Contributes jointly with one other woman. Intends to use the money for house repairs.

SHANTHAMMA: Christian; illiterate
Family situation: Age 35. Married with two children. Husband (rewinder) earns Rs25 per day, works irregularly because of drink.
Control of income: She controls her own income (see text).
Other savings: None at bank. LIC scheme.
Previous *chit* funds: Two (see text). Used money for building and house amenities.
Current *chit* fund: Joined without the knowledge of her husband. Now contributes jointly with Mariamma (below), paying Rs75 per month. Intends to use money for Christmas celebration for the children, and house-painting and repairs. Wants to use future *chit* fund for setting up a reeling unit.

VENKATAMMA: Christian; illiterate
Family situation: Age 35. Unmarried. Lives with mother aged 50, an agricultural labourer, and three younger brothers. Of these two are studying and one is dumb.
Control of income: Venkatamma controls the family income.
Other savings: None at bank. LIC scheme.
Previous *chit* funds: Rs3,000. Used the money for father's medical treatment and funeral.
Current *chit* fund: Joined with mother's consent. Intends to use this and future *chit* funds for brother's education.

MARIAMMA: Christian; illiterate
Family situation: Age 32. Married with two daughters and one son. Husband is a labourer with no regular work. They both take in clothes to mend, and rent out some of the rooms of their house to other poor families. Husband drinks heavily.
Control of income: She controls the family income because of her husband's drinking.
Other savings: None at the bank. LIC scheme.
Previous *chit* fund: Rs 3,000. Used the money for house repairs.
Current *chit* fund: Joined without husband's knowledge. Used rent money. Already drawn money for daughter's training. Intends to use future *chit* fund money for daughters' education and to set up a cycle shop for her husband to work in. Now contributing jointly with Shanthamma above.

SIDDAMMA: Christian; Class 3
Family situation: Age 25 years. Married with three children. Husband reeling supervisor.
Control of income: Husband controls the income but consults her; he does not drink.
Other savings: None
Previous *chit* fund: Rs1,000 used for family subsistence, as reeling work was stopped.
Current *chit* fund: Joined with her husband. Intends to use for daughters' jewellery or to purchase a house site.

Notes

1. These issues are discussed in *World Development 1989*, particularly the articles by McKee and Tendler. The successes and problems of credit provision by SEWA and WWF are discussed in Everett and Savara (1987).
2. The background research for this article was conducted between August 1989 and June 1991 as part of a research project on the silk reeling industry funded by the Economic and Social Research Council, UK, and supported academically by Glasgow University, UK, and the Institute of Social and Economic Research, Bangalore. The bulk of the material for this article, however, comes from an independent study by the authors in July–August 1991 and June–July 1992.

3. The gender division of labour and wage differentials are discussed in more detail in Mayoux et al, 1992; Mayoux, 1992a,c. Women were concentrated in cocoon cooking (81 per cent of labourers) and reeling itself (76 per cent of labourers), for which in Silkapura they were paid Rs12–14 per day. They were also numerous in quality control (70 per cent) and cocoon sorting (69 per cent) for which they were paid between Rs5 and Rs10 per day. They were totally excluded from highly-paid 'male tasks' of rewinding, stifling and supervising, for which men earned Rs20–30 a day.
4. The normal bank interest rate in 1991 was 13 per cent p.a. Under the DRI Scheme the interest rate was 4 per cent for eligible groups. Under SEEUYP it was 10 per cent p.a. with a 25 per cent subsidy.
5. Interest rates varied depending on individual agreement, but a figure commonly mentioned was 10 per cent monthly if security was offered. Unsecured loans carried a higher interest rate, were only available for small amounts and were expected to be repaid in a shorter time.
6. For twelve months each member pays in Rs20 per month, totalling Rs240. After one year these savings are matched by funds from a Christian charity, to make Rs480. Of this, Rs400 is given to the members and the remaining Rs80 put in a fixed deposit. After three years the amount is repaid to the woman with interest.
7. The Life Insurance Corporation (LIC) offers a number of different schemes, including endowment policies under which the policy-holder is eligible for a loan after three years, a 'money bank' policy, under which 20 per cent or 15 per cent of the interest is paid once in five years, and a whole life policy under which the money is paid to a specific party on the policy-holder's death. Interest on loans under this scheme vary, depending on the amount and purpose, between 10.5 per cent and 13 per cent.

References

Ardener, S. (1964), 'The Comparative Study of Rotating Credit Associations.' *Journal of the Royal Anthropological Institute*, XCIV (2): 201–29.
Everett, J. and Savara, M. (1987), 'Institutional Credit as a Strategy Towards Self-reliance for Petty Commodity Producers in India: A Critical Evaluation' in *Invisible Hands: Women in Home-based Production*, A.M. Singh and A. Kelles-Viitanen (eds), New Delhi and London: Sage.
Mayoux, L.C. (1992a), 'Women Reeling Labourers in Kollegal Taluk, Karnataka: A Statistical Profile and Some Issues for Research', *Indian Silk*, February, pp. 1–4.
—— (1992b), *Entrepreneurship and Inequality: A Social Profile of a Scheduled Caste Reeling Community in Kollegal Taluk, Karnataka*, Mimeo.
—— (1992c), *Who Gets the Trickle Down? Gender Inequality and Development in an Indian Industry*, Mimeo.

—— (1993a), 'A Development Success Story? Poverty and Entrepreneurship Development in an Indian Industry' in *Development and Change*, vol. 24: 541–68.

—— (1993b), 'Gender Inequality and Entrepreneurship: Some Issues from the South Indian Silk Industry' in *Development Policy Review*, December.

——, Uma Shankar, V. and Anand, Shri (1992), 'From Rags to Riches? Poverty Alleviation and Development in the Karnataka Silk Reeling Industry', *Indian Silk*, February, pp. 6–26.

World Development (1989), 17 (7). Special Issue on Women's Income Generation, proceedings of Symposium on Expanding Income Earning Opportunities for Women in Poverty: A Cross-Regional Dialogue, Nairobi, 1–5 May 1988.

PART III

Diasporas

12

ROSCAs among South Asians in Oxford

Shaila Srinivasan

This article deals with the prevalence and continuing importance of ROSCAs among the South Asians in the city of Oxford, especially, nowadays, the women. By South Asian is meant essentially those who have migrated from India, Pakistan and Bangladesh. Though it is convenient to speak of national groups such as 'Indians', 'Pakistanis' and 'Bangladeshis', national origin does not appear to be crucial where the formation of rotating credit associations is concerned. Linguistic and regional groupings within the South Asian population seem to be more significant in the genesis of ROSCAs. Of the two groups discussed below, one consists of Punjabi speakers deriving from the northern regions of the sub-continent and the other of Malayalam speakers originating from the extreme south. The Punjabi-speaking group includes Indians as well as Pakistanis, and though this group is predominantly Pakistani Muslim, it also includes Punjabi-speaking Hindus and Sikhs from India, while excluding the Bengali-speaking Muslims from Bangladesh (who were not included in my survey). The second group is predominantly Malayalee Christian but includes a few Malayalam-speaking Hindus and Muslims from the state of Kerala. Thus neither group is homogeneous in religious affiliation, both including Hindus, Muslims and Christians.

The Nature of the Study

The evidence on which this article is based was collected in the course of a survey of Asian shop-keepers and restaurant owners in Oxford.[1] The survey, carried out between September 1989 and May 1990, involved lengthy interviews with owners of small businesses and their family members, and achieved an almost total coverage of the Asian business population. In the early stages of the study, when information regarding the Asians in Oxford was being sought, contact was also made with a small number of Malayalee families in East Oxford. It was found that there were no owners of small businesses amongst them. However, contact with these families was maintained as the researcher, herself a Malayalee from Kerala State, was warmly welcomed into the group. An important form of social interaction within these families was found to be that of the *kuri* (or ROSCA), and one such gathering was attended by the researcher.

Asians in Oxford

The South Asian minorities in Oxford, according to the 1991 census, make up 4.6 per cent of the population of the city; this figure includes 1,541 Indians, 2,092 Pakistanis, 550 Bangladeshis and 881 'other Asians'.[2] Pakistanis thus form the biggest proportion of the Asian population in Oxford, though in Britain as a whole the Indians are the largest Asian group. Their main areas of settlement in the city are East and West Oxford. On the basis of the usual indicators of general housing conditions, including house ownership, and car ownership, the socio-economic status of Asian households compares well with that of all households in Oxford. According to the 1991 census results, the proportion living in owner-occupied housing is the same in both groups. Car ownership is slightly higher among the Asians, and the percentage of households lacking or sharing a bath or inside toilet is about the same in both groups. The main concentrations by occupation are in the bus companies and the car factory. Asians are also to be found in self-employment: they are over-represented in small business ownership, in so far as they constitute only 4.6 per cent of the population but own 12 per cent of the small shops and restaurants in Oxford.

It was this proclivity for business enterprise that prompted my initial interest in ROSCAs. Any attempt to explain the success of business enterprise among certain ethnic groups such as the South Asian ones, as against the lack of it among other ethnic groups such as the West Indian, had to take into account cultural institutions, such as those providing for savings and credit, within the ethnic communities. The role of such economic institutions, which certain groups bring from their country of origin, has been stressed by Light (1972) in his seminal work explaining the over-representation in small business, especially retail trade, of Chinese and Japanese in the United States. Correspondingly, the lack of such institutions among the blacks in the United States, and hence their inability to overcome discrimination in lending practices by banks, is, according to Light, an important factor in their low involvement in business. Evidence of the use of ROSCAs to set up businesses in Britain is provided by Werbner (1981) in her study of Pakistanis in the clothing industry in Manchester. It must, however, be pointed out that though similar institutions are to be found among the West Indians in Britain (Davison describes the 'pardner jackpot' among Jamaicans; 1966:96, 102–3), it does not appear to have encouraged small business activity among them here (Foner, 1977:132). Light (1972:32–6), however, has attributed the business success of West Indians in New York to their participation in ROSCAs, known as 'partners'.

Culturally specific economic institutions such as ROSCAs continue to flourish among Asian migrants in Oxford, but are no longer regarded as an important factor in business start-up. Like pooling of capital, friendly loans, and so on, they appear to have been looked upon as an accepted ethnic resource in the initial stages of Asian business activity. Once businesses are established, however, there is a certain reluctance to draw on this ethnic resource, more formal sources of finance being preferred. The present survey revealed no dependence on these institutions for start-up capital. While respondents did not deny the existence of ROSCAs among the Asian migrant population, they maintained that it was mainly the women who were members of such associations, and that it was not prevalent among the business owners, who were largely male. According to them, the sums of money that changed hands were too small to be of much use in business activity. They also maintained that today there is no difficulty in obtaining loans from banks for business start-up, 81 per cent of respondents having started their businesses with loans from banks. They did, however, admit that in the early stages of immigrant settlement and Asian business activity interest-free loans were obtained through rotating savings and credit associations called *kametis*. This is corroborated by Shaw's 1979–1983 study of Pakistanis in Oxford. She maintains that in the 1960s Pakistani men who moved to East Oxford bought their houses outright. An important reason for this was that *kametis* enabled men to pay for their houses in cash rather than by taking out mortgages. She continues: '[the rotating] form of credit is still used in East Oxford although *kametis* are now mainly organised by women. The sums involved are often quite large. If, for instance, twenty women each pay £20 per week, each woman, when it is her turn, will receive £400. This provides a useful sum for the down payment for a house or a shop' (Shaw, 1988:51). These people are Punjabi speakers.

The nature of the rotating credit institutions found within this group is now described.

Kameti among the Punjabis

The working of the institution called *kameti* is referred to as *parchi katna* or *cutting chits*. Within the Pakistani community in Oxford today three or four women are known to be the organizers of *chit* funds, each of them organizing three or four different ones, so that practically every Pakistani woman is a member of a *kameti*, and will have at least one *chit* 'cut' and often two or three in her name. Many Indian Punjabi women, too, join these *kametis*. A woman who is already a member of one ROSCA may, if requested by a friend who is organizing another, become a member of the second one as well, if she feels able to meet the payments.

Any particular *chit* fund is started with a list of a determinate number of women, all personally known to the organizer, who have agreed to pay a fixed amount, usually £25, into the fund every week. The amount to be paid, the duration for which the fund is to run, and the date of payment to each woman are decided when the list is drawn up. The duration of course depends on the number of *chits* that are 'cut'. For instance, if fifty-two *chits* are 'cut', the ROSCA will run for fifty-two weeks. The number of actual members may well be less than this, as a woman may have more than one *chit* 'cut' in her name.

Members decide by consensus when they would like to get paid, though there is a certain flexibility in this to allow for emergency needs. One of the women in this survey was a member of a *kameti* with fifty-two *chits*, of which she had three in her name. As the weekly amount was £25, she was paying £75 a week into the fund. She had asked for repayment during three consecutive weeks in the month prior to her daughter's wedding. As each *chit* was worth £1,300,[3] she would have the substantial amount of £3,900 to contribute to the wedding expenses. Usually every member anticipates some heavy expenditure, such as a trip back home, the marriage of a daughter or the admission of a child to a private school, and will request repayment according to the expected time of such needs. But if any member is in urgent need of money due to some emergency, such as the death of a family member whose body has to be flown back home, unexpected hospital expenses, or even an unexpected celebration, the *kameti* organizer will ensure that it is paid out of turn to the person in need. The woman whose turn it actually should be is persuaded to give it up for the person in need, and a satisfactory readjustment is brought about.

This is where the organizer has a crucial role to play: so much so that members often feel that the headaches involved in running a fund far outweigh its advantages (which are discussed below). It is the organizer who has to make sure that members keep up their weekly payments and pay on time (usually by the Monday of each week or Tuesday morning at the latest). Women whose contributions fall due may have to face a visit from an irate organizer, reprimanding them for late payment. This, however, is extremely rare, as just the fear of such a humiliating visit apparently suffices to ensure prompt payment. The organizer also has to keep a record of the *chits* that have been paid out, those that remain to be paid, and the times of payment.

Despite these 'headaches', however, a woman wanting, for instance, to put down a deposit on a house may organize a fund on condition that the first payment goes to her, and may 'cut' say five *chits* in her own name. She thus obtains £6,500 without having to apply to a bank for a loan and without having to pay interest. Of course, the cost she has to pay is the management of the fund for the rest of its duration.

The element of trust plays an important part in the functioning of a ROSCA, in that each woman who collects the lump sum is trusted to continue paying in the weekly contributions until all the members have collected their dues. No receipts are taken or given by the organizer for the lump sum paid out or for the weekly contributions paid in. The question 'what if someone does not pay?' gets little response, as non-payment is practically unheard of. While the ROSCA is a business association, those who join it are usually known to each other, involved in many other social activities, and reliant on each other for mutual aid and support. The fact that there is more than an economic relationship between members of the ROSCA contributes to the lack of apprehension regarding non-payment. Social ties act as safeguards against default: respondents feel there would be too much 'shame' involved, they would not be able to hold up their heads in the community, would not be asked to join a ROSCA again, and all this is too big a price to pay.

As noted above, in Oxford the basis of ROSCAs, interestingly, appears to be neither national origin nor religious background but gender (sometimes) and spoken language. Thus the present survey found that Punjabi-speaking Indian Hindus and Pakistani Muslim women unite in the formation of ROSCAs, while Bengali speakers from Bangladesh and Malayalam speakers from South India have their own credit associations. Both the northern and southern groups maintained that speaking the same language allowed members to feel more comfortable with and to trust one another, making it easier for them to unite in a ROSCA. While in theory there were no restrictions on different-language speakers joining a ROSCA, in fact the sort of friendship bonds underlying ROSCA functioning were found only among those who spoke the same language. The business of the ROSCA was usually conducted in the ethnic language, though all the members of the southern group and most of the members of the northern group were fluent English speakers as well. The ROSCA, then, appears to be one instance of social group interaction among Asian migrants in Oxford where ethnicity remains an important factor. Ethnic ties, narrowly defined in terms of regional origin and language and overriding religious and national origin, form the basis of the ROSCAs.

It is interesting to note that for the Punjabi-speakers *kameti* activity does not in itself have a social aspect, in that the women do not get together for food, drinks and a gossip session, as is quite common in many forms of ROSCA in other groups. Members simply ensure that payments reach the organizer before the Tuesday of every week. This job is often carried out by the husbands, who are more mobile. Women who are neighbours may collect their payments and send them off through one of the husbands. There seems to be no attempt to maintain secrecy about *kameti* membership or funds, but *kameti* money is cash over which the woman has control. While she may co-operate with her husband to use the money for family needs or even business purposes, *kameti* money is regarded as the woman's to do with as she pleases. The migrant culture generally ensures that the money is put to constructive use and not frittered away. The Punjabi-speaking women of Oxford see *kameti* payments as compulsory but effortless saving. As one of the women put it:

> If I was saving in a bank, I could miss paying in for a week or two if I wanted to spend money on some unnecessary thing. But I cannot do that with the *kameti* – I *have* to make the payment so I budget my money and don't waste money buying things I don't need – I just don't spend money unnecessarily.

Kameti payments come out of money for household expenses, which the women feel they would normally spend if it did not go into the *kameti*. 'Who would go running to the bank every week with £25?', is a question many women ask. Lack of the interest which would accrue from a bank is not looked upon as a disadvantage of the *kameti* – 'There is neither benefit nor loss . . .' is how these women put it. Though they do not get interest, the capital is safe. The *kameti* also has a certain insurance value, in that in the event of a domestic emergency, a lump sum is often available virtually immediately[4] without the need to apply for a bank loan or pay the very high rates of interest charged by banks for small loans.

The *Kuri* among the Malayalees

Unlike the Punjabi-speaking group, for the Malayalees the meeting of the ROSCA, or *kuri*, is a social occasion. Members get together, usually at the organizer's residence, and partake of refreshments provided by the organizer before getting down to the serious business of the *kuri* or *chitti*. The *kuri* varies from the simple form where the names of members are written on slips of paper, a child being called on to pick out a slip with the winner's name on it, to the more complex form where members bid for the fund. In all forms the number of members, the sum of money, and the duration is fixed for any one cycle. The Malayalee families in Oxford have at some time or another participated in all the different types of the *kuri*. According to one informant, when a *kuri* is first started it might begin in the simplest form. If that *kuri* round was completed successfully without hitches or problems, and the same group wanted to continue for another round, the *kuri* could become more complex, contributions being increased and bidding being introduced.

In the one I attended, there were twelve members who met monthly, paid £500 into the fund, and then bid for the collective amount of £6,000. At the first meeting there was no bidding, as the total amount without any discount went to the organizer. At the second meeting the member most in need of the money bid for the £6,000, offering a discount (possibly of about £50). Another member could have bid a higher discount if considering her need to be greater. While in one association the bidding was known on one occasion to reach a record discount of £500,[5] it usually stops at a discount of around £100, the successful bidder then getting £5,900 from a fund of £6,000. The remaining £100 (the discount) is divided among the other eleven members, so that in this form of *kuri* there is the excitement of the possibility of some extra profit. The profit is substantial for the person who collects at the end of a round when again there is no discount; he or she would also have collected the bonus at ten earlier meetings. Also the person who collects first continues to get the bonus at the following meetings, so that for the first and last collectors there is a form of 'interest', often higher than that offered by a bank. The 'interest', however is envisaged as a 'bonus' rather than a levied interest. The *kuri* is regarded as making financial sense, not in terms of its investment value, but as a means of obtaining interest-free loans, for which a bank would charge very high rates of interest.

To what use is *kuri* money put? While the Malayalees mention the same ones as the Punjabi speakers, such as weddings, trips home, down-payments on houses, house improvements, cars and other consumer items, an important difference is the greater use by the Malayalee group of 'NRI' or Non-Resident accounts in Indian banks. These provide tax-free savings in sterling in Indian banks. Term deposits are free of wealth tax, and interest is free of income tax. The Malayalees from South India living in Oxford often use their *kuri* funds to start term deposits, or simply remit into NRI accounts. Banks in Britain have no attraction for investment purposes for either group, but for different reasons. The Punjabi-speaking group has, on the whole, a more entrepreneurial bent; for them the sort of money growth available from a bank is not at all attractive: their investment money is tied up in ventures from which they can expect much bigger gains. The Malayalees are not involved in such business ventures, and are quite happy to save in banks, but hesitate to approach British banking institutions for various reasons. According to one of the women respondents:

> If you save in a bank here they will ask a hundred and one questions as to where does the money come from, how have you got it, and so on . . . and you also have to pay tax on your savings. [English] people here will go to pubs every evening, eat out, buy expensive clothes, but think that £3,000 or so in a bank account is a big sum. Look at any claim for benefits . . . they want to know how much you have in your bank! And if you have more than £3,000, your chances of getting anything are poor. You work hard to save and then you're penalized for saving! So I prefer to keep my money in a *chitti* – even if I don't get any interest, no questions are asked.

Another important factor in the greater use of NRI accounts by the Malayalees is the continuing influence of the celebrated 'myth of return' amongst them. Though many *kuri* members have been participating in the Oxford *kuri* for more than sixteen years, and have British citizenship, they still think in terms of a return to South India at some time in the future. At least within the Punjabi-speaking entrepreneurial group studied, belief in eventual return to the country of origin was largely absent. As mentioned earlier, the southern group did not include owners of small businesses. The majority of this group, even while admitting that the actual number of returnees within the community was limited, were still governed in their actions by the thought of eventual return to South India. 'You never know . . . you may have to go back', is a feeling expressed by many. In view of this, it is felt that there is greater security in saving in an NRI account which can be operated from 'home' as well.

In the Malayalee group, while women play an active role, both men and women are present and participate jointly, husbands and wives often accepting part ownership of a share. It is usually a man, however, who takes on the organization of the *kuri*, the calling of bids, the choice of members and so on. This is evidently different from the *kameti*, where it is the women who organize and run it, the men playing only a supportive role in the background. Certain tentative explanations could be offered for this, which it must be admitted are impressionistic. One is that the Malayalee women in Oxford are better educated than those from the north of India, and are all employed outside the home, as secretaries, shop assistants, nurses, or in similar jobs. Their economic contribution to the household usually compares well with that of their husbands engaged in factory labour. Their relationship with their men appears to be more overtly egalitarian. Secondly, Malayalee men in Oxford are not as financially secure as those who speak Punjabi, so that they could be considered to be at an earlier stage of financial consolidation, when ROSCAs appear to have greater significance for men. This would tie in with the fact that the men of the northern group were also members of ROSCAs in the 1960s, when they were consolidating their position in Oxford.

Finally, ROSCAs may be seen as indicative of the continuing significance, within certain contexts, of ethnicity and ethnic solidarity in the migrant communities. ROSCAs only flourish because close friendships and social networks based on mutual trust continue to be confined to narrowly defined linguistic and regional groups. Even while one may speak of a pan-Asian consciousness at certain levels, at the level of the ROSCA the divisions within the Asian group become clear, linguistic ties appearing to be the predominant determinants. It is interesting to note the greater autonomy of women in the organization of *kameti* among the less literate Punjabi-speaking women than among the better-educated Malayalee women, who are more comfortable in mixed company, participating with men in *kuri* organized by men. Certainly this study of ROSCAs highlights the cultural differences between the two linguistic groups, each with its own historical background. Even if the Punjabi speakers become more educated, we cannot predict with certainty that gender relations will be sufficiently affected to replicate the current position in the Malayalee community. It will be interesting to see whether ROSCAs will continue to play different roles in the two communities and how women will be affected.

Notes

1. The survey was the basis of a D.Phil thesis on the Asian petty bourgeoisie in Britain.
2. Not including the Chinese.
3. That is, £25 multiplied by 52.
4. Even individuals who have already collected have been known to receive the lump sum again in the event of an emergency, much depending on the ingenuity of the organizer, who may herself advance the money and make sure that accounts are settled in a second round. This was true of the southern group as well.
5. The man who did so was uniformly castigated for 'being silly', 'just wanting to win a point', and so on. The individual concerned was also present when all this was being said. He simply shrugged his shoulders and maintained that he was determined to take the money home that day.

References

Davison, R.B. (1966), *Black British*, London: Oxford University Press.

Foner, N. (1977), 'The Jamaicans: Cultural and Social Change among Migrants in Britain', in *Between Two Cultures: Migrants and Minorities in Britain*, James L. Watson (ed.), Oxford: Basil Blackwell.

Light, I. (1972), *Ethnic Enterprise in America: Business and Welfare among Chinese, Japanese and Blacks*, Berkeley: University of California Press.

Shaw, A. (1988), *A Pakistani Community in Britain*, Oxford: Basil Blackwell.

Werbner, P. (1981), 'Manchester Pakistanis: Life Styles, Ritual and the Making of Social Distinctions', *New Community*, vol. 9, pp. 216–29.

13

A Note on ROSCAs among Northern Somali Women in the United Kingdom

Hazel Summerfield

The Conundrum

While working among predominantly Isaak Somali women in London, I was constantly puzzled that women whom I knew to be on state benefits or low wages and believed not to be participating in the black economy seemed to have access to capital sums of varying sizes. They did not appear to be afraid of 'going into debt'. This was in direct contrast to their white neighbours, who had great difficulty raising lump sums. I heard from the white, and to a lesser extent Asian, communities but not from the Somali of intimidation by illegal money-lenders. In fact the Somali women denied using money-lenders. Further, I knew that many of them did not have access to large kinship networks in the UK. Yet even the poorest appeared to be able to raise air fares to rescue kin from the civil war between the North and South of Somalia which in 1991 led to the formation of Somaliland.

The above drew me to investigate Somali money systems. In this article I will concentrate on one system used almost exclusively by women both in Somalia and the UK: *hagbad.*

Somali Money Accumulation Systems

The Isaaks have various systems for accumulating money to be used either communally or for the benefit of an individual. The system any person chooses seems to be determined by sex and the 'end usage' of the collection. Systems will usually run in parallel and be used to help finance people's total obligations to tribe, clan, kin and self. I will briefly outline the main systems. First I consider three individual or bilateral arrangements and then three types of joint activity. I then concentrate on one form of *hagbad* dominated by women.

1. Wealthier individuals in the Somali community will accumulate money in a bank.
2. An individual can call on a wide kinship network for voluntary contributions for the benefit of himself or his family.
3. Money-lenders exist in Somalia, but they do not claim interest. They are often used so that an individual can fulfil his group or other obligations.
4. The *mag* – Arabic *diya* – is a clan system of accumulating money for the benefit of the clan or tribe or to enable the clan to fulfil a perceived obligation to an individual or another clan. The purpose of the money is decided by men, and is usually known in advance of the collection. The system originated from a clan's blood money obligations and is well documentated by Lewis in *Somali Culture, History and Social Institutions* (1981:21). *Diya*-paying groups are also 'the primary political divisions of the population'. Elders will order a collection either for a specific purpose (such as to raise money for arms for the civil war or to obtain medical treatment for a wounded soldier) or to be kept in a bank against future unforeseen needs. The head of a household has to pay an amount depending on the number of male and female adults in the household and on who is working. Broadly speaking, this is the system used to meet communal obligations and needs. It has been adapted to meet modern political conditions in the homeland to the extent of financing the civil war. The '*mag* groups' are always related males but in the United Kingdom single female heads of households are expected to contribute to the collection.
5. *Box Money* (if collected by men) or *hagbad* (if collected by women) groups consist of friends or relatives each one of whom voluntarily agrees to accumulate money jointly in a bank account for a given period, which could be up to five years. Each individual regularly contributes the same amount and at the end of the period the money, plus interest, is shared out equally. Each individual is free to spend his share as he or she wishes. The groups are normally of single sex. Both sexes use this system of collecting through banks and distributing the capital and interest at an agreed date.
6. The term *hagbad* is also used for ROSCAs organized by groups varying in size from seven to twenty women each, who agree to contribute regularly a fixed equal amount to a fund which is allocated

to members in rotation: each woman is free to spend her share as she wants. The women do not appear to distinguish by language between 'doing a *hagbad*' in which the contributions will be kept in a bank and accumulate interest, and a rotating credit agreement where the money rotates around the group and is always in use.

History and Uses of *Hagbad*

Nobody could tell me the origin of the rotating *hagbad*, but all agreed that it was a very old custom and nearly exclusively used by women. Somali women said they could 'do *hagbad* wherever they are'; in Somalia it is the way a woman can give herself little luxuries such as perfumed soap or a new cooking-pot, or purchase such luxury items as perfume, jewels, clothes or presents for children. However, in only one of the four *hagbad* groups that I investigated was the money used in this way and, perhaps significantly, most of the members were Arab, not Somali. Moreover this group comprised twenty female secondary school leavers who had been neighbours in Aden. It was the only group which had a nearly homogeneous age structure. Money was collected every ten days and spent on shampoo, clothes and jewels. Many women in the United Kingdom told me that back in Somalia in 'good times' they had spent their *hagbad* in the same way, but that now, in London, 'times are hard', and the money is spent on essentials such as gas and electricity bills.

The other three groups consisted of twelve, ten and seven women; one of the women claimed to be in another two groups, one of six and the other of seven people. All the women were based in the United Kingdom, and all agreed that they had exclusive control over how the money should be spent. If they felt that there was any danger that their husbands, children or other relatives would try to direct the use of the money, then they simply did not reveal that they were 'doing a *hagbad*'. It is considered a personal and private matter between the members of the group. In these groups the money was used not only to meet regular household bills (gas and electricity) but when necessary for purchase of children's clothes, kitchen items (pots and pans) or for air fares for relatives; in one case the take-out was donated to a son to facilitate his house purchase.

Better-off women still usually use *hagbad* because of the social interactions involved: to be accepted in a *hagbad* is a sign that you are a trustworthy individual. Two women who had joined *hagbad* in Somalia but not in the United Kingdom were greatly respected and trusted in the community because of their pastoral role. Neither wanted to be involved in a *hagbad* because of the potential acrimony surrounding the pursuit of defaulters to ensure payment (but see below). Thus membership of a *hagbad* group is seen as both positive and negative social interaction. Only one woman among my acquaintances did not use *hagbad* either in Somalia or in England. She was a highly educated woman who before becoming a refugee had a high earning capacity and her own bank account, and had never used *hagbad*. She had a prestigious job in Somalia and hence such a respected status that, when the Government of Siad Barre imprisoned her for political reasons, she was not tortured and the court failed to convict her.

Formation and Structure of a Rotating *Hagbad* Group

New *hagbad* groups are normally initiated by women already in a group. At the end of a rotation some of the women may decide to start another, perhaps with a different size of contribution or length of rotation. Another way is for a woman to announce at a social function that she wishes to form a group. The word goes around, and a group of between six and twenty women forms. The women are not then necessarily related to each other, although they are normally geographically fairly close, and do not necessarily all know each other. All agree that the primary criterion for inclusion must be a reputation for trustworthiness. The women have no effective remedy other than social isolation against a defaulting member. However, in a culture where women have a strong sense of 'sisterhood' and rely heavily on each other socially, emotionally and practically (see Summerfield, 1993) the loss of reputation can be highly humiliating and lead to very real social deprivation. Indeed, nobody I knew admitted to knowing of, or having been in, a *hagbad* with a defaulting debtor. But one woman was in a group where a woman had been paid off and dropped before it was her turn to take the kitty, as she had failed to make two payments. In the same group one woman had lent another the money to fulfil her obligation to contribute (see below). Women told me that in Somalia they would go to a money-lender, or borrow sheep or food, in order to raise the cash to fulfil their *hagbad* obligations, whereas in the United Kingdom members of the group will lend to each other in order to keep the *hagbad* going. For example, in one group the fourth member of the group lent the eighth member £400 of her £500 takings, as the eighth member needed the money to maintain her own contribution and pay her sick father's medical expenses. At the time of interview, £200 had already been repaid and the fourth member expected the rest when it was the debtor's turn to take the kitty.

If a woman dies during a *hagbad* rotation, there seems to be flexibility over her contributions. It was generally felt that her kin, if they were able, should maintain her contributions if she was a debtor but that the matter should not be pressed; similarly, if the deceased was a creditor, the feeling was that her kin would probably need the money. Any money already given out would be considered a product of the general system whereby a Somali is obliged to help a person in need.

The composition of a *hagbad* seems to be fairly flexible; it might perhaps be made up of three groups of related females (each group unrelated to the others) and a few unrelated individuals. The fund rotates on either a weekly, ten-daily or monthly basis. The contribution varies from £10 a week to £100 a month. The women decide at the inception of the group the order of the 'take'. The needier the woman, the earlier she takes. The order is flexible, and if an unexpected crisis occurs the women will telephone around and agree a new order.

Thus to participate in a *hagbad* is to acquire a type of insurance policy against unforeseen need. One woman described how pleased she was, when she heard her father was seriously ill, that she was able to raise her air fare from her *hagbad* group in order to visit him. No interest is paid to late takers of the kitty, but nonetheless it is considered best to take last. 'I will have spent it all by the end unless I take last' seems to be the general sentiment.

Collection

Rotations rarely last longer than a year. Although all the women meet at the beginning of a *hagbad*, they do not necessarily meet again. Even if they decide to vary the order of 'take' because of the unexpected need of a member, variation is done by consent obtained over the telephone or in *ad hoc* meetings.

Sometimes it is left to the individual who is owed the kitty to collect the money, but more usually a very trustworthy woman, who must live in the middle of the group, is selected as the collector. Although she is not paid to act as the collector, it is customary for her to provide food when the women give her their contributions, and for the fund-taker to give her some money as a gift for her children. Men sometimes participate in a rotating *hagbad* group by using a female relative as their representative. In one group a sister represented her brother and a mother represented her minor daughter. The brother could not attend directly as he would not be able to take part in the 'female talk'.

Functions of Hagbad

Rotating *hagbad* seem to be a way in which women can maintain some independence from their men. They are not then reliant on men for the luxuries of life that can increase a woman's feeling of well-being. It also enables them to acquire and maintain their households independently of men, and in a society like that of the Somalis, which has a very high divorce rate, ROSCAs can facilitate a woman's separation from her husband.

Interestingly, no woman admitted to using the fund to buy stock to begin trading; it always seemed to be used for family or personal benefit. In hard times it was regarded as an insurance to maintain the caring aspects of family life: to go towards medical expenses, refugee air fares, or the establishment of a relative in a new home. In easier times it is equivalent to a personal bonus, used to buy non-essential presents for oneself and others. When the Isaak decided to commence the civil war, money was raised among expatriate Somalis around the world. Every household, whether headed by males or females, had to contribute a lump sum which was fixed by male clan elders. The sums were substantial for the individuals and money from rotating *hagbad* was undoubtedly put into the communal 'box'. However, probably because the use of the money was outside the women's control, no woman will admit to having used her rotating *hagbad* money to fulfil clan obligations. *Hagbad* money is seen as 'untied' money, at the disposal of an individual female.

Apart from its fiscal uses, this type of *hagbad* is probably an important psychological resource in that it gives a woman flexibility, independence and security. During the recent civil war it probably helped to feed the families of relatives and gave the women a practical way to show care as their families and homeland disintegrated around them. It is also a way of expressing and maintaining trust between individuals, creating and maintaining bonds of friendship, and responding to another's needs. The flexibility in the order, allowing 'take' according to need, means that the women have an automatic forum in which to express their practical problems. It is a cog in the structure of a society which appears to produce enormously strong and resilient women.

References

Lewis, I.M. (1981), *Somali Culture, History & Social Institutions; An Introductory Guide to the Somali Democratic Republic*, London: Athlone Press.

Summerfield, H. (1993), 'Patterns of Adaptation: Somali and Bangladeshi Women in Britain', in *Migrant Women*, G. Buijs (ed.), Oxford and Providence: Berg Publishers.

14

Gender Differences in ROSCA Participation within Korean Business Households in Los Angeles

Ivan Light and Zhong Deng

Kye is the Korean ROSCA. This paper analyses *kye* participation in the households of Korean immigrant garment manufacturers in Los Angeles. The manufacturers reported the *kye* use of persons in their households in Korea and in the United States. Women were much more likely to participate in *kyes* than men, whether in Korea or in the United States. The difference held for both business and consumer use. However, the women's margin of superiority was greater in the United States than it had been in Korea. Only men who owned very large garment factories reported *kye* participation rates equal to those of women. To explain this increase in women's post-immigration participation we suggest that when Korean households started family firms, women extended their normal financial responsibility to include financial management of the new firm. We also raise the possibility that increased marital instability in the USA contributed to the immigrant women's increased *kye* participation, a suggestion compatible with the findings in Treas (1993) as to why some marriages permit partners to maintain separate bank accounts.

Familiar in many developing countries and a frequent subject of anthropological inquiry (Velez, 1981; Soen and de Comarmond, 1972; Geertz, 1962; Miracle et al, 1980; Wolf, 1991), ROSCAs have also attracted attention in developed countries because of the supportive role they play in immigrant and ethnic minority business enterprise. The provision of investment capital is the most studied issue (Light, 1984; Fratoe, 1986; Werbner, 1990). Obtaining loan capital is an obstacle for all small business ventures, especially for immigrant or ethnic minority entrepreneurs, who lack credit ratings and collateral, or are the victims of ethnic or racial discrimination (Light, 1972: ch. 2; Pryde and Green, 1990; Jackson, 1991). ROSCAs mitigate this problem, first by encouraging saving. Second, ROSCAs make the whole group's savings available to member households for consumption or investment, preventing capital leakage to non-local credit markets. Third, ROSCAs circumvent the slow, unfriendly, and bureaucratic channels of banks and insurance companies, the mainstream financial institutions of market societies (Light, 1977). Finally, ROSCAs are educational institutions in which the more skilled teach money-handling to co-ethnics (Soen and de Comarond, 1972:1178; Geertz, 1962:260; Friedman, 1959:64–5). For these reasons, even in economically developed market societies ROSCAs represent cultural resources that support the consumption, home purchase, and commercial enterprise of groups endowed with the tradition.[1]

Entrepreneurship research has been one of the more active sources of sociological interest in ROSCAs. The principal focus of interest in entrepreneurship research has been how much contribution ROSCAs make to business capitalization and financing. As we have shown earlier, ethnographic and survey research methods yield different results, and firm answers remain elusive (Light, Im and Deng, 1990; Chang, 1990:114). The extent of entrepreneur use of ROSCAs remains unclear. Entrepreneur use of ROSCAs has not seemed to require analysis of gender differences in ROSCA participation, since business firms, not individuals, have been the units of analysis. Hence, the entrepreneurship literature has been indifferent to gender issues in ROSCA participation.

However, other results have compelled entrepreneurship research to examine gender issues. Recent research has found that marital status affects men's entrepreneurship. Lee (1988) found that the availability of the unpaid labour of wives explained why self-employment rates of Korean men exceeded those of Filipino men in Los Angeles. Boyd (1990) reported that married Asian men were more likely than unmarried men to be self-employed. Borjas and Bronars found the same result for the States for men of all ethno-racial categories (Borjas and Bronars, 1989: Table 1). The reasons are unclear. Possibly married men are more ambitious and better organized than unmarried men. Since married men have domestic responsibilities, they probably work harder than unmarried men. But it is also possible that married male entrepreneurs get help from their wives, a form of social capital that supports family firms.[2] This possibility raises the question of the unpaid, ignored, and untheorized contribution of wives to their husband's entrepreneurship. When a wife contributes unpaid labour, her husband's entrepreneurship income will be inflated, since it took two people to earn it (Pedraza, 1991:318).

Therefore, entrepreneurship will appear more highly remunerated per capita than it actually was. Moreover, in a real sense, and often a legal one, the firm will be the joint product of both husband and wife even if census-takers presume that the husband is the firm's founder, owner and chief executive officer (CEO). Therefore statistics will underestimate the entrepreneurship of women.

These findings raise the question of just *how* (not whether) wives support the entrepreneurship of husbands. The gender division of labour is so pronounced in the Korean family itself that it would be astonishing if it disappeared in the family firm. We suppose that in family firms men and women alternate some tasks, as when, for example, spouses take turns in minding the store while the other rests. But we also suggest that a woman's contribution to the family firm is not just to duplicate the labour of her husband and extend its duration. Rather, women's contribution consists partially of specialized tasks that render the family firm a skein of interdependent, gender-linked contributions. A simple example would be a factory in which the husband attends to production and his wife manages the accounting and finance. This would represent a gender-linked division of labour in a family firm.

Beyond this observation, the obvious suggestion is that when families start a business, women extend their domestic responsibilities in ways that support the new business. In many Asian societies accounting is a traditional household responsibility of women, and participating in ROSCAs is one of the ways in which they fulfil this responsibility (Glenn, 1986:39). Werbner found that Pakistani women in Manchester participated in ROSCAs as agents of the family business, thus expanding the women's traditional responsibility for the household budget into the financing of the family business.[3] In this study of Korean ROSCAs in Los Angeles we examine the same issue, assuming that in Korean households women expanded their traditional ROSCA participation to accommodate the needs of the family business. If so, women would participate more in ROSCAs when their family runs a firm than when it does not, and the balance of their participation would shift from consumption towards the cash-flow and capitalization questions that concern businesses.

Kye: A Korean ROSCA

The ROSCA has a centuries-long history in Korea. Its first known use is described in a census volume of 1663. Koreans call their ROSCA '*kye*'(pronounced 'keh', as in English 'ketch'). The word means 'contract' or 'bond,' but is often translated 'voluntary association' (Kennedy, 1973:198). The earliest *kyes* were non-monetary associations for mutual aid between subsistence-farming peasants. Mutual aid *kyes* continue to exist, and Chun identifies funerals, weddings and seasonal ceremonies as occasions for their formation (Chun, 1984:139). Money *kyes* became more important with the commercialization of Korean agriculture and society. Money *kyes* are more common in cities than in the villages. Moreover, rural money *kyes* are commonly interest-free whereas urban money *kyes* have evolved complex methods for the payment of interest to the fund. Janelli and Yim (1988:165) declare money *kyes* 'an extremely popular form of savings and investment in South Korean cities'.

Kennedy finds that money *kyes* became more popular in urban areas after the Korean War. He also maintains that money *kyes* 'successfully competed with other sectors of the money market,' a claim he found confirmed in Bank of Korea publications (Kennedy, 1973:206). Because *kyes* diverted funds from the banking system, Korean banks regarded and still regard them as economic competitors, studying their practices and extent in the hope of emulating their market appeal. Nonetheless, more recent surveys suggest that participation in *kyes* probably peaked in popularity around 1969. In that year's survey of South Korea, the Bank of Korea found that 72 per cent of adult respondents were *kye* members. Another survey found that member households invested about 26 per cent of their monthly income in *kyes* (Vreeland, 1975:241; Kennedy, 1973:206). Subsequent bank surveys of urban Korean households recorded declines in *kye* participation. In 1976 the Bank of Korea found that 42.5 per cent of urban households were *kye* members, and in 1986 only 34.1 per cent were still *kye* members (Janelli and Yim, 1988).

Rural people are usually conservative and slower to change than urban dwellers (for example, peasants retain folk music and costume longer than urban non-manual workers); and so if money *kyes* were simply disappearing one would expect rural and backward populations to retain the practice longer than progressive urban groups. However, contrary to what functionalists would expect, Korea's peasantry included fewer money *kye* participants than Korea's intelligentsia. Yi (1970:70) describes *kye* as 'the only way the poor have' of acquiring lump sums of money, and as 'the most frequent and profitable investment activity of the poor'. But in the mid-1970s 'middle- and upper-income savers' were especially attracted to *kyes*, using their cash withdrawals for 'such costs as children's educational expenses' (Vreeland, 1975:240). It seems likely, therefore, that as numerical participation declined, individual contributions and the size of the funds to be distributed increased. Whether the decline in numbers and the increasing contributions would mean a high grand total of capital involved is not known.

As elsewhere in East Asia, Korean *kye* participants were and are preponderantly women (Moon, 1990:35–6; Benn, 1988:245; Chira, 1987; Gold, 1988). This tendency has encouraged the claim that *kye* is primarily a social institution whose participants do not understand money management. However, in their study of women *kye* participants in Seoul, Janelli and Yim (1988:185) demonstrate that bidders structured their offers in full knowledge of the interest rate advantage of different turns. Although the women did not use mathematical interest formulas, they used 'common sense' and 'crude mathematical intuition' to reach a judgement that was roughly correct. When the women adjusted their interest bids to accommodate social relationships, they knew the cost of it. Another fallacy is that *kyes* involve only 'pin money', and that their function was and is social, not economic. As with a functionalist view of *kyes*, this fallacy rests upon Western assumptions about family roles. Although Korea is a patriarchal society, as noted, women there customarily manage family finances (Kennedy, 1973:155; Benn, 1988:245; Coltrane, 1989). Korean women use ROSCAs to save and invest whatever level of income their households save or invest. As South Korea's saving rate was second only to Japan's in East Asia, this sum was routinely big (Vreeland, 1975:240). Most of the money returned to households from *kye* is utilized for consumption. But, especially in South Korea, where a third of workers are self-employed, the line between household income and enterprise income is frequently indistinct. Possibly, when a family opens a small business, women assume a preponderant role in financing it, extending their traditional responsibility for household finance. This is our basic hypothesis.

Kyes in the United States

Koreans were among the most entrepreneurial of America's immigrants in the 1970s and 1980s (Light and Bonacich, 1988: ch. 1; Min, 1990). In view of the ubiquity and importance of *kyes* in South Korea, the supposition naturally arises that Korean entrepreneurs in the United States used *kyes* to support their numerous firms, a proposition enthusiastically endorsed in the popular media (Harris, 1983:190–98; Goozner, 1987; Gorman 1988:62; Frantz, 1988; Arax, 1988; anonymous, 1992). Reviewing research on Korean ROSCAs in Los Angeles and elsewhere in the United States, Light and Bonacich reported that participation in *kyes* was a frequent practice among Korean Americans, that *kyes* raised substantial sums of money, and that this money often supported the capitalization, expansion, or cash flow of Korean-owned business firms (Light and Bonacich, 1988: ch. 10). Indeed, the use of *kyes* was so widespread in Los Angeles's Korean–American community that Korean banks developed *kye*-like savings plans to compete with them (Frantz, 1988:S4:1).

Methods of Research

Ethnographers dismiss survey research because they do not believe respondents are candid, excluding any hope of measuring participation in *kyes*.[4] It nevertheless seemed to us desirable to obtain the statistical results that only survey research can yield, or at least a more informed estimate of the extent to which *kyes* are used. To this end, when an opportunity presented itself, we undertook a survey of *kye* use designed to minimize the disadvantages of previous survey research while retaining the advantages of the method.

Rather than sampling the whole Korean community or some neighbourhood, as others have done, we located an important Korean trade association in a manufacturing industry. This trade association forms our sampling universe. In June 1987 the Korean American Garment Industry Association (KAGIA) had 368 entrepreneur members in Los Angeles. Each owned and operated one or more garment manufacturing factories. Entrepreneur members represented about half of all the Korean entrepreneurs in the Los Angeles garment industry, and about 11 per cent of the entire garment entrepreneur population of Southern California (Light and Bonacich, 1988: 309). The average entrepreneur member of KAGIA employed forty workers.

The research team explained its scientific purpose to the Director of KAGIA, and thanks to a family friendship connection elicited his co-operation in a study of the use of *kyes* among KAGIA membership. Declining to release his Association's membership list for sampling, the Director agreed to include our questionnaire with the Association's monthly newsletter sent to all members.

Bailey recommends the mailed survey for use when respondents must be assured of anonymity because a topic is sensitive (Bailey, 1982:156). Money is among the most sensitive of research topics (Treas, 1993:727). We therefore developed a self-administered questionnaire of ten items and a letter of introduction explaining the scientific importance of our research and indicating that ROSCAs were not illegal. The questionnaire and letter were translated into Korean, pre-tested and revised before being included with the Association's April 1987 *Newsletter* to the KAGIA membership. At our request, the Association's Director included a communication in Korean, vouching for the *bona fides* of the research and urging members to return the survey questionnaire in the postage-paid envelope provided. We hoped this endorsement would increase the respondents' willingness to participate (Heberlein and Baumgartner, 1978:449).

By 1 June, 1987 we had received seventy-four completed quest-ionnaires, and therefore included a follow-up questionnaire with KAGIA's June *Newsletter*. By 1 September, 1987 we had received 110 replies in all, a response rate of 29.9 per cent of the total KAGIA membership. Although this rate is low, there are three mitigating circumstances (Bailey, 1982:177–8). First, we did not have access to a master list of Association members, and could not identify first-wave non-respondents for additional follow-ups. Second, our research addressed a sensitive subject, discussion of which respondents were already known to resist. Finally, our results are based on 29.9 per cent of the *sampling universe* (roughly half of the Korean garment manufacturers in Los Angeles), not 29.9 per cent of a sample thereof.

Results of the Self-Administered Survey

Interestingly, twenty-two of our respondents were female and eighty-eight male, although the KAGIA Director claimed that only eight of the Association's members were female. However, the Director also indicated that in some cases a woman ran factories nominally owned by her husband or son. In other cases, wives had secretarial and accounting respons-ibilities that apparently included filling out our questionnaire. In any event, we found no statistically significant difference between the replies of male and female respondents as regards factory size or household participation in *kye*, either in the United States or in Korea. Three-quarters of our respondents were between 30 and 50 years old. The average age of male respondents was 42 and of female respondents 44. Table 1 tabulates the answers regarding use of *kyes* in Korea prior to emigration and currently in the United States. Thirty-two of the eighty-three respondents, or 39 per cent of responses from KAIGA members, reported that their household had used *kyes* in Korea before coming to the States, while sixty-one respondents, 73 per cent, indicated participation in the United States. Only 19 per cent of business households had not participated in *kyes* either in Korea or in the United States. Thus our respondents claimed that they used *kyes* more in the United States than in Korea earlier. The increase probably resulted from two causes. First, if entrepreneurs generally use *kyes* more frequently than non-entrepreneurs, as other research has reported, an increase in entrepreneurship following immigration would presumably have increased *kye* use among immigrants. Research has already shown that only one-fifth of Korean American entrepreneurs had been self-employed in Korea prior to emigration (Light and Bonacich, 1988:286–9). Assuming that the same increase in self-employment occurred among the garment makers we surveyed, their increased use of *kyes* as reported by Association members may be a reflection of their increased self-employment in the United States.

Second, owners of small businesses typically fall outside the service market of mainstream financial institutions, and immigrant Korean entrepreneurs probably used *kye* because they found gaps in the American financial system (Derby, 1983:72). However, when *kyes* fill gaps in financial service markets, they supplement mainstream financial institutions that still cannot serve certain communities adequately and often cannot serve them at all.[5] Additionally, Korean immigrant entrepreneurs' increased use of ROSCAs in the United States suggests that the institution facilitated their upward economic mobility. For those who responded to the questionnaire, use of *kyes* was not an 'adaptation to poverty', as described in one study of ROSCAs (Kurtz, 1973; Nee and Sanders, 1985:87–8).

Turning now to the gender of *kye* participants, we wanted to know whether Korean men and women had changed their participation rates in *kye* after arrival in the States. As Table 14.1 shows, of men who did not participate in *kye* while still in Korea, 67 per cent had begun to participate in the USA. On the other hand, of men who had participated in *kye* while in Korea, 30 per cent had given up using them in the USA. The decrease did not annul the increase. In Korea about one-third of the men participated, while after coming to the States the men's participation rate went up to about two-thirds. For women the post-immigration increase in use of *kyes* was even bigger: of women who participated in *kyes* while in Korea, all continued the practice in the United States. Of women who had not used *kyes* when they lived in Korea, 78 per cent turned to them in the USA. Unlike the men, none of the women who had been participants in Korea gave up using *kyes* in the USA. In Korea the

Table 14.1. *Kye* Participation by Householders in Korea and in the USA Reported by Members of KAGIA.

| | Respondents who Participated in Korea | | | | | |
	Males		Females		Total	
Participated in Korea	No	Yes	No	Yes	No	Yes
Not participating in the USA. Per Cent	33	30	22	0	31	19
Participating in the USA. Per Cent	67	70	78	100	69	81
Total	100	100	100	100	100	100
N	42	20	9	12	51	32
Chi-square	0.07		0.93			
d.f.	1		1			
Significance	0.79		0.33			

women's participation rate had been 43 per cent; in the USA it moved up to 90 per cent.

Although men's and women's rates of *kye* participation increased following immigration, prior participation in Korea did not increase the likelihood of either's participation in the USA. Table 14.1 shows no statistically significant change in either men's or women's *kye* participation after immigration. This means that using *kyes* in Korea did not enhance any tendency to use them in the USA. The net increased use was due to new first-time users. Familiar to all Koreans, *kyes* attracted new members when a need appeared.

In Table 14.2 respondents report whether the participants in ROSCAs were the respondent, his/her spouse, both jointly, or neither. Table 14.2 shows that the same number (eleven), but a greater proportion of female respondents reported more *kye* participation than did male respondents. Among these women respondents, 52 per cent said they had been participants in Korea and 82 per cent used them after becoming US immigrants. Men were more likely to report that their wives were the ones who were actually involved (14 per cent in Korea, 26 per cent in the USA) in *kyes*, or that they participated in a *kye* jointly with their wives (12 per cent in Korea, 16 per cent in the USA).

Table 14.2 also shows that *kye* participation increased among both male and female respondents following immigration to the USA. Solo male participation in *kyes* increased from 13 per cent to 34 per cent, an increase of 21 per cent. Solo female participation increased from 52 per cent to 82 per cent following immigration, a gain of 30 per cent. Patterns of participation by household members persisted after immigration. Among those who had participated in Korea, 75 per cent remained participants in the USA. Among men who reported their wives were the ones involved in Korea, 82 per cent reported the same in the USA. This persistence also characterized households in which joint (H + W) involvement was reported in Korea: 86 per cent of these households continued joint *kye* involvement in the USA.

We compared male and female respondents for any gender differences in the percentage of the manufacturing firm's start-up equity that originated in any *kye*, the percentage that originated from a previously concluded *kye* or *kyes*, the percentage that originated from an ongoing *kye* and was subsequently repaid, and the percentage originating from other sources. We also compared the mean size of the garment firms of male and female entrepreneurs. We calculated students' t-score and tested the significance of the difference between all the means because our sample is small. We found no significant mean differences between genders in any of the aforesaid respects.

Participation of Spouse

We asked respondents to estimate the *kye* participation of their spouse and to report their own. Both men and women respondents thought that the participation of their spouse had increased following immigration. However, both men and women placed lower estimates on their spouse's participation than we obtained from the self-reported personal participation of the men and women respondents themselves. Thus, male respondents thought that 14 per cent of their wives had participated in *kyes* in Korea, but 52 per cent of female respondents reported *kye* participation in Korea. Women respondents thought that none of their husbands had been a *kye* participant in Korea, but 13 per cent of male respondents acknowledged participation in Korea. In the USA the same pattern persisted. Men thought that 26 per cent of their wives were *kye* participants whereas 82 per cent of women respondents acknowledged participating. Women thought that 5 per cent of men were participants, but 34 per cent of men acknowledged participation.

Since our respondent men and women were not married to one another, each respondent was describing his or her spouse. Possibly the respondents' accounts were perfectly accurate. We cannot reject that possibility. Since the women respondents may have been more involved in business firms than the wives of male respondents, this is an additional reason to expect differences between husbands' reported behaviour of their wives and replies of the female respondents about their own activities. However, since all our respondents were from the same socio-economic level and the same occupation (garment manufacturing), we would expect broad similarity of *kye* use between the non-respondent wives of the men in our sample and the women respondents in our sample who were, in many cases, the wife of the KAGIA member to whom our questionnaire had been addressed. Similarly, we would expect broad similarity in *kye* use among the husbands of women in our sample and the male respondents in our sample. From this perspective, the systematically low estimates of a spouse's participation, relative to the self-reported participation of opposite-sex respondents, may reflect the respondent's ignorance about her/his spouse's true participation. In other words, the spouses of our male and female respondents were probably more active in *kyes* than our respondents realized. Therefore, when asked to estimate their spouse's participation, our male and female respondents gave answers that indicated much lower rates of *kye* participation for their own spouse than were reported to us by same-sex respondents about themselves.

The same considerations apply to households in which our respondents assured us that neither spouse was a *kye* participant: the respondent told us what she or he knew about her or his own participation and what he or she thought or guessed about the spouse's participation. Thus, discussing participation in Korea, 43 per cent of our women respondents knew that they had not participated and guessed that their husband had not participated either. In contrast, 61 per cent of male respondents knew that they had not participated in Korea, and supposed that their wife had not participated either. Comparing the male and female estimates of household non-participation in Korea, we find that 43 per cent of women respondents came from households in which neither spouse participated whereas 61 per cent of male respondents came from non-participant households. Possibly these reports were completely accurate. However, in view of the much higher participation rates of women than of men, we think it more likely that the male respondents' low estimates of household participation reflected the husbands' *ignorance* of their wives' true participation. Presumably women respondents underestimated their husbands' *kye* participation in Korea too, and underestimated household participation as a result. But since men participated less than women, the women's underestimate of household participation was probably less than the men's.

Why would one spouse not know about the other's true *kye* participation? This could easily happen when husbands and wives communicate little, keep separate financial accounts and exist in gender-distinct social worlds (Treas, 1991). But it could also arise if partners concealed their *kye* participation from each other. The advantages of clandestine participation are obvious: it is then possible for a spouse to have, manage, and build a financial base unknown to the marital partner.

Unlike the USA, where by and large men manage household finances, the gender division of labour in Korea assigns this task to wives. Therefore one would expect that Korean husbands would have only a rough understanding of how their wives actually discharge this responsibility. Male ignorance would, therefore, arise in the normal course of household activities. But it is also true that Korea's strongly patriarchal society gives wives an incentive to build and maintain a financial resource unknown to their husbands, which they themselves control (Hong, 1982:113; Hurh and Kim, 1984:123; Schoenberger, 1989). For both these reasons one would expect Korean husbands to underestimate the *kye* participation of their wives more than their wives would underestimate the participation of their husbands.

Table 14.2 confirms this expectation in both Korea and the USA. If we assume respondents to be in error, and measure this by the difference between a respondent's estimate of the partner's participation in *kyes* and the self-reported rate of participation among opposite-sex respondents, we can compare the size of the estimation errors made by our women and men informants. In Korea women estimated men's participation at zero whereas the men estimated it at 13 per cent, an 'error' of –13 per

Table 14.2. *Kye* Participation by gender reported by KAGIA members.

Respondents:	Yes in Korea		Yes in USA	
	Male	Female	Male	Female
self	11(13%)	11(52%)	28(34%)	18(82%)
spouse	12(14%)	0	21(26%)	1(5%)
both	10(12%)	1(5%)	13(16%)	1(5%)
neither	51(61%)	9(43%)	20(24%)	2(9%)
total	84(100%)	21(100%)	82(100%)	22(100%)

cent. Men estimated women's participation at 14 per cent whereas the women estimated it at 52 per cent, an 'error' of –38 per cent. In the USA, women estimated husbands' participation at 5 per cent, whereas men estimated it at 34 per cent, an 'error' of –29 per cent. Husbands estimated wives' participation at 26 per cent whereas women estimated it at 82 per cent, an 'error' of –48 per cent.

Loglinear Analysis

In order best to examine the associations between gender and *kye* use in Korea and the USA, we use loglinear analysis. Similar to multiple regression models which engage continuous variables, loglinear analysis offers a powerful way to identify relationships between categorical variables. Loglinear models can be applied to tables with more than two variables, and so are useful for uncovering the potentially complex relationships between categorical variables in a multiway cross-tabulation. Compared with the classical chi-square approach, loglinear models offer a systematic evaluation of the relationships between the categorical variables; they also permit us to obtain the quantitative strength (odds ratio) of these relationships, while holding other condition(s) constant.

The first step is to develop a comprehensive set of hierarchical models (see Table 14.3). This includes an independence model (No.1) that assumes no association among any variables, a saturated model (No. 9) that assumes all possible effects are present, and, by deleting interaction terms from a saturated model, all seven possible models between these extremes. Our task is to select the best model from the nine hierarchical models constructed for this case. It should fit the data; and should more than one model fit the data equally well, the simpler would be preferred. If models with and without higher-order interaction terms fit the data well (as judged by insignificant likelihood chi-squares), simpler models are usually preferable to the more complex, since higher-order interaction terms are difficult to interpret. Simpler models contain fewer parameters and more degrees of freedom. By selecting the best model we can be confident that we have found the most parsimonious way of describing the observed data and identifying the associations among variables. Table 14.3 presents the summary statistics required for selecting the best model.

If a model fits the data it should have an insignificant chi-square, indicating that the expected frequencies obtained from this model do not deviate much from the observed cell frequencies. Except for the saturated

Table 14.3. Summary Statistics for Models of Association between Countries, Gender, and *Kye* Participation by KAGIA members.

Model Assumption	Likelihood chi-square	Degree of freedom	P-value
1) no associations	12.56	4	0.014
2) only KO *kye* and US *kye* are associated	10.90	3	0.012
3) only KO *kye* and gender are associated	8.54	3	0.036
4) only US *kye* and gender are associated	7.75	3	0.051
5) associations between KO *kye* and US *kye*, and between KO *kye* and gender	6.88	2	0.032
6) associations between KO *kye* and gender, and between US *kye* and gender	3.73	2	0.155
7) associations between KO *kye* and US *kye*, and between US *kye* and gender	6.09	2	0.048
8) all two-way interactions exist	2.97	1	0.085
9) all associations exist	0.00	0	1.000

model, the only two fitting models are Nos. 6 and 8, since only these have insignificant chi-squares. We compare these two models to choose the more parsimonious. The difference in likelihood chi-square for these two models is 0.73, with 1 degree of freedom. Such a difference is not statistically significant. Thus, model 8 does not improve on 6 but is less parsimonious. Hence model 6 is the better-fitting. We next use its parameters to identify associations between variables.

Table 14.4 presents the parameter estimates from model No.6. Substantively interpreted, they have two implications. First, we note an increase in the likelihood of *kye* participation in the USA relative to participation in Korea. This is the main effect of location in Korea or the USA. In Korea the odds of participation vs. non-participation was 0.8 to 1. In other words, the odds of participation were 80 per cent of the odds of non-participation. In the USA, the odds of participation were 4.5 to

Table 14.4. Parameters for the Preferred Models (from Table 3).

Parameter	Estimates	Standard Error	Z-value
KO *kye*	0.114	0.129	0.877
US *kye*	–0.748	0.198	–3.782
Gender	0.745	0.200	2.728
Gender by KO *kye*	0.257	0.129	1.990
Gender by US *kye*	0.377	0.198	1.907

coding: Gender 1 = male, 2 = female;
   KO *kye* 1 = no, 2 = yes;
   US *kye* 1 = no, 2 = yes.

1.[6] The odds of participation were 450 per cent of the odds of non-participation in the USA. Yet participation in the USA and participation in Korea were independent in the sense that a respondent's participation in Korea did not change his/her odds of participation in the USA. Since model 6 excludes the two-way interaction of participation in Korea and participation in the USA, participation in the two countries was independent. This result confirms what we found in Table 1 above. The likelihood of participating in a USA *kye* was not significantly different whether or not a respondent had participated in *kye* while still in Korea. Therefore we cannot explain *kye* use in the USA by reference to previous *kye* use in Korea. Something in the USA environment inspired *kye* use among Korean immigrants, all of whom were able to respond in this way.

Second, in the USA as in the Republic of Korea gender was the most important factor affecting the likelihood of participation in *kyes*. Immigration did not change this. From the signs of the coefficients, we see that women were more likely than men to participate in *kyes* whether in Korea or in the USA. Everything else being equal, the odds ratio of women to men of participating in *kyes* in Korea was 2.8 to 1.[7] That is: in Korea women were almost three times more likely than men to participate in *kyes*. The ratio increased to 4.5 to 1 in the USA.[8] In the USA both men and women participated more in *kyes* than they had in Korea, but in the USA Korean-born women were 4.5 times more likely than Korean-born men to participate in *kyes*. Although participation increased among Korean men in the USA, when compared with men's participation in Korea, the increase in the probability of men's participation lags behind the increase in women's participation.

This large relative increase in women's use of *kyes* after immigration requires explanation. One possibility is change in the household's economic circumstances upon immigration. All the households in our sample owned manufacturing businesses in the USA though few had done so in Korea. Since entrepreneurs use *kyes* more than non-entrepreneurs, the immigrants' accession to business ownership in the USA pushed all these Korean households into a higher-use occupational category. Therefore a household's use of *kyes* presumably increased after immigration in response to increased occupational need. However, increased *kye* use does not explain the large *relative* increase in women's participation unless we assume that when faced with new financial needs in the USA, Korean business households *expanded women's kye participation in response*.

An alternative explanation is change of marital circumstances attendant upon immigration. Among Koreans as among immigrants generally, the impact of immigration upon marriages has been adverse. Following immigration to the United States divorce among Korean families increased about six-fold, former housewives became full-time workers, marital satisfaction declined, and married women expressed dissatisfaction with non-egalitarian decision-making in the home (Hurh and Kim, 1984:123). Hong (1982:130) found that Korean immigrants in Los Angeles were appreciably less happy in their marriages than other Americans. If Korean women worked more frequently outside the home and were maritally less secure after migration than before, they might increase their *kye* participation in response. Hence these social and marital changes might account for the relative increase in *kye* participation among Korean women following immigration.

Our evidence permits some assessment of these complex issues. Table 14.5 compares the extent and purpose of *kye* participation by men and women respondents with what the men respondents thought was the extent and purpose of *kye* participation by their own wives. The Pearson's chi-square for this 3 x 3 table is highly significant.[9] We asked *kye* participants to indicate whether they had used *kye* funds for business start-up or not. Those who said 'Yes' indicated that business was or had been a purpose of *kye* use. Those who replied 'No' indicated that consumption was the purpose of their participation. When thus requested to state the purpose of their *kye* participation, 42 per cent of women respondents reported that they did not use *kye* funds for business purposes, and 47 per cent said they did. Now, comparing the replies of women and men, we find that women participated more than men in both types of *kyes*, but that their margin of superiority was greater in non-business *kyes* than in start-up (Table 14.5).

We are also able to compare what the husbands guessed about their

Table 14.5. *Kye* Participation by KAGIA Members in Los Angeles by Purpose and Gender. Per Cent.

	Respondents			
	Males	Females	Wives	Total
Non-participants	33	11	0	22
Participant but no *kye*-assisted start-up	28	42	76	41
Participants and *kye*-assisted start-up	40	47	24	38
Total	101	100	100	100
N	61	19	21	101

Chi-square	degree of freedom	significance
19.7	4	0.0006*

* statistically significant

wives' *kye* participation with what women respondents reported about their own. This is a comparison of two groups of women. The differences are striking. Among the wives of male respondents the participation rate was 100 per cent, but 76 per cent participated in non-business *kyes* and only 24 per cent in business *kyes*. Wives used business *kyes* less than either the male or female respondents, but they used non-business *kyes* much more than either. Comparing the participation of the two groups of women, we suggest that the male respondents underestimated the extent of business-related participation by their wives and overestimated the extent of non-business participation. Because the pattern of men's *kye* use diverges more from what they guessed about their wives than it does from what female respondents told us about their actual participation, we suspect that the men respondents saw more gender division of labour in household participation *than actually existed*. To draw a firm conclusion from this would, of course, be premature, for the method-ological reasons explained earlier, but it seems to us the most likely interpretation.

Size of firm offers additional access to the causes and extent of gender difference in use of *kyes*. Table 14.6 compares the use made by male respondents and all females (women respondents + wives) by large and small garment factories. Large factories had forty or more employees; small factories had less than forty. The table shows that size of firm made no difference to female participation in *kyes*. Females showed the same high rate whether their family's factory was large or small. But size of firm did affect the *kye* participation of male respondents. Only 56 per cent of male owners of small firms were participants in contrast to 84 per cent of male owners of large firms. Because of this disparity in men's participation, the gender difference between men and women was statistically significant for small factories. Among owners of small firms, men's participation was less than women's, whereas among the owners of large firms men and women did not differ in their rate of using *kyes*.

Table 14.6. *Kye* Participation among members of KAGIA in Los Angeles by Gender and Firm Size. Per Cent.

	Small firm [less than 40]		Big firm [40 or more]	
	Males	Females	Males	Females
Non-participants	44	5	16	5
Participants	56	95	84	95
Total	100	100	100	100
N	34	21	25	21
Chi-square	7.9		0.55	
d.f.	1		1	
significance	0.002*		0.46	

* statistically significant

Interpreting this result, we hypothesize that as garment factories increased in size, Korean men extended their influence into a zone of operations that among small firms was predominantly a woman's responsibility. These results do not indicate a strict gender division of labour in business-related *kye* participation in either small or large factories. They rather show a movement away from a female-preponderant toward an egalitarian influence as size of firm, and therewith presumably its formality, increased. Since use of the *kye* is an ethnic resource not a universalistic class one, the movement from small to large factory does not involve the shift from ethnic to class resources that Yoon identified as a process of maturing in the Korean firms he studied (Yoon, 1991:303–31). Rather, it suggests a shift of influence within the household such that, with size and formalization of family firms, women's financial role in the business declines from preponderance toward equality.

Discussion

We have suggested that Korean women spontaneously and naturally extended their traditional responsibility for household finance into the business sphere when their family opened a business. In an extreme case, a wife would manage the firm's finances and accounting while her husband managed its operations. If so, this extension of the housewife's traditional role would represent one of the invisible ways in which Korean women contribute to their husbands' entrepreneurship.

Using a questionnaire mailed to members of a Korean trade association in Los Angeles (KAGIA), we have adduced two kinds of supporting evidence. First, although both men's and women's *kye* participation increased following emigration to the USA, women's participation increased more than men's. Since most Koreans who moved into business in Los Angeles had not been self-employed in Korea, the absolute increase in household *kye* participation probably resulted from becoming new members of this high-use occupational category. The relative increase in women's *kye* participation in these Korean business households is presumptive evidence of the extension of women's financial responsibilities from household management to enterprise finance when immigrant Korean families started a business. Second, we observed an increase in male *kye* participation as family firms increased in size. This tended to move *kye* participation from preponderantly female participation toward an equal participation of husbands and wives. This change suggests that women's *kye* participation is one of the unseen ethnic resources that permitted family firms to emerge from immigrant Korean households, but that with business maturity, Korean firms moved away from female preponderance towards gender equality in *kye* participation.

Regarding these results as broadly confirming our tentative hypothesis, we note also that our research turned up some unexpected complexities. The first was methodological. We asked men and women respondents to estimate their spouse's *kye* participation, and found some evidence that although both men and women respondents underestimated the true rate of their spouse's participation, men underestimated it more than women. Since our men and women respondents were not married to one another, we cannot rule out the possibility that respondents accurately reported use of *kye* by spouses in their own unique households, although this seems less likely than respondent error. The possibility of respondent error raises the methodological issue of how much to believe what respondents tell us about their own ROSCA participation *versus* what they guess about that of other household members. If husbands and wives were asked to report their own ROSCA participation and estimate their spouse's, one could determine how much error they report.

If husbands and wives underestimate their partners' participation in ROSCAs, perhaps they also wish to conceal from them their own participation. We found also that husbands knew less about wives' ROSCA use than wives knew about husbands', possibly because wives felt a greater need than husbands personally to control their ROSCA funds. In view of the adverse impact of immigration upon marriage happiness and stability among Koreans in Los Angeles, one might explain the relative increase in Korean women's post-immigration *kye* participation as a social response to changing family roles and expectations. We cannot rule out this possibility.

Interpreting our results, the most striking finding is the absolute and relative increase in Korean women's ROSCA participation after immigration. Although their families' post-immigration shift from wage and salary employment into self-employment would produce this result, in conformity with our hypothesis, so would a deterioration in the stability of marriages in the USA. Since for the Korean women in our sample immigration to Los Angeles occasioned both self-employment and decreased marital stability, both causes might have combined to produce the increased women's ROSCA participation we observed.

Notes

1. Coleman (1988: S103) writes that ROSCAs cannot operate in disorganized groups that lack mutual trust. He evidently supposes that ROSCAs can operate wherever the requisite trust is present. Admittedly mutual trust is a necessary condition of ROSCA operation. However, trust is not a sufficient condition of ROSCA use. ROSCAs embody what Swidler calls a 'culturally-shaped skill'. Cultural skills do not easily cross cultural boundaries. For example, black Americans have never used ROSCAs even though ROSCAs are a West African cultural tradition still used by black West Indians in the United States. See: Coleman, 1988; Swidler, 1986:275; Bonnett, 1981; Light, 1984.
2. Less benignly, one might understand this assistance as another example of 'female labour subordinated' to patriarchalism (Phizacklea, 1988:22). See also: Perez, 1986.
3. 'It is noteworthy that the [ROSCA] associations are usually run by women. It is their circles of trust which underpin the successful functioning of the

associations. Men, competitors in business, save through their wives. The latter sustain the "kommitti" network through their daily interactions with one another' (Werbner, 1990: 315).

4. We have discussed these methodological issues in greater detail in Light, Im, and Deng, 1990.

5. 'Kyes are an important source of working capital for persons, especially new immigrants, who do not qualify for loans from conventional lending institutions' (Carlson, 1988).

6. $(0.8 = \exp(-.11 \times 2))$; $(4.5 = \exp(.75 \times 2))$.

7. $2.8 = \exp. (0.257 \times 4)$.

8. $4.5 = \exp.(0.277 \times 4)$.

9. That result indicates that the variable of the row and the variable of the column are associated; hence the cumulative deviance between observed and expected cell frequencies is significant.

Acknowledgement

The authors acknowledge with thanks a small research grant from the Asian American Studies Center at UCLA. However, only the authors are responsible for errors of fact or opinion in this article.

References

Anonymous. (1992), 'The Kye System', *Asian American Market Report* 2: 2–3.

Arax, M. (1988), 'Pooled Cash of Loan Clubs Key to Asian Immigrant Entrepreneurs', *Los Angeles Times*, 30 October: Sect. 2:1.

Bailey, K. (1982), *Methods of Social Research*, 2nd edition. New York: Free Press.

Benn, N. (1988), 'The South Koreans', *National Geographic* 174: 232–57.

Bonnett, A.W. (1981), 'Structured Adaptation of Black Migrants from the Caribbean: An Examination of an Indigenous Banking System in Brooklyn', *Phylon* 42: 346–55.

Borjas, G.J. and Bronars, S.G. (1989), 'Consumer Discrimination and Self-Employment', *Journal of Political Economy* 97: Table 1.

Boyd, R.L. (1990), 'Black and Asian Self-Employment in Large Metropolitan Areas', *Social Problems* 37: 258–73.

Brooks, N.R. (1988), 'Women Business Owners Thriving in the Southland', *Los Angeles Times* 24 October: Sect. 4:1.

Carlson, T.E. (US Bankruptcy Judge) (1988), 'Findings of Fact and Conclusions of Law,' in re: Case Number 3-87-01598-T-LK, Soon Duk Cabling and Rodolfo Cabling vs. Young Hwan Chang, et al., United States Bankruptcy Court for the Northern District of California, 5 October.

Chang, E.T. (1990), *New Urban Crisis: Korean-Black Conflicts in Los Angeles*, Unpublished Ph.D. Thesis, University of California, Riverside, CA.

Chira, S. (1987), 'It's Clubby, It's Thrifty, and It Can Cover the Bills', *New York Times* 19 November: Sect I:4.

Chun, K-S. (1984), *Reciprocity and Korean Society: an Ethnography of Hasami*, Seoul: National University Press.

Coleman, J.S. (1988), 'Social Capital in the Creation of Human Capital', *The American Journal of Sociology* 94: S95–S120.

Coltrane, S. (1989), 'Demographic Trends in the Division of Household Labor', paper presented at the *60th Annual Meeting of the Pacific Sociological Association*, Reno NV, April 15.

Derby, J. (1983), 'The Role of the Tanomoshi in Hawaiian Banking', *Social Process in Hawaii* 30:66–84.

Frantz, D. (1988), 'Hanmi Bank Uses Ancient Asian Lending Practice to Help Koreans', *Los Angeles Times*, 5 October: Sect. 4:1.

Fratoe, F. (1986), 'A Sociological Analysis of Minority Business', *Review of Black Political Economy* 15:5–29.

—— (1988), 'Social Capital of Black Business Owners', *Review of Black Political Economy* 16:33–50.

Friedman, M. (1959), 'The Handling of Money: A Note on the Background to the Economic Sophistication of Overseas Chinese', *Man* 59:64–5.

Geertz, C. (1962), 'The Rotating Credit Association: A "Middle Rung" in Development', *Economic Development and Cultural Change* 10:241–63.

Glenn, E.N. (1986), *Issei, Nisei, War Bride*, Philadelphia: Temple University.

Gold, S.J. (1988), 'Refugees and Small Business: The Case of Soviet Jews and Vietnamese', *Ethnic and Racial Studies* 11:411–38.

Goozner, M. (1987), 'Age-Old Tradition Bankrolls Koreans', *Chicago Tribune*, 19 July, Sect. 7:1.

Gorman, C. (1988), 'Do-It-Yourself Financing', *Time* July 25:62.

Harris, M. (1983), 'How the Koreans Won the Greengrocer Wars', *Money* 12:190–8. March.

Heberlein, T.A. and Baumgartner, R. (1978), 'Factors Affecting Response Rates to Mailed Questionnaires', *American Sociological Review* 43:447–62.

Hong, L.K. (1982), 'The Korean Family in Los Angeles', Ch. 5 in *Koreans in Los Angeles*, edited by Eui-Young Yu, Earl H. Phillips, and Eun Sik Yang. Koryo Research Institute and Center for Korean American and Korean Studies, California State University, Los Angeles.

Hurh, W. M. and Kwang Chung Kim (1984), *Korean Immigrants in America*, London and Toronto: Associated University Presses.

Jackson, J. (1991), 'Racism is the Bottom Line in Home Loans', *Los Angeles Times* 28 October: B5.

Janelli, R.L. and Yim, D. (1988), 'Interest Rates and Rationality: Rotating Credit Associations among Seoul Women', *Journal of Korean Studies* 6:165–91.

Kennedy, G.F. (1973), 'The Korean Fiscal Kye (Rotating Credit Association)',

Unpublished Ph.D. Thesis. University of Hawaii.

Kurtz, D.F. (1973), 'The Rotating Credit Association: An Adaptation to Poverty', *Human Organization* 32:49–58.

Lee, H-K. (1988), *Korean and Filipino Immigrant Women in the Los Angeles Labor Market*, Unpublished Ph.D. Thesis, University of California at Los Angeles.

Light, I. (1972), *Ethnic Enterprise in America: Business and Welfare among Chinese, Japanese, and Blacks*, Ch. 2, Berkeley: University of California Press.

—— (1977), 'Numbers Gambling Among Blacks: a Financial Institution', *American Sociological Review* 42:892–904.

—— (1984), 'Immigrant and Ethnic Enterprise in North America', *Ethnic and Racial Studies* 7:195–99.

—— and Bonacich, E. (1988), *Immigrant Entrepreneurs*, Berkeley and Los Angeles: University of California, chs. 1, 4–7.

——, Im, J.-K. and Deng, Z. (1990), 'Korean Rotating Credit Associations in Los Angeles', *Amerasia* 16:35–54.

Min, P. (1989), *Some Positive Functions of Ethnic Business for an Immigrant Community: Koreans in Los Angeles*, Final Report submitted to National Science Foundation, December, ch. 5.

—— (1990), 'Problems of Korean Immigrant Entrepreneurs', *International Migration Review* 24:436–55.

Miracle, M.P., Miracle, D.S. and Cohen, L. (1980), 'Informal Savings Mobilization in Africa', *Economic Development and Cultural Change* 28:701–24.

Moon, O. (1990), 'Urban Middle Class Wives in Contemporary Korea', *Korea Journal* 30:35–6.

Nee, V. and Sanders, J. (1985), 'The Road to Parity: Determinants of the Socioeconomic Achievements of Asian Americans', *Ethnic and Racial Studies* 8:87–8.

Pedraza, S. (1991), 'Women and Migration', *Annual Review of Sociology* 17:303–25.

Perez, L. (1986), 'Immigrant Economic Adjustment and Family Organization: The Cuban Success Story Reexamined', *International Migration Review* 20:4–20.

Phizacklea, A. (1988), 'Entrepreneurship and Gender', in *Enterprising Women*, Sallie Westwood and Parminder Bhachu (eds), London: Routledge.

Pryde, P. and Green, S. (1990), *Black Entrepreneurship in America*, New Brunswick NJ: Transaction.

Schoenberger, K. (1989), 'Korea: It's Suffer, not Suffragette', *Los Angeles Times* 16 October, Sect 1:1.

Soen, D. and de Comarmond, P. (1972), 'Savings Associations among the Bamileke: Traditional and Modern Cooperation in Southwest Cameroon', *American Anthropologist* 74:1170–79.

Swidler, A. (1986), 'Culture in Action: Symbols and Strategies', *American*

Sociological Review 51:273–86.

Treas, J. (1991), 'The Common Pot or Separate Purses? A Transaction Cost Interpretation', in *Gender, Family, and Economy*, Rae Lesser Blumberg (ed.), Newbury Park: Sage.

—— (1993), 'Money in the Bank: Transaction Costs and the Economic Organization of Marriage', *American Sociological Review* 58:723–34.

Velez, C.G. (1983), *Bonds of Mutual Trust: The Cultural Systems of Rotating Credit Associations among Mexicans and Chicanos*, New Brunswick: Rutgers University.

Vreeland, N. (1975), *Area Handbook for South Korea*, 2nd ed., Washington, D.C.: U.S. Government Printing Office.

Werbner, P. (1990), *The Migration Process: Capital, Gifts and Offerings Among British Pakistanis*, New York: Berg Publishers.

Wolf, D.L. (1991), 'Female Autonomy, the Family, and Industrialization in Java', in Rae Lesser Blumberg (ed.), *Gender, Family, and Economy*, Newbury Park: Sage.

Yi, K-T. (1970), *Modern Transformation of Korea*, translated by Sung Tong-Mahn, Seoul: Sejong Publishing Co.

Yoon, I-J. (1991), 'The Changing Significance of Ethnic and Class Resources in Immigrant Business: The Case of Korean Immigrant Businesses in Chicago', *International Migration Review* 25:303–31.

15

Gold Coins and Coffee ROSCAs: Coping with Inflation the Turkish Way in Northern Cyprus[1]

Jane Khatib-Chahidi

Introduction

This chapter deals mainly with a form of ROSCA found in the Turkish Republic of Northern Cyprus (TRNC) called *altın günü*, literally 'gold day'. Groups of women hold afternoon gatherings on a rotating basis in their homes. The hostess provides light refreshments while the guests present the hostess with a 'gift' in the form of a non-currency gold coin, a piece of gold jewellery, or a sum of money equivalent to a predetermined amount of gold. The women in such groups are often colleagues at work, friends and neighbours. They include housewives as well as many working women.

Variations on the same principle are also found in Northern Cyprus: objects such as ornamental silver-backed mirrors may be given instead of gold, in which case the term *gümüş günü* ('silver day') will be used; some groups present the hostess with money in pounds sterling or German marks. As in other countries, ROSCAs operate among employees in several government offices, including the Central Bank and the Finance Office, and in other institutions, but in these cases the participants may be both men and women, and the giving of the fund will rarely be accompanied by a social gathering.

Without exception all informants say the custom of *altın günü*, its derivatives and other forms of rotating savings and credit associations come from mainland Turkey. This being the case, and since, to date, ROSCAs in Turkey have received little mention in previous publications, information about such associations in Turkey will be included in the Discussion section of this chapter.[2]

An Example of *Altın Günü*: Primary School Teachers

For several years now twenty primary school teachers in the age-range 25–35, most of whom work in the same school in Kyrenia, have formed an *altın günü* association. They were not previously involved in any regular social gathering with each other. They meet approximately every two weeks on a weekday afternoon[3] in the house of the person whose turn it is to receive the collective 'gift'.

The cycle starts at the beginning of the school year in September, and finishes by the end of the summer term in June. The reasons given for not holding gatherings in the summer months are that people go away and that they have many visitors, usually relatives from London. This means that the women concerned, although on holiday from school, have less time to socialize. The summer is also the time when most weddings and circumcisions take place. Since hundreds, sometimes thousands, are invited to the celebrations associated with these events, they affect the social life of all sections of the community.

At the beginning of the cycle it is agreed what the 'gift' will be and what refreshments will be offered. The actual order of rotation is also decided at this stage by drawing numbers. During the cycle participants may exchange turns with each other if their position in the cycle is inconvenient. The exact day of the week for the two-weekly gathering is decided upon from one gathering to the next, depending on the members' and hostesses' other commitments.

In the year 1991–2, when I attended two of the *altın partisi* (gold party) gatherings, the teachers were giving a gold coin, a *cumhuriyet,* popularly known as *altın para* (gold money), which weighs 7.2 grams. In December 1991, when the Turkish lira (TL) was approximately TL 10,000 to the pound (sterling), gold was about TL 60,000 per gram. Thus each month each member contributed about £4.50 towards the £85.50 required for the two coins, except in the month when it was her turn to be the hostess: the hostess does not contribute to the gift she receives.

The money for the coins was collected before each monthly meeting by a teacher who had volunteered to do this. The collection took place shortly after they received their monthly salaries and after this teacher had checked on the current rate of gold to determine what each member should contribute.

The refreshments, provided and served by the hostess, sometimes helped by a friend, were Turkish coffee followed by tea and two cakes, one savoury, one sweet. Several of the women were on diets and so did not eat the cakes but took their share home with them. The hostess spent about £10 on refreshments. The gatherings lasted just over an hour. Some women brought their children, who played outside if they were older, or stayed with us if they were toddlers. All the women had taken some trouble with their appearance.

Within this *altın günü* group another *altın* fund operated: eleven members who had children below the age of twelve gave a collective gift, a half *cumhuriyet* (worth about £22) for each child's birthday as it occurred. The mother in each case gave the birthday party, to which she invited the other mothers, all of whom are close friends as well as colleagues at work. The women concerned said they had decided to introduce this second *altın* fund because it was better collectively to give something of worth to their friends' children than give individual presents that they described as useless.

A year later (1992–93) the teachers' group has shrunk to thirteen members. Most of them have become very weight-conscious, so they have decided to serve 'slimming' dishes instead of the sweet and savoury cakes of past years. This appears to have introduced a certain element of competition into the gatherings, each hostess trying to serve something different and non-traditional which is both non-fattening and tasty. There have also been changes in the contribution, its collection, and the form in which it is given: each member contributes the equivalent of one gram of 24-carat gold, which is collected at the school by the hostess of the preceding gathering and presented to the current hostess in the form of money. In September 1992, when the cycle started, each member contributed TL 82,000 (approximately £6.30); in May 1993 the contribution was TL 110,000 (about £7.10 at the then exchange rate). Several of the teachers are quickly investing the money they receive in a plain gold 22-carat bangle to ensure that they save it. Another change made in 1993 is that they have agreed if possible not to bring children to the gathering.

The birthday *altın* fund is still operating. It has increased to twelve members, who although all teaching in the same school are not now all members of the *altın günü* association. The current members decided in September 1992 to increase their contribution for the children's birthday gift to give a whole *cumhuriyet*. They pointed out that nowadays one would think nothing of spending TL 50,000 (about £4 then) on an individual gift, but there was nothing of value that one could get for that amount of money. The contribution for the first birthday was about £4; in May it was about £4.40.

The teachers, and indeed all Turkish Cypriots, are acutely aware of the weakness of their currency against the dollar, pound or mark, and of the high rate of inflation in their economy. All government employees, including teachers, receive bi-monthly cost-of-living increments to their salaries, but they all feel these increases fail to reflect the true rate of inflation. The teachers view gold as a safe investment. They explained that it was better to save in gold coins or unworked gold, as then one did not pay extra for the workmanship, a cost which one could not recoup when selling. This was the reason given in 1993 by some of the teachers for the choice of the plain gold bangle: unlike the gold jewellery they normally wear, it was no item of beauty. The *altın günü* gatherings were valued in both social and economic terms: they were something interesting to do in the winter months, giving an opportunity to talk to friends and colleagues, which was not possible during school hours; and they were seen as useful in that they encouraged saving.

Two Other Examples of *Altın Günü* Associations

The Group of Friends

This group (1992–93), also in Kyrenia, had fifteen members at the beginning of the cycle in January 1993, and subsequently it grew to sixteen.[4] The members, all in the 28–40 age range, include several housewives, two retired government employees (it was possible until recently to retire after as little as ten years' service and receive a small pension), two bank employees, and a woman who works with her husband in his business. The original members all knew each other before starting the *altın* group, and some have been friends since their schooldays. They had not previously formed any rotating social gathering, however. This is the second year that they have had an *altın günü* association. Unlike the teachers, they continue their two-weekly meetings during the summer months, another cycle starting directly after the previous one ends. They meet on Saturday afternoons from September to May because this is the only time those who work can be free; in the summer months, when government offices change to summer hours, they meet on a weekday afternoon.

Each member except the hostess contributes equally towards the cost of a plain gold 22-carat bangle weighing approximately 14 grams. It is brought to the meeting by one of the members who is related to a jeweller. The collection for the bangle is made at the meeting itself and then given to the jeweller by the same member. The contribution in January 1993, when I attended the first meeting of the cycle, was TL 70,000 (about £5.40). At subsequent meetings the contribution was proportionately less because of the additional member.

The refreshments served by the hostess each time are Turkish coffee, followed by tea and two cakes, one sweet, one savoury. It was decided from the beginning that no children were to be brought. The gathering I attended started about 2.30 p.m. and finished by 4.00 p.m. There was a discussion about introducing some kind of game such as bingo at the next gathering (subsequently they have sometimes done so), and about an evening out together in February to include their husbands (this did not materialize as no date suggested was convenient for everyone). All the guests had obviously dressed up for the occasion, many looking as though they had just been to the hairdresser.

Several of the women in this group are participating in more than one gold association: four belong to two, three to three. One of the bank employees is involved in a rotating fund with thirty of her male and female colleagues at work, where the contribution each month is £5, given in sterling.

The members of this *altın günü* association viewed the gatherings as a way to keep in regular touch with friends. Unlike the teachers, who mainly work in the same place and live more or less in the same locality, the workplaces and homes of this group are more dispersed. They also stressed the economic side of the gatherings: because of inflation and the falling value of the Turkish lira, it was best to save in gold.

The Group of Neighbours

In November 1991 an *altın günü* association of twelve women in the age range 30–55 started in and around a large block of flats some miles from Kyrenia. The members were mainly neighbours, although one in the group, the mother of another member, came from a village some twenty miles away. The group was started by a teacher, the older sister of a member of the teachers' group described above. Other members included the local hairdresser, two local restaurant owners, and several housewives. Each member contributed the equivalent of one gram of gold, and the gatherings were held approximately every two weeks over a six-month period. According to one member, the plan was that each member should buy a piece of gold jewellery with the fund she received on her gold day and then show it to the others when they next met. According to another, there was no need to buy jewellery, and no need to show what one had done with the money. Most of the members did, in fact, invest in gold jewellery, sometimes adding something to the amount they received in order to get a piece they particularly wanted.

At the first meeting two members sent the money but did not attend. The husband of one had forbidden her to join such an association; she asked the others not to tell him and it was agreed that she would send the money each time, sometimes attend the parties, but not give a party when it came to her turn. It was said that the other member who was absent from the first meeting did not come because she thought the former would attend and they were not on speaking terms. Subsequently two other women who were not on speaking terms did not attend each other's parties but sent their contributions.

Despite the animosity between certain members of this group, there were no defaulters and the parties were described as 'great fun', 'a good way of getting people together'. The gatherings lasted two to three hours, and games such as bingo were played.

Discussion

The Incidence of altın günü *Associations*
Without a full survey, which was beyond the scope of this study, it is impossible to give accurate figures for the incidence of *altın günü* and simple money ROSCAs in Northern Cyprus. Nevertheless, certain trends can perhaps be discerned from information received during the course of the research. *Altın günü* groups are becoming increasingly popular but are unevenly distributed geographically and socially: in Kyrenia they are extremely common, and they have spread to a few nearby villages; in Nicosia (the capital), Famagusta, and Güzelyurt (Morphou) far fewer women form such associations.[5] The only villages where they are reported as being commonplace are where settlers from mainland Turkey predominate.[6] Second, the members of *altın günü* groups are more likely to be middle-income, middle-class (in terms of Turkish-Cypriot society), and women who are or have been salaried or involved in their own or their husbands' businesses. If they are housewives, their husbands will be relatively well off. However, several of the wealthier women and those considered upper class whom I questioned were somewhat dismissive of such gatherings; poorer women, if they work in an organization and earn enough to save, are more likely to be collecting a sum of money to spend on non-luxury goods than saving in the form of gold. The simple money ROSCA is found more in government offices in Nicosia than elsewhere, but even so several government employees I asked were unaware of their existence.

The foregoing comments contrast with the situation described in Turkey, from where the custom of *altın günü* and other forms of ROSCAs is said to have come to Northern Cyprus. Cases are reported of wealthy women in Ankara and Istanbul throwing lavish all-day *altın günü* parties in hotels, where each guest's gift to the hostess is a whole *cumhuriyet*, usually referred to as an *altın*. ROSCAs involving both women and men are extremely common in a variety of workplaces: among teachers and secretaries in universities and schools, office-workers in factories, car mechanics in garages, cleaners in public offices. These sometimes involve much larger contributions than those in Northern Cyprus.

Some of the employees in an aircraft assembly factory in Turkey are participating in a fund where the contributions are more than TL 1 million per month and linked to the price of a new car. The cycle extends over several years, each member, as her/his turn comes round, being given the opportunity of buying a new car. The group has been able to negotiate a good discount on the price of new cars because they are buying regularly. One member of the group, who has received his turn already, bought a second-hand car instead of a new one, and thus had some cash in hand for other purposes.

In one provincial town near Izmir *altın günü* gatherings are described as so popular that they have replaced much of the family visiting of the past, women seeing relatives regularly only if they are in the same *altın günü* group. Older women reported not wanting or not needing to join such groups, but feeling obliged to do so because a refusal would mean social exclusion or seem unneighbourly. One such woman, who had initially referred to her *altın günü* as 'my day' because she was embarrassed to admit that she was involved in this type of entertaining, now openly refers to her 'gold day'; she has also recently chosen new sitting-room furniture with a view to its appropriateness for entertaining the two *altın günü* groups to which she now belongs. Although in Turkey, as in Northern Cyprus, *altın günü* with a social gathering is considered specifically a women's activity, one case of a mixed gathering was mentioned: a group of retired army officers and their wives held their gold coin afternoon parties in the local officers' club.

Economic Aspects of the altın günü Association

(i) Why Gold? Exchange rates are a daily subject of conversation in Northern Cyprus. With depreciation of the Turkish lira over 60 per cent a year, and inflation rates around the same level, Turkish Cypriots are well aware how much they stand to lose if they save in Turkish lira. Excess Turkish liras are quickly turned into a foreign currency, usually sterling.[7] Even children can be seen changing their holiday-job earnings into pounds.

By giving gold, or linking their contributions to the price of gold, the women in *altın günü* groups feel they are ensuring that the 'gift' received by each member of the group is approximately the same, even though their contributions paid in Turkish lira may fluctuate throughout the cycle. When they select gold, it is with this idea firmly in mind: the 'gift' should be equal for all participants, those whose turn is later not suffering a loss because of inflation.

My Turkish informants all stressed this aspect too: one said she always recommended groups involved in simple money ROSCAs (*para günü*) to link their contributions to the price of gold; another, on hearing that the cleaners in the Turkish Cypriot university where she worked were concerned at the falling value of their *para günü* fund (contributions of TL 100,000 per month), immediately said she must tell them how to compensate for inflation by using the gold rate for determining their monthly contributions.

Over the period 1988–92 the women who chose gold would actually have done better to choose German marks, if they had been thinking purely in terms of a return on their investment. During this period gold traded in the area at a fluctuating rate of $350–$420 per ounce, the actual local price in Turkish lira depending on the exchange rate of the Turkish lira against the dollar and the purity of the gold. Some groups do, in fact, operate with marks, and certain shopkeepers in Famagusta who trade in non-essential items regularly price their goods in marks or Cypriot pounds (the currency of Greek Cyprus) as a practical way of keeping pace with inflation. If in addition they had banked their savings, the women could have received interest in 1991 of 70–80 per cent for Turkish lira and 9 per cent for sterling, the German mark and the US dollar. By taking the risk of lending their pooled savings outside the banking system, they might have doubled or trebled these rates[8]. However, gold for Turks and Turkish Cypriots alike has a symbolic and practical value which puts it in a different category from money. 'Gold, incorruptible, shining, a symbol of wealth and beneficence, is often associated with divinity' (Delaney, 1991:120n). Gold in various forms – coins, amulets, jewellery – is given by close relatives for births, circumcisions and weddings. It is the gift *par excellence* which is rarely inappropriate. Gold coins are also very practical: they can be easily exchanged for money when in need, or for a piece of jewellery that can be worn. Some Turkish women to whom I spoke also saw gold as a safer way of keeping their money, as their husbands were less likely to borrow it![9]

(ii) Altın Savings as a Proportion of Income. Writers such as U Tun Wai (1992:343) have referred to 'the untapped savings capacities'

that the existence of ROSCAs indicates for governmental and non-governmental organizations in lower-income countries. It is therefore useful to look at the amount of savings the *altın günü* represents in relation to individual income in Northern Cyprus. In 1992, when the minimum wage was set at £80, a newly-qualified teacher earned about £160 net per month, one with ten years' experience about £200. This can be compared with the monthly net income of a government under-secretary or university lecturer of around £420. These government salaries for teachers compare favourably with most private sector earnings but to make ends meet most married male teachers with children need second jobs, often in the form of private teaching, as well as working wives.

For the teachers in the *altın günü* group described above, the £4.50 contributed each month, when it was not their turn to receive the gold coin, represented approximately 2.25 per cent of their net monthly income if they had worked for ten years. Over the whole year, however, because teachers receive an extra month's salary, the percentage of net income contributed dropped to around 1.6 per cent; for those involved in the birthday *altın* fund the figure would be 2.5 per cent. These calculations exclude the cost of the one-off expense of being the hostess, which represented more than 23 per cent of the value of the coin. Thus although the party costs are not, as one husband jokingly suggested, the equivalent of the gold coin received, they are not negligible in relation to what the teachers earn or to the value of the savings. They also preclude any purely economic interpretation of the custom.

Clearly the Turkish Cypriot teachers in this group are demonstrating little 'untapped savings capacity' potential in their *altın günü* association. Compared with figures such as an average of 17 per cent of total salary for one *pasanaku* contribution in Bolivia, given by Adams and Canavesi (1989:231), and figures ranging from 12–30 per cent in Asia and Africa given by Bouman (1979:256), the teachers' contributions/savings as a proportion of income are low. Their entertainment costs are also relatively high compared with those of ROSCAs like the Nigerian *esusu:* these were estimated at less than 3 per cent of the annual funds flow (Okorie and Miller 1976, cited by Bouman 1979:262). However, the teachers' *altın günü* association may well represent the lower end of the scale: some members in the two other groups I described will earn approximately the same or less than the teachers but contribute proportionately more each month of the cycle for two grams of gold; some, as I indicated, belong to several groups. Contributions in Turkey seem also to represent a higher proportion of monthly income: a Turkish university lecturer gave a figure of 4–5 per cent per month for her one *para günü* and one *altın günü* group combined, and an older, widowed woman the equivalent of 6.25 per cent of her monthly income for the two *altın günü* associations to which she belonged.

(iii) Financing of Contributions: Non-salaried Women. Those of my Turkish Cypriot informants in *altın günü* associations were all either employed or self-employed. Thus they were not in the position of a housewife who may be dependent upon her husband for spending money. An indication that some housewives may finance their contributions from savings on housekeeping money, unbeknown to their husbands, was gained from the comment by a male informant that his sister was distinctly uneasy when he asked her, in front of her husband, how much money she contributed to the *altın* group to which she belonged. My Turkish informants, commenting on the popularity of the *altın günü* form of ROSCA particularly among housewives, said that husbands are often happy to see their wives saving rather than spending, so may not mind giving them the money to participate in a group; however, women will often not disclose that they are participating in more than one group, and will pay the additional contributions by economizing on the housekeeping money.

In Turkey, too, it is reported that some women who do not go out to work finance their contributions by making handicrafts to sell; sometimes they sell them at the *altın günü* gathering to supplement their income. Some *altın günü* associations also collect money from each 'guest' to pay for the refreshments offered at the gathering instead of these being the hostess's responsibility.[10]

(iv) Altın günü Savings: To Keep or Spend? Most Turkish Cypriot women seem to keep their gold in the form of coins or jewellery. Although they may sometimes cash it to buy a needed piece of household equipment, they do not seem to participate in *altın günü* associations in order to save for anything other than buying jewellery to keep, and even this purpose seems secondary to the social gathering (see below). The *para günü* in sterling, German marks or Turkish lira, without a social gathering, may be used when the purpose is to raise money for an item of capital expenditure.

In Turkey, where contributions are sometimes much bigger in proportion to income than is usual in Northern Cyprus, some women are said to be investing the gold they receive through *altın günü* associations in real estate; others are investing in items for the home, or using it to supplement the household income.[11] One of my Turkish informants, now a university professor, found her stock of gold coins extremely useful when she returned to Turkey after field research abroad and her first pay cheque took several months to come through. The popularity of *altın günü* associations among housewives was attributed partly to the fact that the gold coins saved gave such women some individual security and financial independence from their husbands.

Social Aspects of the altın günü Association

Although saving in gold makes good economic sense, in that it helps to counteract the effects of high inflation, this should not obscure the important social role of *altın günü* associations when they are accompanied, as they normally are, by a party. For the Turkish Cypriot women involved in them this social aspect seems in fact more important than the savings the associations represent, however useful these may be for converting into gold jewellery or more rarely into cash for more basic requirements. In social terms, each teacher's capital outlay on refreshments in 1991–92, for example, can be viewed as an excellent investment: for one party given, costing £10, nineteen were provided in return; to this can be added the bonus of enforced savings exceeding £40, which could be converted into a piece of jewellery, in itself an item of social value.

The *altın günü* associations in Northern Cyprus are gatherings of women who are, by and large, social equals and often friends. That they frequently choose to give the gold object itself (the coin or bangle) rather than the money underlines, I suggest, the social rather than the economic value of this type of ROSCA: gold represents the ideal gift for someone for whom a gift of money would be inappropriate; it preserves the idea that it is indeed a gift, rather than an economic transaction. The rotating fund as a gift was also stressed by a Turkish informant (a university professor) who insisted that the *altın* given to the hostess by the guests collectively at each party was a way of making 'a worthwhile gift' (her words) to the hostess, instead of the individual gifts often presented by guests when they have been invited to someone's home.[12] Such an interpretation virtually excludes any economic connotation to the *altın* gatherings; it also perhaps minimizes the fact that for many unsalaried Turkish women gold coins and gold jewellery represent easily realizable cash in times of need, which can be replaced at a later date when their financial position improves.[13] Another Turkish university teacher, expressing similar feelings to the first one, described the falling value of a rotating fund in Turkish lira, of which she was a member, as being of little importance as it was 'between friends' who were not in need of money; the expensive silk scarf she had been able to buy with her *para günü* (money day) gift was for her a beautiful memento of her friends in Ankara whom she was sorely missing in her present post in Northern Cyprus.

Turkish Cypriot women regard *altın günü* parties as something interesting and fun to do. Unlike the men, who can frequent the coffee-house, club or cheap eating-place in their leisure time, the social life of married women – unless accompanied by their husbands or male relatives – is largely confined to each other's homes. None of the three groups I describe had been meeting regularly before they formed their *altın günü* association, although rotating afternoon women's gatherings are commonplace. The introduction of the *altın*, in fact, appears to have prompted them to enter into a regular social commitment which two groups (of the teachers and of the friends) found enjoyable and worth repeating.

Similar and additional feelings were expressed by several Turkish women about *altın günü* parties. An old Turkish lady described how the *altın günü* association comprising neighbours in her apartment building enabled women not from Istanbul, and therefore very lonely, to get to know each other: only three of the twenty participants in this group were from Istanbul. In this group, too, the *altın* parties provided an occasion for the women to show off their culinary skills with a variety of dishes from their home regions. The competitive display of food described for this group contrasts strongly with the effort made by Turkish Cypriot and Turkish women from a town near Izmir to keep things on a more equal basis. Among the latter it was said that, to avoid competition, some groups had introduced a rule that two other members of the group should prepare the refreshments for the party in the hostess's house, rather than allow her to provide them herself.[14]

Another Turkish source stated that *altın günü* gatherings in Turkey provided an opportunity for women to display their best clothes and jewellery and demonstrate their culinary talents, and for mothers to find suitable spouses for their sons.[15] Except for the last item, this also seems to apply in Northern Cyprus. In addition the same source cited examples of *altın günü* associations in Malatya (eastern Turkey) which confine membership to relatives, with the stated purpose of strengthening family ties. This can perhaps be seen as a reaction and antidote to the extreme popularity of *altın günü* associations, which my other Turkish informants saw as weakening social interaction within the extended family in favour of extra-familial links with friends, neighbours and work colleagues.

The Origins of the altın günü *Association*

(i) Northern Cyprus. For Turkish Cypriots there is no question that the *altın günü* association as described in this chapter is originally a Turkish custom. They see no similarity between it and other Turkish Cypriot customs, present or past.

No one remembers exactly when this form of gathering started, but most agree that it was after 1974, the year when the Turkish army intervened in support of the Turkish Cypriot community and the northern third of the island became the Turkish Federated State of Cyprus (1975), subsequently the Turkish Republic of Northern Cyprus (1983). Only one person thought she had heard about such parties before that date and as far as she remembered they were *gümüş günü* (silver day) ones. One person suggested that the custom had actually come to Cyprus with the Turkish soldiers' wives.

In their insistence that it is an imported custom and nothing like their own, one can sense a certain ambivalence in the feelings Turkish Cypriots still have about *altın günü* gatherings, even though they are so popular in Kyrenia. This may be because the imported custom has introduced a financial element into what used to be, and for many older women in Northern Cyprus still is, a social gathering between friends and neighbours: the rotating coffee/tea-party. This is sometimes referred to as *arkadaş toplantısı* (friends'/colleagues' meeting), although older women may use the term *kabul günü* (literally 'acceptance day' but usually translated 'reception day').[16] In their desire to distance themselves from the financial aspect, I suggest, they stress the foreign origin of the whole custom, including those parts of it which are definitely part of their own culture.[17]

The rotating element, albeit an irregular one, and the collaborative effort for individual gain,[18] a distinguishing feature of the *altın günü* association and any other form of ROSCA, are also present in other Turkish Cypriot customs. Villagers used to pool their labour to build houses for each other and harvest the crops. Circumcision and wedding celebrations also bear distinct similarities to *altın günü* associations, at any rate to the outsider: the gifts given (gold for close relatives, money otherwise) to the circumcised boy and the bride and bridegroom represent a savings (or credit) fund to which large sections of the Turkish Cypriot community will have subscribed in relatively fixed amounts which are dictated by the closeness of the giver's relationship to the receiver, and the former's known financial and social status within the community.[19] The refreshments offered to the guests are similarly standardized at the majority of *düğün* (wedding) celebrations in Northern Cyprus towns: they consist of a macaroon wrapped in a tissue, a cigarette and sometimes a non-alcoholic drink.[20] It is in fact this very equality of the content of such celebrations, even if their venue varies according to wealth, that is echoed in the Turkish Cypriot *altın günü* associations I have described.

(ii) Turkey. As to the origins of *altın günü* associations in Turkey, the possibilities are almost as numerous as the people questioned. The editor of a leading Turkish paper saw them as originating in ancient customs prevalent among Turkish tribes who settled in Anatolia: in order to get to know neighbouring tribes, they would visit them, bearing gifts of surplus produce; the tribe visited would reciprocate with their different surplus products when they returned the visit.[21] This interpretation supports the claim that the custom came from the rural areas to the towns and cities. However, in contemporary village studies such as those by Stirling (1965), Roper (1974) and Delaney (1991) there is no mention of any form of *altın günü* association among the women. Others say the custom originated in Ankara and Istanbul in the 1960s and spread to the provincial cities and towns, in particular in the 1980s when inflation became a serious problem.

The National Folklore Research Department of the Ministry of Culture in Ankara described *altın günü* associations as similar to the rural custom of *imece:* people helping each other with tasks that individual households would find difficult, such as the construction of buildings and periodic work on the land. The *altın günü* association was seen as the city equivalent of *imece,* its purpose being to save money. However, it was suggested that women initially formed such associations more for social reasons (having a good time together and forming friendships) than to save money; as people's standard of living improved, the associations became more a means of acquiring credit to purchase items for the home. According to the same source it was the *altın günü* association, practised mainly by women, that gave rise to this and the other forms of ROSCA now prevalent in many government and business organizations.[22]

From the foregoing it is clear that in the absence of more detailed research in mainland Turkey the origins of *altın günü* associations are open to many different explanations, any of which could be correct. In Turkey, as in Northern Cyprus, rotating gatherings of friends and neighbours (mentioned by Aswad 1974:15) are commonplace. In the provincial town referred to above, rotating gatherings of women also take place for various purposes other than a purely social one. Some groups now spend the afternoon dancing, because with television offering entertainment at home, and many newly-wed couples eliminating *düğün* (wedding) celebrations, occasions for dancing are becoming increasingly rare. A handicraft rotating gathering was mentioned, at which each woman exchanged tuition in some skill she had (such as dress-making, ceramics or making artificial flowers) in return for tuition in some other craft. This was described as a more interesting and enjoyable way of learning than attending 'boring' evening classes.

The only published source I have been able to find which may have some bearing upon the origins of *altın günü* associations in Turkey appears to be that by Arpi Hamalian (1974). She describes the *şirket* ('partnership'), a form of ROSCA accompanied by a rotating gathering practised by the Armenian women in Lebanon, many of whom were refugees or the descendants of refugees originally from Turkey. Although she saw the *şirket* as a new pattern of social integration in response to the breaking of community and family bonds as a result of their refugee situation, her informants recognized features of the *şirket* in earlier institutions that existed in their communities before the Armenian exodus from Turkey: for example the *ikhaniyat* (brotherhoods) formed by young men or women practising the same craft which, while similar to the guild system, operated independently of it. She also saw similarities between the Lebanese *şirkets* and the assemblies of elders (*majlis*) in Armenian towns and villages in Turkey in past centuries and the 'prayer-visiting' type of meetings which, according to Hamalian, developed in Turkey in the nineteenth century. The latter are extremely popular in present-day Turkey among devout Muslim women (although not common in Northern Cyprus). Hamalian also reports the existence of *şirkets* among Armenian village men for the purpose of saving money in Ottoman Turkey.

Hamalian's article on Armenian women's *şirkets* in Lebanon thus suggests several possible lines of inquiry regarding the origins of *altın günü* associations in Turkey. It is doubtful, for example, whether the antecedents she cites were confined to the Armenian community in Ottoman Turkey; and even if some were, as one of my male Turkish Cypriot informants perceptively remarked, it is perhaps among minority group customs that one should look for links with contemporary Turkish customs such as *altın günü* gatherings, which are mainly confined to that major minority group: women!

Conclusion

The Turkish *altın günü* appears to be a unique form of ROSCA in the literature on the subject to date. Although Nayar (1992:196–7) mentions that the savings of the Indian poor may be in the form of gold and jewellery, and Ardener (1964:208) mentions the *khatta* savings of Sudanese women to buy gold ornaments for their daughters' weddings, the Turkish *altın günü* as practised by Turkish and Turkish Cypriot women demonstrates a more financially sophisticated approach to gold than its mere collecting as savings or gifts: the application of a gold standard, whether the fund is given as gold or as money. It is this single-minded adherence to a gold standard that keeps the *altın günü* so uniquely simple to administer.

Bouman (1979:258), commenting on ROSCAs in general, says, 'Simple schemes have the beauty of simplicity.' The *altın günü*, in administration and organization, represents one of the most basic forms of ROSCA: similar to the consumer-durable rotating fund in concept but much more flexible because the 'commodity money' is gold. There is no need for written rules, book-keeping, receipts or records; not even an overall organizer is required when this function also rotates, as it can, from one hostess to the next. The erosion of the fund through inflation over the cycle period, which causes many of the complications in ROSCAs elsewhere and requires compensatory mechanisms, is neatly avoided. There is no need for discounting and auctioning, or for calculating complicated interest rates: the linking of the contribution to the prevailing (albeit fluctuating) gold rate is accepted by all as an equitable way of maintaining the value of the gift.

This method of countering inflation, supremely elegant in its simplicity, and avoiding any question of interest, would seem an attractive proposition for areas of the world where the Islamic prohibition on usury (*riba*), which includes interest on capital, is likely to be strictly adhered to. Hansen (1991:540–41) comments on the fact that Turkey has had a long history of interest control related to religious doctrine, and that Islamic fundamentalists are currently pressing for adherence to Islamic principles in this respect. Although Turkey is a secular state, religious observance is strong in many sections of the population, which is not the case in Northern Cyprus. My research, of necessity limited to information obtained from Turkish people in Northern Cyprus and written communications with others in Turkey (see note 2), suggests a far higher incidence of ROSCAs, including *altın günü*, in Turkey with its population of over 60 million, than in Northern Cyprus, with its population of around

167,000; also the involvement of people from a much wider range of social and occupational classes. Thus they may be a potentially far more economically significant factor in the country as a whole. As such, ROSCAs in Turkey would seem to warrant more research by social scientists, especially economists, than they appear to have received so far.[23]

Reverting to *altın günü* in Northern Cyprus, the ready adoption of this Turkish custom by some Turkish Cypriot women may well be due, as I have suggested, to its similarity to their own customs where economic and social factors are combined (circumcision and wedding celebrations), and their rotating gatherings of neighbours and friends. As I also indicated, the participants are, almost by definition, not in urgent need of money: they are neither rich nor poor; they represent the middle-ranking sections of society, for whom the *altın* fund is seen as savings which may be spent in the future rather than as an interest-free loan or credit. Indeed, the idea of the fund as a gift to the hostess virtually excludes the use of the terms 'borrower' and 'lender', just as their choice of the gold standard excludes the notion of interest.

The rotating gathering amongst women in Turkey and Northern Cyprus is clearly a valued and long-established custom, whether in the form of the more formal *kabul günü* described by Aswad (1974) and Benedict (1974) for Turkey, or the friends' and neighbours' groups – with or without the *altın* – in both countries that I have mentioned. For most married women, whether working or housewives, who have the time to spare and the need for social interaction, the rotating gathering in each other's homes remains the most socially valued and acceptable form of entertainment, rarely objected to by any husband, and affordable on a modest income. While governments and aid agencies have found participation in family-planning programmes is greater when linked to a ROSCA (see Bouman and Moll, 1992:215; Hospes, 1992:231), many Turkish and Turkish Cypriot women seem to have found that friends, colleagues and neighbours are more inclined to commit themselves to holding a party and regularly attending those of others when the cycle is linked to an *altın* fund.

Notes

1. I am greatly indebted to many Turkish Cypriot friends and to my former colleagues at the Eastern Mediterranean University (EMU) in Famagusta for

help in this research. In particular I wish to thank Tomur and Ahmet Ergüven, who helped me throughout and commented on the final draft; Utku and Burhan Gürdal, who first introduced me to *altın günü*; Dr Jonathan Warner, Lecturer in Economics at EMU, who so kindly supplied me with economic information and relevant comments; Dr Nilüfer Narli and Firuzan Güyer, who gave me much first-hand information on the subject in Turkey; and Selda Mansour who, with her relatives, was able to give me further valuable information on the custom in provincial Turkey.

2. The information on Turkish ROSCAs was obtained from Turkish informants in Northern Cyprus (tourists, visitors and university teachers), and from written communications with others in Turkey (academics, and staff of the National Folklore Research Department of the Ministry of Culture, Ankara).

3. Working hours for primary school teachers are 8.00 a.m.–12.45 p.m. Monday to Friday, and 2.00–4.00 p.m. one afternoon per week. Thus they are free on the other four afternoons.

4. The sixteenth member was a teacher from the primary school teachers' group who arranged to take me to this gathering. Although she was acquainted with several members of the group, they were not her close friends. They liked her and decided to ask her to join, which she did.

5. For many Turkish Cypriots Kyrenia (Girne in Turkish) enjoys a higher standing than other cities of Northern Cyprus. It has more tourists; those living in the capital, Nicosia, regularly come to its restaurants; wealthier Turkish Cypriots in their teens and twenties, and the growing population of foreign students at the various universities, flock to it at weekends for its nightlife; and whereas most shops elsewhere close down on Saturday afternoon and Sunday – reminiscent of British practice in colonial times, perhaps – Kyrenia stays open. Is there, one wonders, a link between the greater commercial activity of Kyrenia and the greater incidence of *altın günü* among its inhabitants?

6. This information was obtained from a well-known Turkish Cypriot journalist. According to her, these settlers are extremely poor but their social gatherings regularly include an *altın* gift, which may be a ring of very little real value. This was the only example given of the *altın günü* custom among poorer Northern Cypriots.

7. Their choice of sterling rather than the German mark or the US dollar can be attributed in part to their British colonial past, sterling being the foreign currency with which they are most familiar. The Cypriot pound – now the currency of Greek Cyprus, but before 1974 of the whole island – was linked to the British pound after independence in 1960, and held at parity to it until the early 1970s; currently (June 1993) one Cyprus pound is £1.29. Also Northern Cyprus, with its population of around 167,000, has strong financial and kinship ties with the United Kingdom, whose Turkish Cypriot community, living mainly in London, is about the same size.

8. Arpi Hamalian describes how the simple *şirket* (a form of ROSCA among

Armenian women in Lebanon) developed in the 1950s and 1960s into a profit-oriented loan institution: the money collected would be lent to members for commercial use by their relatives (Hamalian, 1974:77).

9. This does not seem to be the case in rural areas, however. Delaney (1991:120) describes how the *başlık* (brideprice), part of which is given to the bride in the form of gold jewellery, is often taken back by the husband to finance some economic venture.

10. Written communication from the National Folklore Research Department, Ministry of Culture, Ankara.

11. Ibid.

12. In this respect the *altın günü* association would appear to resemble the tea parties with compensating presents for the hostess which are a feature of some ROSCAs in South Africa (Kuper and Kaplan 1944, cited by Ardener, 1964:207, and the chapter by Burman and Lembete in this book); and also the ROSCAs of groups of well-to-do Bolivian women which aim to buy an expensive birthday gift, in rotation, for their members (Adams and Canavesi, 1989:221). The latter case is similar to the children's birthday *altın* fund operating in the Turkish Cypriot teachers' group.

13. See below, footnote 17.

14. A young Turkish woman who had been living abroad for several years was shocked to hear this: in the past, she said, it would have been inconceivable for visitors to someone's house to provide the refreshments.

15. Written communication from the National Folklore Research Department, Ministry of Culture, Ankara.

16. The *kabul günü*, as practised by élite groups in two provincial areas of Turkey in the early 1970s, has been described by Benedict (1974) and Aswad (1974). Aswad contrasts the socially stratified *kabul günü* of the related leading families with those of the lower-middle classes, whose gatherings were more socially homogeneous; she also mentions the popularity among women of the more informal rotating gatherings of friends (Aswad 1974:15). In Northern Cyprus the term *kabul günü* appears to have shifted its meaning, and does not correspond to the big rotating gatherings based on a monthly cycle, at which several participants might hold reception days on the same day, as described by Aswad and Benedict. Several Turkish Cypriots in their early twenties were unfamiliar with the term; those in the *altın* groups I describe who knew it considered it an élite custom of the past. The women who currently use the term are over fifty, and when they refer to their *kabul günü* it is more likely to be a select gathering of close friends at which, as with the *altın günü*, the length of each cycle is determined by the number of participants and how often they decide to meet.

17. To illustrate the point that the *altın günü* custom must have come from Turkey, an educated Turkish Cypriot woman told me how her daughter's Turkish friend had readily sold a gold bracelet to pay for a trip to Cyprus, whereas it would never have occurred to her daughter to use her jewellery

in this way.

18. Sofia Koufopoulou's apt description of a ROSCA at the workshop held in Oxford in January 1992.

19. The fact that teachers do not hold *altın günü* gatherings during the summer months may not be just because of other social commitments. During these months, like all Turkish Cypriots, they will be attending such celebrations, sometimes two or three in one weekend. A teacher and her husband, a government employee, estimated that they had to allocate at least TL 300,000 (roughly £20) a month from June to October for wedding and circumcision gifts. Clearly, for teachers with no extra sources of income, it would be extremely difficult to meet such expenses and also contribute to an *altın* fund.

20. This is in marked contrast to such celebrations among Turkish Cypriots in London, who often have sit-down receptions in a hotel, sometimes paid for from the money given by the guests at the *düğün* itself. Over the past two or three years some wealthy families in Northern Cyprus have started giving lavish wedding receptions for their children, but these remain isolated cases.

21. This informant advised me to ask the National Folklore Research Department in the Ministry of Culture for the source of this information. The latter did not, however, mention such a possible origin in their reply (see footnote 22).

22. No published sources were cited for the information given.

23. How far the Islamic prohibition on interest, strictly adhered to in very few Muslim countries, affects the incidence of ROSCAs and the forms they take is not clear from recent writings. Shanmugam (1989), writing on Malaysia, and Bouman and Moll (1992) and Hospes (1992), writing on Indonesia, do not mention religion as a factor affecting participants' choice of scheme, although Bouman and Moll say that auctioning and discounting to counteract inflation seldom occur (1992:215). Hospes mentions the increasing popularity of *arisans,* and the fact that some are organized around religious issues; in others the *arisan* group is itself a religious praying society (1992:230–34).

References

Adams, D.W. and Canavesi de Sahonero, M.L. (1989), 'Rotating Savings and Credit Associations in Bolivia', *Savings and Development*, vol. XIII, no. 3, pp. 219–35.

—— and Fitchett, D.A. (1992), *Informal Finance in Low-Income Countries,* Boulder, San Francisco, Oxford: Westview Press.

Ardener, S. (1964), 'The Comparative Study of Rotating Credit Associations', *Journal of the Royal Anthropological Institute*, vol. 94, Part 2, pp. 201–29.

Aswad, B.C. (1974), 'Visiting Patterns Among Women of the Elite in a Small Turkish City', *Anthropological Quarterly*, vol. 47, pp. 9–27.

Benedict, P. (1974), 'The *kabul günü*: Structural Visiting in an Anatolian Provincial Town', *Anthropological Quarterly*, vol. 47, pp. 28–47.

Bouman, F.J.A. (1979), 'Financial Technology of an Informal Savings and Credit Institution in Developing Economies', *Savings and Development*, vol. III, no. 4, pp. 253–76.

—— and Moll, H.A.J. (1992), 'Informal Finance in Indonesia' in D.W. Adams and D.A. Fitchett (eds), pp. 209–223.

Canavesi de Sahonero, M.L. see Adams, D.W. and Canavesi de Sahonero, M.L. (1989).

Delaney, C. (1991), *The Seed and the Soil: Gender and Cosmology in Turkish Village Society*, Berkeley, Los Angeles, Oxford: University of California Press.

Hamalian, A. (1974), 'The *şirkets:* Visiting Pattern of Armenians in Lebanon', *Anthropological Quarterly*, vol. 47, pp. 71–92.

Hansen, B. (1991), *The Political Economy of Poverty, Equity, and Growth: Egypt and Turkey*, World Bank Comparative Studies, Oxford: Oxford University Press.

Hospes, O. (1992), 'Evolving Forms of Informal Finance in an Indonesian Town', in D.W. Adams and D.A. Fitchett (eds), pp. 225–38.

Moll, H.A.J., see Bouman, F.J.A. and Moll, H.A.J. (1992).

Nayar, C.P.S. (1992), 'Strengths of Informal Financial Institutions: Examples from India', in D.W. Adams and D.A. Fitchett (eds), pp. 195–208.

Roper, J. (1974), *The Women of Nar*, London: Faber and Faber.

Shanmugam, B. (1989), 'Development Strategy and Mobilising Savings through ROSCAs: The Case of Malaysia', *Savings and Development*, vol. XIII, no. 4, pp. 351–66.

Stirling, P. (1965), *Turkish Village*, New York: Wiley.

Wai, U Tun (1992), 'What Have we Learned About Informal Finance in Three Decades?', in D.W. Adams and D.A. Fitchett (eds), pp. 337–48.

16

Women's Use of ROSCAs in the Caribbean: Reassessing the Literature

Jean Besson

Rotating savings and credit associations (ROSCAs) have been reported from the Caribbean region for nearly half a century, and are more widespread among Caribbean peoples than Ardener's (1964) pioneering cross-cultural survey of ROSCAs indicated. This chapter will first indicate the wide distribution of ROSCAs in both the Caribbean region and its diaspora. A brief overview of the structure, organization and function of selected examples of ROSCAs from the anglophone, hispanophone and francophone Caribbean will next be given. Against this background, preliminary research on Caribbean women's use of ROSCAs will be highlighted. It is then argued that such participation in ROSCAs is a significant aspect of women's status and their contribution to Caribbean culture-building and development; this extends the writer's critique of Wilson's thesis that the Caribbean 'indigenous' counter-culture of 'reputation', established in response to colonial 'respectability', is male-oriented (Besson, 1993a, cf. 1993b; Wilson, 1969, 1973). The chapter concludes with suggestions for further research on women's use of ROSCAs in the Caribbean region and the diaspora.[1]

Distribution of Caribbean ROSCAs

ROSCAs have been reported in the Caribbean region since Melville and Frances Herskovits first identified the *susu* in Toco, Trinidad, in the 1940s as part of their thesis of African cultural survivals in Afro-America (Herskovits and Herskovits, 1947:76–7, 292; cf. Herskovits, 1941). As Ardener's classic article on ROSCAs noted, the Herskovitses also drew attention to similar institutions in Barbados and Guiana, known as the *meeting* and *box money* respectively (Ardener, 1964:208). Ardener (ibid:208) noted, however, that R.T. Smith's subsequent study of British Guiana provided no evidence of ROSCAs: 'R.T. Smith, writing of British Guiana, did not describe rotating associations. He did give details of a family fund known as the "canister", but this does not, apparently, rotate among subscribers (1956:68, 85–6)'. A later account by R.T. Smith did, however, identify ROSCAs among Afro-Guyanese, known as *throwing a box*: '"Throwing a box" is a form of savings institution which is extremely widespread and involves all the 'hand holders' in a weekly or monthly contribution of a fixed amount of money, the total sum being drawn by each participant in turn' (1964:315–16). Ardener (1964:208) also noted the detailed study by Katzin (1959a) of ROSCAs called 'partners' in Jamaica, also reported by M.G. Smith and Kruijer (1957). M.G. Smith's later work on the plural society in Jamaica referred to these ROSCAs by the alternative names of partner and *susu* (1965:168).

Since Ardener's survey (1964), which usefully located Caribbean ROSCAs in a cross-cultural perspective, such associations have been more widely identified throughout the Caribbean region. Norvell and Wehrly (1969) reported a ROSCA known as *san* in both rural and urban contexts in the Dominican Republic, and a similar institution called *esu* in the Bahamas (personal communication from D.J. Crowley (1967) to Norvell and Wehrly); Philpott (1973:172) noted ROSCAs called *boxes* in Montserrat; while Laguerre (1982, 1990) has reported ROSCAs for both Haiti and Martinique. In Martinique these were known as *sousou*, as in Trinidad but with a different spelling (Laguerre, 1990:140 n1). In Haiti, where ROSCAs were found both in rural areas and among urban slum dwellers, such associations were variously known as *sangue, solde* and *comble* (Laguerre, 1982:55–6). The persistence of partners or *pardners* has also been noted by the writer for rural Jamaica (Besson, 1974, I:209), and by Austin (1984:50) and Harrison (1988:113) for urban Kingston. Barrow (1986), Clarke (1986) and Senior (1991) also referred to ROSCAs in the Caribbean region, including the *sou sou* [sic] in St. Vincent (ibid:146).

ROSCAs have also been reported among Caribbean migrants in the United States and Britain. In a comparison of West Indian migrants and American blacks in New York in the 1970s, Light (1972:32–6) identified ROSCAs among West Indians, and as noted by Foner (1977:132), 'attributes West Indian success in New York to a traditional institution: rotating credit associations (known as "partners" to Jamaicans) which, he argued, provided West Indians with an important source of capital for business ventures. American blacks, by contrast, lacking traditional credit associations, have been more dependent on banks and lending institutions for credit, which they were frequently denied (Light, 1972:36)'. In a more recent study of migrants from the Dominican Republic in New York in the 1980s, the existence of the *san* was also noted (Sassen-Koob, 1987:283).

In Britain, Patterson (1965) and Davison (1966) noted the widespread existence of partners among Jamaican migrants in London in the 1950s and 1960s respectively, Davison noting a 25 per cent membership of partners in his sample (cited in Foner, 1979:167). Patterson hypothesized that such ROSCAs would 'fade away' as West Indian migrants became more familiar with banks (1965:349, cited in Philpott, 1973:172), and Foner's later study of Jamaicans in London in the 1970s found little evidence of partners in her sample (1979:167). However Philpott not only reported the persistence of *boxes* among Montserratian migrants in the 1970s, but also contended that this institution 'has been greatly enhanced in the migrant situation' (1973:172; cf. Philpott, 1977:110–11). Moreover, Foner was not entirely consistent in her report on the apparent insignificance of partners among Jamaican migrants in London (1979:167) for she noted elsewhere (1977:132), in a comparison of Jamaicans in London and New York and a related critique of Light's (1972:32–6) thesis that ROSCAs were responsible for West Indian entrepreneurial success in New York, that:

> The fact that 'partners' are found among Jamaicans in England as well as in New York seems to undermine Light's argument, however. It is true that Jamaicans in England may well have amassed financial resources for real-estate investment through 'partners'. Indeed, many Jamaicans (and other West Indians) are home owners here. Yet, it is unclear why they do not invest more of their savings in small-scale businesses, like so many Jamaicans in New York (Foner, 1977:132).

Structure, Organization and Function of Caribbean ROSCAs

As the previous section indicates, there is an emerging literature to be tapped on the structure, organization and function of Caribbean ROSCAs. This section provides a brief overview of selected examples: partners in Jamaica (Katzin, 1959a; cf. Besson, 1974; Austin, 1984; Harrison, 1988); the *box* in Guyana, Montserrat and among Montserratians in Britain (R.T. Smith, 1964; Philpott, 1973, 1977); the *san* in the Dominican Republic and among Dominican migrants in New York (Norvelle and Wehrly, 1969; Sassen-Koob, 1987); and the Martinican *sousou* (Laguerre, 1990). Together these examples cover a time span of some thirty years, and draw on the anglophone, hispanophone and francophone variants of the Caribbean and the region's diaspora in the United States and Britain.

Katzin's analysis (1959a) identified the basic structure of Jamaican partners as a 'banker' and a number of 'throwers' ranging from ten to twenty. The banker initiated and organized the partners, which lasted for the same number of weeks as there were throwers. Contributions to the fund varied in different groups, ranging from a few shillings to a pound or more per week at the time of Katzin's study, but were consistent within a given group. The banker consulted each thrower as to his or her position for receiving the 'draw'. The banker, who usually received a gratuity from throwers, was also responsible for ensuring that each thrower met his or her obligations. Throwers who drew late in the rotation were prevented from defaulting by the fact that they could not retrieve the contributions already paid. Sanctions for those who drew early were the knowledge that their default would become widely known and prevent them from being admitted to other partners; and the fear of physical reprisals and court prosecution.

The function of partners, as analysed by Katzin, was to raise capital for unusually large financial obligations. These included school tuition fees for children; payments on house or land; and, in the case of petty traders, purchasing goods for restocking stalls. The main reasons for participating in the informal institution of partners, as opposed to banks, were that the former provided a personalized context for raising capital and a means of forced saving, and did not carry the danger of government taxation (Katzin, 1959a:439). Subsequent reports of partners in Jamaica by the writer (Besson, 1974, I:209), Austin (1984:50) and Harrison (1988:113) confirmed the continuing relevance of Katzin's basic model.

R.T. Smith's account of the structure and organization of the Afro-Guyanese institution of *throwing a box* has already been cited in clarification of the Guyanese case, indicating 'a weekly or monthly contribution of a fixed amount of money' by 'hand holders', each participant drawing the total fund in turn (1964:315–16). R. T. Smith also elucidated the function of the box, which provided capital accumulation for 'consumer goods of one kind or another, including household furnishings and clothes, both of which are generally renewed or renovated for the big festive season of Christmas' (ibid:316).

Philpott stated that in Montserrat *throwing a box* was sometimes done for small sums, but that with the escalation of this form of savings among

Montserratian migrants in Britain the *box* was thrown for sums as large as '£250–£300 in a two-week period if he [sic] has the last hand in one box and the first hand in the following one' (1973:172). The size of such groups ranged from eight to twenty-five, members contributing 'a fixed amount each week to the central organizer or "banker" who distributes the total sum (the "hand") weekly to members in a pre-arranged order' (ibid:172). Migrants regarded the *box* as a method of compulsory saving, and large sums saved in this way were sometimes deposited in banks. However, the idea of 'keeping the money working' in further mutual aid rotations was valued more highly than deposits in banks (Philpott, 1973:173). The first migrants had often used *boxes* to finance the subsequent migration of relatives from Montserrat, and recruitment to such groups was usually on the basis of common island identity; this served especially as a sanction against defaulting, as defaulters could be more easily traced and their misdemeanour more readily made known.

The *san* identified by Norvell and Wehrly (1969) for the hispanophone Dominican Republic was similar in structure, organization and function to the ROSCAs described above for anglophone Jamaica, Guyana and Montserrat. However, *san* also provided an interesting variation on the theme by incorporating the risk element of the Dominican national lottery. *San* consisted of a 'leader' and a specified number of 'players', who could take it in turns to be leader and who might also be workmates, kin or friends. 'Each player is assigned a number at random to be used in selecting a winner and he [sic] agrees to contribute a specified amount of money at regular intervals', while the leader 'serves as an administrator' and 'in return for his services, he usually extracts a toll'; different forms of *san* existed as a result of variations in 'the leader's time and manner of extracting his toll' (ibid:46). The fund rotated, as 'once a player's number has been selected, he continues to contribute but cannot win again' (ibid:46). However, there was a 'built-in propensity for players to lose' (ibid:49); for example in a *san* with ten players, while those who won draws in weeks one to five gained some financial advantage, those who drew from weeks six to ten 'are sacrificing use of funds during the duration of the game in addition to paying a fee for participating in the game' (ibid:48).

Despite this element of potential financial loss *san* was used extensively, especially among lower income groups, to 'mobilize credit, fractionalize risk and circumvent moneylenders'; and to 'finance large consumer durable purchases, or to finance weddings and other festivities' (Norvelle and Wehrly, 1969:49). Of particular significance was the use of *san* by vendors, who were considered a credit risk by banks, to raise working capital for marketing. This function closely paralleled that of partners as described by Katzin (1959a, 1959b, 1960) for the Jamaican peasant marketing system. When middle-income groups in the Dominican Republic participated in *san*, its functions included financing shopping trips to Puerto Rico (Norvell and Wehrly, 1969:49). Among Dominican migrants in New York, *san* was used 'to finance the documents, travel, and initial settlement costs involved in coming to New York', and might have contributed to 'the rising number of small shop owners in the community' (Sassen-Koob, 1987:283; cf. Light, 1972:32–6).

Laguerre's (1990) analysis of the *sousou* formed part of his wider case study of Caribbean urban poverty in Fort-de-France, the capital of French Martinique. The study focused on the social reproduction of urban poverty and the coping strategies of the urban poor, who were often migrants from impoverished rural areas of the island. The *sousou* was studied in two aspects: it provided cash for the daily needs of individuals and their families and friends, but also provided capital which fed the system of inequality. Moreover *sousou* participation was typical of all classes.

Laguerre's chapter on such associations (1990:113–40) is rich in detail on their structure, organization and functioning, including modes of recruitment; order of rotation; sanctions and risk-solving; advantages and disadvantages; forms of exchanges; and the niches (family, yard, workplace and friendship networks) where the *sousou* was found. Of particular interest are the seven variants of the *sousou* that Laguerre identified: the acephalous yard or family *sousou*, without a head; the *sousou* with a treasurer, the most common form; the *sousou* with double membership; the *sousou* with associate membership; and three variants of *sousou* networks in which two or more *sousous* were connected by the common participation of one or more member: e.g. an individual could belong to more than one *sousou*, serve as treasurer to more than one, or be treasurer of one and member of another.

Caribbean Women's Use of ROSCAs

In their pioneering work on the Trinidadian *susu*, the Herskovitses noted that 'both men and women may belong to these groups, which may, however, also be restricted to persons of one sex', citing as an example a '*susu* group . . . made up of Public Works Department employees' who might be either male or female (Herskovits and Herskovits, 1947:77). However such employees, for example, worked on the roads and there were many more men than women in road-gangs (ibid:47). Women, however, especially older women, played a significant role in Toco culture, including the economic life of the community (ibid:8–10). Thus 'selling in the market is definitely women's work' and 'their earnings are their own' (ibid:49, 292). This begged the question, especially in the light of Katzin's later study of the use of partners by Jamaican higglers (1959a; cf. Laguerre, 1982:55), of the role *susu* played among Trinidadian female marketeers.

Over forty years after the Herskovitses' study, Laguerre in his research on the Martinican *sousou* gave an example of the commonest form of *sousou*, the *sousou* with a treasurer, in which all but one of the participants were female (1990:120). However, although this research was recent, Laguerre provided no detailed information on women's use of *sousous*, though in his earlier study of Haiti he noted that many women, especially market women, participated in *sangue* (1982:55). This lack of gender differentiation typifies much of the literature on Caribbean ROSCAs. For example, Philpott mentioned that 'estate workers and female shop clerks would sometimes "throw a box" for small sums in Monserrat' (1973:172), but provided no further information on women's use of the *box* in either Montserrat or Britain. Moreover, in his previously cited statement on participation in the *box* among Montserratians in Britain, Philpott assumed that participants were male (1973:172). R.T. Smith (1964) provided no information on Guyanese women's use of the *box*, and neither Norvell and Wehrly (1969) nor Sassen-Koob (1987) provided any insight into women's use of the Dominican *san*. This omission was especially significant in the case of the Dominican Republic in view of the marketing context in which the *san* was most usually mobilized (Norvell and Wehrly, 1969:49–50), since participants in such post-slavery Caribbean marketing systems are primarily female (Katzin, 1959b, 1960; Herskovits and Herskovits, 1947:49; Mintz, 1960; 1989:214–24). Moreover Norvell and Wehrly (1969:52) assumed that both leader and players in the *san* were male (1969:46,52).

However, most informants who discussed partners with the writer in rural Jamaica (Besson, 1974, I:209) were female, and there is some detail on women's use of partners in Jamaica in the studies by Katzin (1959a), Austin (1984) and Harrison (1988). There is also some general information on Caribbean women's use of ROSCAs in the recent 'Women in the Caribbean Project' (WICP), based at the University of the West Indies. This included brief references by Barrow (1986:164) and Clarke (1986:115) to women's use of the *meeting* in Barbados, and slightly fuller information on women's use of ROSCAs in Senior's (1991) study of women's lives in the English-speaking Caribbean. The remainder of this section reviews the contributions by Katzin, Austin, Harrison and Senior. In her classic study of partners in Jamaica, Katzin (1959a) provided perspectives on both class and gender differentiation. She noted that nearly all sectors of the population with relatively regular incomes participated in partners. However, Katzin cited only middle-class and working-class participation by 'middle-class clerks and minor government officials, domestic servants, gardeners, workers and petty traders' (ibid:439). She also noted that both bankers and throwers could be either men or women. In her own fieldwork on the predominantly female occupation of higglering, Katzin found that partners was 'probably the most important single source of capital' (ibid:439; cf. Katzin, 1959b, 1960). Moreover, she observed that many such petty traders,

> both urban and rural, obtained the capital to begin trading by working at some other type of employment, usually domestic service, and participating in a partner until they had accumulated the necessary cash. Some, who had lost their capital through a prolonged period of bad luck in the market, worked as domestic servants and participated in a partner until they had enough money to resume trading. Other anthropologists [i.e. M.G. Smith and Kruijer 1957:89] reported partners in rural areas whose members were mostly workers and petty traders (Katzin, 1959a:439–40).

Katzin also observed that middle-class employers attributed 'their inability to keep domestic servants for long periods' to their servants' participation in partners for the purpose of resuming petty trading, and concluded that 'undoubtedly, many women alternate between higglering and domestic service' (1959a:439na). In his analysis of the Jamaican peasant marketing system, Mintz commented:

> In describing their fellows, many market women have told the writer that 'one week she gains and the next she loses, but she'd rather be a higgler and make a shilling than work in someone's house.' In a country where over 70,000 adults, most of them women, are employed as domestics . . ., where labor is relatively plentiful, where average incomes are low, where no social barrier prevents lower-class women from working, and where the only economic alternative to marketing is domestic labor, it is easy to see why many women choose to be higglers (Mintz, 1989:223).

This preference for higglering is especially understandable in view of the negative symbolism of domestic service in Caribbean post-slavery societies.

Austin's (1984) study of class-cultures in Kingston, Jamaica, which compared the middle-class neighbourhood of 'Vermount' with the working-class neighbourhood of 'Selton Town', identified partners in the latter and argued that this institution 'exemplifies the relations of mutual dependence which characterize the working class networks of Selton Town' (1984:50). Austin also contended that 'partner is primarily a female institution by means of which housekeeping money is stretched as far as possible' (ibid:50). Harrison's study of women in the urban informal economy of the Kingston slum of 'Oceanview' also noted the significance for such women of the role of banker 'in rotating credit networks called "partners"' (1988:113). This observation was made in the context of Harrison's observation that 'social networks – or very fluid and diffusely structured social relationships organized primarily around kinship, co-residential, and/or peer ties – constitute the basis for much of the socioeconomic activity within the informal economy' (ibid:112).

Senior's study included some brief but sensitive observations on women's use of ROSCAs, 'known variously as "meeting turn", "credit turn", "partner", "throwing box" and "sou-sou"' in the English-speaking Caribbean' (1991:146). In defining the Caribbean ROSCA, Senior, like Herskovits and Herskovits (1947:292), argued for an African origin from the Yoruba. She also highlighted the element of trust central to the ROSCA:

> Yoruba-derived, it is widely used by people of Afro-American origins to save and to meet financial obligations. It functions according to networks of kin, friends or co-workers. What is most important to the functioning of the 'sou sou' is that participants trust each other. Particularly important is the position of the 'banker'. Each set time period – week, month or fortnight as agreed – a network of people contribute a 'hand' or set sum of money to the banker. Each set period, the total take is paid out to one person in turn – the 'meeting turn' or 'credit turn'. By this means poor people can count on getting their 'hand' or 'turn' to meet heavy obligations such as a down payment on an appliance, children's clothes or school fees, or payments of debts. Women in the WICP discussed the importance of the 'sou sou' in helping them to meet their responsibilities (Senior, 1991:146).

This function of the ROSCA in helping women to meet such financial obligations included obtaining an advance in emergencies which could not be obtained from banks, and also raising funds for major purchases beyond the means of house money – one example being a Singer sewing machine. A typical weekly 'throw' was twenty Caribbean dollars; this could be shared with a 'pal', each of whom contributed and received two half-shares of ten dollars (ibid:147).

Senior's study showed that Caribbean women's use of ROSCAs was part of a wider pattern of participation in kinship and friendship networks of mutual aid in which cash, goods and services were exchanged among women. These networks were of major significance in the survival strategies of Caribbean women, often Eurocentrically described as having 'no visible means of support' (Senior, 1991:139; cf. Barrow, 1986:164–5; Clarke, 1986:114–15). Elsewhere, for example in Olwig's (1981, 1985) study of the Afro-Caribbean family system on the former Danish West Indian island of St. John, recognition of similar networks has shifted attention from the Eurocentric analysis of the so-called 'matrifocal family' to bilateral kinship networks of exchange.

The next section briefly considers Caribbean women's use of ROSCAs in the light of the writer's critique of Wilson's thesis that the Caribbean counter-culture of 'reputation' is male-oriented, while women uphold Eurocentric colonial values of 'respectability' and inhibit indigenous development (Besson, 1993a, cf. 1993b; Wilson, 1969, 1973).

Women, ROSCAs and Reputation

Peter J Wilson (1969, 1973) has advanced the concepts of 'reputation' and 'respectability' for the social anthropology of anglophone Afro-Caribbean societies. Respectability is rooted in the colonial system of social stratification based on class, colour and wealth and Eurocentric culture, life-style and education. It is perpetuated especially by the white churches, the European institution of legal marriage and Eurocentric educational systems.

Reputation, by contrast, is an 'indigenous' counter-culture based on the ethos of equality and rooted in personal, as opposed to social, worth.[2] It is a response to colonialism and a solution to the scarcity of respectability. In its most literal sense, the dynamics of reputation are played out in peer group *crews* in rum-shops, through the public display of oral skills and boasting of virility; in titles and nick naming; and in participating in anti-establishment activities. In this context reputation in the anglophone Caribbean parallels *machismo* in hispanophone Caribbean societies such as Puerto Rico (Wilson, 1969:71–3). In the wider sense, the value system of reputation is rooted in the solidarity of common kinship and equal inheritance of land; in entrepreneurship; and in membership of Afro-Caribbean cults, especially the Rastafari movement. Wilson saw reputation as essentially the preserve of lower-class Afro-Caribbean males, arguing that Afro-Caribbean women uphold Eurocentric respectability – a situation stemming historically from their proximity, as concubines and house slaves, to the colonial masters during slavery days. He further argued that for indigenous development to be achieved Caribbean women must move from respectability to reputation (Wilson,1973:233–4).

Wilson's model has been widely drawn on by theorists of the Caribbean region and its diaspora (e.g. Dirks, 1972; G. Brana-Shute, 1976, 1979; C. Wright, 1984). However, as shown in detail elsewhere (Besson, 1993a), Wilson's thesis, based primarily on the tiny Colombian/Catholic-controlled anglophone/Baptist island of Providencia, does not elucidate the writer's long-term in-depth fieldwork in the Jamaican Baptist free villages of Trelawny parish, at the very heart of the Caribbean plantation-peasant interface.[3] For here women are at the core of a peasant culture of resistance, rooted in dynamic Caribbean culture-building, established and maintained in response to imposed colonial and neo-colonial styles of life and the persisting post-slavery plantation system (cf. Mintz, 1989:132–3). Women are also central to the peasant economy and indigenous development. An alternative analysis, which finds support in data from the wider Caribbean region, explores Afro-Caribbean women's complex historical and contemporary role in slave resistance and anti-slavery nonconformist (Baptist) churches; in the creation of creole kinship, landholding, economic and religious institutions; and in local status systems and procreation (Besson, 1993a; cf. Besson, 1993b).

Seen from this perspective, the emerging literature on Caribbean women's use of ROSCAs suggests that participation in such associations may be a significant aspect of women's involvement in the Caribbean counter-culture of reputation, both in the more literal sense of establishing reputations based on personal worth, and in the wider sense of culture-building and indigenous development.

For example, on the theme of reputation as personal worth, Katzin noted that to be a banker in Jamaican partners 'is a mark of prestige and a validation of economic status', and that 'a thrower selects a particular partners mainly on the basis of the reputation of the banker' (1959a:437); while among throwers, the fear of loss of reputation was a sanction against defaulting (ibid:438). Likewise Philpott noted this sanction as significant among Montserratian migrants who *throw a box* in Britain (1973:173). Similarly, in his discussion of sanctions against defaulters in the Martinican *sousou*, Laguerre stated that 'it is possible to put pressure on members of the individual's family, or to threaten his or her reputation' (1990:127). Laguerre also argued that: 'Particularly in the case of someone who has had a bad reputation, the opportunity to write off the debt to society is a benefit. Such an individual can use the *sousou* to rebuild the confidence of the community' (ibid:133). In Haiti 'a *sangue* is formed when an individual of good reputation invites friends and relatives to join him [sic] as a co-member' (Laguerre, 1982:56), and fear of loss of reputation was a sanction against defaulting among participants (ibid:59). Harrison (1988:113) also identified the significance of peer networks beyond the domestic sphere for women in the informal urban economy of Kingston, Jamaica, including bankers in partners.

As Herskovits and Herskovits (1947), Katzin (1959a), Philpott (1973), the writer (Besson,1974), Austin (1984), Barrow (1986), Clarke (1986), Harrison (1988), Laguerre (1982:55, 1990) and Senior (1991) all provided evidence of female participation in Caribbean ROSCAs, the above status dynamic of reputation in such ROSCAs seems as applicable to women as to men. This status aspect was also identified by Norvell and Wehrly (1969:51) for the *san* in the Dominican Republic, which as noted previously functioned especially within the context of the internal marketing system. While, as observed earlier, these authors gave no account of women's use of ROSCAs, their emphasis on the marketing context suggested extensive female use of *san*, participants in post-slavery Caribbean marketing systems being primarily female. Likewise participation in *susu* may have contributed to the high status of women observed by Herskovits and Herskovits in Toco, Trinidad; as they noted, not only did women dominate the marketing system, but also their earnings were their own (1947:8–10, 49).

This interpretation of Caribbean ROSCAs and reputation, in the sense of contributing to personal status, is supported by Ardener's comparative analysis. For Ardener noted that ROSCAs 'may enhance the social status of participants. Sometimes it is the organizer who gains status by demonstrating his [sic] powers of leadership and administrative ability . . . Sometimes, on the other hand, it is acquired by members who join an association in order to assist the organizer, and who thereby demonstrate their generosity . . . Sometimes mere membership confers prestige' (1964:220). Ardener also observed that fear of loss of reputation was a significant sanction against defaulting: 'A person may hesitate long before destroying his reputation before a large circle of friends or relatives' (ibid:218).

The significance of Caribbean women's use of ROSCAs for the wider meaning of reputation, namely, culture-building and indigenous development, must be set within the theoretical context of the interpretation of the origin and persistence of Caribbean culture. As noted previously, the Herskovitses argued for an African origin of the

Trinidadian *susu*, as part of their wider thesis of African cultural survivals in Afro-America – an argument reinforced by identifying the linguistic derivation of *susu* from the Yoruba *esusu* (Herskovits and Herskovits, 1947:292; Herskovits, 1941; cf. Senior, 1991:146). This argument could also be extended to the Martinican *sousou* (Laguerre, 1990) and the Bahamian *esu* reported by Crowley, who interpreted both the *esu* and Trinidadian *susu* as arriving 'more or less simultaneously with Chinese, East Indian and African immigrants' (personal communication from Daniel J. Crowley, 1967, cited in Norvell and Wehrly, 1969:45). However, Crowley's contention that such ROSCAs were derived simultaneously from Africa and Asia seems to over-stretch the 'cultural survival' thesis.[4] Katzin also argued for the African origins of ROSCAs in Trinidad and Jamaica, but her 'belief' regarding the African origin of Jamaican partners and Trinidadian *susu* is likewise weakened by her supporting observation that a similar institution exists 'among American Indians [sic] in Peru' (1959a:440, 440na).[5]

The interpretation of Caribbean culture as reflecting African survivals has also been more recently reassessed, especially by Mintz and Price (e.g. Mintz, 1970, 1989; Mintz and Price, 1976, 1992). In their examination of the birth of African-American culture, with particular reference to the Caribbean region, Mintz and Price stated that 'one of our major postulates ... [is] that neither social context nor cultural traditions alone can explain an Afro-American institutional form ... and that the development of institutions must be viewed in their full historical setting' (1976:33). From this viewpoint, they contended that 'the organizational task of enslaved Africans in the New World was that of *creating institutions*, institutions that would prove responsive to the needs of everyday life under the limiting conditions that slavery imposed upon them' (Mintz and Price, 1976:10, emphasis added). In this context, the role of the African cultural heritage in the Caribbean has been reinterpreted, with more emphasis on 'the implicit "grammatical" principles' generating new, dynamic, Caribbean creole forms rather than 'static "retentions" or "survivals"' from specific West African cultures (ibid:27); for Caribbean slaves were brought from various African societies and their cultures could not be transferred intact (ibid:4–11).

Thus while Yoruba survivals could account for the retention of *susu* in some parts of the Caribbean such as Trinidad, this would not explain the widespread distribution of ROSCAs throughout the Caribbean region, whose Afro-Caribbean populations derive from many African societies. While it could then be argued that ROSCAs are widely found in Africa (see Ardener, 1964:204–8), the 'cultural survival' thesis would not sufficiently account for the role of ROSCAs in the Caribbean. Moreover, as Ardener's cross-cultural review of ROSCAs showed, such associations were found not only in Africa and the New World (including Indo-America), but also in Asia and Europe (ibid:202–4, 208); they also appeared to be absent among Americans of African descent in the United States (ibid:208; Light, 1972:36, cited in Foner, 1977:132).

A more meaningful explanation of the widespread existence of ROSCAs in the Caribbean region, bearing in mind that they have been found especially among lower income groups such as peasant marketeers and rural–urban migrants, may be located within the dynamic historical context of Caribbean culture-building in response and resistance to the pronounced experience of colonialism, slavery and the plantation system (Mintz and Price, 1976, 1992; Mintz, 1970, 1971, 1989).[6] From this theoretical perspective Mintz has contended that 'Caribbean peasantries represent *a mode of response* to the plantation system and its connotations, and *a mode of resistance* to imposed styles of life' (ibid:132–3). Thus, for example, Caribbean peasant marketing systems, despite their contemporary formal similarities to those of West Africa, have been shown to be historically derived from the Caribbean plantation-generated 'proto-peasant' adaptation, and to reflect creole institution-building and cultural resistance to slavery and the plantation system (Mintz, 1955, 1960, 1970, 1971, 1983, 1985, 1989:131–250).[7] In assessing the role of African survivals in this proto-peasant marketing system, Mintz has pointed out that, while women dominate post-slavery Caribbean peasant markets as in West Africa, reports of proto-peasant marketeers have provided no evidence that women outnumbered men and family groups; and that in Jamaica, where the proto-peasantry was most pronounced, the first market 'was English, not African, in conception and form' (ibid:196, 210–12; cf. Mintz and Price, 1976:40–2).

Pursuing this approach, the writer has also shown that the customary land tenure systems of Caribbean peasants, such as the widespread kin-based institutions of *family land*, are not, as others have argued, passive survivals from either Africa or Europe; nor do they, as such, inhibit Caribbean development as some writers have contended. Instead they are dynamic cultural creations by Caribbean peasantries, established and maintained in response and resistance to Caribbean agrarian relations and colonial legal codes. For the cognatic descent systems at the heart of *family land* differ from the unilineal systems predominant in Africa, including Ashanti landholding groups (from which it has been argued *family land* derives), being structurally closer to Pacific landholding systems. In the Caribbean context cognatic descent maximizes freehold land rights and kinship lines among the descendants of chattel slaves, who were not only denied legal land rights and kinship by their masters but were also regarded as property themselves. Moreover the cognatic descent principle reflects, more fully than unilineal descent, women's contribution to culture-building and indigenous development (Besson, 1979, 1984a, 1984b, 1987a, 1987b, 1988, 1992a; 1992b; 1993a; 1993b; cf. Besson and Momsen, 1987; Momsen, 1993).[8]

From this perspective of culture-building the origin and role of ROSCAs in the Caribbean may be reassessed. For example, Katzin's classic study of partners in the predominantly female occupation of higglering in Jamaica is consistent with the thesis of institution-building and development (cf. Laguerre, 1982:55). Thus in addition to her African-ist hypothesis, which as noted earlier does not entirely stand up to closer scrutiny, Katzin herself related ROSCAs in Trinidad and Jamaica to the 'stage' of 'economic development' in these societies (1959a:440); that is, to a process of indigenous development. Such an interpretation is also borne out in the microcosm of the free villages of Trelawny parish, Jam-aica, studied by the writer, at the heart of the Caribbean plantation-peasant interface. For here partners was seen to be an integral part of the peasant culture and economy, created and maintained in the face of the persisting plantation system and imposed colonial/neo-colonial styles of life (Bes-son, 1974, 1984a, 1984b, 1987b, 1988, 1992a, 1992b, 1993a, 1993b).

This interpretation of Caribbean ROSCAs as representing creole institution-building also throws light on a related new phenomenon in Trinidad, where Herskovits and Herskovits (1947) first identified the *susu*. For in Trinidad and Tobago in 1992 the writer found the institution of *susu land* currently being created, in a society whose land is being taken over by corporate plantations, tourism and increasing urbanization.[9] Thus not only have ROSCAs in Trinidad been recognized by law (Herskovits and Herskovits, 1947:292), but their ethos is also now guiding post-colonial agrarian indigenous development. This parallels the situation elsewhere in the decolonizing Caribbean, such as Barbados and Jamaica, where the principles of customary *family land* are transforming colonially-derived agrarian legal codes (Besson, 1984a:76 n9, 1987b:111, 1988:55; Carnegie, 1987:97 n3).

Future Research on Caribbean Women's Use of ROSCAs

The preceding reassessment suggests a number of related directions for future research on Caribbean women's use of ROSCAs. First, the review reveals that ROSCAs are more widespread in the Caribbean region than Ardener's (1964) path-breaking cross-cultural survey indicated. Future research in both rural and urban contexts in the Caribbean may therefore usefully identify further examples of ROSCAs with their structure, organization and function, including their articulation with other aspects of socio-economic life. For example, the writer's enquiries in the anglophone/francophone Windward Island of Dominica in 1993 suggest that such associations, known as *sub* (an abbreviation of *subscription*), are widespread and regarded as the 'backbone' of the informal economy. Initial evidence also suggests that such ROSCAs may be joined by 'anyone who is working', women as well as men, and that participation entails regular contributions, each member receiving the fund in turn.

Second, ROSCAs have been shown to exist in anglophone, hispanophone and francophone Caribbean societies; this begs the question of their presence in the former Scandinavian and Dutch Caribbean territories. Researchers on Suriname, the former colony of Dutch Guiana, have highlighted networks of mutual aid and exchange among both men and women, as well as some aspects of the dynamics of reputation (G. Brana-Shute, 1976, 1979:31–40; R. Brana-Shute, 1976). Networks of exchange have also been central to cultural adaptation and resistance on the former Danish West Indian island of St. John, and their ethos has remained a significant basis of cultural identity in the contemporary American Virgin Island tourist society (Olwig, 1981, 1985; cf. Besson, 1989).[10] Such data suggest that ROSCAs may exist in these contexts, and could usefully be identified and explored.

Third, as the above reassessment reveals, much of the literature on Caribbean ROSCAs has lacked gender differentiation, and some authors have assumed that participation in such groups has been entirely or primarily by males. Yet as the review has also shown, evidence is emerging of significant use of ROSCAs by Caribbean women. Future research on Caribbean ROSCAs is therefore not only needed, but should also explore more fully Caribbean women's role in them.

Fourth, in this context an especially promising field for future research is women's use of ROSCAs in Caribbean marketing systems, which historically derive from the proto-peasant adaptation and have been female-dominated throughout the post-slavery period. Katzin's (1959a, 1959b, 1960) study of partners among female higglers in Jamaica provided a useful model for such research; and as has been shown, data from Trinidad and the Dominican Republic have also been suggestive (Herskovits and Herskovits, 1947: 8–10, 47, 49, 77, 292; Norvell and Wehrly, 1969). Laguerre also noted that in Haiti the *sangue* was used especially by market women (1982:55). The writer's information on the use of *sub* by women as well as men in Dominica, mentioned above, is also relevant here. For Dominica's Roseau Market is rooted in the proto-peasant adaptation to the slavery past and has remained a primarily female sphere throughout the post-slavery era. Commuting female hucksters from this mountainous and fertile Windward Island also provide neighbouring islands such as Antigua and Barbuda with food.

Fifth, the writer's research among the peasantry of Trelawny, Jamaica, suggests that ROSCAs may also be significant in generating a new stage in the Caribbean peasant marketing system, namely informal international import higglering. The Trelawny peasant marketing system, which culminates in the market-place in the parish capital of Falmouth, is a classic example of Caribbean post-slavery peasant marketing rooted in the proto-peasant past. Falmouth market was established in the late eighteenth century, at the zenith of Jamaican plantation slavery and the heart of Jamaican slave society, as a dimension of the proto-peasant economy created by the Trelawny slaves in resistant response to the plantation system (Besson, 1987b:119–21). Like other such markets in Jamaica, the Falmouth proto-peasant market was held on Sundays – around the water tank in the centre of the town at what later became known as Market Square.[11] In 1800 a shed was built for this market, previously conducted by slaves squatting in the streets to sell their food produce (Ogilvie, 1954:43, P. Wright, 1973:56).

After Emancipation in 1838, Falmouth market became consolidated at this same site as a post-slavery peasant market in the face of the continuing monocrop export-oriented sugarcane plantation system that still encompassed Trelawny's fertile land; and in the late nineteenth century a market-place was built on this site to accommodate the peasant market (Ogilvie, 1954:43). During many of the writer's years of fieldwork in Trelawny, in the late 1960s and 1970s, the contemporary peasant market, maintained especially by female higglers, continued to be held in this same market-place. The market by then was thrice weekly: the main food markets on Fridays and Saturdays, and a supplementary dry goods *Ben' Down* market on Wednesdays with several stalls laid out on the ground outside the market-place.[12] In the late 1970s a new market-place was built at the edge of Falmouth for the still-expanding peasant market.

By the 1990s a new stage had been reached in the Falmouth market, namely the development of informal international import marketing. Higglers now regularly commute by air to Curaçao, Panama, Miami and New York, buying retail and wholesale for resale in the Falmouth market-place. Such goods include clothes, shoes, bales of cloth, cosmetics, crockery, pots and pans, and domestic electrical appliances. As a result the Wednesday *Ben' Down* market has expanded, overflowing onto the streets for several blocks beyond the market-place. Higglers have therefore been instructed by the state to move these stalls off the streets, thus paralleling the higgler–state tension of the proto-peasant past (see Mintz, 1989:197–8; Simmonds, 1987:37–8). These attempts to contain the *Ben' Down* market seem, however, to have made little impact, as Falmouth *Ben' Down* is now the island's best-known and largest rural dry-goods market; higglers come in droves from all over Jamaica. The peasant marketing system is also being transformed elsewhere in the Caribbean, such as at Fort-de-France, French Martinique, where higglers commute especially from Haiti (Laguerre, 1990:152–3).[13] Follow-up enquiry by the writer in Fort-de-France in 1993 confirms the persistence of this pattern, while as noted above there is evidence of hucksters similarly commuting from Dominica to neighbouring islands such as Antigua and Barbuda.

From the writer's fieldwork among the Trelawny peasantry, women are known to participate in partners as a feature of the traditional peasant economy, as well as being the main participants in the contemporary internal marketing system. In the 1990s the writer also observed women playing a major role in informal international import higglering.[14] It is therefore likely, especially in view of Katzin's (1959a) study on the role of partners among Jamaican female higglers, that ROSCAs are a significant source of capital accumulation in the current transformation of Falmouth market.

Preliminary enquiry on this hypothesis by the writer in 1993 confirms that partner is indeed in operation among higglers in the Falmouth *Ben' Down* market. An example of the role of such associations is a woman who participates in a partner with fifty-four members, each of whom contributes 200 Jamaican dollars per week and receives a rotating fund of approximately Ja.$10,800 in turn. Researching this hypothesis more fully could reveal both continuity and change in Caribbean women's use of ROSCAs and the region's peasant marketing system. In addition, with the expansion of *Ben' Down* market through informal import higglering, men also are entering the primarily female sphere of marketing; and initial data suggest that such men are likewise involved in partners. An example is a male higgler who participates in two overlapping associations, one of which has thirty members who contribute Ja.$200 per week and receive a fund of Ja.$6,000 in turn. Further research could also uncover competition for reputation between women and men in this formerly female sphere.

A sixth direction for research is the role of ROSCAs among Caribbean peoples – both men and women – in the overseas diaspora. As appears from the preceding review, ROSCAs have been found among migrants from the Dominican Republic, Montserrat and Jamaica in the United States and Britain. However, more work is needed on both the continuing role of ROSCAs among such migrants and women migrants' use of them. For example, in both these contexts, ROSCAs may be contributing not only to entrepreneurship, but also to house deposits and savings for Christmas, holidays and return or circulatory migration. Preliminary enquiry by the writer on the current use of ROSCAs among Caribbeans in Britain suggests that in the 1990s such associations are still being used by Guyanese, Jamaicans and Barbadians. An example is an all-female Barbadian migrant *meeting turn* in London, in which each participant's 'hand' or contribution is £100 per month; the *meeting turn* is used to generate savings for large outlays, including return visits to Barbados. This *meeting turn* had been going on for six months and was in indefinite operation (personal communication to Jean Besson from Rosemary Mallett, 21 September, 1992).[15] ROSCAs may also be contributing to the growing transnational Caribbean Carnival tradition in Britain, Canada and the United States (Cohen, 1980, 1982, 1993; Manning, 1990). Such associations may also exist not only among anglophone and hispanophone Caribbeans in North America and Britain, but also among migrants from the French and Dutch Antilles, Suriname and French Guiana in the Netherlands and France.

A seventh question, most relevant to southern Caribbean territories such as Trinidad and the Guianas and their overseas migrants, is the differential use of ROSCAs by Caribbeans of Asian and African descent in the wider context of Caribbean institution-building and development.[16]

Finally, an eighth direction for research is the institution of *susu land* currently being created in Trinidad and Tobago. With this new mode of indigenous development, in the society where Herskovits and Herskovits (1947) first identified the Caribbean ROSCA, we come full circle to the theoretical debate about African cultural retentions and Caribbean cultural creativity. *Susu land* is being created nearly five hundred years after African slaves were first brought to the Caribbean region.[17] This suggests the active use of African symbols to create Caribbean institutions, rather than passive cultural survivals; the symbol of the Yoruba *esusu* may have been so used to create Caribbean ROSCAs.[18]

Notes

1. I wish to thank participants in the Workshop on Women's Use of Rotating Credit Associations at the Centre for Cross-Cultural Research on Women, Oxford, for their comments on an earlier draft of this chapter presented at the Workshop; and Shirley Ardener and Sandra Burman for helpful editorial comments.

2. Reputation is 'indigenous' in the sense of being an Afro-Caribbean counter-culture deriving from the descendants of imported plantation slaves; the truly indigenous Amerindian population of the region having been almost totally eradicated following the Columbian conquest of 1492.

3. Trelawny parish was the heart of Jamaican and Caribbean plantation slave society, an important area of slave resistance, and the vanguard of the nonconformist anti-slavery struggle, the Baptist free-village system and the post-emancipation peasant movement. Trelawny's fertile land remains encompassed by plantations – two vast corporate 'centrals' and several *properties* or large estates – which constrain the persisting peasant villages (Besson, 1984a, 1984b, 1987b, 1988). Long-term fieldwork in Trelawny was conducted during the period 1968–93 and funded in part by the Social Science Research Council, the Carnegie Trust for the Universities of Scotland and the University of Aberdeen Travel Fund.

4. The statement by Norvell and Wehrly (1969:45) that Ardener (1964:201–9) 'reported that occurrences [of ROSCAs] in the new world were limited to Barbados, Guiana, Peru and Jamaica' is not quite accurate; Ardener (ibid:204, 208), drawing on the Herskovitses' work (1947), also cited the example of the Trinidadian *susu*, a point that Norvell and Wehrly (1969:45) attributed to Crowley (1967).

5. More specifically, Katzin stated that 'In my opinion the practice [of ROSCAs in Jamaica and Trinidad] is probably of *African origin*, and it is reasonable to assume that similar institutions exist elsewhere in *Africa* and in other *New World Negro societies*' (1959a:440, emphasis added); she footnoted that 'The writer is encouraged in the belief that informal mutual savings groups are present in other areas by the fact that Dr. Bernice Kaplan reports a similar institution among *American Indians* in Peru' (ibid: 440na, emphasis added). The question of African survivals in Caribbean ROSCAs and the contemporary distribution of ROSCAs are, however, two separate points and should be dealt with as such rather than confused as in Katzin's argument. Katzin's discussion of the Trinidadian *susu* drew on the work of the Herskovitses (1947).

6. The Caribbean is the oldest sphere of Western overseas colonialism and has experienced the longest and most pronounced impact of the Columbian conquest in the Americas (Mintz, 1989:22–3, 302). The resistant response to colonialism in the Caribbean has likewise been extreme, and the region has been described as manifesting 'the most remarkable drama of culture-building

in the modern world' (Mintz, 1980:15). Thus for example slave rebellion and the emergence of peasantries were more pronounced in the Caribbean than in the United States (Genovese, 1981; Mintz, 1989). This differential impact and response may account for the presence and absence of ROSCAs among peoples of African descent in the Caribbean and United States respectively, noted by Ardener (1964:208) and Light (1972:32–6, cited in Foner, 1977:132). For as the present chapter argues, ROSCAs, which are found especially among the peasantries and rural-urban migrants, reflect Caribbean culture-building.

7. The 'proto-peasant' adaptation initially derived from the planters' need to feed the slaves, in a context in which warfare between European colonizers in the Caribbean disrupted food imports and made their importation costly. The pattern that emerged in the eighteenth century therefore was that in colonies where plantations had marginal mountainous land, such land was allocated to slaves as 'provision grounds' to grow their own food; while in flatter territories most land remained devoted to sugar cane and there was reliance on food imports. However the slaves developed the proto-peasant economy beyond the planter rationale, producing surpluses on their provision grounds for sale in internal markets (Mintz, 1989:151–2, 180–213).

8. In a cognatic system descent is traced through both sexes and men and women are equally significant. If cognatic descent groups or corporations remain unrestricted, as in the case of Caribbean family land, they not only overlap but also rapidly increase in size. Such a system differs from the Ashanti case, where landholding corporations are not only matrilineal but also therefore restricted. Moreover even in matrilineal systems men play the most significant roles as mother's brother/sister's son. In addition to Ashanti provenance, Caribbean family land has also been variously attributed to survivals from English, Napoleonic and Roman–Dutch legal codes. For a fuller assessment of these 'cultural survival' arguments see Besson, 1984a, 1987a, 1987b, 1992a.

9. Research in Trinidad and Tobago in 1992, when the writer encountered the phenomenon of *susu land*, was made possible by grants from the British Council, the University of the West Indies, St. Augustine Campus, and Goldsmiths' College, University of London. Unfortunately time did not permit research on *susu land*, but the essence of this institution appeared to be that freehold land rights were being gradually acquired through instalment payments (to the government) paralleling *susu* contributions. *Susu land* therefore seems to be both a new mode of establishing land settlements and a new form of indigenous development (cf. Besson and Momsen, 1987).

10. While St Johnian society is anglophone, it was forged under Danish colonialism. St John was sold to the United States in 1917 along with the other Danish West Indian islands of St Croix and St Thomas (Olwig, 1985).

11. The Falmouth market was the subject of the classic Duperly daguerreotype of a Jamaican market around 1840, just after emancipation, featured for

example on the cover of Craton (1978) and in Holt (1992:165). This shows that even at that time much marketing was still conducted in the open around the water tank in Market Square. When Falmouth market was established, in the late eighteenth century, the Jamaican proto-peasant slaves were the main food suppliers in the island and as a result of their marketing activities controlled at least 20 per cent of the island's currency, in small coins. Thus the slaves not only challenged their masters' classification of them as property, but also acquired resources and skills that later became the basis of the post-emancipation peasantry (Mintz, 1989:159, 199, 200).

12. The *Ben' Down* market is so called because vendors and purchasers have to bend down to the goods laid out on the pavement. This mode of marketing parallels that of the proto-peasantry in Falmouth in the late eighteenth century; for especially before the market shed was built, in 1800, the proto-peasants laid out their foodstuffs and squatted on the streets (Ogilvie, 1954:43).

13. Such developments mark not only a new stage in the Caribbean peasant marketing system, but also a new variant of the region's migration tradition.

14. An increasing number of men are also participating in informal international import higglering. This parallels the situation among the proto-peasantry, in which men and family groups were significant (Mintz, 1989:211).

15. I am grateful to Rosemary Mallett both for this information and for permission to include it in this publication.

16. As these territories were the Caribbean region's expanding plantation frontier around the time of emancipation, they received large imports of Asian indentured plantation labour.

17. The first importations of African slaves to the New World were to the Caribbean around 1505 (Mintz, 1989:59).

18. It is therefore important, as Mintz has noted, to distinguish between African origins and the symbolic role of African culture: 'such origins are far less significant than the continuing creative employment of forms, whatever their origins, and the symbolic usages imparted to them' (1989:20). The case of Saramaka wood-carving, where Africanisms were a recent innovation, is an example (Mintz and Price, 1976:27).

References

Ardener, S. (1964), 'The Comparative Study of Rotating Credit Associations', *Journal of the Royal Anthropological Institute* XCIV: 201–29.

Austin, D.J. (1984), *Urban Life in Kingston, Jamaica: The Culture and Class Ideology of Two Neighbourhoods*, New York: Gordon and Breach.

Barrow, C. (1986), 'Finding the Support: A Study of Strategies for Survival', *Social and Economic Studies* 35 (2): 131–176.

Besson, J. (1974), 'Land Tenure and Kinship in a Jamaican Village', 2 vols,

Unpublished Ph.D. Thesis, University of Edinburgh.

—— (1979), 'Symbolic Aspects of Land in the Caribbean: The Tenure and Transmission of Land Rights among Caribbean Peasantries', in *Peasants, Plantations and Rural Communities in the Caribbean*, M. Cross and A. Marks (eds), 86–116, Guildford: University of Surrey; Leiden: Royal Institute of Linguistics and Anthropology.

—— (1984a), 'Family Land and Caribbean Society: Toward an Ethnography of Afro-Caribbean Peasantries', in *Perspectives on Caribbean Regional Identity*, E.M. Thomas-Hope (ed.), 57–83, Liverpool: Liverpool University Press.

—— (1984b), 'Land Tenure in the Free Villages of Trelawny, Jamaica: A Case Study in the Caribbean Peasant Response to Emancipation', *Slavery & Abolition* 5(1): 3–23.

—— (1987a), 'A Paradox in Caribbean Attitudes to Land', in *Land and Development in the Caribbean*, J. Besson and J. Momsen (eds), 13–45, London: Macmillan.

—— (1987b), 'Family Land as a Model for Martha Brae's New History: Culture-Building in an Afro-Caribbean Village', in *Afro-Caribbean Villages in Historical Perspective*, C.V. Carnegie (ed.), 100–32, Kingston, Jamaica: African-Caribbean Institute of Jamaica.

—— (1988), 'Agrarian Relations and Perceptions of Land in a Jamaican Peasant Village', in *Small Farming and Peasant Resources in the Caribbean*, J.S. Brierley and H. Rubenstein (eds), 39–61, Winnipeg: University of Manitoba.

—— (1989), 'Review of Karen Fog Olwig's *Cultural Adaptation and Resistance on St. John*', *Plantation Society in the Americas* 2(3):345–8.

—— (1992a), 'Freedom and Community: The British West Indies', in *The Meaning of Freedom: Economics, Politics, and Culture after Slavery*, F. McGlynn and S. Drescher (eds), 183–219, Pittsburgh: University of Pittsburgh Press.

—— (1992b), 'Free Villagers, Rastafarians and Modern Maroons: From Resistance to Identity', paper presented to the Conference, *Born Out of Resistance: Caribbean Cultural Creativity as a Response to European Expansion*, Utrecht.

—— (1993a), 'Reputation and Respectability Reconsidered: A New Perspective on Afro-Caribbean Peasant Women', in *Women and Change in the Caribbean*, J. Momsen (ed.), London: James Currey and Bloomington: Indiana University Press.

—— (1993b), 'Religion as Resistance in Jamaican Peasant Life: The Baptist Church, Revival Worldview and Rastafari Movement', in *Rastafari and Other African-Caribbean Worldviews*, B. Chevannes (ed.), London: Macmillan (in press).

Besson, J. and Momsen, J. (1987), 'Introduction', in *Land and Development in the Caribbean*, J. Besson and J. Momsen (eds), 1–9, London: Macmillan.

Brana-Shute, G. (1976), 'Drinking Shops and Social Structure: Some Ideas on Lower-Class West Indian Male Behavior', *Urban Anthropology* 5 (1): 53–68.

—— (1979), *On the Corner: Male Social Life in a Paramaribo Creole Neighborhood*, Assen: Van Gorcum.

Brana-Shute, R. (1976), 'Women, Clubs, and Politics: The Case of a Lower-Class Neighborhood in Paramaribo, Suriname', *Urban Anthropology* 5 (2): 157–85.

Carnegie, C. V. (1987), 'Is Family Land an Institution'? in *Afro-Caribbean Villages in Historical Perspective*, C.V. Carnegie (ed.), 83–99, Kingston, Jamaica: African-Caribbean Institute of Jamaica.

Clarke, R. (1986), 'Women's Organisations, Women's Interests', *Social and Economic Studies* 35 (3): 107–55.

Cohen, A. (1980), 'Drama and Politics in the Development of a London Carnival', *Man* (N S) 15: 65–87.

—— (1982), 'A Polyethnic London Carnival as a Contested Cultural Performance', *Ethnic and Racial Studies* 5 (1): 23–41.

—— (1993), *Masquerade Politics: Explorations in the Structure of Urban Cultural Movements*, Oxford: Berg.

Craton, M. (1978), *Searching for the Invisible Man: Slaves and Plantation Life in Jamaica*, Cambridge, Mass: Harvard University Press.

Davison, R.B. (1966), *Black British: Immigrants to England*, London: Oxford University Press.

Dirks, R. (1972), 'Networks, Groups, and Adaptation in an Afro-Caribbean Community', *Man* (N S) 7 (4): 565–85.

Foner, N. (1977), 'The Jamaicans: Cultural and Social Change Among Jamaicans in Britain', in *Between Two Cultures: Migrants and Minorities in Britain*, J.L. Watson (ed.), 120–50, Oxford: Basil Blackwell.

—— (1979), *Jamaica Farewell: Jamaican Migrants in London*, London: Routledge and Kegan Paul.

Genovese, E.D. (1981), *From Rebellion to Revolution: Afro-American Slave Revolts in the Making of the New World*, New York: Vintage Books.

Harrison, F.V. (1988), 'Women in Jamaica's Urban Informal Economy: Insights from a Kingston Slum', *Nieuwe West-Indische Gids* 62 (3 & 4): 103–28.

Herskovits, M.J. (1941 [1990]), *Myth of the Negro Past*, Boston: Beacon Press.

—— and Herskovits, F.S. (1947), *Trinidad Village*, New York: Alfred A Knopf.

Holt, T.C. (1992), *The Problem of Freedom: Race, Labor, and Politics in Jamaica and Britain, 1832–1938*, Baltimore: Johns Hopkins University Press.

Katzin, M.F. (1959a), '"Partners": An Informal Savings Institution in Jamaica', *Social and Economic Studies* 8: 436–40.

—— (1959b), 'The Jamaican Country Higgler', *Social and Economic Studies* 8 (4): 421–40.

—— (1960), 'The Business of Higglering in Jamaica', *Social and Economic Studies* 9 (3): 297–331.

Laguerre, M.S. (1982), *Urban Life in the Caribbean: A Study of a Haitian Urban Community*, Cambridge: Schenkman.

—— (1990), *Urban Poverty in the Caribbean: French Martinique as a Social*

Laboratory, London: Macmillan.

Light, I. (1972), *Ethnic Enterprise in America*, Berkeley: University of California Press.

Manning, F.E. (1990), 'Overseas Caribbean Carnivals: The Art and Politics of a Transnational Celebration', *Plantation Society in the Americas – Carnival in Perspective*, 47–62.

Mintz, S.W. (1955), 'The Jamaican Internal Marketing Pattern: Some Notes and Hypotheses', *Social and Economic Studies* 4: 95–103.

—— (1960), 'Peasant Markets', *Scientific American* 203: 112–22.

—— (1970), 'Creating Culture in the Americas', *Columbia University Forum* 13: 4–11.

—— (1971), 'Toward an Afro-American History', *Cahiers d'histoire mondiale* 13: 317–31.

—— (1980), 'Cultural Resistance and the Labor Force in the Caribbean Region', paper presented to the Cornell University Conference *Latin America Today: Heritage of Conquest*.

—— (1983), 'Reflections on Caribbean Peasantries', *Nieuwe West-Indische Gids* 57 1/2): 1–17.

—— (1985), 'From Plantations to Peasantries in the Caribbean', in *Caribbean Contours*, S.W. Mintz and S. Price (eds), 127–53, Baltimore: Johns Hopkins University Press.

—— (1989 [1974]), *Caribbean Transformations*, New York: Columbia University Press Morningside Edition.

Mintz, S.W. and Price, R. (1976), *An Anthropological Approach to the Afro-American Past: A Caribbean Perspective*, Philadelphia: Institute for the Study of Human Issues.

—— (1992), *The Birth of African-American Culture: An Anthropological Perspective*, Boston: Beacon Press.

Momsen, J. (ed.) (1993), *Women and Change in the Caribbean*, London: James Currey and Bloomington: Indiana University Press.

Norvell, D.G. and Wehrly, J.S. (1969), 'A Rotating Credit Association in the Dominican Republic', *Caribbean Studies* 9 (1): 45–52.

Ogilvie, D.L. (1954), *History of the Parish of Trelawny*, Kingston, Jamaica: United Printers.

Olwig, K.F. (1981), 'Women, "Matrifocality", and Systems of Exchange: An Ethnohistorical Study of the Afro-American Family on St John, Danish West Indies', *Ethnohistory* 28: 59–78.

—— (1985), *Cultural Adaptation and Resistance on St John: Three Centuries of Afro-Caribbean Life*, Gainesville: University of Florida Press.

Patterson, S. (1965), *Dark Strangers: A Study of West Indians in London*, Harmondsworth: Penguin Books.

Philpott, S.B. (1973), *West Indian Migration: The Montserrat Case*, University of London: Athlone Press.

—— (1977), 'The Montserratians: Migration Dependency and the Maintenance of Island Ties in England', in *Between Two Cultures: Migrants and Minorities in Britain*, J.L. Watson (ed.), 90–119, Oxford: Basil Blackwell.

Sassen-Koob, S. (1987), 'Formal and Informal Associations: Dominicans and Colombians in New York', in *Caribbean Life in New York City: Sociocultural Dimensions*, C.R. Sutton and E.M. Chaney (eds), 278–96, New York: Center for Migration Studies of New York.

Senior, O. (1991), *Working Miracles: Women's Lives in the English-Speaking Caribbean*, London: James Currey and Bloomington: Indiana University Press.

Simmonds, L. (1987), 'Slave Higglering in Jamaica 1780–1834', *Jamaica Journal* 20 (1): 31–8.

Smith, M.G. (1965), *The Plural Society in the British West Indies*, Berkeley: University of California Press.

Smith, M.G. and Kruijer, G.J. (1957), *A Sociological Manual for Extension Workers*, Jamaica: Caribbean Affairs Series.

Smith, R.T. (1956), *The Negro Family in British Guiana: Family Structure and Social Status in the Villages*, London: Routledge and Kegan Paul.

—— (1964), 'Ethnic Difference and Peasant Economy in British Guiana', in *Capital, Saving and Credit in Peasant Societies*, R. Firth and B.S. Yamey (eds), 305–29, London: Allen and Unwin.

Wilson, P.J. (1969), 'Reputation and Respectability: A Suggestion for Caribbean Ethnology', *Man* (N S) 4 (1): 70–84.

—— (1973), *Crab Antics: The Social Anthropology of English-Speaking Negro Societies of the Caribbean*, New Haven: Yale University Press.

Wright, C. (1984), 'Cultural Continuity and the Growth of West Indian Religion in Britain', *Religion* 14: 337–56.

Wright, P. (1973), *Knibb 'The Notorious': Slaves' Missionary 1803–1845*, London, Sidgwick and Jackson.

Appendix

The Comparative Study of Rotating Credit Associations[1]

SHIRLEY ARDENER

THE TERM 'rotating credit association', as used by Geertz (1962), seems to be the most apt so far devised for institutions which have previously been called *esusu* or contribution clubs, or have been included in the wider groups of thrift, loan, and benevolent associations. A satisfactory definition is still lacking. For example, Geertz writes: 'The basic principle upon which the rotating credit association is founded is everywhere the same: a lump sum fund composed of fixed contributions from each member of the association is distributed, at fixed intervals and as a whole, to each member in turn' (Geertz 1962, p. 243). This description is too restrictive, and does not allow the inclusion of all the examples quoted by Geertz himself. Contributions are not, in fact, always fixed (see, for example, the case from Keta, Ghana, in Little 1957, pp. 579–96), and the whole of the lump sum is not always received by a member (see, for instance, Ardener, S. 1953). Further, the use of the term 'sum' is not satisfactory, as it may seem to imply that contributions can be made only in cash and not (in part or in whole) in kind, as with some Japanese or Chinese associations (Embree 1946, p. 141, among others). The wide variety of structure found, not only in different communities, but sometimes within one single community, makes it necessary to pare to essentials any definition which is to be comprehensive, in order to isolate the common elements. I would suggest the simple one: *An association formed upon a core of participants who agree to make regular contributions to a fund which is given, in whole or in part, to each contributor in rotation.* This embodies 'the essential principle of rotating access to a continually reconstituted capital fund' mentioned by Geertz (1962, p. 243), but includes also the notion of regularity. The two elements of rotation and regularity are, I think, the essential criteria, if we are usefully to distinguish these associations from the whole range of mutual benefit clubs and co-operative undertakings. Associations in which all contributions are held by an official or 'banked' and are not distributed on a rotary principle are, by this definition, excluded.[2]

A simple type of rotating credit association would be of this kind: Ten men meet every month and contribute one shilling each to a fund which is straightway handed over to one of their number. The following month another member receives the fund, and so it continues, members receiving in rotation, until at the end of ten months, each member will have put in ten shillings and received ten shillings. This appears at first sight, perhaps, to be an equitable mechanism for saving. It will be seen on closer examination, however, that the first member to receive the fund becomes a debtor to all the other members and remains one until the last contribution has been made; the last member to receive it becomes a creditor to all the other members throughout; while the other eight members move in turn from being creditors to debtors. As has often been recognized, therefore, the advantages to all members are not equal. Some of the most important differences between associations are in the ways in which the advantages and disadvantages are distributed or balanced between members. Associations also differ in size, qualifications for membership, structural complexity, and in many other ways. Their social and economic significance also varies from one community to another.

In view of the wide geographical range of these institutions, it is perhaps surprising that no real comparative work had been published before Geertz's recent study, which includes, besides new data on Java, summaries of a number of studies by other writers. The present paper is based upon an independent analysis on which I have been engaged for some time, and which I believe may complement Geertz's work. It begins with a short review of the distribution of these associations, and the literature on them known to me; this includes some useful material put at my disposal by Polly Hill, and, for completeness, brief references to the works which have already been summarized by Geertz. Also included is some information obtained from research workers, civil servants, and graduate students, from various countries, whom I interviewed in Oxford. This, although incomplete and possibly sometimes imprecise, suggests fields for further enquiry, and supplements the literature, in which there are numerous short accounts and brief references tucked away in various works, but not many specific studies, and fewer still with 'case material' detail. Consideration is then given to the many structural and other variations found. After this, some of the material on the social and economic significance of these associations is drawn together and discussed, and, at the end, a tentative field-guide for the study of these institutions is provided. Within the limits of this paper, it is only possible to touch the surface of the subject, especially for particular areas, but it is hoped that it will draw forth further material, of which there must be a good deal.[1]

DISTRIBUTION

Asia. By the end of the nineteenth century, rotating credit associations were well-developed in China, and were described in detail by A. H. Smith (c. 1899, p. 152 ff.). Although the number of members was generally small the time-span of each complete rotation was often long, since meetings were usually held only once or twice a year. The long time-spans made these associations especially vulnerable to anything (such as famine or war) which might unbalance the economy and lead to their breakdown by default among members (A. H. Smith c. 1899, p. 157). Their organization had much in common with more modern counterparts in China, such as those described by Kulp (1925, p. 190 seq.), Fei (1939, pp. 276, 268–9), Fei & Chang (1948, pp. 120–1), and Gamble (1944; 1954).

Various methods of allocating the fund have been in use. One was by throwing dice, another by auctioning a discount, while a variant of the latter required written tenders in place of verbal bids; such methods are discussed below, pp. 211–15. Sometimes interest was paid by some members to the others. In some associations complex mathematical formulae were necessary in order to determine the amount of contribution required of members at each meeting. Thus in one notable instance, the contributions of those members who had not yet received the fund (the creditors) were determined as follows: fund – [organizer's subscription + (number of debtors × debtor's subscription)] ÷ number of creditors. Small wonder then, as Fei commented, that the complexity of this system was too difficult for every villager to understand (1939, pp. 270–3). Geertz's generalization that, in Asia, 'the tendency is towards the development of complex methods of calculating interest payments and of distributing those payments among the members of the association' (1962, p. 249) applies in this case. Nevertheless, even in China, associations with relatively simple structures are found (such as the *hui hui* association in Fei 1939, pp. 273-4). Indeed, not all villages had these institutions; Yang states of Taitou village in Shantung Province that 'no organized credit society, such as the old Yao-hui or the new credit co-operative society exists' (1947, p. 153).

Purcell gives evidence of rotating credit associations among the Chinese in Malaya. The indigenous terms *kongsi* and *hui* appear to be difficult to distinguish; they can be applied to 'secret societies' as well as to benevolent societies (Purcell 1948, p. 78 note; Ward 1954, describing *kongsi* in Borneo, deals mainly with their political aspect and does not mention rotating credit associations).[4] Burridge (1962, personal communication) noted the existence, in 1954, of small rotating credit associations among the Malays in Johore, in which the fund was allocated by auction. They were normally described by the same Malay terms as were used for savings banks, but one informant said that they were called *tonti* (probably from English 'tontine'; for the use of 'tontine' in a Malayan context see W. L. Blythe, quoted in Purcell 1948, p. 78 note, see also below, note 6). Rotating credit associations are said to be found among women, but not among men, in Indian communities in Malaya (Sharma 1962, personal communication).

Jacques (1931) gives a detailed account, which is also discussed by Freedman (1957), of one association among Chinese in Sarawak. A full description of the role they play in Java is given by Geertz (1962, pp. 243-6), and although no details are at present available, it seems that they are also found in Timor (Cunningham 1962, personal communication), the Philippines (Pagaduan 1962, personal communication) and in Hongkong (Ho 1962, personal communication).

In India, a type of rotating credit association, known as *kameti* (probably from English 'committee'), started among women in urban areas at about the turn of the century and is still found to-day. Groups of from five to fifteen women living near each other, pay small sums monthly (from two to twenty-five rupees), first allocations of the fund being made, by general agreement, to those considered to be in greatest need of them. A more formal type, known as 'Chit Fund Groups', was started more than fifty years ago, mostly in Madras and to some extent in Travancore and Kochin, all areas of comparatively high literacy. Gradually they spread northwards, and some southern Chit Fund organizers opened branches in the north. The last five years have seen their rapid development in Delhi. They have much in common with some of the more complex Chinese types, but are now commercially organized, sometimes with State registration, with the keeping of accounts and registers of contributors, and with the issuing of receipts and the like. The organizers often advertise, stating the amount of reserves, and sometimes giving such details as recommendations from patrons and guarantors. One organizer sometimes runs several Chit Fund Groups, perhaps of different sizes (usually from 100 to 200 members), and with different contribution rates. Methods of allocating the funds vary, but the system of auctioning discounts is most common, written tenders also being found (see below, pp. 212-13). A small percentage usually goes to the organizer and a further percentage is sometimes also funded for the covering of bad debts (Chawla; Gupta; Srivastava; 1962, personal communications.)

Krishnan gives four types of Chit Fund in vogue in the Tambrapani area of Madras State: (1) Thattu Chit, in which allocations are made by simple lottery; (2) Auction Chit, in which the Dutch-auction method of under-bidding is used; (3) Sahaya Chit, a benevolent type usually found among relatives for the help of needy kinsmen; and (4) Lottery or Prize Chit, in which there is an element of gambling. He also states that there are Chit Funds for specific purposes, such as Grain Chits, Cloth Chits, and the like (quoted in *All-India Rural Credit Survey* 1954, pp. 65–7). Mayer gives brief details of an institution in Malabar called *kuri*, which may not come within our definition, because of the apparent absence of regularity in the payment of contributions (1952, pp. 122–4). Geertz (1962, p. 249 note) also states that Notteboom has referred in passing to some associations in India.

In the urban areas of Vietnam, associations, like some of the Indian Chit Funds, are organized by commercial managers; in the Vietnam material, however, all managers happen to be women (Nguyen Van Vinh quoted in Geertz 1962, pp. 253–4). Embree (1946, especially pp. 138–53) gives a very detailed and interesting account of rotating credit associations in Japan, where they have existed a long time—a document mentioning them dated 1275 is extant. Different types are found, many of which are similar to some Chinese associations.

West Africa. The most commonly used term for the rotating credit association in the literature on West Africa is *esusu* (or its variants), a term generally assumed to be of Yoruba (Nigeria) origin. Bascom (1952) suggests that *esusu* was an ancient institution among the Yoruba, contributions having been made in cowries before British currency came into use. Certainly it existed in 1843, for Crowther's Yoruba vocabulary of that date gave details of small rotating credit associations among the Egba (a Yoruba people), and noted that the term *esu* was used for contributions. Burton, after quoting Crowther's later edition of 1852, added: 'Even at S'a [Sierra] Leone, the Egba keep up this system' (I am not sure whether this is Burton's own addition of 1865 (pp. 287–8), or was from Crowther of 1852). M. & J. Herskovitz (1947, pp. 76–7, 292) believed that the use of the term *susu* in Trinidad for similar associations showed that the system had been taken there by Yoruba slaves. This has been accepted by Bascom and others, Bascom, in fact, using the Trinidad evidence to establish 'that it was part of Yoruba culture during the period of the slave trade'. This will be touched upon again below.

As I have shown elsewhere (S. Ardener 1953), rotating credit associations proliferate among the Mba-Ise Ibo of Nigeria. The most usual terms in Mba-Ise for these associations are *oha* ('public') or *contribution*. Although they are of great economic and social importance in many areas now, they appear to be of comparatively recent origin. Green (1947, p. 44) puts their introduction into Umueke Agbaja, a little to the north of Mba-Ise, at about 1927. Further south, they appear to have existed earlier, since A. Martin (1956, p. 22) states that Ibibio near Calabar claim to have copied the system from the Ibo in about 1913. The Ibibio system as she describes it appears to be similar to that in Keta, Ghana, which is discussed below. Jeffreys (1951) points out that the term *osusu* (whether used only of rotating associations is not explicit) is now in use among the Ibibio, although it did not appear in Goldie's Efik dictionary of 1872; this, however, is not proof of its absence in the language then. Jeffreys also gives details of an official enquiry in Abak (Ibibio) which revealed that *osusu* existed in all parts of the junior civil service and that many members of the Native Court bench were connected with associations involving hundreds of pounds. (The institution of *umanamana* among the Ibibio, as described by Jeffreys, is not a rotating association.) Isong (1958) gives more recent details of these associations among Ibibio in Eket. Forde (in Forde & Scott 1946, p. 76) did not find rotating credit associations among the Yakö or other Cross River peoples of Nigeria.

L. & P. Bohannan (1953, p. 49; P. Bohannan 1962, personal communication to P. Hill) describe credit associations among the Tiv of Nigeria, some forms of which (known as *adashi*) rotate, and others (known as 'meetings') which do not. In 1951 the Tiv were extremely suspicious of the latter. These appear to have come from the Ibo, who were thought by Tiv to use them in order to get money to buy Tiv slaves for sacrifice (for the use of the term 'meeting' for rotating credit associations by Ibo, see Green 1947). By 1953 the Tiv had taken up the 'meeting' which seems to have been rapidly replacing age-sets.[5] The term *adashi* has a correlate in *dashi* among the Nupe of Nigeria. There it was used for rotating credit associations to which traders, craftsmen and the like belonged. Although wives of farmers used the system, farmers themselves did not, 'nor have they apparently ever done so' (Nadel 1942, pp. 271–3). Jeffreys (1951) notes that *adashi* (from Pidgin English *dash*, 'to give') appears in Bargery's Hausa dictionary of 1932, but not in Robinson's dictionary of 1906 (but again, this is not proof of its absence in the language). Rotating credit institutions also appear on the Jos Plateau of Nigeria, among small groups of wage-earners (Sheni 1962, personal communication).

Rotating associations are found in various parts of Cameroon. Among the Nsaw, Kaberry (1952, pp. 119–20) states, they are 'an adaptation of traditional custom'. In 1947, the women of Mbandi (Mbembe), Fungom village, Ngie, Aghem, Zhoaw, and Mashi reported to Kaberry that they knew of these associations, commonly known by the Pidgin English word *djanggi*, which were of recent introduction. The women of Bali, Bamessi, and Ngwo also reported the existence of these associations (Kaberry 1962, personal communication). Chilver also has some unpublished information on such associations in Bali, as well as in Meta (personal communication). At the end of the last century, an interesting manuscript on the history and customs of Bamum was begun under the direction of Chief Njoya, in his own orthography. It includes detailed rules laid down by Njoya for the control of what appear to have been rotating credit associations. These dealt with the fines (in cowries) which were to be levied on defaulters, and on organizers who took bribes (Martin (transl.) 1952, pp. 112–13, 118); it is interesting to note that Njoya would not support the levying of interest on any loans. Rotating credit associations are also found on a small scale among the Bakweri and among the plantation workers (who come from many different areas) at the coast (Ardener, Ardener & Warmington 1960, pp. 178–82 and *passim*). In Duala, associations are found composed of small groups of workers in the same establishment (Guilbot 1956, p. 105); among the Bulu, associations are 'largely confined to salaried labourers and civil servants' (Horner cited in Geertz 1962, p. 255), which suggests that the system there may be of recent inception. Kaberry states (1962, personal communication) that the women of Benakëmë in Esimbi did not know of these associations in 1947, and Ruel, in his discussion of voluntary associations among the Banyang, does not offer any evidence of these institutions. He does give details of a loan club which was introduced in 1951, but this does not rotate (1955, p. 377 seq.). In the Cameroons, to summarize, it would appear that in certain areas, such as on parts of the Bamenda-Bamum Plateau, rotating credit associations existed before the circulation of European currency; in other areas they are of recent introduction (almost certainly not older than the plantation industry); and in some they are not found at all.

Rotating credit associations are also found in Ghana in the larger towns but not, Hill believes (1962, personal communication), in rural areas. They do not seem to exist in Akwapim, for instance Brokensha (1962, personal communication) confirms that they do not exist in Larteh. Hill suggests that, in Ghana, they are unlikely to spread into areas where farmers can raise capital by pledging their farms, although pledging of land among the Mba-Ise Ibo of Nigeria did not inhibit the development of rotating credit associations there (cf. also A. Martin 1956). The Gã people of Accra may have learnt of them from immigrants, some, but not all, of whom use them. The latter may deny that such associations exist, as 'the lottery element seems slightly disreputable. . . . A group of Nigerian Ijaw were insistent that their mutual benefit society had no element of *susu*' (Hill 1962, personal communication; the *Report of Enquiry with regard to Friendly and Mutual Benefit Groups in the Gold Coast*, 1954, also mentions the existence of *susu* among the Gã). Little gives details of an association in Keta, Ghana, in which most members were women, and in which the order of rotation was determined by seniority. The contributions were not fixed and the size of the fund therefore varied. The fluctuations of the fund gave an element of chance which added 'spice to the normally dull business of saving' (Little 1957, p. 584). Hill notes that rotating credit associations also exist in government offices in Ghana, and that the system 'has spread so rapidly in southern Ghana that it is now regarded as a social evil' (personal communication); the *Ghana Evening News* (12 March 1962, Brokensha) reported that 'over 500 women have been advised at a mass rally held here that the "susu" system of saving was both "dangerous and primitive" and urged to save with the Ghana Commercial Bank'.

Banton (1957, p. 187) states that a thrift club was introduced into Sierra Leone by the Nova Scotians as early as 1794, but he does not say whether or not this was a rotating association. As noted above, by 1865 rotating credit associations were certainly in use among the Egba Yoruba in Sierra Leone. In 1885, according to Fyffe (1962, p. 422), they were known as *asusu* and any member who defaulted in the payment of contributions could be prosecuted in the courts. Rotating credit associations were in use among the Susu of Sierra Leone at least about the 1880's (according to Khalu 1962, personal communication), contributions being made in kind before European currency was available (an instance of default in the payment of a contribution of a cow is remembered).[6] Guilbot (1956) refers to associations called *ndjonu* in Dahomey. Baeck makes reference to two savings associations in the Congo: *kitimo* among the Bakongo (1957, p. 165), and *ikilemba* in Leopoldville (1961, pp. 168–9), which may possibly be rotating associations.

Central and East Africa. A very simple institution known as *chilemba* ('piling up', cf. *ikilemba* above) appears in Northern Rhodesia. In its most common form, two wage-earners agree to give part of their monthly wages to each other in turn, and a man may make several such bilateral agreements. Occasionally three men join together in such an arrangement. Sometimes 'doubling' takes place: a partner may return twice the amount of money given to him, in order to improve his credit position (Mupansha 1962, personal communication). It may be argued that where, as is usual here, only two participants are involved, the term 'association' is inappropriate. However, the elements of rotation and regularity appear, and the existence of groups of three participants shows that *chilemba* may be regarded as an embryonic form of the institution.

Rigby (personal communication to P. Hill) gives evidence of true rotating associations in the peri-urban villages in Nyasaland and Northern Rhodesia. These associations were normally composed of not more than half-a-dozen people of the same tribe who lived and worked together. He did not come across them in Ugogo in the villages away from the railway line, but in Dodoma and other small towns they were very common. In Dodoma they were formed mainly by non-Gogo, as the population was mainly non-Gogo; in smaller places along the railway line, railway employees and others, many of whom were Gogo, belonged to them. In Bulawayo, Southern Rhodesia, Brokensha (1962, personal communication) estimates that, in 1959, three-quarters of the 60,000 Africans in employment belonged to rotating associations. Gussman has some unpublished material on these associations in Southern Rhodesia also, according to the Sofers (1951, p. 108) who give details of a system found among wage-earners in Jinja, Uganda, which appears to be similar to *chilemba*. Gutkind & Southall (1956, pp. 162–3) also describe briefly small rotating associations among wage-earners in Mulago, Kampala.

South Africa. Rotating credit associations are found among the Indians of Natal. Known as *chita* (Hindi) or *chitu* (Tamil) they are restricted in membership, unlike many of the present Chit Funds of India, to a few relatives or friends or both. They have 'no officials, and no special sociability and a single specific monetary fund' (Kuper 1960, p. 93). In the Union of South Africa, among the Bantu-speaking people, two types of rotating association are found in the urban areas, and have been described in excellent detail by Kuper & Kaplan (1944, pp. 178–86). One type, *mahodisana*, was composed only of women; the name was said to be of Sotho origin and to mean 'make pay back to each other'. The second type, *stokfel*, was open to men and women, and was a cluster of small sub-associations each with its own officers. The organizations of these two types are said to have been more complex (in 1944) than at their inception (the precise date of which is not known but 'informants who have grown up in the location can remember these societies in operation when they were children' (p. 179). The term *stokfel* is said to be Afrikaans, although the derivation is obscure (the spelling 'stockfair' is used by Phillips (n.d., p. 293) and Hellman (1948, pp. 43–5). Feasting and other forms of entertainment played an important part in both types of association, and Kuper & Kaplan believe that they may have developed from the series of 'tea-parties' which used to be given by hostesses who received compensating presents from the guests. A form of 'doubling' exists (see below p. 211). Kuper & Kaplan also state: 'A similar system is to be found among some European factory workers in South Africa. A few friends will organize themselves into a savings club. Each worker will then receive a fixed part of the wages of his fellow workers in turn' (p. 183 note). No further details are given.

Sudan and Egypt. Rotating credit associations seem to have been introduced into the Sudan about fifteen to twenty years ago. Known as *sanduk* (meaning 'box') or, especially among women, as *khatta* ('putting down'), they appear to have started among members of the middle age-group of women in the central townships who wanted to collect sums to buy gold ornaments for their daughters' weddings. Later the uses to which the fund was put were more varied. These associations have spread to the more rural areas in the south, where they are restricted mainly to small groups of wives of senior civil servants and similar status-holders. These women mainly come from the central area, and may represent the daughters of the generation who first began to use the system. Men sometimes contribute to these associations through their wives, but in places like Khartoum it is not rare nowadays to find men openly joining them (Khogali; Gadalla; Bashir; Karar; personal communications). These associations were not found in the Southern Sudan among the Nuer by Evans-Pritchard, nor among the Dinka by Lienhardt (1962, personal communications); nor do they appear among the Azande (see below, p. 221).

Rotating credit associations have existed in Egypt for 'more than fifty years' and are known as *gameya* (meaning 'association'). In the rural areas membership is confined to women, but in urban areas men, women and children belong to them. Membership is usually restricted to from five to twelve persons (Ebeid, personal communication).

The West Indies and the Americas. As has been noted above, rotating credit associations exist in Trinidad under the name of *susu*. In Barbados and Guiana the terms 'meeting' and 'boxi money' respectively are said to be used for these associations (M. & F. Herskovits 1947, p. 292). However, R. T. Smith, writing of British Guiana, did not describe rotating associations. He did give details of a family fund known as the 'canister', but this does not, apparently, rotate among subscribers (1956, pp. 68, 85–6). In Jamaica a true rotating system known as 'partners' is found, and has been described in detail by Katzin (1959; see also Smith & Kruijer 1957, p. 33), who also quotes Kaplan for the existence of savings associations among the American Indians of Peru. There does not seem to be any documentation on rotating credit associations among American negroes. As Hill notes (personal communication), Myrdal (1944, p. 955) gives details of other forms of mutual benefit association and it seems unlikely that he would have overlooked the rotating credit type, had it existed.

Europe. In Scotland and the north of England, saving clubs called *menages* existed in 1825, which Jeffreys takes to have been rotating credit associations. In 1933 a Scottish magistrate described in some detail associations which clearly rotated and which were also called *menages* (Jeffreys 1951, quoting Oxford English Dictionary; Shennan 1933, p. 81). Kuper & Kaplan (1944, p. 183 note) state that associations exist in some mining districts of England, organized for the purpose of 'mail-order purchase of such things as blankets and shoes which are normally very large items in a low income group. The privilege of using the pool is decided by lot. The element of chance lends excitement to this form of saving'. As can be seen, it is not clear whether or not every member will receive the pool. Dennis, Henriquez & Slaughter, in their description of an English mining community, give no details of rotating associations (1956). Christmas and 'slate' clubs are well-known in England, but these are excluded from the discussion here by definition.[7]

Origins. Although very little attention has been paid to the origins of these associations, the present evidence suggests that they have not developed independently in each community in which they are found. Among the Ibibio of Nigeria, for instance, these associations are said to have been borrowed from the Ibo about fifty years ago.

Yet the modern Ibibio system described by Martin is very different from that found among the Mba-Ise Ibo. Evidence of borrowing may, as in this case, seem to complicate the problem of accounting for present-day differences between two systems. Such evidence should not, however, be dismissed as irrelevant.[8]

In the Sudan, rotating credit institutions may be of even more recent introduction than they were among the Ibibio, and it should not be hard to find evidence to test such hypotheses as borrowing from immigrants or from modern Egypt. Mention was made earlier of connections between Trinidad, Sierra Leone, and Yoruba country through the various forms of the term *esusu*. Although it is generally believed that the system was taken to the West Indies by Yoruba slaves, the mechanism for this transfer has never been rigorously examined. As noted above, the Egba Yoruba had a rotating system in Nigeria in 1843, and in Sierra Leone in 1852 or 1865. It is possible that they took the system to Sierra Leone, but the possibility cannot be ruled out that those Egba who returned from Sierra Leone in considerable numbers from about 1839 brought the custom with them to Yoruba country. (For this dating see Biobaku 1957, p. 26.) Hill's suggestion (personal communication) that 'immigrant groups, owing to their insecurity, may develop *susu* although they did not have it at home', may be borne in mind here. Thrift clubs of some sort, it will be recalled, existed in Sierra Leone as early as 1794. It would also have been possible for the institution to have gone from Sierra Leone to the West Indies through free labour.

In other parts of the world some valid historical connexions could probably be set up. The possibility of overlapped borrowing is not precluded—in South Africa and Malaya, for instance, where various immigrant groups are found. Even the idea of a single centre of origin for an institution with such distinctive features should not be lightly rejected, but it would be hard to make out a convincing case.[9]

Associations could have grown up independently in many different ways; for instance, from the obligations of kinsfolk to assist each other in times of distress, or with the payment of bride-wealth. In some communities, development may have come from the custom that relatives and friends should make contributions to a host at feast-giving, in order to compensate him for items consumed. Compensating gifts often exceed the cost of feasts, giving profit to the host. Firth (1946, pp. 176–82) gives details of profitable feast-giving among Malays; Ibo church marriage feasts are another example.[10] Kaberry suggests that the rotating associations among the Nsaw of Cameroon developed from palm-wine drinking clubs (1952, pp. 119–20), and Kuper & Kaplan state that among the Bantu-speakers of South Africa they may have developed from the now outmoded 'tea-party' (1944, p. 179; and above, p. 207). It may be that in some communities, rotating credit associations evolved through the need to formalize uncodified traditional obligations as traditional sanctions weakened, by introducing the concepts of regularity and rotation which distinguish these associations. Some associations, on the other hand, instead of being adaptations of existing institutions, may have been innovations designed to meet entirely new needs to which the traditional forms could not be adapted to respond. Some clues may be provided by the composition of associations. Those composed of rural women may have sometimes had different beginnings from associations composed of urban traders of mixed ethnic origin, even where both types are found among one people. The conditions required for the growth of these associations need

o

much more attention. A modern currency is not necessarily, as some have imagined, one of them (see also below, pp. 211 and 221).

The following analysis considers some of the main structural and other features encountered. It is presented in a form which may be of use, not only for a fuller understanding of the institution, but also as a framework for the systematic collection of further field material, and to this end it has been summarized as a field-guide at the end of the paper.

Membership. The total number of members may range from a handful to several hundreds. Membership may be based on one or more criteria, of which the following have been found: sex, age, kinship, ethnic affiliation, locality, occupation, status, religion, and education. Perhaps other criteria, such as political affiliation, also exist. The eligibility of some or all of the members of a rotating association may sometimes be contingent upon membership of another association. For example, Ibo yam-title and age-grade associations, among others, often organize rotating credit subsidiaries in which the 'management' is restricted to members of the parent association, while ordinary membership may or may not be restricted (S. Ardener 1953, p. 133). In such cases the criteria for membership of the parent associations indirectly determine the qualification for membership of some or all of the members of the subsidiaries. In some instances these subsidiaries appear to overshadow the other activities of the parent association (they may also reinforce them, cf. Geertz 1962, p. 248). Occasionally a group of people may hold a single joint membership in an association (in Japan a whole *buraku* (a village-subdivision 'of about twenty households') may have such a joint-membership, the fund being used for communal purposes, Embree 1946, pp. 143, 24).

Organization. The roles of all members may not be the same: an association may have one or more organizers or officials. Among the Mba-Ise Ibo, for instance, such officials as 'President', 'Secretary', 'Treasurer', 'Food-taster', 'Sanitary Inspector' and the like, were not uncommon. Sometimes, as in some Indian Chit Funds, the organizers are professionals. The membership may sometimes be divided into groups, each having separate officials in addition to the general officials of the association. Among the Yoruba of Nigeria, for instance, membership is divided into 'roads' (Bascom 1952); among the Mba-Ise Ibo, it is grouped under 'head-men' (S. Ardener 1953); the South African *stokfel* appears to be organized by a committee of the sub-association officials (Kuper & Kaplan 1944). Some associations may also have distinct branches, as do, for instance, some of those in India, Vietnam, and Ghana.

Other characteristics may include: the keeping of records, the issuing of receipts (sometimes specially printed books and other stationery are used, see Freedman 1959, p. 64, among others), written constitutions, lists of rules and regulations (Kuper & Kaplan 1944, p. 181; S. Ardener 1953, p. 131, for instance), and even advertising (Chawla 1962, personal communication). Uniforms may be worn (as in the *mahodisana* of South Africa (Kuper & Kaplan 1944, p. 183), and other paraphernalia required; for instance, special soup-bowls were used in one association among the Ibo of Nigeria (S. Ardener 1953, p. 140). Special forms of entertainment and special songs may also be found.

Contributions. Individual contributions (sometimes called 'shares' or 'hands') may be in cash or in kind, or a combination of both. Contributions in kind are sometimes treated in the same way as cash contributions, being collected and handed over to members in rotation (as for instance in Japan where contributions are sometimes rice seedlings, Embree 1946, p. 139), or they may be in the form of refreshments and consumed. Requirements may not be the same on this point for all members. The organizer in some Chinese associations, for example, may be required to make his contributions only in the form of feasts, while other members pay only in cash, or he may be obliged to contribute both in cash and kind (see, for instance, A. H. Smith *c.* 1899, pp. 155–6). In some associations the organizers do not contribute at all, and do not receive a fund (as for example among the Nupe of Nigeria; Nadel 1942, p. 372).

Regularity in the payment of contributions has been singled out as one of the criteria distinguishing rotating-credit from some other institutions. In any specific study the frequency with which contributions are made and the time required to complete the rotation should never fail to be noted. At the completion of a rotation an association may or may not be perpetuated or reformed. A procedure for speeding things up can be found among the Ibo: periodically (usually at every fourth meeting) contributions are doubled, and two members receive funds (S. Ardener 1953, p. 130). In South Africa a totally different form of 'doubling' takes place. A member may sometimes, if he wishes, independently double his own contribution, thereby giving the recipient of the fund a bonus. When the roles of the two members are reversed, however, the member who received this enlarged contribution must, if possible, double this amount as his own contribution in return. Sometimes the members of the sub-associations of the *stokfels* of South Africa, when one of their number is to receive the fund, simply double the amounts of contributions they pay (Kuper & Kaplan 1944, pp. 180–1; cf. also 'doubling' in *chilemba* in Northern Rhodesia). In some associations a member is allowed to make more than one contribution and receive more than one allocation of the fund (Embree 1946, p. 142; S. Ardener 1953, p. 130).

Payment of contributions may take place in a special meeting house, or at a member's house (usually that of the member taking the fund); or contributions may be collected by one of the organizers, or taken to the organizer's house or office; or they may be made elsewhere, such as in the market-place, at a beer-hall, or at the member's place of work.

The fund. The size of the fund (sometimes called the 'pool', 'take-out', or the like), the amount of individual contributions, and the number of members, are clearly interdependent, and it is possible sometimes to deduce one of these from the other two (it is obvious that, in a simple case in which ten members contribute equal amounts into a fund which totals ten shillings, then each member's contribution is one shilling). In some complex associations, as we shall see, this is not possible.

At the beginning of this paper it was pointed out that, in an association in which all members contribute equal and fixed amounts throughout, the advantages are nevertheless not equal to all. That is to say: all members but the last to receive the fund get interest-free loans of decreasing magnitude for decreasing periods, and all but the first give interest-free loans of increasing magnitude. The method by which the order is determined is therefore of much importance. In certain, usually small, associations, such as the *kameti* of India, the order is reached by general agreement, those members considered to be most in need of cash being put first (Chawla 1962, personal communication; the Meta of Cameroon offer another case, Chilver 1962, personal communication). In other associations, the order is determined by the organizer (or organizers) who may perhaps take into account a member's needs, whether he will offer a gift or bribe, or a number of other considerations. Organizers determine the order among the Nupe of Nigeria, for example (Nadel 1942). In other associations the order of allocation may be settled in advance by known criteria, as is done, for instance, among the Bulu of Cameroon, where the criteria are those of age and kinship seniority (Horner, quoted by Geertz 1962, p. 255). The rotation may also be determined by lot; the lottery element is considered by some to add excitement (e.g. Kulp 1925, p. 194; Little 1957, p. 584; Kuper & Kaplan 1944, p. 183 note), but is regarded by others as 'slightly disreputable' (Hill 1962, personal communication and above p. 206; cf. Fei 1939, p. 274). More rarely, the order of rotation may be decided by recourse to divination, as among the Yoruba (Bascom 1952, p. 67 and note 15).

In some associations, however, the amounts of contributions and of funds are not constant. In these, allocation of the fund is sometimes by auction. The principle may be illustrated as follows: the fund may nominally be one hundred units, but a member who requires it may offer to accept ninety instead. Another member may bid against him by offering to take a lower fund: the member offering to take the lowest fund gets it. At the beginning of the rotation, when many members are competing for the fund, it will tend to be relatively small. As the number of members waiting to receive grows fewer, and their chance of receiving comes nearer, the amount of the fund regarded as the minimum acceptable tends to rise. The last man does not need to bid at all, but automatically receives the full fund. The size of the fund is reflected in the size of the contributions which make it up. The members who receive low funds made up of low contributions must continue to pay the higher contributions required towards the end of the rotation. They will therefore have paid out more in contributions than they received in their funds. The difference may be regarded as a *de facto* interest charge on the loans they received at the beginning of the rotation. The members who receive towards the end will, conversely, have contributed less than the amounts they took out, and they may be said to have received interest. By this system of bidding, the order of rotation, the amounts of contributions and of funds are determined, and the advantages or disadvantages of any particular position in the rotation are to some extent balanced. (See model 4, page 214, below, and cf. the *Kwangtung Piao Hui* system given in Fei 1939, p. 274.)

Alternatively, bids may refer to the amount of contributions considered acceptable, instead of the amount of funds, the effect being the same. Or again, instead of bidding *down* the amount of fund they will accept, members may bid *up* the amount of fund they are prepared to forego, or, in other terms, to bid for discounts (instead of offering to accept a fund of ninety units in place of a nominal hundred, a member offers to accept a discount of ten, which may be pushed up by competitive bidding; cf. the system in some Indian Chit Funds, for example (also A. H. Smith *c*. 1899, pp. 154–5). Written tenders may take the place of bids in some associations (see Kulp 1925, p. 191, among others). This may add an extra element of chance, for when a member puts in his own tender, he has no means of telling whether or not any other tenders which may be submitted are truly competitive or are merely put in to frighten him into raising his offer (Freedman 1959, p. 65).

It is possible for 'interest' to be paid without the use of either bids or tenders. This can be done by fixing in advance a sliding scale in such a way that members at the head of the rotation consistently contribute larger amounts than those at the end, the funds remaining constant (Fei 1939, p. 274). Although not documented, a sliding scale could also be so arranged that both contributions and funds are smaller at the beginning of the rotation, all members contributing larger amounts towards the end than those which they contribute at the beginning. Where sliding scales are employed, the order of rotation must be determined by one of the methods discussed earlier, such as by lot. The pattern of payments in an association using a sliding scale may resemble the pattern of one in which bidding is employed. In the former however, the amounts of contributions and of funds are known in advance, whereas in the latter they are not, but depend on the degree of competitiveness among members. Contributions and funds may both fluctuate in size, as in Keta, Ghana. There, a member who has not yet received may make contributions to any fund of whatever magnitude he wishes. After having received a fund, however, he must return to subsequent recipients contributions equal to those received from them. By careful recording, the amounts a member contributes and receives are made equal (Little 1957; cf. A. Martin 1956).

Methods are not always as straightforward as has so far been suggested. Thus, in some associations, the contributions a member makes when he is a debtor (i.e. after having received a fund) are different from those he makes when he is a creditor (i.e. before receiving a fund). In such associations, the contributions of the debtors are constant, and are at a higher rate than those of the creditors. The contributions of the latter are determined by one of three ways: they may be at a constant, fixed rate (cf. A. H. Smith *c.* 1899, p. 155, note; it should be noted, however, that Smith gives a simplified scheme); they may be at a predetermined but declining rate (Fei 1939, p. 271, note); or they may be determined by auction among the creditors. In the latter case, the amounts of the creditors' contributions decrease, although, because of the increasing number of larger contributions paid by the debtors, the fund increases in amount (Embree 1946, pp. 139–40). The creditors' contributions decline not, I think, because the competitors are reluctant to 'win' the fund, as Embree supposes, but because of their relationship to the size of the contributions of the debtors. Near the end of the rotation, creditors, instead of *paying* contributions may even *receive* amounts (Embree 1946; Fei 1939). The situation may be even more complicated, for the organizer may make contributions at a different rate altogether. Associations are also found in which two methods of allocating the fund alternate: bidding taking place for one fund, and lottery for the following fund, and so on (Embree 1946, p. 145). Such complexities may be noted, although they need not detain us longer here.

It will be generally clear that the size of contributions, the method by which this is determined, the method by which the fund is allocated, whether or not interest is paid, and whether or not the contributions are fixed in advance, are all related. To illustrate the kind of relationship possible between contributions and funds, some simplified diagrammatic models are given. Consider, for this purpose, only the following variables:

(i) All members receive equal funds.
(ii) Funds are not all equal.
(iii) All members pay identical contributions.
(iv) Members' contributions are not identical.
(v) A member's contributions remain the same throughout.
(vi) A member's contributions may change.

(It has been assumed for convenience that members contribute to the funds which they themselves receive; this does not necessarily happen in all actual associations.)

1.	Members	Contributions			Total paid	Fund received
		1st	2nd	3rd		
	A	10	10	10	30	30
	B	10	10	10	30	30
	C	10	10	10	30	30
		30	30	30		

This model involves variables (i), (iii) and (v). (The system in Mulago, Uganda, described by Gutkind & Southall (1956), for example, appears to be based on these.)

2.	Members	Contributions			Total paid	Fund received
		1st	2nd	3rd		
	A	10	10	10	30	27
	B	9	9	9	27	27
	C	8	8	8	24	27
		27	27	27		

3.	Members	Contributions			Total paid	Fund received
		1st	2nd	3rd		
	A	Kind	Kind	Kind	3 × Kind	20 + Kind
	B	10	10	10	30	20 + Kind
	C	10	10	10	30	20 + Kind
		20 + Kind	20 + Kind	20 + Kind		

Models 2 and 3 involve variables (i), (iv) and (v). (Compare the example given by Fei (1939, p. 274, note). The examples from China in which the organizer supplies only feasts resemble model 3 (see, for instance, Kulp 1925, p. 191).)

4.	Members	Contributions			Total paid	Fund received
		1st	2nd	3rd		
	A	8	9	10	27	24
	B	8	9	10	27	27
	C	8	9	10	27	30
		24	27	30		

In this model variables (ii), (iii) and (vi) obtain. (Such a pattern may be found where bidding is employed, for instance.)

5.	Members	Contributions			Total paid	Fund received
		1st	2nd	3rd		
	A	10	9	8	27	27
	B	9	10	10	29	29
	C	8	10	10	28	28
		27	29	28		

This model involves variables (ii), (iv) and (vi). (The example from Keta, Ghana, embodies these variables. So, it is clear, does Martin's Ibibio case.)

The variables discussed, and the models given, are not enough to demonstrate exactly all schemes actually encountered. They have been simplified and regularized: bids, for instance, would not necessarily rise in such a neat progression. Real associations are frequently a good deal more complex. For example, Fei & Chang (1948, p. 120) give a scheme in which variables (i) and (iv) apply generally, but (vi) applies only to the organizer, while (v) applies to the rest of the members (in this case, both contributions and funds are, nevertheless, fixed in advance). Smith (c. 1899, p. 156) describes a system in which (ii) and (iv) apply generally, but (v) applies to the organizer, and (vi) to the rest of the members.

It will be noted that in models 1 and 5 no interest is paid, all contributors putting in amounts equal to those which they receive back. In models 2 and 4 interest is paid by A and received by C, while B neither gives nor takes interest; if there were more than three members, the interest paid would theoretically decrease to a vanishing point in the middle of the rotation, and the interest received would gradually increase from this point towards the end of the rotation. The methods by which interest is distributed in models 2 and 4, however, are not the same. In 2 it is achieved by having different contributions for each member, while the funds remain equal; in 4 contributions are all equal, while the funds vary. In model 3, whether or not interest is paid, and by and to whom, depends on whether the contributions in kind of A equal, exceed or fall short of the value of ten, which is the amount of the contributions paid by B and C.

Transferability. The fund itself may or may not be transferable. Among the Ibo, for example, a member may arrange (with the head-man through whom he pays his contributions) for his right to receive a fund in the future to be transferred to another person (S. Ardener 1953, pp. 135–8; and cf. Embree 1946, p. 142 for Japan). This is an important concession. An Ibo association may have between 200 and 300 members, and a contributor may have to wait a long time before he can get access to the fund. If he urgently needs money, it is possible for him to borrow from someone (not necessarily a member) to whom he transfers his right to his fund in settlement. He continues to pay his contributions to the association, and in so doing gradually divests himself of his debt. When his fund becomes due it goes to the lender of the money. Usually interest is allowed for in such transactions, and the amount charged will frequently depend on the chances of the money-lender (who is often one of the head-men) obtaining the fund quickly, but it is often lower than the prevailing rate in the community.[11] Debts, such as for bridewealth, may also be settled by the transfer of a right to a fund. In some associations the use to which a fund may be put is restricted—for instance, to the buying of umbrellas (Embree 1946, p. 148), or tools (A. Martin 1956, p. 22), or cloth (S. Ardener 1953, p. 134) or to marriage payments (Fei 1939, p. 268).

Deductions from Fund. In some associations, the whole of the fund is kept by each member in turn; in others deductions are made. These may be deposited in a special pool for lending out. In some Ibo associations this pool, known as 'the box', is important, and high rates of interest are charged for loans from it. Often 'the box' is treated as if it were a member of the association, 'making' contributions and 'receiving' a fund, which is added to its lending capital (S. Ardener 1953, p. 135). The money in this pool at the end of the rotation is usually divided among members. Sometimes, as in some Indian Chit Funds (Chawla, personal communication), deductions are required for a contingency fund, for use in case of losses from defaulters. Deductions may also be made for payment of officials, or for the provision of entertainment, and the amounts may be fixed, or left to the discretion of the recipient of the fund. It is also necessary sometimes for *ex gratia* gifts or bribes to be given overtly or surreptitiously to organizers, in order to compensate them for their pains, or to receive preferential treatment in the allocation of the fund. To a contributor, these deductions may be regarded almost as interest charges or administrative costs, and they may substantially reduce the value of his fund.

Sanctions. A rotating credit association obviously cannot function unless all members continue to keep up their obligations. The pressure of public opinion within the membership may be enough to ensure this. It is interesting to note the very great importance placed upon these obligations in some communities. In associations based on kin, default may be prevented by the 'acknowledged social obligation between relatives' (cf. Fei 1939, p. 269). Often payment of contributions is regarded as a 'solemn duty' (see, for instance, Kuper & Kaplan 1944, p. 181), and other debts may be incurred in order to do this. In Japan there 'is nothing dishonourable in a debt as such', but to have a debt in a rotating credit association and be unable to pay is 'very dishonourable indeed' (Embree 1946, p. 147); in South Africa, 'the fact that members get into debt while making these contributions does not in any way discredit *mahodisana* or *stokfel* with some Africans' (Kuper & Kaplan 1944, pp. 183–4).[12] The member who defaults in one association may suffer to such an extent that he may not be accepted as a member of any other. In some communities the rotating credit institution has become so rooted in the economic and social system that exclusion would be a serious deprivation. An illustration of the way in which these institutions may be embedded in the economic system comes from Bulawayo: 'An attempt was made to introduce fortnightly pay in the Municipality, which employed 5,000 African workers: it threw the rotating system completely out of balance, and riots were threatened before the system reverted to monthly pay' (Brokensha 1962, personal communication). In Mba-Ise (Nigeria) much of the opposition to the introduction of Pioneer Oil-mills was put in terms of fear of resulting collapse of these associations (E. W. Ardener 1953, pp. 921–2). A member may go to great lengths, such as stealing (S. Ardener 1953, p. 139) or selling a daughter into prostitution (Embree 1946, p. 147), in order to fulfil his obligations to his association; failure to meet obligations can even lead to suicide (Embree 1946, p. 147).

There are several ways in which the association may act directly to minimize default.

A member whose reliability is suspect may be placed towards the end of the rotation, and sometimes he may be given only half his share at once, and he must wait until later for the second half (Bascom 1952, p. 65). A member may be required to sign a contract, either when joining the association, or when he receives a fund. Sometimes he must give some form of security, or find a guarantor. A defaulter may be fined by the association, and in the last resort proceedings may be taken against him in the courts (see, for example, S. Ardener 1953, p. 131; Fyffe 1962, p. 422; for an interesting unsuccessful case see A. H. Smith c. 1899, pp. 158–60). The legal validity of the contract between a member and an association may vary: rotating credit associations may, for instance, be the subject of special legislation (as in Madras State of India) or the ordinary legislation relating to the recovery of debts may be regarded as sufficient protection for both the association as a whole and for individual members. The attitude of government departments and other agencies, such as the press (see above, p. 206) and religious organizations may be important. It is interesting to note that among the Ibibio 'the older men maintain that it was the spread of christianity which made possible sufficient mutual cooperation for [rotating credit associations] to develop' (A. Martin 1956).

FUNCTIONS AND OTHER ASPECTS

The functions of rotating credit associations, their relation to some other institutions, and their place in the general economic and social patterns of the societies in which they occur need some consideration.

The most obvious function of these associations is that they assist in small-scale capital-formation, or more simply, they create savings. Members could save their contributions themselves at home and accumulate their own 'funds', but this would withdraw money from circulation: in a rotating credit association capital need never be idle. If, instead of being saved at home, money were given to a treasurer to keep, he could put it into circulation until it was transferred back to the subscribers. Sometimes the chances of embezzlement are high, however: an advantage of the rotating credit institution is that each fund (or part of it) is immediately possessed by one of the contributors and cannot be embezzled. There remains, of course, the risk that a member may default, but as we have seen, sanctions are normally strong enough to reduce this.

In many of the countries for which there is documentation, savings can be made in post office (or other) savings banks, where deposits are for practical purposes absolutely secure. Amogu (1956, p. 203), however, has shown that in Nigeria, absolute security is not an overriding consideration with the majority; the measure of security provided in rotating credit associations is considered adequate. Post office savings banks do provide interest and give speedy access to deposits, which some associations do not. On the other hand, savings banks may be disliked for fear that incomes may be made known to tax or other government departments (Katzin 1959, p. 439; cf. the withdrawal of money for fear of its confiscation by Government, in Kuper & Kaplan 1944, pp. 185–6). As Amogu pointed out (1956), post offices and the like are frequently less accessible than rotating credit associations, although it must be emphasized that this is not always the case, especially in towns.

It has often been said that one of the advantages which rotating credit associations possess, in contrast to savings banks, is that they are less impersonal. The environment of banks and the conduct of officials may appear intimidating. Also it has been suggested that the forms and other procedures of savings banks may confound the less educated. Although this is generally true, it has been seen that in some rotating credit associations, procedures may also be more complex than the ordinary member can understand, and written documents are often required. Even where inaccessibility or the procedural complexities of banks offer no obstacles, the rotating credit association may still occur, and indeed members may employ some of the facilities of banks in connexion with them. In the Sudan, for instance, a group of bank employees themselves formed a rotating credit association in which one of the members made the payment of his contributions through the bank; he made out a series of suitably post-dated cheques in favour of each member which he handed in a bunch to the organizer (a woman) to be distributed at the appropriate times (Bashir 1962, personal communication). This member had joined the association for another advantage: the element of compulsory saving. The importance attached to a committed obligation to save and pay contributions has already been mentioned. I have shown elsewhere the great driving force this may give to economic activity (1953, p. 138).

Rotating credit associations also, of course, provide credit on the sort of small scale in which banks are not normally interested. Amogu (1956, p. 208) has pointed out in the case of the expatriate banks of Nigeria, that, even where they are interested, bank officials may be hyper-cautious, perhaps partly because they may not be able easily to assess the reliability of those seeking loans; organizers of rotating credit associations may be in a more favourable position to do this. (The decision to allow a member to join an association may itself be a recognition of his reliability; however, an association, as noted above, can sometimes take steps to minimize risk of default.) The commercialization of rotating credit associations in India suggests, however, that bank officials may not necessarily be at a great relative disadvantage in assessing credit-worthiness everywhere.

Credit may also be sought from money-lenders, but in many communities the rates of interest charged are very high, perhaps 100 per cent per annum, whereas in rotating credit associations interest charges, where they exist, are usually somewhat lower. This is probably because, as we have seen, the sanctions inducing a member to repay his loan in an association are comparatively strong. A person may hesitate long before destroying his reputation before a large circle of friends or relatives, but object less perhaps, to ruining it with one money-lender. It is often much easier to divest oneself of a debt piecemeal by paying contributions than with the one lump-sum repayment which money-lenders often require, and default is therefore less likely (cf. Nguyen Van Vinh, quoted in Geertz 1962, p. 254). The difference in risk probably accounts partly for the difference in interest charges. It has been noted in Sarawak (Jacques 1931), where bidding is employed, that should any doubts as to the stability of an association arise, high bids invariably follow, since members become anxious to secure what they can, lest the association should collapse (high bids, as has been seen, are equivalent to high interest charges).

The hire-purchase system is a possible alternative to rotating credit institutions in some places. A disadvantage is that the use to which credit may be put is normally restricted to particular items, although this is true also of the comparatively few associations in which funds may be restricted to particular uses (see above, p. 216). Another disadvantage of hire-purchase is, again, that creditors are often not easily able to assess credit-worthiness, nor easily able to apply sanctions on defaulters (whatever their legal powers), and consequently charges may tend to be high. (For an example of the ineffectiveness of hire-purchase sanctions in Nigeria, where rotating credit associations are normally strong, see Wells & Warmington 1962, pp. 104–5. Kuper & Kaplan 1944, p. 183, imply that among the Bantu-speakers of South Africa, rotating credit association debts have priority over hire-purchase debts.) An important advantage of hire-purchase, on the other hand, is that all who make use of it obtain credit and do not give it, whereas in a rotating credit institution, all but the first member in the rotation must give credit before they obtain it, and in fact the last member never receives credit.

Isong has remarked of associations in Nigeria that 'it can safely be said that from the standpoint of modern business methods, the system is unbusinesslike'. He regards it so because in Nigeria no interest is paid (Isong 1958, p. 118; cf. Geertz 1962, p. 254, 'another indication of the business-like nature of the *ho* [in Vietnam] is the fact that the gap between the open-market interest rate and that of the rotating association is not so wide as in the traditional cases'). Apparently unaware of forms of the institution elsewhere in which, one way or another, interest is charged, he proposes a scheme in which a rate of three per cent is levied. The 'unbusinesslikeness' of associations in which no interest can be gained by waiting does not prevent some members from actually preferring (even 'clamouring') to wait till near the end of the rotation, as he himself noted (Isong 1958, p. 120, note 10; cf. Katzin 1959, p. 437). This may be because such members prefer to have their funds available to be applied for in time of trouble. To them the association is a form of insurance society. The element of insurance exists where compassionate grounds determine to some extent the order of allocation, or where a member may obtain the fund by some form of bidding. Where the order of rotation is flexible and interest charges are made, in whatever form, the burden of the latter is likely to fall upon those who urgently require a fund, and the benefit to accrue to those who do not. If no interest is charged, the interest thereby foregone is lost to those who did not need to call for an early place in the rotation. This loss may not be begrudged because it may indicate that no sudden calls for cash occurred. The interest foregone may possibly be regarded as the cost of insurance placed upon those who did not need to make a claim. It is also possible to question the advantage of levying interest on general grounds, for it may tend to favour the richer members, those more able to wait and enjoy the benefit of the interest paid by the rest (cf. Embree 1946, p. 146—rich men 'can afford to wait until the last meeting before winning, thus paying in least and taking out most. From this results a situation whereby the more substantial members of the community act as bankers to their less substantial neighbours'). One feature of rotating credit associations in some communities, such as among the Mba-Ise Ibo, is that, through them, the less wealthy members have been able to accumulate cash and compete with richer persons (S. Ardener 1953, p. 140).

A subsidiary aspect of rotating associations which perhaps has not been sufficiently brought out, is that they function to some extent as money markets. Quite apart from their built-in features—the rotating fund and, sometimes, a loan fund—they may act as exchanges where money can be raised. Members who have not yet received their funds, and even non-members, may perhaps be able to obtain loans from those members who have received funds, news of which is usually easily obtainable. (See, for instance, Gamble, quoted in Geertz 1962, p. 252, who says 'of the eight members of the particular association studied [just south of Peking, China] . . . four used the fund they received for business expenses or ventures, seven loaned it out to others, and only three used it for family expenses'.) Loans may also be obtainable from the organizers or officials of the association, who often, as among the Ibo, become the money-lenders of the community (S. Ardener 1953, p. 136; cf. Nguyen Van Vinh, quoted in Geertz 1962, pp. 253-4, for Vietnam). Members who have not received their funds may also be able to obtain credit by transferring their rights to receive future funds, as already described.

It is not only the financial aspects of these associations which merit consideration: for instance, the ambivalent role of kin is of interest. In certain areas the close kin-group formed the basis of the membership, and, as noted already, the obligations towards associations were regarded, in parts of China, rather as an extension of kinship obligations. In Luts'un, China, however, close kin did not usually join the same association, because it was not considered easy to maintain the organizer-subscriber relationship between kin, nor wise to attempt to exploit kinship obligations for what were regarded as ordinary business transactions (Fei & Chang 1948, p. 121). Among the Yoruba, associations composed of close male kin were prohibited in case frictions arose which could disrupt the harmony of the kin-group (Bascom 1952, p. 67). Fei has shown that in Eastern China kinship often formed the basis of membership of these associations and when associations broke down during a depression this 'had far-reaching consequences in disrupting the existing kinship ties' (1939, pp. 269-70). In urban areas, rotating credit associations, in common with other forms of voluntary association, often tend to support the solidarity of neighbourhood or other groupings (in Java for instance, see Geertz 1962, p. 248). Kuper & Kaplan state that 'the extent to which bonds of friendship induced by local proximity are developing emerge from the organization of [rotating credit associations]. . . . How far this bond is replacing the already weakened kinship bond with its obligations of support and aid cannot be exactly determined'. However, members of these associations were among the first to be turned to when burial collections, and the like, were being made (Kuper & Kaplan 1944, pp. 184-5; see also Little 1957).

Rotating credit associations may enhance the social status of participants. Sometimes it is the organizer who gains status by demonstrating his powers of leadership and administrative ability (Kulp 1925, p. 193). Sometimes, on the other hand, it is acquired by members who join an association in order to assist the organizer, and who thereby demonstrate their generosity (Fei 1939, p. 269). Sometimes mere membership confers prestige. In South Africa, for instance, 'a recognized motive in joining these associations is prestige,' through them you may become known 'not only as generous but also as reliable' (Kuper & Kaplan 1944, p. 184). The position of a member in a rotating credit association may be somewhat different from that of one in many other types of loan association. Although we know that all members but the last in the rotation receive credit, often they may barely be aware of the fact; they frequently do not think of their funds in terms of loans. Each contributor, as already noted, has a 'right to a fund', provided he fulfils his obligations. Even if he should need to plead for an early place in the rotation, this only brings into question *when* the right is to be exercised, not the right itself. Where bidding is permitted, the recipient of the fund has the satisfaction of having dominated those bidding against him. In the case of most other loan associations, a member who requires money is largely in the position of a supplicant. In a rotating credit association, the recipient of a fund, far from suffering loss of dignity, is often the member of honour or host at a feast or some other form of entertainment.

GENERAL REMARKS

Geertz has described the rotating credit association as a 'middle-rung' institution. He sees it as a product of a 'shift from a traditionalistic agrarian society to an increasingly fluid commercial one', as an 'educational mechanism in terms of which peasants learn to be traders, not merely in the narrow occupational sense, but in the broad cultural sense' (1962, p. 260). I have suggested elsewhere, that among the Mba-Ise Ibo the transition from a mainly agricultural to a predominantly trading economy was success-ful, largely because of the development of these associations (1953, p. 128), but I am not convinced that these associations were in any sense a 'product' of this shift; they may have been partly, at least, causative. In either event, one is left with the problem: why do these associations flourish in some societies which have made this transition, while they are less important in others which have also done so? The institution does not seem to exist at all among the Azande of the Sudan; yet the Azande 'have been using money for about fifty years', and 'everybody wants more money'. Among the Azande, 'almost all families were found to save money when possible; some said they were saving for large purchases, usually bicycles, and others explained their savings in terms of social emergencies' (Reining 1959, pp. 39, 40, 42). The absence of rotating associations among the Azande has had to be deduced: writers only rarely specifically refer to the absence of these associations in particular communities; such negative evidence could be of great interest. Here is a group in which there are pressures to save for ends which appear to be similar to those found in many groups which utilize rotating credit associations in order to achieve those ends. Why then have they not developed among the Azande? Geertz's notion of peasants learning to be traders, even in the broadest sense, is also inadequate, if only because in some communities associations are confined to non-trading wage-earners.

Especially open to question is the concept which Geertz presents of a continuum, ranging from 'traditionalistic' associations with stress laid on 'ritualistic, solidarity-strengthening elements', to associations which are more 'rationally oriented', being increasingly concerned with the financial probity of members and leaders, the legal enforceability of obligations, and with more complex patterns of organization and commercial calculation. Also questionable are the positions which he allocates to some associations on this continuum: he moves from 'the village *arisan* [of Java], the Japanese *ko*, or the Bulu example, towards the Indo-Chinese *ho* and the case Ardener reports for the Mba-Ise [Ibo], or Little for Keta'. To take the example of the Japanese *ko*, these vary widely in type, and include associations which are registered, which have legal, stamped documents, and in which sureties are required. 'The original borrower registers some land or property, e.g. house (property must be insured) as surety for debt. ... Other members, when they have won, must also register indebtedness and surety, each time for fifty yen less than the previous man in case of a fifty-yen *ko*' (Embree 1946, pp. 143–4). Such a degree of organization would surely place these types of *ko* towards the end of any such continuum.

One should beware of assuming that the 'economic' or 'rational' aspects always predominate in the more sophisticated institutions or those with larger memberships. In a small association among a group of wage-earners more stress may be placed on purely financial return than it is in some much larger ones having more complex structures. Geertz has suggested that when more information on urban associations in Africa is available, this may show 'some of the same sort of movement towards increased economic rationality that their counterparts in Asia show' (1962, p. 258). He cites the case for Keta, Ghana, as a possible example of this increased rationality. The present evidence does not entirely support this. As we have seen, much greater stress is laid upon feasting and social prestige in some urban associations among the Bantu-speakers of South Africa, than it is among some rural Ibo (the benefit in joining these South African associations is not primarily economic. 'The sum of money put into circulation gives little material benefit, but does confer prestige' (Kuper & Kaplan 1944, p. 184). Even where associations are organized professionally, such 'uneconomic' aspects as feasting and conviviality may be important. In Vietnam, for instance, where associations are comparatively businesslike (with government registration, the keeping of books, and so forth), feasting is still required, and meetings must be 'gay' and 'elegant' (Nguyen Van Vinh cited by Geertz 1962, p. 254). Classification of associations into 'rational' and 'irrational', 'economic' and 'non-economic', 'traditionalistic' may lead us nowhere.

Geertz has also suggested that as the form becomes 'more and more like a specifically economic institution' it is perhaps 'self-liquidating', being replaced ultimately by banks, co-operatives, and other economically more rational types of credit institution' (1962, p. 263). Isong, on the other hand, came to the conclusion with regard to Nigeria that 'this indigenous institution deserves a place in our programme of economic development' (1958), and the All-India Rural Credit Survey recommended their incorporation into co-operative societies (this has already been done in Sierra Leone according to Khalu 1962, personal communication). The persistence of the institution in communities in which banks and co-operatives exist, such as in Great Britain, Japan, and South Africa, and the recent formation of an association by bank employees in the Sudan, suggests that there is still a place for these institutions alongside 'other economically more rational' types of institution. Any mechanism of saving or credit deserves the attention of economists, but these institutions also merit further study by social anthropologists and sociologists (in *Economic Anthropology*, Herskovits 1952, a standard textbook, there is not even a reference to any form of rotating credit association), not only because they have been shown to possess remarkable powers of survival, and because they illustrate the manifold forms an essentially identical institution can take in different societies, but also because they cannot be understood in terms of 'economic' motive alone.

POSTSCRIPT

In 1962 it was possible for thirty-three collaborating scholars to publish *Markets in Africa* (P. Bohannan and G. Dalton, Editors, a volume of nearly 800 pages) without any consideration being given to this important capital-forming institution. One may indeed agree with Firth (1964. p. 17) that 'the formation and use of capital constitutes one of the least developed aspects of socio-economic study'. (The paucity of references to *capital* in the index of this large volume—namely six—would also appear to confirm this.) However, the position has recently been improved by these associations' having received some attention (but not very much) in *Capital, Saving and Credit in Peasant Societies* (Firth and Yamey, Editors, 1964), published since this present essay was written, where Benedict gives some material for Mauritian Indians, Dewey for Java, Epstein for New Britain, Smith for British Guiana, Swift for Malaya and Topley for Hongkong. Katzin also makes a reference to these associations in *Economic Transition in Africa* (Herskovits and Harwitz, Editors, 1964). Lévi-Strauss states that, although kinship has been one of the main concerns of those gathering ethnographic material in the last fifty years, the amount of usable material in relation to that actually collected remains disappointingly small (1963 (1952), p. 300). And in discussing the present condition of studies of social structure he says: 'Surprisingly enough, it is at the very moment when anthropology finds itself closer than ever to the long-awaited goal of becoming a true science that the ground seems to fail where it was expected to be the firmest: The facts themselves are lacking, either not numerous enough or not collected under conditions insuring their comparability' (p. 315). If this can be said of topics commanding the centre of attention in social anthropology, it is not surprising to find a parallel situation in the study of economic behaviour, a field which Lévi-Strauss admits has in the past been suspect among anthropologists (p. 297). Thus we find Firth recently (1964, p. 15) complaining that contributions by anthropologists to the analysis of economic institutions have not yet been very impressive. He also suggests (p. 16) that their studies in this field are apt to be selective and not systematic. Certainly I arrived at similar views when I came to consider the small segment of economic activity examined in this paper. While there will always be a great dependence on well-documented socio-economic studies on circumscribed areas these can no longer be too inward looking, but must also be increasingly 'usable'; there will also be an increasing need for more detailed study of selected topics in a wider setting. One of the basic problems of systematic analysis is the recognizing and isolating of phenomena; the breaking down of large groups into smaller groups capable of being precisely defined and analysed in greater detail. In this paper I have attempted to isolate according to clear criteria one type of institution which has received comparatively little treatment so far in the literature, and to draw attention to some of the variables relevant to its analysis.

FIELD-GUIDE

Note. The characteristics discussed on pp. 210–17 are summarized in question form below, for the use of field-workers. It will be necessary, in order to understand this guide, for reference to be made to the appropriate sections in these pages. The discussion of the social and economic functions of these associations, and their relation to other institutions, has not been summarized: the factors involved and their permutations will depend on the society in which the investigations are undertaken. The points raised in the relevant sections of this paper would clearly be the minimum which should be considered. Similarly, investigation into origins, which has been given a brief section below, will require consideration of a wide range of historical and linguistic evidence, the interpretation of which will require special caution (see note 7). This guide cannot, therefore, be exhaustive, and additional questions will be required in particular investigations; it has been included mainly as an *aide memoire*, because I am aware from experience how easily some of the more obvious and basic questions of fact may escape one in the field.

The absence of rotating credit associations in any particular community should be recorded.

1. *Membership*
   (a) How many members are there?
   (b) Is the qualification for membership the same for all?
   (c) Is qualification for membership determined by one or more of the following criteria?
   - (i) Age
   - (ii) kinship
   - (iii) ethnic affiliation
   - (iv) locality
   - (v) occupation
   - (vi) status
   - (vii) education
   - (viii) religious affiliation
   - (ix) political affiliation
   - (x) other criteria
   (d) Is qualification for membership determined by affiliation to another association, and if so what is the required qualification for membership of the parent association?
   (e) Is joint-membership by a group permitted?

2. *Organization*
   (a) Are the roles played by all members identical?
   (b) If there are officials or organizers, what are their titles and functions?
   (c) By what criteria are they selected?
   (d) Does the association have branches?
   (e) Are members organized into sub-groups?
   (f) Are records kept, receipts given, and the like?
   (g) Is there a 'constitution' or set of formal rules?
   (h) Are specially printed books and stationery in use?
   (i) Are uniforms, or any other paraphernalia in use?
   (j) Are any forms of refreshment or entertainment found?
   (k) Are advertisements in use?

3. *Contributions*
   (a) Are contributions made in cash, in kind, or both, and is this requirement the same for all members?

(*b*) Do all members contribute?
(*c*) Do all members contribute equal amounts?
(*d*) Do the amounts a member contributes remain constant?
(*e*) Do members pay different contributions after having received a fund from before?
(*f*) What are the amounts of contributions?
(*g*) How are these amounts determined and are they fixed in advance?
(*h*) Does any form of 'doubling' occur?
(*i*) May a member make more than one contribution to each fund?
(*j*) What is the frequency of payment?
(*k*) On what date did the current rotation begin, how long is it expected to last, and is it likely to be renewed?
(*l*) Where is payment made?
    (i) at a meeting house
    (ii) at a member's house
    (iii) at the organizer(s')'s house or office
    (iv) at the market-place
    (v) at the members' place-of-work
    (vi) elsewhere

4. *Fund*

(*a*) What are the amounts of the funds, and do they remain constant?
(*b*) Are the amounts predetermined?
(*c*) Are the uses to which funds may be put restricted by the association?
(*d*) Are funds transferable?

5. *Order of Rotation*

(*a*) Is the order of rotation determined by general agreement?
(*b*) Or by predetermined criteria (if so what are they)?
(*c*) Or by the organizer(s)?
(*d*) Or by any kind of auction, or tender?
(*e*) Or by lot?
(*f*) Or by divination?
(*g*) Or by other means?
(*h*) Do different methods alternate?

6. *Interest*

(*a*) Is any form of interest paid?
(*b*) Is it determined
    (i) by use of a formally fixed rate?
    (ii) by any form of auction or tender?

7. *Deductions from fund*

If there are any deductions made from the fund (in addition to any interest charges) are these for

P

(a) a loan fund,
(b) a contingency fund,
(c) for entertainment of members,
(d) for officials?
(e) If for officials,
 (i) what form (gifts, bribes, etc.) do they take?
 (ii) Are the amounts predetermined?

8. *Sanctions*
 (a) Are written contracts required:
  (i) when joining the association?
  (ii) when receiving a fund?
 (b) Are guarantors required?
 (c) Is security required?
 (d) What is the legal position?
  (i) Are contracts ordinarily enforceable in the courts?
  (ii) Has special legislation been enacted?
 (e) What are the general attitudes towards these associations of:
  (i) the public,
  (ii) the state,
  (iii) other agencies (such as the press, or religious orders)?

9. *Origins*
 (a) When were rotating associations first known?
 (b) What is the earliest record of their existence?
 (c) How did they originate?
 (d) What nomenclature and terminology are in use?

NOTES

[1] This essay was awarded the Wellcome Medal for Anthropological Research in 1963.

[2] This would exclude, for instance, one of the examples from Nigeria given by Ajisafe, and quoted by Isong (1958, p. 113). Other aspects of this definition will be illustrated by the material in the text, but it may be noted here that the phrase 'formed upon a core of participants' takes into account associations in which the officials do not contribute although they receive funds, or do not contribute or receive at all. Although the term 'regular' in this context would normally mean 'at equal intervals of time', a hypothetical association in which contributions were made and distributed on members' birthdays might still be included, since the intervals, although not equal, would form a 'regulated' sequence known in advance to all members. The commonly found general social obligation to make gifts at marriage feasts would not normally fulfil all the criteria. In this paper, the term 'fund' refers to one collection of contributions, unless otherwise qualified; the plural, 'funds', refers to more than one such collection.

[3] This paper has gained greatly in style and clarity from the detailed criticisms of Edwin Ardener. I am indebted to Polly Hill for putting at my disposal personal communications and other material which she had begun to collect towards a similar project. Dr D. Brokensha, Mrs E. M. Chilver, and Dr P. M. Kaberry made available further material when this paper was in draft. I also acknowledge those informants who helped me in this country and whose names will be found among the references. My own first-hand experience of rotating credit associations in West Africa was obtained during various periods of field-work with Edwin Ardener in Nigeria and the Cameroons since 1949.

[4] Purcell notes that one secret-benevolent society organized the T'ai-p'ing rebellion, which A. H.

Smith says led to the downfall of many rotating credit associations in China and brought them into dis-credit (Purcell 1948, pp. 79–90; Smith *c.* 1899, p. 157).

[4] Bohannan also states that 'certainly it [the 'meeting'] replaced age-sets for the Ibo'. There was no evidence that rotating credit associations were replacing age-sets among the Mba-Ise Ibo in 1951: in fact they provided a useful means of financing age-set ceremonies. (However, for the Nsei of Cameroon, cf. Schmidt, cited in Jeffreys 1951.)

[6] My informant maintained firmly that the word *susu* ('to subscribe in rotation') was indigenous to the Susu language. (The ethnic name Susu is of course a coincidence.) However, in view of the evident age of the institution in the Sierra Leone area the word may still be a loan, entering the language even more than a century ago. The term appears to be used also for systems of reciprocal entertainment which, because they have no 'fund', cannot strictly be classed as rotating credit associations: the host for the occasion being the only contributor. It was even extendable to the notion that witches may 'contribute' children to be 'eaten' in rotation by their comrades!

[7] 'Tontine', mentioned above in connection with Malaya (Burridge), has been used in English for a type of assurance society in which the annuity is shared by subscribers to a loan, the shares increasing as subscribers die until the last survivor takes all (see *Concise Oxford Dictionary*). The writer has come across the usage as an alternative for 'slate-club' in the south of England. (There is a Tontine Street in Folke-stone.) The term 'tontine' comes from the name of a Neapolitan banker, Lorenzo Tonti, who proposed a type of loan scheme to Mazarin in 1653, which apparently had been known in Italy. It was introduced into France by Louis XIV in 1689 (*Larousse*).

[8] Claims of borrowing may sometimes be made by people unable to account otherwise for a new institution, and must, of course, be supported by other evidence. Even where borrowing has taken place, the source given may not be the true one. Linguistic data must also be treated with caution. Evidence of borrowed terminology and nomenclature is not proof of borrowed institutions. Nor is the absence of borrowed terminology proof that institutions were not borrowed. It is possible for both terminology and institutions to be borrowed, but from different sources. Martin and Jeffreys use the terms *esusu* and *osusu* in an Ibibio context. If these terms are normally used by Ibibio themselves, this evidence must be considered together with the claim of borrowing from Ibo (for the Mba-Ise, at least, did not normally use these terms).

[9] China may well have had priority in the development of the institution in Asia (although Japan has our earliest available date). I have considered and rejected the possibility of a link between China and West Africa, through indentured Asian labour and emancipated Africans in the West Indies, because Indian labour reached the West Indies only at the end of the 1840's, and Chinese labour arrived even later, that is: after our first reliable West African date (1843). Any tempting hypothesis of the development of the Chinese *she* or *she-chu* (terms from Smith *c.* 1899, p. 153) into West Indian *susu* or its West African variants, becomes also improbable, because of the dating of the term *esu*.

[10] This leads us into ritual gift exchanges, potlatches, and similar institutions: no-one has, however, demonstrated that any of the particular institutions mentioned lead directly to the establishment of rotating credit associations.

[11] The power to transfer funds may have wide ramifications. For instance, one member of an Ibo association bought a bicycle, at a price somewhat higher than the current market value, by transferring his right to a fund to the seller. He thereupon sold the bicycle at the current price, and obtained cash. His loss on the transaction, as he had calculated in advance, was considerably less than the interest which would have been charged had he borrowed the money at current rates (S. Ardener 1953, pp. 136–8).

[12] Brokensha (personal communication) writes of Bulawayo, Southern Rhodesia (where in 1959 about 45,000 Africans in employment belonged to some credit association) that he never heard of any case of any member refusing to pay his contributions, 'this was regarded as *the* priority payment, before all else,' and he knew of no cases which came to court.

REFERENCES (1)

All-India Rural Credit Survey 1954, vol. 2.
AMOGU, O. O. 1956. Savings in an African Economy. *Social and Economic Studies,* 5, no. 2, 1956.
ARDENER, E. W. 1953. A Rural Oil-palm Industry: 2 The Opposition to Oil Mills. *West Africa,* 3 Oct.
ARDENER, E. W., ARDENER, S. & WARMINGTON, W. A. 1960. *Plantation and Village in the Cameroons.* London.
ARDENER, S. 1953. The Social and Economic Significance of the Contributions Club among a Section of the Southern Ibo. *Conference Proceedings,* West African Institute of Social and Economic Research.

BAECK, L. 1957. Une Société Rurale en Transition: étude sociologique de la region de Thysville. *Zaire*, no. 2.

BAECK, L. 1961. An Expenditure Study of the Congolese Évolués of Leopoldville, Belgian Congo, in *Social Change in Modern Africa*, A. Southall (ed.).

BANTON, M. 1957. *West African City*.

BASCOM, W. R. 1952. The Esusu: A Credit Institution of the Yoruba. J. R. ANTHROP. INST., **82**, pp. 63–69.

BASHIR, H. 1962. Personal communication.

BIOBAKU, S. O. 1957. *The Egba and Their Neighbours, 1842–1872*.

BOHANNAN, P. 1962. Personal communication to P. Hill.

BOHANNAN, P. & BOHANNAN, L. 1953. *The Tiv of Central Nigeria*.

BROKENSHA, D. 1962. Personal communication.

BURRIDGE, K. 1962. Personal communication.

BURTON, R. 1865. *Wit and Wisdom from West Africa*.

CHAWLA, H. L. 1962. Personal communication.

CHILVER, E. M. 1962. Personal communication.

CROWTHER, S. A. [1843]. *Vocabulary of the Yoruba Language*.

CUNNINGHAM, C. 1962. Personal communication.

DENNIS, N., HENRIQUES, F. & SLAUGHTER, C. 1956. *Coal is Our Life*.

EBEID, A. H. 1962. Personal communication.

EMBREE, J. 1946. *Suye Mura*.

EVANS-PRITCHARD, E. E. 1962. Personal communication.

FEI, H. T. 1939. *Peasant Life in China*.

FEI, H. T. & CHANG, C. I. 1948. *Earthbound China*.

FIRTH, R. 1946. *Malay Fishermen*.

FORDE, C. D. & SCOTT, R. 1946. *Native Economies of Nigeria*.

FREEDMAN, M. 1957. *Chinese Family and Marriage in Singapore*.

FREEDMAN, M. 1959. The Handling of Money: A Note on the Background to the Economic Sophistication of Overseas Chinese. MAN 1959, 89.

FYFFE, C. 1962. *A History of Sierra Leone*.

GADALLA, I. 1962. Personal communication.

GAMBLE, S. D. 1944. A Chinese Mutual Savings Society. *Far Eastern Quarterly*, **4**, cited in Geertz 1962.

GAMBLE, S. D. 1954. *Ting Hsein: A North China Rural Community*, cited in Geertz 1962.

GEERTZ, C. 1962. The Rotating Credit Association: a 'Middle Rung' in Development. *Economic Develop ment and Cultural Change*, 1, no. 3.

Ghana Evening News, The, 12 March 1962.

GREEN, M. M. 1947. *Ibo Village Affairs*.

GUILBOT, J. 1956. Study of the Labour Force at Duala, summarized in *Social Implications of Industrialization and Urbanization in Africa South of the Sahara*.

GUPTA, S. C. 1962. Personal communication.

HELLMANN, E. 1948. *Rooiyard*.

HERSKOVITS, M. J. 1952. *Economic Anthropology*.

HERSKOVITS, M. J. & HERSKOVITS, F. S. 1947. *Trinidad Village*.

HILL, P. 1962. Personal communication.

HO, S. K. 1962. Personal communication.

HORNER, G. Summarized in Geertz 1962.

ISONO, C. N. 1958. Modernisation of the Esusu Credit Society. *Conference Proceedings*, Nigerian Institute of Social and Economic Research.

JACQUES, E. W. 1931. A Chinese Loan Society. MAN 1931, 216.

JEFFREYS, M. D. W. 1951. Le associazioni 'Osusu' nel' Africa Occidentale. *Rev. Etnog.*

KABERRY, P. M. 1952. *Women of the Grassfields*.

KABERRY, P. M. 1962. Personal communication.

KARAR, K. 1962. Personal communication.

KATZIN, M. F. 1959. 'Partners': An informal savings institution in Jamaica. *Soc. and Econ. Stud.*, pp. 436–440.

KHALU, M. C. S. 1962. Personal communication.

KHOGALI, A. 1962. Personal communication.

KRISHNAN, V. 1954. The Tambrapani Ryot, unpublished thesis, summarized in *All-India Rural Credit Survey*.

KULP, D. H. 1925. *Country Life in South China*.

KUPER, H. 1960. *Indian People in Natal.*
KUPER, H. & KAPLAN, S. 1944. Voluntary Associations in an Urban Township. *African Stud.*, **3**, pp. 178–186.
LIENHARDT, R. G. 1962. Personal communication.
LITTLE, K. 1957. The Role of Voluntary Associations in West African Urbanization, *Amer. Anthrop.*, **59**, pp. 579–96.
MARTIN, A. 1956. *The Oil Palm Economy of the Ibibio Farmer.*
MARTIN, H. (transl.) 1952. *Histoire et Coutumes des Bamum.*
MAYER, A. C. 1952. *Land and Society in Malabar.*
MUPANSHA, I. 1962. Personal communication.
MYRDAL, G. 1944. *An American Dilemma.*
NADEL, S. F. 1942. *Black Byzantium.*
PAGADUAN, L. 1962. Personal communication.
PHILLIPS, R. c. 1939. *The Bantu in the City.*
PURCELL, V. 1948. *The Chinese in Malaya.*
REINING, C. C. 1959. The Role of Money in the Zande Economy. *Amer. Anthrop.*, **61**, pp. 39–43.
Report on Enquiry with regard to Friendly and Mutual Benefit Groups in the Gold Coast, 1954, cited by Hill 1962.
RUEL, M. 1955. The Banyang of the Southern Cameroons, unpublished D.Phil. Thesis, Oxford.
SCHMIDT, A. 1951. Cited in Jeffreys 1951.
SMITH, A. H. c. 1899. *Village Life in China.*
SMITH, M. G. & KRUIJER, G. J. 1957. *A Sociological Manual for Extension Workers in the Caribbean.*
SMITH, R. T. 1956. *The Negro Family in British Guiana.*
SOFER, C. & SOFER, R. 1951. *Jinja Transformed.*
SOUTHALL, A. W. & GUTKIND, P. C. W. 1956. *Townsmen in the Making.* Mimeographed edition.
VINH, NGUYEN VAN 1949. Savings and Mutual Lending Societies (*Ho*), *Yale Southeast Asia Studies*, 1949; summarized in Geertz 1962.
WARD, B. 1954. A Hakka Kongsi in Borneo, *J. Orient. Stud.*, **1**, pp. 358–70.
WELLS, F. A. & WARMINGTON, W. A. 1962. *Studies in Industrialization: Nigeria and the Cameroons.*
YANG, M. 1947. *A Chinese Village, Taitou, Shantung Province.*

REFERENCES (2)

BENEDICT, B. 1964 Capital, Saving and Credit among Mauritian Indians, in Firth & Yamey 1964.
BOHANNAN, P., & DALTON, G. 1962. (eds.) *Markets in Africa.*
DEWEY, A. 1964. Capital, Credit and Savings in Javanese Marketing, in Firth & Yamey 1964.
EPSTEIN, S. 1964. Personal Capital Formation among the Tolai of New Britain, in Firth & Yamey 1964
FIRTH, R. & YAMEY, B. S. (eds.) 1964. *Capital, Saving and Credit in Peasant Societies.*
HERSKOVITS, M. J. & HARWITZ, M. (eds.) 1964. *Economic Transition in Africa.*
LÉVI-STRAUSS, C. 1963 (1952). *Structural Anthropology.*
MEYER, E. 1940. Kreditringe in Kamerun. *Koloniale Rundschau*, **31**, no. 2/3.
KATZIN, M. F. 1964. The Role of the Small Entrepreneur, in Herskovits & Harwitz 1964, pp. 179–98.
MORRILL, W. T. 1963. Immigrants and Associations: the Ibo in Twentieth Century Calabar. *Comparative Studies in Society and History*, **5**, no. 4, pp. 424–48.
OTTENBERG, S. 1955. Improvement Associations Among the Afikpo Ibo. *Africa*, **25**, pp. 1–28.
RUEL, M. 1964. The Modern Adaptation of Associations among the Banyang of the West Cameroon. *Southwestern Journal of Anthropology*, **20**, no. 1, pp. 1–14.
SMITH, R. T. 1964. Ethnic Differences and Peasant Economy in British Guiana, in Firth & Yamey 1964.
SWIFT, M. G. 1957. The accumulation of Capital in a Peasant Economy. *Economic Development and Cultural Change*, July 1957, pp. 325–37.
SWIFT, M. G. 1964. Capital Saving and Credit in a Malay Peasant Economy, in Firth & Yamey 1964
TOPLEY, M. 1964 Capital, Saving and Credit among Indigenous Rice Farmers and Immigrant Vegetable Farmers in Hongkong's New Territories, in Firth & Yamey 1964.

Subject Index

(page numbers in bold print refer to Appendix)

Name Index

Printed in the United States
by Baker & Taylor Publisher Services